Education, Travel and the "Civilisation" of the Victorian Working Classes

Education, Travel and the "Civilisation" of the Victorian Working Classes

Michele M. Strong
Associate Professor, University of South Alabama

First published 2014 by
PALGRAVE MACMILLAN

Palgrave Macmillan in the UK is an imprint of Macmillan Publishers Limited,
registered in England, company number 785998, of Houndmills, Basingstoke,
Hampshire RG21 6XS.

Palgrave Macmillan in the US is a division of St Martin's Press LLC,
175 Fifth Avenue, New York, NY 10010.

Palgrave Macmillan is the global academic imprint of the above companies
and has companies and representatives throughout the world.

Palgrave® and Macmillan® are registered trademarks in the United States,
the United Kingdom, Europe and other countries.

ISBN 978–1–137–33807–5

This book is printed on paper suitable for recycling and made from fully
managed and sustained forest sources. Logging, pulping and manufacturing
processes are expected to conform to the environmental regulations of the
country of origin.

A catalogue record for this book is available from the British Library.

A catalog record for this book is available from the Library of Congress.

Typeset by MPS Limited, Chennai, India.

Contents

List of Figures

Acknowledgements

Like many of the workers' travels described in this book, my first trip abroad was made as an "educational tour." I would like to begin this acknowledgement by conveying my gratitude to the people and institutions that made research in the United Kingdom possible. Research and writing for this project was funded by grants from the University of North Carolina at Chapel Hill and the University of South Alabama in Mobile. I am also grateful to the History Department at Trinity University, San Antonio, which helped fund research in 2004, when I was a visiting Assistant Professor. Many curators, archivists, and librarians (and civilians, too) helped guide me through the archives. Kevin Smyth, General Secretary of the Working Men's Club and Institute Union, kindly brought me up to date on the WMCIU's history and made sources available to me even while the club headquarters underwent reconstruction. Gordon Fox introduced me to the Working Men's College and carefully selected interesting documents from its archive to help with my project. Paul Smith graciously welcomed me to the Thomas Cook archive – summer after summer – while Joy Hooper and Jill Lomer directed my attention to its many treasures. Their friendship in subsequent years has been the best treasure of all. I am also grateful for the expert help and warm friendship of Susan Bennett, former curator of the Royal Society of Arts archive and currently Honorable Secretary of the William Shipley Group for RSA History; and, Brenda Weedon, former archivist at the University of Westminster archive. Brenda Weedon's successor, Elaine Penn, has been enormously helpful in tying up loose ends for which I am grateful. Thanks are also owed to the intellectual generosity of Piers Brendon, former Keeper of the Archives at Churchill College, Cambridge. It would have been madness to write this book without consulting him first or his book on "the great man," Thomas Cook. Back in the USA, Tommy Nixon at Davis Library (UNC-CH) helped me launch the project at a time when sources about British, working-class travelers were difficult to imagine, much less find. Kathy Jones and members of the ILL staff at the University of South Alabama Library have helped me conclude the project with quick and expert responses to every book request.

Much of my work has been shaped in conversation with scholars and friends. At UNC-CH, I could not have hoped for a better advisor than Lloyd Kramer. His spirit of intellectual adventure guides me still. Discussions with James Hevia, Jeanne Moskal, Donald Reid, Jay Smith, Richard Soloway, and Susan Thorne sharpened my analysis. David Anderson, Chris Endy, Mariola Espinosa, Cora Granata, Doina Harsanyi, Brandon Hunziker, Leah Potter, Bianca Premo, David Sartorius, and Susan Thuesen also offered important insights at various stages of my early thinking and writing. At the University of South Alabama, my work has benefited greatly from a department that both values and supports new scholarship. I owe a special debt of gratitude to the Chair, Clarence Mohr, and to my colleagues Frye Galliard, Mara Kozelsky, and Rebecca Williams for their encouragement, comments on an early chapter draft, and advice about the publishing process. Chapter 5 came into being as conference papers on imperial networks at the Southern Conference of British Studies and at the American Historical Association. I want to thank Alan Lester and Philippa Levine for their insights and encouragement. In many conversations over the years, Douglas Bristol also contributed to my thinking about networks, class, and power, for which I am grateful. Alice Ritscherle and Jeffrey Harris generously read the entire manuscript in its early and late stages (respectively) and offered astute comments, editorial turns of phrase, and laughs. I am eternally grateful. All errors, needless to say, are my own.

My appreciation extends to the people and institutions involved directly with the publication of this book. De Gruyter Saur granted permission to reproduce my chapter, "'Clothing Britain's Legions' with 'Intellectual Weapons' and 'Sound Science': The Artisan Exhibition Tours and the Rise of Modern Educational Travel, 1867–1889," edited by Franz Bosbach and John Davis, in *Die Weltausstellung von 1851 und ihre Folgen/The Great Exhibition and its Legacy, Prince Albert Studies*, 20 (Munich: K.G. Saur, 2002; Reprint, Berlin: De Gruter Saur, 2012), which comprises portions of Chapter 3 and Chapter 4 of this book. Cambridge University Press and the *Journal of British Studies*, granted permission to reprint my article, "Class Trips and the Meaning of British Citizenship: Travel, Educational Reform, and the Regent Street Polytechnic at Home and Abroad, 1871–1903," in Chapter 5 of this book. I want to thank the anonymous readers and, especially, editors Elizabeth Elbourne and Brian Lewis at *JBS*, for their enormously helpful comments and suggestions. Many thanks also go to Clare Mence, Commissioning Editor, for supporting this project and to Alec McAulay, for his patience and valuable expertise. I also wish to convey my deep appreciation to the anonymous readers of the sample chapters and the completed manuscript.

I dedicate this book with love and respect to my sister, Dominique, whose own educational tour is about to commence. Bon voyage!

Introduction: Grand Tours and Workers' Tours: Rethinking Victorian Travel and Education

Grand Tours and Workers' Tours: Rethinking Victorian Travel and Education

Sifting through his morning correspondence, Peter Le Neve Foster would have paused at a rough envelope postmarked 5 November 1878, the return address, "Peckham House Lunatic Asylum, London," scrawled in the corner. It was a letter from Alexander Kay, an unfortunate Scottish joiner with whom he had corresponded since the 1867 "Artisan Tours" of the Paris Exhibition. Foster had neglected to respond to Kay's September post. Yet here was another letter to pester and perhaps sadden him with the musings of a man who had lost his mind, his capacity for self-government, and his freedom.

Foster, the Secretary of the Society for the Encouragement of Arts, Commerce, and Manufacturers (SA), had been a key organizer of the 1867 Artisan Tours, in which 84 skilled craftsmen (including Kay) had reported on the Paris Exhibition. A quasi-governmental institution, the SA was dedicated to the progress of British industry through national programs such as adult education classes. The SA thus viewed the artisan tours as important pedagogical innovations to improve workers' education, their livelihoods, and the prosperity of the nation. The SA also anticipated that the tours would improve relations between the middle-class organizers and the artisans, many of whom would win the franchise in the forthcoming 1867 Reform Act. Kay, however, writing from a lunatic asylum a full decade later, had come to a far different conclusion about the educational utility of the tours, and questioned the intentions of the organizers.

Although Kay began his letter congenially enough, saluting Foster as "My dear friend of 1867," he quickly descended into an odd rant. "I have not received a reply to my September letter," Kay remonstrated, "but you are well aware that it is very undesirable to lose old friends. As in fact there seems [sic] to be plenty of sharks. But as the Whaler fleet this year have demonstrated the scarcity of whales, we must not be anxious to throw the Jonahs

1

overboard as there are so few whales to save them although [there are] any quantity of Sharks ready to destroy them." The Biblical allusion must have startled Foster, for Kay's words not only expressed his despair at being left to the mercies of fate in a world teeming with sharks, but ultimately condemned Foster and the SA for casting him into a sea of ruin. Continuing his missive, Kay railed against the injustice of his arbitrary "confinement" to the "dens of Whoredom and infamy." He moaned over the poverty that made him vulnerable to the power of social superiors, to employers, and to the judgment of medical men. And, most of all, he lashed out at the duplicity of middle-class reformers who offered working people a vision of social mobility – so long as they obeyed the ideological tenets of self-improvement and class conciliation. In other words, Kay viewed his captivity in Peckham as a symptom of class inequalities rather than the outcome of mental derangement.[1]

In the context of Kay's life, revealed in this and other letters written to Foster over the course of a decade, the parable of Jonah and the whale made sense as a metaphor for class struggle and as an indictment of the British class system. Kay's existence as a "Jonah" was not only dictated by a fickle God, but was subject to the noblesse oblige of an inconstant aristocracy (whales) and to the mean self-interest of the middle classes (sharks).[2] The SA embodied this amalgamation of class interests. Members included industrialists, scientists, educationists, and radical politicians, as well as the Prince of Wales, who, as the society's president, had set his imprimatur upon the SA's various educational programs. Furthermore, the SA worked closely with voluntary educational organizations such as the Workingmen's Club and Institute Union, whose middle-class officers had collaborated with the SA to send an additional 3000 working men (and a few of their working-class wives) across the Channel to the Paris Exhibition in 1867.

To Kay's mind, it appeared that he and his fellow artisan travelers to the 1867 Paris exhibition had misplaced their trust in the SA. His letter sputtered and fumed at the "doings of the Society of Arts in their professed endeavourment to diffuse Knowledge in the terms of technical education guilds of learning &c &c.," and castigated "all the dishonourable arrangements of the Committee of the Society of Arts in connection with the Working Classes, in many of which the whims of the Revd. H. Solly has been pandered to also Mssrs Pratt, Mundella &c [the officers of the Workingmen's Club and Institute Union] ... and other professionals."[3] The working men had hoped to gain so much for themselves, their class, and Britain through their "educational" tours of the exhibition. But to Kay, there was no appreciable benefit from cooperating with the upper classes or in his self-cultivation as an artisan intellectual. Indeed, although Kay's decade-long correspondence with Foster reveals a personal relationship of patronage and perhaps respect which, from Kay's perspective, rested on his artisanal skills, book learning, and civic enthusiasm for public improvements, it also reveals a life fraught with worry over employment, the desperate health of loved ones, and brutal housing conditions. In this final letter from Peckham, therefore, Kay's words expressed bitter disillusionment. Hardly a Samuel Smiles self-help narrative of rags-to-riches working-class heroism, Kay's life had become a series of tragic disappointments.[4] As such, it reflected the fortunes of many more ordinary and aspirational working people, even among the so-called "artisan aristocracy," who banked on the liberal promise that they could better their circumstances through middle-class educational provisions, such as the artisan exhibition tours.

Like Kay's diatribe against the SA and its Artisan Tours which, until now, had been relegated (with other workers' letters) to the obscurity of alphabetized bundles in the SA's archive, this book reveals a historical formation that, by all current accounts, never existed, but was swallowed up – if not by aristocratic "whales" or by "whoredom and infamy" – then, in Edward Thompson's words, by "the enormous condescension of posterity."[5] This study proposes to examine working people's responses to the exhibition tours and other travel experiences beyond the British Isles, and to place them within the social, political, and cultural contexts of Britain's education history, particularly with reference to the institutional formation of modern study abroad. As Kay's letter suggests, such tours helped shape working people's perceptions about the politics of class, culture, and knowledge and thus offer an unusual window into working people's responses to modernity and their contributions to what has become one of the most lucrative niche travel industries today, an industry that largely excludes them.

The artisan tours of the 1867 Paris exhibition represented just one of many new pedagogical technologies that emerged in the second half of the nineteenth century, and which conferred an educational value to working-class travel abroad. As this book will show, the artisan exhibition tours and other predecessors of modern study abroad were the outcomes of industrialization, the professionalization of science and industry, and international economic competition. They therefore furthered the public and private interests of capital and contributed to the educational travel practices of the professional or business-oriented middle classes. Indeed, founded in the age of industrial capitalism, the artisan tours made science and technology the locus of educational travel, challenging the primacy of the "classical" Grand Tour typically associated with liberal arts curricula.[6] However, working-class people were not only agents in the capitalist transformation of education and mass tourism, but the objects of rule and subjects of reform. This book thus explores working-class struggles for active citizenship in the British nation through education, but does so by examining the creation of educational travel programs that, as Kay lucidly surmised, reformers used to win and maintain popular support for middle-class values and objectives. This book thus looks at the rise of modern educational travel as a cultural response to working-class demands for inclusion in the nation, and middle-class attempts to contain them.

Scholars have traced the origins of modern educational travel to a variety of cultural practices, from the classical Grand Tours of seventeenth-century aristocrats to Britain's Central Bureau for Educational Visits and Exchanges established by UNESCO's National Co-operating Body for Education in the immediate post-World War Two era.[7, 8] While these multiple lines of descent suggest the diverse ways in which educational travel has been conceived and practiced historically, they neglect specific nineteenth-century modes of foreign study that presage today's university language programs, vocational work/study classes, and holiday-learning tours abroad. This historical oversight may be related to the fact that the social underpinnings of educational travel today, as in the days of the Grand Tour, are those of the affluent classes. However, it is with and for the working classes that many modern forms of educational travel took shape. This book will demonstrate that the intersection of Victorian working-class autodidact traditions, a protracted liberal educational reform movement, the exigencies of international economic competition abroad, and the need for social control at home, produced some of the underlying conditions for the formation of study abroad in the nineteenth century.

The Grand Tour has often been cited not only as the origin of modern educational travel, but as a precursor to modern leisure travel generally. The Grand Tour typically consisted of three years of leisurely travel on the European continent. Accompanied by tutors, young (male) aristocrats completed their university education by visiting sites of classical learning before assuming their adult roles as titled and wealthy landowners upon their return home.[9] In the eighteenth century, however, the aristocratic class of leisure travelers on the European continent was vastly outnumbered by the gentry, the professional classes, travel writers and even workers on the "journeyman's tramp" who practiced their own form of the "Grand Tour." In these socio-economic groups, "educational travel" became a more generalized program of self-improvement in which an acquaintance with European culture and scientific knowledge in transit constituted an edifying holiday.[10] Consequently, to look to the aristocratic Grand Tour, as József Böröcz argues, "as the only source of world-wide cultural patterns regarding contemporary" modern leisure travel is "empirically untenable." Instead, Böröcz suggests that scholars interrogate nineteenth-century patterns of international industrial capitalism and the two classes that manned the industrial revolution: the bourgeoisie and the working class. Such an analysis would take into account not only new transportation technologies that facilitated mass tourism, but structural components that fueled the commercialization, standardization, and normalization of travel as a cultural commodity – including workers' demands for shorter working hours and the free time to pursue leisure.[11]

Böröcz and others have highlighted the importance of infusing class into travel analyses to better understand modernity in terms of class formation, industrialization, democratization, nation building, internationalism, and the formation of individual and collective identities. While such studies primarily explain middle-class travel and tourism, there have been calls to make these investigations more inclusive.[12] David Engerman suggests exploring consumer culture to locate working people's contributions in shaping the popular "urge" to travel abroad.[13] More expansively, James Clifford challenges scholars to develop a global and comparative understanding of the cultural modernities revealed in travel practices, meanings, and their representation. Clifford thus calls on historians of travel to step beyond narratives of the leisured classes – beyond the "heroic explorer, aesthetic interpreter, or scientific authority" – to explore knowledges created through the transcultural encounters of "subaltern" travelers such as migrants, servants, interpreters, and guides. Understanding mobility as a metaphor for "the modern" thus opens windows onto multiple and overlapping experiences and identities, including those of working-class travelers that are every bit as significant as those of elites.[14] However, except for internal analyses of British seaside resorts, camp holidays, and the "day tripper," few scholars of British travel and tourism have responded to Clifford's call.[15]

Scholarly preoccupation with domestic working-class leisure travel makes sense since greater numbers of working people traveled for pleasure within than outside of Britain. Although the rise of real wages gave an estimated 70 to 85 percent of working-class families the financial wherewithal to indulge in occasional seaside holidays during the last quarter of the century, mass (working-class) excursions to the continent were more costly and time-consuming, and thus rarer.[16] In addition, as John Benson observes, the social composition of most continental tours perhaps intimidated working people, preventing them from much more than imagining such a journey.[17] Conversely, at working-class seaside resorts, as Peter Bailey argues, working people could drop the ruse of "respectability" and enjoy themselves outside the range of the middle classes' disciplining gaze.[18] The fact remains, however, that working people did travel on the continent and elsewhere in the world, both individually and en masse. Two questions, therefore, need to be addressed: why have scholars neglected this singular aspect of modernity, and furthermore, given such prohibitions, *how* and *why* did working people overcome such obstacles to travel beyond Britain's shores?

In answering the first question, it should be noted that until very recently, the common cant of British social and cultural historians has been to argue that the working classes lived insular, isolated lives and were little concerned with the outside world. According to this perspective, consumerism and a "defensive" conservative localism "consoled" the working classes for existing social and political inequalities.[19] One consequence of this view is that studies on working-class leisure have largely failed to explore British workers' identification with people and places outside their local haunts. Jonathan Rose's densely researched history of autodidact reading practices and subjectivities is a case in point. Finding little evidence of working-class engagement with Europe or even the Empire, Rose concedes that workers may have treasured news of the "Holy Land" and entertained a utopian vision of the United States as a land paved with "streets of gold," but argues that they exhibited little concern with foreign affairs or even with the economically crucial issues surrounding Britain's imperial mission. These conclusions need to be qualified, not least of all because Rose's sources include working-class members of the Toynbee Travelers Club, who made successive tours of the European continent in the late Victorian era and who wrote about their travels and the books, it should be noted, that they read to prepare for their journeys.[20]

Complicating this blanket perception of British working-class isolationism and apathy are recent works that touch on working people's construction of national, imperial and international identities through their varied encounters with the wider world – from their ideological and financial support of missionary work in the colonies to their radical engagements with European socialism and nationalist movements.[21] *Education, Travel, and the "Civilisation" of the Victorian Working Classes* contributes to this dialogue by exploring the rise of modern educational travel and explaining how and why some working people dared to venture beyond their villages, towns, and cities. To understand the significance of working-class travel, however, historians need to transform normative concepts of study abroad.

Sociologists have defined educational travel today as an activity in which "the traveller chooses to travel, as well as makes other decisions such as when and where to journey, based on the interest in learning."[22] This pat definition clearly demarcates today's university study-abroad programs or adult-learning holidays from vacations characterized by "Club Med" hedonism, but it has little relevance for most educational travelers during the nineteenth century. Drawing on ideologies of rational recreation and self-improvement in which labor, leisure, and learning were seen as complementary rather than antithetical activities, many people who traveled abroad for any number of reasons – work, health, leisure – would have placed their experiences meaningfully in a general educational framework. In short, travel was broadly defined as a form of education rather than as a leisure activity alone. Study abroad thus emerged within a cluster of discourses, practices and meanings about education before becoming a well-defined niche in the commercial travel industry or an essential part of higher learning curricula.

In investigating how educational practices and ideologies became invested in nineteenth-century travel experiences, this study owes much to histories of culture and state formation that combine materialist and linguistic analysis to understand relations of social and cultural power. This book uncovers the ways in which modern study abroad developed alongside a liberal educational reform movement that was part and parcel of what the authors of *The Great Arch* describe as a "cultural revolution," one in which the "educational idea," the "statistical idea," and the "sanitary idea," the "three great 'ideas' which energized the system of national improvement," helped avert a social revolution and secured "bourgeois civilization."[23] In the context of working-class travel, the educational reform movement promoted two broad goals: to educate the expanding electorate for responsible citizenship, and to make skilled British workers competitive with the increasingly educated and advanced industrial workforce of Europe and the United States. In pursuit of these goals, working-class "educational" travel emerged within a set of new pedagogical technologies produced by civil society and often supported or adopted by the state to educate the masses. One outcome of these technologies was the bureaucratization of culture, such as museums that operated as sites of public instruction or, in Michel Foucault's terms, as circuits of knowledge/power that sought to assert ontological authority, define class, gender, and national identities, and regulate behavior.

Drawing on Foucault (and his interpreters for the British context), particularly with regard to his later concept of liberal "governmentality," this book demonstrates that educational travel became a varied field in which to exercise direct and indirect power. Ian Hunter's work on the role of government in modern education explores disciplinary technologies of pastoral governance as a function of civil society in the Protestant emphasis on self-examination for self-regulation, a practice that originated in voluntary, religious schools; and, as it was put to work in "purpose built" state schools, to assist with governing at a distance.[24] Middle-class reformers will use travel, much like "pastoral technicians" used the schoolhouse and playground, as a cultural resource with which to deploy technologies of social discipline and surveillance over the working classes, and to inculcate liberal values that would ready (in their estimation) the working classes for participation in the nation as self-regulating subjects and citizens. This book, therefore, also examines travel in terms of cultural citizenship, which anthropologist Aihwa Ong explains as a "process of self-making and of being made within webs of power linked to the nation state and civil society." Indeed, Ong uses Foucault's concept of governmentality as a corrective to Corrigan and Sayer's state-centered approach. For Ong, the disciplinary role played by non- governmental institutions and social groups (civil society) was (and is) equally pernicious in the exercise of power.[25] As many others have shown, the early Victorian state was predicated on liberal notions of individual freedom and laissez faire. Thus, the informal function of disciplining (or educating) subordinate populations often fell to voluntary, philanthropic, and charitable organizations, as well as quasi-governmental groups, such as the Society of Arts. Within them, individuals motivated by personal quests for spiritual or, as Seth Koven shows, psycho/sexual self- realization, or motivated by broader ideological contests between philanthropy and socialism, as Lauren Goodlad also shows in examining Victorian liberalism in the context of pastoral governance, sought to bridge class boundaries by cultivating inter-subjective relationships with working people that they hoped would establish, as Goodlad stresses, moral equality.[26] Consequently, power was wielded through a coercive state and its apparatuses, but also through civil society and its institutions in defining normative behaviors and values, and, in this instance, in shaping working-class mobility to specific personal, social, economic, and political ends. Either way, the point was to regulate behavior at a distance, whether its object of disciplinary power, the British working-class subject, traversed the streets of London, Paris, or, for that matter, Bombay. Reformers' attempts to orchestrate working-class travel experiences, however, were often mediated through cross-class conflicts over the purpose, practice, and content of education.

Underpinned by political and class interests, education, like culture generally, was contested terrain. Before the fall of Chartism in 1848, radical artisans challenged the middle-class monopoly on parliamentary power and its disciplinary intrusions into their lives by creating not only a separate and unifying (working-class) public sphere, but also an autonomous sphere of educational activity. Rejecting both voluntary and state forms of education, they, as Geoff Eley explains, articulated "through the medium of educational practice a searching critique of the existing political system."[27] This critique continued after Chartism, but was tempered by middle-class attempts to "contain" and "neutralize" popular opposition through compromise and consensus, leading to new interpretations of liberal ideology. While "classical" liberalism, with its emphasis on *laissez-faire* and the individual citizen, did not vanish from the Victorian political landscape, it no longer dominated. Proponents of the "new" liberalism accepted the necessity of an interventionist state, but also state partnership with civil society that was to ameliorate the moral failure of capitalist society without threatening its overthrow. Margot Finn's book on internationalism and the post-Chartist Lib–Lab alliance, shows how cross-class engagements with French socialism, nationalist movements, and insurgent republicanism established common ground in which to critique classical liberalism, and reveals the influence of working-class activists in giving shape to the new liberalism of the late nineteenth century.[28] The development of educational travel reflects this dynamic. Workers may not have possessed the means to produce mass tours, but in collaboration with middle-class organizers, they helped shaped their meaning, purpose, and practice.

Indeed, in the mid- to late-Victorian era, class identity and class consciousness did not produce a coherent political dynamic of "class warfare," although class-conscious working people agitated for a new place in the social, political, and economic order. Thus, as Finn argues, the new liberalism would not have taken the progressive form it did without the constant pressure from working-class activism that it sustained. However, working people agitated for sociopolitical change within the system as well as against it, and members of the middle class were likewise divided between reformist and radical politics.[29] This book, therefore, accepts the correlation between class identity and class ideology, but emphasizes that these labels comprise overlapping groups and by no means represent fixed, consistent categories. Indeed, the development of organized educational travel put multiple identities and interests into play (and into conflict).

In mapping the growth of modern educational travel in this period of developing class identities, this book traces Victorian Britain's transition from classical liberalism to the new liberalism. The history of educational travel offers a unique entrée not only into the shifting and fraught relationships between working-class and middle-class Britons, but also into a reevaluation of liberal ideology that would determine working people's access to education and, consequently, to social and economic mobility. This book, therefore, considers the individual and collective experiences of working men and women, primarily (although not exclusively) London artisans, as well as young apprentices and clerks, who traveled abroad as participants in an educational reform movement spearheaded by middle-class liberals. This examination will also contribute to an understanding of how the new liberalism was conceived and practiced by analyzing the challenges that the democratization of travel and education posed for middle-class "containment" of working-class politics. To bring to light these working-class experiences and the middle-class efforts to control them, this study examines four institutions during the Victorian era that drew workers into transnational travel.

Thomas Cook & Son was one of Britain's first modern tourist agencies. Founded during the Chartist era in the early 1840s, Cook's agency developed a philosophy of leisure travel grounded in rational recreation, patriotism, and class harmony. Historians unfailingly note the working-class origins of Cook's early tours in the temperance movement, but tend to focus their analyses on the middle classes, his primary clientele.[30] Conversely, this study has used the archival resources, particularly the agency's pamphlet collection and company organ, *The Excursionist*, to trace the practical expression of Cook's philosophy and commercial philanthropy in his "educational" tours for workers. Specifically, it examines how Cook's collaboration with middle-class reformers between the 1840s and 1870s produced tours for workers that were intended to foster cross-class interaction rather than division, as well as a new mass market for travel and tourism.

The Working Men's Club and Institute Union (WMCIU), was a social club founded in 1862 by the Rev. Henry Solly, a Unitarian minister (and one target of Kay's wrath in his letter to Foster). The WMCIU provided working men with opportunities for rational recreation and cross-class cohesion. The WMCIU turned the 1867 Paris exhibition, for example, into a site of leisure and learning for 3000 British workers. Even though middle-class WMCIU officers and financial supporters devised ways to deploy governmental power through club activities (such as the tours), by 1867 they had also begun to modify their own ideological frameworks to accommodate the rise of working-class politics and to redress the failures of the liberal state. Based on the WMCIU's institutional records and other supporting evidence, including the minute books of the International Workingmen's Association, this analysis reveals co-existing aims connecting middle class and working-class leaders that complicate patronizing views of the "Lib–Lab alliance" as it has been traditionally defined. However, it also recognizes the WMCU's primary function as an instrument of social control, as Richard Price argued four decades ago in one of the few scholarly analyses of the WMCIU.[31]

The Society of Arts (SA), a voluntary organization for the promotion of arts, manufacturers, and commerce founded in London in 1754, originally functioned as an informal think tank for improving British industry. With origins in the Enlightenment, the SA linked progress to developing educational provisions for workers and nationalizing standards of technical education. One manifestation of the SA's commitment to working-class education was its instrumental role in helping to organize several artisan tours for select groups of highly skilled craftsmen and industrial operatives to continental exhibitions between 1867 and 1889. The Society of Arts intended these tours to convince workers and employers alike that educational reform was both necessary and realizable given European educational models and practices. Indeed, SA members (government bureaucrats, scientists, industrialists, and public intellectuals) helped promote and fund the tours in order to correct a perceived technology gap as well as a deficiency of taste in British design that threatened the nation's industrial and economic supremacy. In so doing, they reshaped working-class education and the role of travel within it. As Anthony David Edwards has argued in examining the impact of international exhibitions on British educational policies, the economic and technological threat from abroad compelled organizations, like the SA and its affiliates, to campaign for educational reform.[32] The artisan reporters themselves gave voice to these concerns in their reports which were published for public consumption. While historians have used these reports to substantiate or dispute claims about Britain's economic decline, here they are used to delve into workers' subjectivities, and their fashioning of public identities and personas. Indeed, many artisans used the reports as a public forum in which to critique the liberal state, primarily with regard to educational provisions for working people.

The Young Men's Christian Institute (the Polytechnic), was a vocational school and social club founded by Quintin Hogg, a wealthy philanthropist and powerful City merchant. It began in Long Acre, London, in 1871 and expanded operations in 1882, when Hogg leased a more spacious building, known as the Royal Polytechnic on Regent Street. Meshing the previous establishment's name with its own, it became the London Regent Street Polytechnic and Young Men's Christian Institute, or, more familiarly, "the Poly." By 1900, the Polytechnic had evolved into a state-funded social and educational institute for thousands of young men and women in London's wage-earning classes, reflecting not only the intervention of the state in secondary and adult education, but a measure of success for the technical education reform movement.

Indeed, one outcome of the artisan tours and the technical education movement was the 1889 Technical Instruction Act that allocated monies to the building and maintenance of technical schools, many modeled on the Regent Street Polytechnic, which had already developed curricula that included educational travel. Thus, the Polytechnic succeeded the artisan tours as the means of exposing working people directly to continental industry and design, as well as the organizational framework for study abroad. This analysis of the Polytechnic's institutional records, travel brochures, and weekly magazine, will illustrate how its institutional ethos defined travel and tourism as a duty of citizenship – an ideology that it backed with "co-operative" and "educational" tours and its very own travel agency, the Polytechnic Touring Association. Although education historians sometimes note the Polytechnic's origins in philanthropy or the technical education movement, and although travel historians occasionally proffer a nod to the Polytechnic Travel Association, only this book examines them together and links them to the broader question of state formation in light of emerging liberal ideology.

Except for the Polytechnic, each of these institutions organized working-class travel in the form of "artisan" or "workingmen's" tours.[33] The five artisan tours examined in this book all deployed working Britons to continental Europe. The first tour, which took place during Whitsuntide in 1861, was originally organized as a demonstration of class solidarity with French workers by British working-class radicals, but was commandeered by middle-class social reformers who turned it into a mixed-sex, cross-class, and cross-Channel demonstration of rational recreation. The 1861 tour is significant, in part, because many of the same actors – the middle-class reformers and working-class militants – played central roles in the organization of the 1867 artisan tours, reflecting continuity in the ideological and practical formation of educational travel practices. The remaining four tours were exhibition tours. All but one of the tours were to Paris (1861, 1867, 1878, 1889), the exception being the 1873 tour to Vienna. The SA and the WMCIU conducted the 1867 tours to the Paris Exhibition, while two Midland affiliates of the SA conducted the 1873 tours to Vienna. The SA again organized artisan tours of the Paris Exhibition in 1878, while a Mansion House Committee (government committee of the City of London) conducted the 1889 artisan tours of the Paris Exhibition.

It was with these tours of European exhibitions that the modern practices of educational travel can be seen to coalesce in response to rising concerns over economic competition abroad and democratization at home. This book thus contributes to the rapidly expanding literature on the multiple modernities of international exhibitions. The exhibitions have been the focus of extensive cross-disciplinary research into nationalism, liberalism, and imperialism that inform the analysis. Several studies have examined the Great Exhibition as a site of identity formation, for example, where exhibition organizers sought to involve all segments of British society in the affirmation of British national and imperial identities.[34] Tony Bennett's concept of the "exhibitionary complex," reveals a twofold manipulation of the spectator's gaze. The exhibition projected an idealized, celebratory image of the British Empire at its industrial and political apogee that sought to win the "hearts and minds" of Britons for their government's national and imperial projects. Exhibition visitors were thus invited to play the roles of subjects and objects of their own gaze, absorbing and interpreting the Crystal Palace's "messages of power" while simultaneously policing each other's participation in British triumphalism. Bennett also stresses that the exhibitions were designed to facilitate the desired interpretations of the "exhibitionary complex"; exhibition spaces were systemically ordered to showcase a hierarchy of civilizations, with Britain in 1851 represented as the most enlightened and exalted zenith of human achievement.[35] Sensitive to these manipulations, some artisans contributed to their ideological claims, while others mocked their conceits. This book thus also draws on Paul Greenhaugh's analysis of the civilizational hierarchies represented at European and American exhibitions. As Greenhaugh shows, the themes of peace, education for the masses, trade, and "progress" were common to the exhibitions at all venues, and the common framework of Western imperial hegemony in which they were articulated.[36] Although some historians, such as Peter Hoffenberg, have analyzed audience response at the exhibitions, the recent proliferation of exhibition studies has produced little scholarship on the testimonies of British workers.[37] With regard to exhibitions domestically, Susan Barton has explored the participation of working-class organizations in the 1851 Great Exhibition and the interaction of workers with middle-class organizers such as Thomas Cook and the Society of Arts.[38] The few studies that address British workers participation at exhibitions outside the United Kingdom have done so only in passing.[39] This book, therefore, takes readers on a different journey than is customary in the exhibition literature. While it examines middle-class motives for organizing the exhibition tours, it also explores artisans' motives for participating and their responses to the exhibitions.

The artisans touring the continental exhibitions were only able to explore Europe with the collusion of middle-class organizations, but they arrived in Paris and Vienna with their own agendas and their own perspectives. Their life experiences (and those of the Polytechnic students in geographically broader contexts), became part of the dialectical process of identity construction and self-representation that gave meaning to their travels. The analysis is thus attentive to illuminating the class- and gender based subjectivities of these writers and the conscious and unconscious meanings revealed in the narrative tropes and strategies that they employed. It is these processes that are explored in close textual readings of workers' letters, reports, and travel journals in the following chapters.[40]

Chapter 1, "'A True Agent of Civilisation': Travel and the 'Educational Idea,' 1841–1861," explores the educational climate of rational recreation and reform during the early- and mid-Victorian period and explains the disciplinary function of organized travel based on the utilitarian and governmental ideal of the "educational idea." It also shows how Thomas Cook & Son, a rising commercial institution, subscribed to the "educational idea" in disseminating a popular discourse of educational travel. This discourse gained momentum in 1851 when Cook, as well as other travel agents and social reformers, encouraged ordinary workers – preferably under their auspices – to visit the Great Exhibition in London's Hyde Park. The chapter concludes in 1861, a decade after the Great Exhibition, with a case study that examines how middle-class reformers deployed the "educational idea" in taking control of a politically charged Paris tour organized by a London committee of radical workers. Transforming the tour into an education in patriotism and social amelioration, the middle-class organizers shepherded 1600 tourists across the Channel. In spite of reformers' best efforts to orchestrate workers' travel experiences, these and similar tours gave workers access to a form of power with which to shape collective class and international identities. This chapter thus lays the historical and thematic groundwork for analyzing the educational and political climates surrounding the organization of artisans' tours to world exhibitions in subsequent chapters.

Chapter 2, "Turning the 'Educational Idea' on its Head: The Lib–Lab Alliance and the Organization of the 1867 Working Men's Exhibition Tours," complicates the patronizing view of the "Lib–Lab alliance," as historians have traditionally defined it, by examining the collaboration of middle-class reformers and labor leaders in the Working Men's Tours of the 1867 Paris Universal Exhibition. Sponsored by the Working Men's Club and Institute Union (WMCIU), the tours led over 3000 British workers on sightseeing tours of Paris and the exhibition. The analysis opens with a meeting of the London chapter of the International Workingmen's Association (IWA) and its plan to organize workers' tours of the 1867 Paris exhibition. Seeking to transform "governmental power" into working-class power, the IWA imagined that culture and education could be used as tools of working-class emancipation from the bourgeois state. Mass tours of the Paris exhibition not only promised to stimulate workers' intellectual engagement with French culture, from high art to industrial craft design, but also an identification with working-class causes that extended beyond national borders. However, like organizers of the 1861 tours, the IWA needed capital and the power of the state to get its tours off the ground. The project was ultimately brought to fruition by the Working Men's Club and Institute Union (WMCIU), an institution steeped in middle-class ideology, but one whose infrastructure and influence were up to the task. The planning committee of the WMCIU tour devised ways to deploy governmental power from beyond the club room to across the Channel. Indeed, organizers conceived workers' itineraries and lodgings as manageable sites of control, some basing their vision on the knowledge and experience gained as colonial administrators charged with educating or imposing order on indigenous populations. However, these plans (if not their underlying disciplinary intent) still required the sanction of labor leaders to make the tours successful, turning travel into another site for cross-class negotiation in a political rapprochement that reflects workers' contributions to the development of the new liberalism in the mid- to late-Victorian era. Indeed, in the process of collaboration, labor leaders challenged middle-class reformers' ideological framework to accommodate the rise of working-class politics and to redress the failures of the liberal state. An unintended consequence for their middle-class supporters, the tours promoted some workers' radical articulation of travel as an education in internationalism and class identity.

Chapter 3, "'The Lessons of Paris,': The Artisan Imagination and the 1867 Working Men's Exhibition Tours," takes a closer look at the tours by analyzing 84 "Artisan Reports" that were subsidized and published by the Education Department and the Society of Arts. Organizers encouraged workers to critique Britain in constructive ways and with patriotic aims. Although the artisan reporters were expected to offer a comparative analysis of foreign and domestic life, labor, and leisure, their analyses led to mixed responses, often in favor of French rather than British social, political, and cultural mores. While the reports served a public function in communicating information, they also allowed the reporters to examine their own lives, beliefs, and values in new environments and contexts. Rife with discursive tensions, their narratives reveal the interplay of patriotic, national, imperial, class, occupational, and gender identities.

Chapter 4, "The Technical Education Movement and the Artisan Exhibition Tours of Paris and Vienna, 1867–1889," explores how the 1867 tours offered a blueprint for three subsequent artisan exhibition tours and how they became linked to a movement for reforming Britain's education system. It examines the tours' organization, sources of funding, and itineraries, as well as the publication of the reports and the workers who produced them. These tours expanded, formalized, and institutionalized a form of educational travel by defining new categories of knowledge to be derived from study abroad and by ritualizing a selection process that privileged some workers over others for the post of "artisan reporter." This process parallels the social divides within educational travel; both the artisan tours and educational travel, generally, were promoted in terms of patriotism and the common good, but ultimately became the purviews of a privileged few. Indeed, tour organizers identified those who could be usefully deployed abroad to study continental educational, cultural, and labor practices that tour organizers considered crucial to the national well-being. Only select workers were in a position, therefore, to benefit from education and examinations that emphasized technical skills and knowledge. This chapter thus establishes the links between education and economic, social, and geographic mobility. Chapter 5, "Class Trips and the Meaning of British Citizenship: The Regent Street Polytechnic, 1871–1903," examines the outcomes of the artisan tours and the changing face of education for young wage earners in the late nineteenth century. In 1889, the passage of the Technical Instruction Act led to the provision of state and municipal funds for the development of technical schools. After nearly four decades, the educational reform movement had at last succeeded in getting tax monies funneled to local county councils to support technical education committees and to fund new and existing technical schools for the artisan classes. The London Regent Street Polytechnic was one such beneficiary. Founded by middle-class philanthropy, the Young Men's Christian Institute, or "Polytechnic," sought to incorporate working-class youth into the nation by exposing its members to the outside world. The Polytechnic's institutional ethos privileged informal as well as formal travel experiences at home and in the empire as a function and duty of citizenship. Travel permeated its social and educational programs, from its language clubs to its plumbing courses, to produce recognizably modern forms of study abroad. In addition to organizing group trips abroad, the Institute invited guests from around the world to Regent Street, reflecting the normalization of empire in the everyday life of the metropole. The analysis contextualizes this travel ethos and links it to the "educational idea" and the educational reform movement discussed in earlier chapters. It thus reintroduces Thomas Cook & Son and other actors who represent the protracted nature of educational reform and the enduring interest in educational travel into the last quarter of the nineteenth century and beyond. The analysis also situates within the new liberalism, the Polytechnic's travel practices, such as the establishment of its own travel agency, which offered inexpensive "Co-operative and Educational Tours" for its students and the public alike. Indeed, an examination of the collective representations of "mass" tours in the *Polytechnic Magazine* reveals a new form of travel writing that was an active expression of cultural citizenship, reflecting the ideological transition from individualism to collectivism characteristic of the new liberalism. Although the Polytechnic sought to create collectivities through travel as an antidote to the alienation of mass society and the problems of democratization, travel also became a site of gender and class conflict within the Polytechnic that mirrored inequalities and tensions in wider society. This chapter illustrates, therefore, the limits of liberal reform by defining citizenship, in part, by access to educational travel.

The analysis in Chapter 5 ends, for all intents and purposes, at the turn of the twentieth century, after the momentum for expanding adult education with opportunities for travel faltered under the pressure of not only conservative reaction to liberal progressivism, but from the inherent contradictions within liberalism itself, an outcome that Alexander Kay sensed even within the confines of Peckham House. The book concludes, however, in another time and another house, pursuing the contradictions of liberalism and the fate of study abroad into the present. The book's final pages return to working-class disillusionment and the meaning of travel in ruling-class rhetoric. The conclusion, "Goody, Gordon, and Shilpa Shetty 'Poppadom': The Politics of Study Abroad from the New Liberalism to New Labour," thus follows an everyday Briton beyond the borders of council house poverty to India, and follows leaders of the land to the lecture halls of the new metropolitan center, the United States, to call into question the rhetoric of "globalization" and the reinvention of study abroad as the *sine qua non* of a new kind of citizenship.

1
"A True Agent of Civilisation": Travel and the "Educational Idea," 1841–1861

> The Continental tourist obtains something more than mere pleasure. He procures increased health and information. To him the world is no longer a sealed book [for] never before did the British people know so much about the early and modern history of their neighbours across the channel. ... In this increasing familiarity of the British people with the nations of the Continent are to be detected the germs of results far grander, far more powerful, than even statesmen or philosophers have yet ventured to dream of. People are gaining experience and wisdom, and with these will come a day of better things. There is nothing like travel to remove the strong crust of prejudice which hardens around poor human nature. It expands the mind and teaches people to be more tolerant in their ideas. No wonder that the old brutal sports of the multitude are fast declining in popularity. When the masses are provided with the proper facilities, they are to be found preferring the romantic marvels of Matlock to a prize-fight, or the art-treasures of Chatsworth to a racing-match. Is not then the excursion system a true agent of civilisation? After all, the cause of social and intellectual progress does owe a little to Cook's Excursions.[1]

Thomas Cook, the nineteenth-century founder of the global travel agency, Thomas Cook & Son, is often celebrated as a pioneer of the modern package tour, an entrepreneur who contributed to the rationalization and democratization of travel by coordinating transport, food, and lodging before the era of nationalized railways or chain motels. Yet, as the quotation above illustrates, Cook also viewed himself as a cultural ambassador between Britain and the world, and between Britain's past and its future. Working for "the cause of social and intellectual progress," Cook's excursions not only helped ordinary Britons become cosmopolites by introducing them to their continental "neighbours," but they helped "the masses" discard the vulgar leisure attractions of a bygone era for more "elevating" pursuits such as trips to scenic sites, country estates, and art galleries.

Over the course of his career, Cook maintained these themes in sundry pamphlets that advertised his tours, offering potential excursionists the means of travel and promising that positive results would arise from the experience. In so doing, Cook contributed to an emerging discourse about culture and its utility that was allied with the "educational idea." A feature of the Victorian climate of utilitarian reform, the "educational idea" was linked to the "statistical idea" of liberal governance in which members of civil society and state officials assembled "facts" in order to educate and regulate the populace using sound scientific knowledge. Thus the educational idea gave direction and coherence to seemingly diverse projects. These included public lending libraries, museums, savings banks, and even municipal sewage systems (the "sanitary idea") that taught the "poorer population" the qualities of respectability, sobriety, thrift, and hygiene, qualities that promised to bring them within the pale of civilization.[2] Invested with these educational properties, travel also became an instrument of public instruction.

Cook's excursions (along with the tours of other early travel entrepreneurs) should be counted among these educational projects in applying a utilitarian rationale to culture as a public resource. Travel organizers not only infused excursions with a moral purpose, but they developed technologies that permitted travel's benefits to be distributed through the general population. Within this reformist climate of proliferating ideas, modern travel practices – or, the technologies that put travel (the travel "idea") into motion – emerged as innovative pedagogical tools for individual and national improvement.

This chapter reconstructs the climate of educational reform and the ethos of improvement that will lead to the tour of over 3000 working men to the 1867 Paris exhibition. A colossal event that required the resources of civil society and the state to realize – Cook, prominent men in civil society, state bureaucrats, and working people, each had a role to play in making the Workingmen's Paris Exhibition Tours come to pass. Ultimately, their actions contributed to the formation of educational travel as a form of power that served different interests, from the state's effort to regulate the population to labor leaders' struggle for inclusion in the civic and political life of the nation. The purpose of this chapter, therefore, is to explain how the largest mass tour of British workers to the continent became invested with an educational and moral imperative and the different meanings it assumed as a "true agent of civilisation."

From "Pests" to "Citizens": Education, Rational Recreation, and Liberal Governance

Steam and steel – the twin pillars of modern industrial progress – helped give rise to nineteenth-century mass travel, with steamboat voyages across the

Channel in the 1820s, and passenger rail service a decade later. However, for labor leaders, reformers, and eventually the state, these engines of change also signaled the human and governmental costs of industrialization, costs that called into question the welfare and governance of an expanding and increasingly impoverished and alienated urban proletariat. Responses to these problems varied. Many urban workers addressed the question of industrialization in the 1830s and 1840s through Chartism, a series of protest movements that sought, with either "physical" or "moral" force, to eradicate economic hardship, political disenfranchisement, and social inequality. Middle-class reformers and government bureaucrats took a different approach to the welfare crisis of industrialization. They conducted statistical inquiries that identified and quantified social problems, and they legislated solutions, such as the 1834 Poor Law Amendment Act and the 1835 Municipal Reform Act, which would make the population knowable, manageable, and productive. They had thus begun collecting the bricks and mortar that would constitute, in Michel Foucault's terms, the "carceral city."

As Foucault writes in describing the mechanisms of modern social governance, reformers assembled a "multiple network of diverse elements – walls, space, institution, rules, discourse" that were "intended to alleviate pain, to cure, to comfort – but which all tend[ed], like the prison, to exercise a power of normalization."[3] These "elements" included culture, which in the form of education and recreation became a means for the governance of extended populations. As such, reformers' views on culture's utility as a governmental technology deserve some scrutiny, for they influenced how travel – on steamboats and passengers trains – could be used to improve Britain's increasingly industrialized society. In their hands, organized working-class travel, like mass education, would require trained guides and specially constructed environments to get the most educational value out of the travel experience and to effectively transform the urban working poor into productive citizens.

Drawing on Foucault, scholars stress the ambition of British reformers and the state to manage urban populations by guiding individuals into becoming self-regulating citizens.[4] Education venues became the primary site for achieving this objective. Ian Hunter argues that the modern school system emerged in the late nineteenth century as a "hybrid of two radically autonomous 'technologies of existence.'" The first was an "apparatus of government that sought the social transformation of the citizenry in accordance with the objectives of the state." The second was a "system of pastoral discipline that operated by inculcating the means of ethical self-reflection and self-cultivation."[5] In one example, Hunter explains this duality with regard to the Scottish reformer, David Stow, and the historical formation of the "playground." An important early proponent of national education to better control the poor, Stow was appalled by the criminality and immorality that he confronted each day in walking through Glasgow's polluted and densely populated Saltmarket district. Determined to rescue a few Saltmarket children "for whose souls and bodies no one seemed to care," Stow founded a popular school in which such "pests to society" would learn to behave themselves as moral beings.[6] In observing these specimens of urban squalor and vice, Stow determined that their regulation required a purpose-built environment, one that included a playground where children would learn how to conduct themselves within a "free" space. While simulating the freedom pauper children experienced on the streets, the playground contained one crucial difference: specially trained teachers in pastoral governance, professional educators who would "incorporate the sympathetic demeanors of both the spiritual guide and the caring parent" to help steer (rather than coerce) their pupils into using freedom to make principled behavioral choices in any circumstances and conditions. Under the teachers' supervision, therefore, children's natural exuberance could be gently tamed and channeled into moral behavior.

Building on this concept, Stow's disciple, Samuel Wilderspin, recommended that playgrounds include fruit trees as a way of "appeal[ing] to the child's judgment." Wilderspin argued before the Select Committee on the Education of the Poorer Classes in the 1830s that:

> The child moves in a society of trained beings [the teacher and other children], and the next time he stops and looks at a fine cherry he looks about to see whether there is anybody within view. Doubtless he is restrained from taking the cherry by fear, but in process of time, by moving among restrained playfellows, he has that command over himself which enables him to resist temptation.[7]

This conceptual and pedagogical shift from coercion to conscience appealed to reform-minded, utilitarian bureaucrats. James Kay-Shuttleworth, a Poor Law Commissioner and first secretary to the committee of the privy council on education in 1839, endorsed these tactics, regarding such early ethical training as cost-effective means for securing state interests. Impressed with the new "sympathetic" role devised for school teachers who, in the eyes of their pupils, would be seen as kind friends rather than coercive tyrants, Kay-Shuttleworth argued that these methods could be expected to produce social and political contentment, empty out workhouses and prisons, and maximize the state's human resources by nurturing productive, healthy, and, crucially, self-regulating citizens.[8]

Despite these early forays into disciplinary power at pauper schools, it would take three decades of subsequent parliamentary inquiries to establish national elementary schools based on this logic. In the meantime, however, reformers tackled the equally important question of adult education. If reformers felt that indigent children required expert guidance and special play environments to become self-regulating citizens, they believed that their parents were equally in need of instruction. Yet, devising environments for the social training of adults posed a special set of problems if reformers expected to maintain Britain's liberal ethos of individual freedom and minimal government intervention. Compulsory adult education was out of the question except, perhaps, in the final instance when punishment concluded the disciplinary life cycle behind prison walls.[9] Reformers approached this dilemma, therefore, by looking at culture in new ways that allowed the state, assisted by civil society, to govern at a distance through culturally elevating activities. Museums, libraries, and galleries – sites of "rational recreation" – provided the means by which working people would voluntarily and pleasurably learn to regulate themselves, often guided by unobtrusive pastoral agents, just as their children learned their lessons from sympathetic teachers and the school playground.

The middle classes had originally constructed the ideology of rational recreation with a concern for their own self-betterment. Peter Bailey writes that early in the century, the middle classes confronted the "process of developing a new culture within the unique matrix of a maturing urban industrial society," in which recreation played a significant part in their daily lives and identities. This process was particularly evident by the mid-Victorian period, when economic affluence matched a proliferation of new goods and services, and the leisure time to enjoy them.[10] At issue, however, was that "in a work-oriented value system leisure represented the irresponsible preoccupations of a parasitic ruling class or the reckless carousing of an irrational working class."[11] Moralists resolved this tension with the ideology of rational recreation, a concept and practice that managed to reconcile work and leisure.

Steeped in the work ethic that had made them prosperous yet uncomfortable with the very concept of a holiday, middle-class Victorians viewed rational recreation as a justification for productive, improving play. In this line of thinking, enjoyment and relaxation were understood as necessary companions to work, as they restored the mind and body for even greater exertions. Phrased another way, "work and play were antithetical in form only; in purpose they were part of a single natural process in which work was sovereign."[12] What mattered most, then, was how and where leisure time was expended. Quiet employment at home with book or needle, restful days spent at holiday health spas, and self-improvement at literary and scientific clubs became acceptable mediums for productive leisure. And what was good for the middle classes was good – even an imperative – for the working classes.

In seeking to establish liberal governance, reformers assessed the utility of culture to achieving this goal, particularly its deployment among the working classes through diverse forms of rational recreation. Tony Bennett's analyses of government and culture, for example, show how reformers throughout the Victorian era applied a utilitarian calculus to culture in determining its positive civilizing effects. This eventually led to the bureaucratization of culture in the establishment of public libraries, galleries, museums, and exhibitions in the second half of the nineteenth century.[13] These "set of educative and civilizing agencies," as Bennett remarks in his influential study of the "exhibitionary complex," were crucial to modern state formation.[14] An important champion of culture and its governmental utility was the brilliant and energetic civil servant, Henry Cole. Bennett lists Cole's influence in a number of capacities. As a member of the Society of Arts, Cole was the "architect" of the 1851 Great Exhibition, the "founder" of the South Kensington Museum, and the first "effective" head of the Department of Art and Science. Through such agencies, Cole envisioned a positive role for government in society by virtue of its "multiplying the circuits" in which ordinary people would have access to culture and its benefits. Indeed, Cole's vision extended to all of Britain, not just the metropolitan center. Thus, Cole wanted *objets d'art* housed in London museums to circulate in provincial museums, further multiplying their civilizing effects. The passing of the Museum Bill of 1845 and the Libraries Act of 1850, which enabled town councils to construct public institutions for the "instruction and amusement" of their citizens, demonstrate how persuasive the discourses surrounding rational recreation and the utility of culture had become, although such programs would still require ideological support to maintain their viability late in the century.[15]

Justifying government expenditure on these agencies of civilization, reformers insisted that they would more than pay for themselves, just as Kay-Shuttleworth had argued in promoting his concept of the elementary school. Even as late as the 1880s, as Bennett explains, these arguments persisted. The political economist, William Stanley Jevons observed, in a discussion of public libraries, that such investments would:

> Not only [be] repaid many times over by the multiplication of util-
> ity of the books, newspapers, and magazines on which it is expended,
> but it is likely ... to come back fully in the reduction of poor-rates and
> Government expenditure on crime. We are fully warranted in looking
> upon Free Libraries as an engine for operating upon the poorer portions
> of the population.[16]

Jevons, like earlier reformers, clearly articulated the relevance of culture in social reform projects from a standpoint that considered both the moral and fiscal outcomes of public institutions, and regarded it as a power, an "engine," in which to develop the population's "capacities."[17] Viewing culture as a powerful governmental resource to effect social change and the inner transformation of individuals, Jevons and his ideological forebears hoped to transform the idle poor into an industrious poor by turning to the "exhibitionary complex," the links between museum, library, art gallery, and exhibition, rather than to the workhouse or prison alone, to create governable populations.[18] Thus, while the middle class originally developed the ideology and practices of rational recreation in defining their identity in opposition to the ruling and working classes, their concerns over the growth of unregulated urban masses made opening culture to working people a necessity, inspiring new techniques of liberal governance.[19]

This, then, was the context of the educational idea, which would intersect with travel, becoming, for people like Cook, the "travel idea." Like other rational recreation activities, educational travel became another way in which reformers used culture to help instruct and regulate a governable and self-governing society, turning "pests" into "citizens." Multiplying culture's utility, travel encouraged an engagement with sites of learning both at home and abroad. Railways and steamships, therefore, provided the circuits with which people had access to culture, broadening their intellectual and cultural horizons and their sense of themselves as individuals, as members of society, as British citizens, and – if Cook had his way – as members of a common humanity.

Cooking-up the Travel "Idea"

Like Stow, Kay-Shuttleworth, and Cole, Thomas Cook harnessed culture to the idea of education and self-improvement, promoting a view of mass travel as a "public service." Taking the lead in this "great public work," as he often announced in his advertising gazette, *The Excursionist*, Cook viewed mass tourism "as his mission to humanity," which he realized in part by taking on the pastoral role of guide.[20] Although his primary clients proved to be shopkeepers, schoolmasters, ministers, physicians, small factory owners, and managers, he continually sought to bring travel within the reach of the working classes. As a rule, however, working people found Cook's Tours economically prohibitive. In an age when work and wages were rarely stable, even the best-paid artisan would think twice before surrendering ten or more pounds for an extended tour of the Continent. Moreover, few could forgo employment for the period of time necessary for a trip abroad, be it a week, a month, or longer. Nevertheless, Cook attempted to help workers overcome these obstacles by organizing short excursions, such as day trips to scenic sites and famous country estates, and by promoting holiday savings clubs and specially priced package tours for large groups of workers.

Several factors influenced Thomas Cook's lifelong commitment to working-class travel. The first was his humble Derbyshire origins. Upon leaving school in 1818 at the age of ten, Cook began his working life as a gardener's assistant and later became a carpenter, a printer of religious tracts, and an itinerant preacher. From these formative years, Cook understood the drudgery of manual labor and the constant worry of making ends meet that dominated working people's daily lives. This empathy was reinforced by the "hungry forties," a period marked by severe unemployment and poverty, but also by radical solutions to these problems, including the repeal of the Corn Laws and Chartist demands for the franchise. Persuaded by the principles of classical economics and liberal internationalism, Cook supported limited democracy and free trade as well as voluntary solutions to poverty and class hostilities.[21]

Cook's initial goals as a travel entrepreneur reflect these liberal and nonconformist beliefs and values. Cook seized the opportunity presented by the growth of the railways to use travel as a means for earning a living, but also as a platform for proselytizing the good life, one based on Christian morality, hard work, and importantly, sobriety. With other social reformers of the period, Cook viewed alcohol as a fundamental cause of working-class indigence. While Cook understood that trade and employment cycles, as well as disease, drought, and famine contributed to the misery of the working classes, he also believed that the evils of drink exacerbated these conditions. Cook's occupational transition from an itinerant preacher to a travel entrepreneur thus began with a temperance extravaganza in 1841, in which he chartered a train that transported between 400 and 600 teetotal passengers 11 miles from Leicester to Loughborough. In Loughborough, excited spectators and brass bands greeted Cook's first excursionists, who also enjoyed, if Cook's account of the event is to be believed, uplifting speeches on the slavery of drink and the freedom of sobriety. Elated with the success of this first excursion and "inspired," as Piers Brendon writes, "by millenarian hopes of redeeming an entire people," Cook encouraged the crowd to cheer "for Teetotalism and Railwayism!!!" and promised more excursions in the years to come. He soon fulfilled this promise, carving out a path that led to the creation of a global travel network. Along the way, he also assumed the pastoral role of a kindly teacher and guide to novice travelers.[22]

From these early temperance excursions, Cook developed a wider program of domestic and foreign travel that included new technologies of seeing and learning. Like emerging museum technologies such as catalogues and descriptive labels, Cook's promotional literature plainly explained what sites tourists would encounter on their journeys and what to value in their tours. Commercializing the self-help ethos, Cook even included a didactic how-to article in *The Excursionist* for aspiring travel writers. "The value of a diary to the tourist who wishes to remember accurately all that he may have seen is incalculable," he moralized, "yet comparatively few persons know how to keep one." He thus advised his clients to fashion their travel diaries much like a popular tour, always keeping in mind "system, brevity, and exactness."[23]

By the 1880s, Thomas Cook & Son had so perfected the business principles of "system, brevity, and exactness" that the agency expanded from its base in London (previously, Leicester), and became an imperial institution with offices around the world. This expansion was due in large part to Cook's willingness to risk hard-won capital in innovative organizational schemes, from conducted package tours to all-inclusive coupons that allowed tourists to travel on their own, but with transportation and lodging reassuringly secured by Cook's in advance. These changes shifted the focus of Cook's firm from the working class to the middle, and even the upper, classes. In the late 1870s, Cook's son made it a point to torment the competition by publicizing the firm's growing list of royal clients. But Thomas Cook did not abandon the rank and file altogether. His deeply held religious beliefs sustained his commitment to working-class tourism and infused his vision of travel with an ethos of ecumenical cosmopolitanism.

As a New Connexion Baptist, Cook believed that good works paved the road to salvation. This conviction, Brendon writes, lent a missionary zeal to all of Cook's travel schemes, including finding ways to make travel affordable to all but the very poor. Sometimes called the patron saint of travel, Cook believed that through travel "man has been brought nearer to man and nearer to his Creator," an ideology that blended well with his liberal politics and social activism.[24] Cook thus anticipated that travel – from day trips to European tours – would help to resolve conflicts that impeded the progress of all mankind, from social tensions at home to political tensions abroad. Embracing all working people – those who toiled with their minds as well as with their hands – Cook propagated an inclusive language about travel's personal, social, and international benefits, always referring to its broad educative function.[25] Not everyone, however, greeted the advent of passenger trains and the development of the excursion system with Thomas Cook's ardor for progress and vision of reform.

The political implications of mass mobility produced significant anxiety in the upper ranks of society. As Brendon observes, "the word 'mob' stemmed from 'mobile,' and British rulers had always regarded lower-class mobility as a threat." British rulers feared that the railways would facilitate Chartist organization and its rise to power, that train travel encouraged "the lower orders to go uselessly wandering about the country," and that the "railway revolution" permitted a "dangerous tendency to equality." The railway companies concurred. Brendon reminds us that the railways not only divided the passenger trains into a three-tiered class system that reproduced class hierarchies, but initially policed access to their services. "Anyone wanting to buy tickets," Brendon writes, "had to apply twenty-four hours in advance giving name, address, place of birth, age, occupation, and reason for the journey. Only thus could the station agent satisfy himself that 'the applicant desires to travel for a just and lawful cause.'"[26]

Regulation of rail travel, however, soon gave way to the profit motive and, in the end, the railway interests endorsed mass travel. Elites – members of the aristocracy, the upper-middle classes, and public intellectuals – rebelled. The development of anti-tourism, as literary critic James Buzard remarks, thus paralleled the growth of mass tourism. When the Kendall and Windermere line opened the Lake District to day trippers, for example, Wordsworth decried the invasion of his precious lakes by "artisans and labourers, and the humbler classes of shopkeepers [who] should not be tempted to visit particular spots which they had not been educated to appreciate."[27] Others similarly resented the influx of tourists to what were once their exclusive haunts of aesthetic, healthful, or spiritual consumption – be they the Swiss Alps, Mediterranean promenades, or Roman catacombs. Consequently, when Cook (and his rivals) began escorting "the millions" into Europe and then around the world, insisting upon travel's educational and ecumenical properties, a sustained polemic against the democratization of travel emerged that constructed culturally status-and-class laden distinctions between the authentic, educated, and lone traveler, who Buzard dubs the "anti-tourist," and the inauthentic, ignorant mass tourist or excursionist.[28]

Standing up to his critics, Cook first formulated his philosophy of travel's educational value in a tract titled *Pleasure Trips Defended*, published in 1846 and reprinted in 1854. As the title suggests, as early as five years after his first temperance excursion, Cook found it necessary to publicly confront critics who sniffed disapprovingly at the development of mass tourism. In response to the narrow interests of this cultural elite, Cook's rhetoric joined the world together in fraternal brotherhood while at the same time it joined a nation together under the banner of rational recreation and self improvement, the reformer's remedy to the problems of a modern industrial society.

Legitimating mass tourism as a rational and progressive movement, Cook announced that travel was a gift of science which had inspired men with "new feelings and animated [them] with new hopes," with none so powerful as "Railways and Locomotion." The opening of a new railway in a backward town, Cook proclaimed, "is [thus] an omen of moral renovation and intellectual exaltation." Previously, Cook explained, "a 'visit to a watering place' was a luxury beyond the reach of the toiling artizan or mechanic." But in the new age of modern mass travel all may "revel in the delights of nature and go forth to inspect objects of artistical magnificence ... and thus the broad distinctions of classes are removed without violence or any objectionable means."[29] While science and locomotion made mass mobility possible, the experience of travel itself, Cook continued, also changed the "minds and morals of men," and was thus a transformative experience. Travel, wrote Cook:

> provides food for the mind; it contributes to the strength and enjoyment of the intellect; it helps to pull men out of the mire and pollution of old corrupt customs; it promotes a feeling of universal brotherhood; [and] it accelerates the march of peace and virtue, and love.

Moreover, the process of travel, of leaving home to experience other cultures, Cook insisted, brings an "increase of self-knowledge, ... [an] enlargement of [the] mind, ... a deepening of charity, [and] a warmer and enduring patriotism." Addressing his critics directly, Cook queried, "Are not all these valuable objects?"[30] A progressive view of mobility, Cook's rhetoric ultimately claimed that travel functioned as a leveling mechanism that did away with petty class and cultural differences at home and abroad, and educated all in a profound love for humanity and the noble pursuit of knowledge.

Cook's philosophy, therefore, echoed the educational idea of other Victorian reformers. Like Stow's schools, travel under Cook's pastorship, became a liberal technology that could bring all Britons into the light of civilization. Infusing the language of travel with the utility of culture, Cook used *The Excursionist* over the course of his career to reiterate the themes of inner transformation – of education, virtue, patriotism, and internationalism. Further, he continued to frame his philosophy in ways that reached out to Britons of every class, subscribing to the evolving democratic ideals of liberal society. In this vein, Cook wrote about tourism in generally class-inclusive terms, and occasionally drew his readers' attention to individual working men who, having recognized the rational benefits of travel, availed themselves of his tours. For instance, recounting his first mass tour of the continent, a short excursion to Calais in 1855, Cook made an example of one working man, "a model for his 'order,'" who "managed to enjoy a treat worth ten times the labour and self-denial at the price of [£10] of which it was secured." The lesson to be gleaned by this worker's tour, Cook informed his audience (and critics), is that while "many a working man who spends £20 a year in 'drink and bacca' would stand appalled at the idea of appropriating half that sum to a trip on the Continent. ... all are not spendthrifts ... there *are* wise and thoughtful and prudent working men ... who ... toil hard for the means of recreation and improvement."[31] Although Cook contributed to the dominant discourse by contrasting the vulgarity, immorality and drunkenness of the working classes with this condescending valorization of one "rational" worker-traveler, he nonetheless responded to a genuine consumer demand in offering his socially diverse clients "an educational course – a system of practical teaching of the highest value."[32]

Eventually, Cook's ideas would win the approval of the state, of social reformers, and of working people themselves, and seemed to promise unlimited expansion. Yet, while these individual instances of worker travel gratified Cook, his aspiration to truly effect social change required that the working classes *en masse* also become active participants in traversing the world – in acquiring a taste for travel. Nowhere was this promise of rational and improving travel better exemplified than at the 1851 Exhibition in London. Millions attended the Exhibition, many of whom had their travel and lodging coordinated by Cook, and perhaps their outlook on travel and tourism shaped by Cook as well. The Exhibition thus gave people a reason to leave the familiar comfort of home and a new way of thinking of travel in terms of recreation. Indeed, according to Hugh Cunningham, it spurred an unprecedented interest in leisure travel.[33]

"Paxton's College": Travel, Education and the Great Exhibition

After the 1851 Great Exhibition, Cook stood poised to expand his travel operations beyond the midlands to the rest of Britain. Cook's 15-year association with the Great Western Railway and his personal association with Joseph Paxton (the architect of the Exhibition building and a member of the Royal Commission) secured him semi-official status as a special excursion agent for the Exhibition. With characteristic enthusiasm for improvement projects of every kind, and with an eye to improving his firm's prospects, Cook agreed to print Exhibition propaganda in *The Excursionist* including workers' prize essays. Many workers responded positively to the event, such as one anonymous "working man" who referred to the Exhibition as "Paxton's College" and as "a great School of Science, of Art, of Industry, [and] of Peace and Universal Brotherhood."[34] This perspective echoed Cook's own philosophy of progress and must have been all the more gratifying to him because it was voiced by a "working man."

Exhibition organizers would have viewed this working man's testimony as a triumph in meeting their goals as well. The Great Exhibition was the first international fair to bring the world's industries, manufacturers, and producers together in a show of "friendly rivalry," the oft-repeated phrase of Exhibition literature. Located in London's Hyde Park, and held in a specially constructed glass enclosure popularly known as the Crystal Palace, the Exhibition hosted a series of competitions that won Britain the lion's share of prizes. The British press celebrated this feat as the crowning glory of a free people and good governance. But, for many Exhibition organizers, the dissemination of liberal principles at the Crystal Palace was the prize they valued most.

Orchestrated by a Royal Commission and the Society of Arts, the primary Exhibition organizers were cut from a wide swathe of liberal cloth, representing the mid-century patchwork pattern of Radical, Whig, and Peelite interests. Under their direction, the Great Exhibition became not only a showplace for British manufacture, but a platform from which to articulate and affirm a range of liberal tenets, such as free trade, national independence, and international harmony. All told, organizers intended the Exhibition to persuade both foreign and domestic audiences of Britain's leading role in civilizational progress as evidenced by its industrial prowess and social stability.[35] Prince Albert, for example, took a special interest in cultivating an Anglo- German liberal alliance. Consequently, he organized tours of Britain's most prestigious cultural and political institutions, enabling German visitors to draw comparisons with their own states.[36]

Domestically, the Exhibition functioned as a locus of educational technologies designed to win hearts and minds, and to discipline bodies. Bennett demonstrates that these technologies had been in play at regional exhibitions for decades. Promoted by mechanics' institutes and other voluntary organizations, small-scale exhibitions proliferated in provincial towns and cities prior to 1851, and served several instructional purposes. First, exhibitions offered workers illustrations of exemplary industrial equipment, processes, and products in their trades. In studying and understanding the mechanics of the process or emulating the craftsmanship on display, workers could improve their own skills and contribute to the excellence of national industry. Equally instrumentally, they taught workers to conform to middle-class norms of public comportment. Exhibition organizers, for example, distributed special guidebooks which "trained" workers to behave and dress with decorum so as to become integrated into the "spectacle" of an ordered society – as an object of admiration (a respectable worker) – rather than an object of disorder and derision.[37] Susan Barton argues that this form of exhibition pedagogy (of informal technical education) also operated as part of a larger ideological project. Familiarizing workers with the "ethos of industrialism," exhibition organizers hoped to win their acceptance of the social order.[38] According to contemporary testimony, their aims were more than rewarded at the 1851 Exhibition. Originally lining the streets and paths of Hyde Park with an expectant cavalry, ready to charge at Chartist mobs and foreign agitators, government officials sighed with relief when "the people" proved calm and orderly from the first day to the last. In "The Harmonizing & Ennobling Influence of the Great Exhibition," Cook celebrated this accomplishment (and the governmental technologies that went into it) in *The Excursionist*. In it he printed a speech delivered to the Merchant Tailors' Company by an unnamed Royal Commissioner of the Exhibition. First acknowledging workers' contributions to the nation's prosperity on display at the Exhibition, the commissioner commented:

> I hope I may say in the language not of dishonourable pride, that I witnessed, and I am sure they witnessed with admiration and respect, the self-imposed order, discipline, and regularity [cheers] with which this free people confident in their free institutions guard and protect the treasures entrusted to their charge, and, without the need of military force, without the need of coercion, they themselves maintain that order which is the greatest and highest proof of a few and enlightened people.[39]

Evidently, the early exhibitions had done their work. They had socialized workers to behave and dress respectably and to use their free time productively. For Cook, however, what would have been more revelatory about the Great Exhibition was not the capacity of the working class for public decorum or self improvement, but the broad articulation of a new ethos of travel, one that was more widely disseminated than he could have hoped through the pages of *The Excursionist* alone. Travel to exhibitions and other sites of rational recreation now had the sanction of government as a public and national good.

Because the Royal Commission wanted the Exhibition to not only multiply culture's utility, but to represent social harmony in Britain, it took strong measures to ensure working-class attendance. Barton shows, for instance, that organizers originally intended to establish a working-class committee to help galvanize workers' interest in attending the Exhibition. Early on they enlisted support from a number of prominent Chartists. The Royal Commission, however, disbanded the subcommittee when some Chartist leaders concluded that the event was geared to subvert working-class politics and to lure working people into accepting the economic principles of laissez faire. Bearing this setback, organizers pressed ahead with a campaign that included conducting provincial organizational meetings, distributing promotional circulars, setting-up travel and savings clubs, establishing cheap accommodations in London, and procuring reasonable railway fares. In response, nearly 300 working-class groups formed their own local committees (often, but not always, headed by prominent citizens and progressive employers of large firms) to organize their own savings banks, transport, and lodgings in London. Without question, travel, in Barton's words, had "caught on."[40] However, while the Royal Commission wanted the Exhibition to convey a particular message and to produce certain results, Barton shows that working-class visitors brought their own expectations and agendas to the Crystal Palace. Constituting three-quarters of the six million visitors to the venue, artisans and mechanics hoped to derive a number of benefits from their journey to London. The Chartists among them wanted to make the Exhibition a venue for reviving their cause and advancing the ideas and aims of socialism. The trade unionists wanted to use the Exhibition to meet with other domestic and foreign labor organizations. In addition, members of mechanics institutions (many of whom were Chartists and trade unionists) wished to promote educational improvement. Some even predicted that the Exhibition would conclusively demonstrate their respectability through their impeccable public behavior, while their artisanal skills and taste in design – on display for all to see – would at last end upper-class contempt for working men.[41]

The Great Exhibition (and subsequent exhibitions) thus became a site for imagining the trajectory of progress into the future. Competing interests at each spectacle sought to manipulate that imagination, although none of them successfully monopolized it. The 1851 Exhibition operated, therefore, as a site for liberal propaganda and governmental disciplinary technologies, which accustomed ordinary Britons to travelling the rails for leisure purposes, and, as an unintended consequence (but one discerned by early critics of passenger trains and working-class mobility), accustomed workers to traveling en masse for specific political, social, and cultural aims that served their class interests. Indeed, working-class visitors brought their own perspectives to the exhibitions which their upper- and middle-class organizers could hope to redirect, but never control. Organizers and workers carried these varied interests with them into subsequent workers' tours, both at home and abroad, to continental exhibitions and elsewhere, making travel and tourism a contested cultural terrain that seemed to confirm the worst fears of early railway critics. Indeed, the Great Exhibition had established patterns of travel that reformers would wrestle to control once workers set their sights on producing their own excursions of the European continent for their own educational purposes.

"Simply for Amusement and Instruction": The Workingmen's Paris Excursion of 1861

For Cook, the 1851 Exhibition had demonstrated that a travel revolution was possible and that he was the man to lead it. Although the Exhibition was an ephemeral event, it realized the wide scope of his philosophy with thousands of working people willing to travel for rational recreational purposes. Thereafter, Cook stepped up his efforts to attract working-class travelers. In the 1850s he offered domestic working-class excursions such as "Cook's Moonlight Trips" to the Manchester Exhibition of "art treasures." Further afield, Cook also escorted an assortment of well-to-do English artisans, mechanics, and middle class schoolmasters, doctors, and shopkeepers into Scotland and Ireland.[42] In the 1860s, however, Cook set his sights on opening the European continent to all.

A decade after the Great Exhibition, working-class tourists began to cross the Channel, sometimes with Cook, but just as often without him. Working people had become enamored with foreign travel, but not necessarily with Cook's tours. Never one to shirk a challenge or neglect an opportunity, Cook made pointed overtures to working-class organizations with travel plans of their own. In the month of June in 1863, for example, Cook remarked in *The Excursionist* that during a brief trip to Paris he had encountered "numerous groups" of British workmen whose trips had been arranged by "the Working Men's Committee in London." Though "enjoying themselves most heartily," he was able to enhance their experience by arranging cheap tickets to Versailles and back, which they "gratefully" accepted. Cook estimated (based on sources he deemed reliable) that 700 workers at most, had participated in the tours, although the French and English papers had inflated the numbers to over 2000. A month later, Cook courted working-class tour groups directly in *The Excursionist*, stating that all "Working Men's Clubs for Paris are respectfully informed that we are prepared to co-operate with them, and to afford, on the most liberal terms we are able to offer, the facilities of our Paris Trips," noting that his firm possessed the experience and infrastructure necessary to make the organization of foreign tours easy and affordable.[43] Cook even appealed to politically subversive organizations for their patronage, such as the International Workingmen's Association

(IWA), an organization comprised of English trade unionists and continental émigrés dedicated to defending "humanity" from ruling-class greed and oppression.[44] Noting an upcoming IWA congress in Brussels in 1868, Cook suggested that those delegates who could spare two or three extra days abroad might take advantage of his special excursions to Waterloo, now a tourist attraction.[45] Perhaps some took him up on his suggestion, for sightseeing was an acceptable part of their meetings abroad. *The Bee-Hive*, a radical working-class paper published by the labor leader George Potter and edited by the former Chartist, Robert Hartwell, reported that the delegates of the Second Congress at Lausanne used a Monday afternoon to visit the city's museum, cathedral, and "other Lions of the Place."[46]

Cook had thus begun accompanying travelers to the continent with some regularity in the 1860s, including working-class tourists. Although he faced competition from the working classes themselves, as the London "Working Men's Committee" attests, he insisted that the financial success of his tourist enterprises up to this point had given him more flexibility than even his most formidable competitors to "assist the humbler classes in many of their laudable attempts to improve and gratify themselves and their fellows."[47] One such venture was a seven-day Whitsuntide excursion of 1673 British travelers to Paris in May of 1861.[48] Philanthropic and propagandistic in nature, it opened foreign travel to ordinary people while serving to promote Cook's Tours and the educational idea. Like many of the large 1851 Exhibition excursions, this event required Cook's travel expertise and also the active support of political and industrial elites, who were coming to view working class travel abroad as a means of regulating working people at home.

The Whitsuntide excursion of 1861 constituted Cook's second mass tour of Paris. He had conducted an excursion to the French capital in 1855, but was prevented from repeating the experiment by the railways, which had refused to lower their prices to accommodate Cook's "economical" travelers.[49] In 1861, however, the climate was more conducive to cooperation as a new free trade agreement with France, devised by Richard Cobden, had abolished the necessity of passports between the two countries (although the authorities still required travelers to register their names at the French border). Indeed, Cobden's free-trade rhapsody of the fraternal marketplace not only guaranteed the free flow of goods and services between Britain and France, but the exchange of people and ideas through increased travel. Long tantalized by travel narratives describing the attractions of Paris, British would-be travelers wanted to see with their own eyes the celebrated city and, as their numbers attest, responded to Cook's advertisements with enthusiasm.[50]

Although the tour was advertised as a "Workingmen's Excursion," Cook assured his readers that all who worked, whether with "head or hands," "male or female," "young or old," were welcome to join them.[51] With prices that varied depending on second or third class railway tickets and equivalent accommodations in Paris (consisting of single or shared rooms at over 20 hotels and boarding houses), middle-class travelers also took advantage of Cook's arrangements, seemingly not minding having to rub shoulders with working-class subordinates if it meant seeing Paris on a shoestring.[52] Despite the presence of middle-class tourists, however, the tour was a "workingmen's excursion" through-and-through. Subsidized for that purpose by philanthropists and reformers, it bore all the disciplinary markers of the educational idea.[53]

The tour originally got off the ground as an alternative to an excursion proposal by a corps of Army Volunteers who intended to march down Paris's boulevards in full dress uniform.[54] Given that the Volunteer Movement had mobilized that very year to protect Britain from the possibility of a French invasion (Napoleon III had modernized his navy with steel-bottomed boats), this paramilitaristic scheme generated a slew of articles and letters in *The Times,* thundering the public's disapproval.[55] Seizing the opportunity that this public denouncement had produced, a "body of English workmen," whose members included the chair-maker and former Chartist, Benjamin Lucraft, wanted to organize a tour that would allow earnest workers, instead of uniformed troops, to visit the country and meet with the people. To do so, they formed a "London Workingmen's Committee" (the likely predecessor to the 1863 "Working Men's Committee in London"), with the radical barrister, J.J. Merriman, as its president. Merriman then wrote to the influential secretary of the Peace Society, Henry Richard, stating their ambitions (portions of which were published in *The Excursionist*). First, the workers wanted to "inspect the public buildings, institutions, and places of resort in the French capital"; and, second, they wanted to "shake hands with the Parisian *ouvriors* [sic], and assure them that whatever may have been the case many years ago, this nation has now no other feeling towards France but that of good will." As Merriman explained, unlike the Volunteers, the excursion was to be "moral" and "pacific," and would have "no direct political object or character." Thus, the excursion was to be a "visit of pleasure, from which it is hoped some profit may, however, ultimately accrue to England and France." These goals were certain to appeal to Richard, who, in another round of networking, approached Paxton (now a Liberal MP) and Cook for help with organizing the tour.[56]

The "London Committee of Workingmen" had originally attempted to make its own arrangements, but found it rough going – a common experience in this early stage of continental travel.[57] The difficulties were many. First, while internal travel and short excursions were becoming routine by the 1860s, mass travel abroad still remained a complex enterprise, often requiring the expertise of travel agents. Organizers needed to navigate not only foreign-language barriers, but a labyrinth of domestic and foreign railway timetables, exchange rates, and lodging options. Mass tours also tended to require surplus capital, the approval of well-placed British and foreign officials, and personal or business contacts with railway managers and hotel owners. Working-class-travel organizers, therefore, needed assistance from middle-class elites whose business influence and social and political networks could simplify and expedite the process. Middle-class reformers, as the working-class organizers were well aware, were only too willing to help with advice, financial subsidies, and other organizational necessities if given sufficient latitude to shape such tours in ways that conformed to their ideas of rational recreation.

Cook, for instance, promoted the workingmen's excursion as a "great national" project with benevolent "international" implications. He also legitimated the project by announcing that the tour had the support of "gentlemen" who had "risen 'from the ranks' of the industrial population" and whose stature would convince the "French authorities that the project had the sympathy of eminent men, well-known in connection with the great Progression Movements of the Age." In addition to Paxton, they included the railway magnates Thomas Brassey and Sir Morton Peto; the Liberal MP and brewer, Michael Thomas Bass; the paternalist employer Titus Salt, who would assist two hundred of his own factory workers to participate in the Whitsuntide Paris tours; the editor of the politically liberal *Lloyd's Weekly Newspaper*, Blanchard Jerrold; the industrialist and future architect of the 1870 Education Reform Bill, W.E. Forster; and the radical MP and president of the tour committee, Austin Henry Layard.[58] Radicals and reformers, industrialists and parliamentarians – the tour's many supporters illustrate the comingling of multiple interests as travel's utility broadened to match the expansion of educational technologies and, it should be emphasized, liberal trade practices that had spurred a resurgence of labor activism.

Indeed, liberal governance through travel-as-culture offered tour sponsors a pedagogical means for influencing working class opinion at a critical juncture in international trade relations. Although 1848 saw the last Chartist petition before parliament, working-class agitation had not been quelled by the Chartist defeat, as many workers persisted in their demands, with the new model unions acting as seedbeds of post-Chartist radicalism. Trade unions had reentered the public sphere during this period with the London builder's strike in 1859, the creation of the London Trades Council in 1860, and the launching of *The Bee-Hive* newspaper in October, 1861.[59] Through trade unionism, workers continued to agitate for social equality, the franchise, and an end, as the trade union activist, George Howell expressed it in an early editorial of the *Operative Bricklayers' Circular*, to the "tyranny of capital and oppression of employers."[60] While, as Margot Finn writes, this labor activity was bereft of a "coherent theory of economics," labor leaders refused to be wooed to the tenets of laissez-faire economics.[61] In remaining united on this score, they also reaffirmed their "international fellowship" with "workers from France, Italy, Belgium, Holland, Hungary, and Poland."

This commitment recognized their mutual interests in the internationalization of labor through liberal capitalism and would have its strongest articulation in the formation of the International Workingmen's Association and the First International in 1864.[62]

In response to this labor activity, some middle-class leaders in parliament and industry adjusted their views on laissez faire to stem the tide of working class militancy. The positivist movement, for instance, rejected the ideology of "self interest" to foster social collectivities. Other radicals sought to build alliances by promising support for labor arbitration and the extension of the franchise. And still others joined working-class leaders in developing internationalist understandings through their mutual support of European nationalist movements.[63] But, in forming alliances with labor, they wished to do so on their own terms. With regard to the 1861 tour, this meant that organizers wished to orchestrate the contexts in which workers' met with their *confrères* on the continent and to shape the lessons to be gleaned from their time abroad. Indeed, once the tour was taken up by Cook the "body of English workingmen" who had originally promoted the tour nearly disappeared from the narrative. Instead liberal reformers and pundits dominated the discourse surrounding the meaning and purpose of the tour.

Some in the liberal press, for example, turned the tour into a vehicle for demonstrating the viability of political economy with direct reference to free trade between Britain and France. Commenting on the proposed tour, the *London Review*, a journal that represented radical liberal interests, remarked that French workmen would initially resent seeing British working-class tourists in Paris. Well-dressed and enjoying a leisure holiday, the British workers would seem to be enjoying themselves at the expense of French workers' own livelihoods. However, once they realized that it had been protectionism rather than free trade that had placed them in desperate economic straits, they would shake hands with their new friends from across the Channel and stroll down the Parisian boulevards "arm in arm," understanding, at last, that with the new commercial agreement in place, prosperity awaited them just around the corner.[64] Needless to say, radical workers, like Lucraft, would have questioned this celebratory narrative, and reformers knew this.[65] They anticipated, nevertheless, that exposure to working-class conditions on the continent might chip away at labor's long held antipathy to economic liberalism. This expectation placed a lot of faith in the transformative power of travel. But, it was a conviction that the tour organizers and supporters shared, as Layard's letters and speeches illustrate.

Aside from Cook, Layard probably influenced the tenor of the tour more than any other committee member. Layard, the famous excavator of Nineveh and MP for the working-class borough of Southwark, had made his early reputation in parliament as a staunch radical. He spurned aristocratic privilege at all levels of government, supported European nationalist movements, and even empathized with the instigators of the India uprising. In the 1860s he continued on this path becoming known as both "a man of the people" and a social reformer who championed the extension of the franchise for respectable working men. In 1861, Layard's enthusiasm for radical causes worried his closest friend, Lord Cowley, the British Ambassador to France, who cautioned that "we are living in an age when the too great power of the people must be kept in check."[66] Cowley need not have worried. Although a "man of the people," Layard exercised paternalistic restraint in his dealings with the working classes.[67]

Layard believed in the governmental power of culture. As a Vice President of the National Book Union for the Dissemination of Sound Literature among the Working Classes, Layard lent his time and influence to promoting the "Book Union Bill" which, while "appealing to all Friends of National Education" was rejected by the House of Lords.[68] Layard also stood on the board of trustees for both the British Museum and the National Gallery and, well acquainted with Cole, shared his commitment to making all public institutions more conducive to "the comfort and convenience of those who are to use them."[69] As Commissioner of Works and Public Buildings, Layard also endorsed the Sunday Movement that petitioned for working people's access to museums, parks and other institutions of rational recreation on their one full day off from their labor. Layard, thus shared with utilitarian reformers the desire to multiply culture's utility, and appeared as committed as Cook to developing the educational efficacy of travel.

A series of communiqués from Layard to Cowley, who assisted the tour's organization from the Paris embassy, illustrate Layard's ambitions for the excursion. Although Layard repeatedly stressed that the aim of the tour was simply one of "amusement and instruction" with no "political character or function" whatsoever, its perceived utility as a medium for change was unquestionably political.[70] Writing to Cowley in early March of 1861, he confessed that he "look[ed] upon the scheme as highly useful because the more our working classes see of the world, the more rational and intelligent they get and the less likely to be led astray by dangerous and designing men."[71] As he continued in another letter, "I think the visit of these men will be good – it will open their eyes a little and make them less apt to think too much of themselves."[72]

Layard did little to disguise these expectations. During a crowded promotional meeting at the London Whittington Club, attended by journalists and, reportedly, 1000 prospective tourists, Layard urged the excursionists to refrain from "allowing any political feeling to be mixed up in their proceedings, nor yet, to allow themselves to be dragged into any conduct that would detract from the dignity and credit of England."[73] Indeed, *Lloyd's Weekly Newspaper* reported that Layard was emphatic in stating that the tour had nothing to do with the "Volunteer excursion," of which he "disapproved," and in a pointed warning to other agitators (perhaps radical republicans in the crowd who would have objected to the "tyranny" of Napoleon III) stated that the French had the "undoubted right of selecting the system they desired." Indeed, if "any excursionist should turn the visit to Paris into political capital" he would likely, and quite rightly, find himself in a "French prison." Appealing instead to their identities as respectable working men, Layard urged them to "conduct themselves in a manly and gentlemanly manner" and reminded them of the "welcome" addition of "ladies" on the tour. Turning then to the subject of recreation, he also urged them to use this opportunity to "learn a good deal" about the French capital that may be of use to London and the country. Indeed, Layard not only regarded educational travel as a technique for developing self-regulating subjects, but as a means for promoting the transformation of England's dangerous urban spaces into what Patrick Joyce terms "liberal cities" – areas open to inspection through their rational organization. Layard thus suggested that the excursionists examine the changes made to Paris which had transformed it from a dirty and crowded medieval city into a pristine and orderly modern metropolis. Layard then directed their attention to housing. Was the French government's answer to workers dwellings suitable for England? That question, he remarked, should be of the upmost interest to them during their time abroad.[74]

Layard had set the terms of their cross-class collaboration long before a single ticket had been issued. Yet, perhaps seeking to dispel the Ambassador's apprehensions or just as likely his own, Layard confided to Cowley that Paxton and Cook had "assured me steady, intelligent men" and, as a precautionary measure, had also "promised me faithfully to keep a careful watch over those who go."[75] Moreover, Layard intended to accompany the tourists and to meet with them each day, and would thus be there to "assuage matters" if any signs of "political agitation" emerged.[76] The tour, therefore, was carefully orchestrated to keep the excursionists "in check." No matter how respectable they may have promised to appear and to behave, working-class tourists, like Stow's ragged children, would be closely monitored by their guides to ensure conformity and compliance with the goals that had been established for the tour.

According to reports, the tour progressed without a hint of trouble. Layard, Paxton, and Cook had seen to it, but the French authorities had a hand in keeping order as well. Cook had met with officials at the Palais de Justice in mid-March, a month prior to the tour, seeking "any friendly aid the authorities might be able to afford, in the event of very large numbers availing themselves of the Excursion arrangements." Told that "France was open to all who enter and conduct themselves in compliance with her laws," Cook, with coded pleasantries, informed his readers that he was "pleased" to learn that "the very efficient Police system, combined with the services of the Guard de Paris, answered all needful protection and practicable assistance."[77] Thus, had Cook and his assistants been unable to contain their charges, the French police would have stepped in to restore order.

Cook found this out for himself when his excursionists, all 1,673 of them, congregated at the Champs Elysées to begin their exploration of the city. Before they could organize the day's itinerary, however, the police ordered the excursionists to disperse as an unauthorized public assembly, causing momentary confusion before they sorted themselves into small groups. Led by "captains" whose leadership qualifications rested on their willingness to take responsibility for the group and who could converse (however poorly) in French if necessary, the tourists marched off to inspect shops, art galleries, parks, monuments, and government buildings. Thus, despite Cook's careful planning, the tour encountered unexpected difficulties. As the tourist agent in this enterprise, Cook's job was to manage the tours' seamless unfolding. *The Illustrated London News,* therefore, scolded Cook for his lack of foresight, remarking that he should have received authorization to assemble his troops of tourists before setting off across the Channel, as everyone knew that France was little more than a police state.[78] Cook failed in other respects as well. The British workmen, for example, never met up with their French counterparts. Cook (perhaps after his preliminary meeting with the Paris authorities) had determined that "it was not deemed advisable to make any arrangements for a fraternal gathering in the French capital; indeed, this could not have been effected without very great inconvenience and difficulty." Nor had Cook thought to arrange invitations to Paris workshops, which the *Illustrated London News,* again finding fault with Cook's expertise, asserted were what "ought certainly to have been one of the objects of an 'excursion of British workmen.'"[79]

But Cook was not to blame for every misstep. Beyond Cook's control, for example, was a rogue petition penned by members of the excursion that conveyed to the French people a message that not one of the organizers could have anticipated. The original working men's committee had hoped to express their solidarity with French workers, while the press had hoped to promote economic liberalism. But, some excursionists took it upon themselves to endorse the Second Empire with effusive praise for Napoleon III and his security forces in a petition that the government organ, *Le Moniteur,* disseminated throughout France. As reported in the working-class weekly, *Reynolds's Weekly Newspaper,* the self-described voice of "extreme Republicans," 89 excursionists had grossly misrepresented British working people by signing a petition that not only thanked the Prefect of Police and Napoleon III for their hospitality, but gushingly intimated that the French working class lived under a benevolent and just ruler who had created the conditions for material prosperity and social equality, evident for all to see in the "splendid city of Paris and its environs." The one redeeming factor to note, *Reynolds's* suggested by way of comfort, was that the majority of excursionists, the remaining "1611 British subjects," had declined to "affix their signatures to that toad-eating, tuft hunting address that the *Moniteur* wishes to convert into political capital."[80]

Despite these mishaps and misunderstandings, there was little in the British papers to suggest that the tour should never have taken place. The Paris correspondent for the *Daily Telegraph,* for example, encouraged more tours, but with some caveats. Weighing in on the petition debacle, he remarked that its circulation throughout France should "induce caution for the future." If tourists wanted to see the real Paris they needed to peer beyond the façade of the city center. But, to attain access to the "real" Paris required tourists to avoid "fuss" and to "keep clear ... of all political questions."[81] Without reservation, *The London Review* also expected to see many more working-class tourists out and about in Europe after "rapturous tales" started circulating about the Whitsuntide tour of Paris. "From the Black Country, from smoky Birmingham and Sheffield, from Glasgow, Newcastle, Preston, Bolton and Leeds, prosperous operatives will form themselves into groups and put themselves under the auspices of professional excursion contrivers."[82] The *London Review's* optimism was, for the most part, justified. After 1861, individuals and small groups of working men (and perhaps their wives as well), continued to travel the continent for "leisure and instruction," if not always under the careful guidance of reformers or in as large numbers as hoped, as the cost continued to be prohibitive. Nevertheless, Cook and other reformers continued to seek opportunities for conducting large excursions, as numbers were what counted if a social good was to arise out of a travel revolution.

Cook lost revenue in the venture. But, as he explained in *The Excursionist,* it had been worth the losses it incurred. As a "labour of love minus profit," he wrote, it was "just one of those numerous instances in which my experience, position and perseverance were made contributary to a great public object." Indeed, the "moral power" of aiding "the interests of humanity," he stressed, was reward enough.[83] Cook therefore, had achieved his goals. He had taken an important step toward democratizing mass travel to Europe and, managing, as Brendon notes, to combine "business with idealism," had instilled the masses with the travel ethos, an ethos that Cook hoped would produce domestic and international harmony – as well as future financial victories for his firm.[84]

For the other reformers invested in the tour, the Whitsuntide excursion had similarly shown that travel to the continent, despite its contingent nature, could be embraced as a form of rational recreation. The *Illustrated London News* berated Cook for his failings as a travel agent, but it was also pleased to report that the "gentlemanly and orderly conduct of the visitors has left a most favourable impression in the minds of the Parisians," demonstrating the viability of governmental technologies at a distance.[85] Moreover, the tour had proven a medium for cross-class interaction that, in the case of the "body of working men," had produced a collaboration of sorts, if an unequal one. The travel idea had thus been put to the test and had met with a measure of success both at home and abroad.

Conclusion

With the upsurge of working-class militancy in the 1860s, reformers wanted to confront working-class politics head-on and influence, change, and tame it to harmonize with liberal goals and values by whatever means possible – including through travel. Cross-class cooperation, therefore, influenced the form, function, and meaning of workers' travel abroad. On the reformers' part, their assistance in organizing working-class tours carried the taint of social control. Orchestrating the contexts in which British workers fraternized (or not) with their foreign counterparts on the continent and defining the value of tourist sites, liberal reformers placed workers' tours within the framework of rational recreation. This intervention, as with other forms of leisure sponsored by the upper classes, sought to diffuse the radical potential of working-class groups and communities. New educational technologies designed for pauper children offered models for this project, by seeking to produce reflexively self-regulating citizens, thus maintaining the ethos of individual freedom and minimal government intervention – the central tenets of liberal government. In addition, Cook's perception of his pastoral role in the travel industry contributed to how travel was conceived as an "agent of civilisation." Temperance excursions and the 1851 Exhibition had given travel entrepreneurs, such as Cook, a vision of what was possible in creating a travel revolution as a form of rational recreation, while the 1861 Workingmen's Excursion to Paris offered reformers such as Layard an opportunity to test the governmental principles of the educational idea in the context of travel abroad. The 1867 Paris Exhibition, as the following chapters show, would offer the right set of circumstances to put travel as a governmental resource to further use – and on the largest scale to date. Replete with a purpose-built environment designed for working-class visitors, the 1867 Paris Exhibition and the Workingmen's Paris Exhibition Tours would epitomize the liberal expression of "governing at a distance."

Like the workers' tours of the 1851 Great Exhibition and the 1861 Whitsuntide Tour, different interests would compete to establish the meaning and purpose of workers tours to the 1867 Exhibition. But, unlike the earlier tours, they were organized on the eve of the 1867 Reform Bill, which enlarged the franchise for male householders and empowered "respectable artisans" with political citizenship. A different dynamic thus emerged between middle-class reformers and working-class activists in producing, for the second time, arrangements for working-class tourism in Paris. In the intervening six years, a different dynamic also emerged between France and British tourists. The Second French Empire was authoritarian and statist, but by 1867 its economy was second only to Britain in Europe. Napoleon III's program of economic modernization included legalizing workers' strikes in 1864, winning, in some quarters, popular support for his rule. Consequently, Paris in 1867 was far more accommodating to tourists, even those who wished to peer beyond the lighted boulevards and into the workshops and homes of ordinary people. But, this is to anticipate. For now it should be evident that the organizers of the 1867 Paris Workingmen's Tours would pay little heed to the *Daily Telegraph*'s cautionary advice. Trusting the logic of liberal governmentality to produce the desired results, they surrounded the tours with as much "fuss" as was due 3000 British artisans and mechanics – many newly enfranchised – who were to cross the Channel for the first time and experience for themselves, the meaning to be made of a Paris excursion.

2
Turning the Educational Idea on Its Head: The Lib–Lab Alliance and the Organization of the Working Men's 1867 Exhibition Tours

At an October 1866 meeting of the General Council of the International Working Men's Association (IWA), also known as the First International, Eugene Dupont, a maker of musical instruments and the IWA's Corresponding Secretary for France, made a proposal that for a short time turned this London association of socialists and labor leaders into a tourist agency. Dupont suggested establishing a "Special Committee" to assist "British Workingmen and others" to visit the 1867 Paris Exhibition.[1] The council, as it turned out, needed little persuasion. Some members, such as Benjamin Lucraft, had participated in the 1861 "Workingmen's" tour, and had acquired organizational experience prior to Layard and Cook's intervention.[2] Perhaps Lucraft wished to repeat the experiment? In addition, the IWA's Parisian branch assured Dupont of their eagerness to "cooperate heartily" with the council. They, like Lucraft, also had wisdom to impart, having organized the visits of worker delegates to the 1862 International Exhibition in London.[3] Yet, despite their initial enthusiasm, the IWA led the project for only a short while. Almost as soon as the IWA assembled the Special Committee, it handed the reins over to the Workingmen's Club and Institute Union – a middle-class network of social and educational clubs that pursued a domestic civilizing mission among the artisan classes. The WMCIU, needless to say, invested the tours with a different meaning and purpose than the IWA. Nevertheless, members of both organizations managed to surmount their differences long enough to form a loose collaboration, albeit with the WMCIU playing the leading role, that culminated in the planned tours of over 3000 workers.

At first glance, the IWA and the WMCIU made an unlikely pair. In scattered references, historians have characterized Dupont as unwavering in his support of Marx and the "social revolution."[4] Surely he viewed both groups as historically determined adversaries? His contemporaries at the Whiggish political and literary magazine, *The Edinburgh Review,* certainly would have come to this conclusion. In an 1871 essay that reviewed hot-off-the-press reports on the Paris Commune, the author traced the September Revolution and its bloody conclusion back to the 1862 London International Exhibition and the deputation of Parisian workers who visited it to observe industrial conditions and to meet with trade union representatives. This experience, the author argued, had led to additional visits and the radicalization of international-ist thought with the 1864 formation of the IWA. Dupont's correspondence (printed in the review) confirmed this radicalization. Taunting ruling elites during the 1871 Paris Commune, he concluded a letter to the Lyon chapter of the IWA with the slogans "Down with the Middle Classes!" and "Long live the International!" – sentiments that called for class conflict, not cooperation.[5]

Despite its members' commitment to democratic and socialist principles, the First International found it necessary to reach out to its ideological adversaries for help with the 1867 Paris Exhibition excursions. Indeed, the IWA discovered (much like the initial working-class organizers of the 1861 Paris tour) that mass "working-class" tours abroad would, of necessity, have to rely on support from outside their organization. Although five years had passed since the 1861 Paris tour, arrangements for large scale ventures still required not only the expertise of professional travel agents, but the patron-age of well-to-do liberal reformers. However, since 1861 the dynamics of this relationship had shifted. After the defeat of the Liberal Reform bill in June 1866., Liberal reformers recognized that they needed working-class support to get their agenda through parliament and to keep their party in power in the upcoming elections. Without at least the tacit acceptance of their incre-mentalist platform by working-class trade union leaders, the Liberals faced political stalemate. Middle-class progressives thus sought to retain working-class support by making concessions to ideas and practices that challenged liberal orthodoxy, such as socialism, trade union activism, and the efficacy of parliament in social reform.[6] It was in these circumstances, therefore, that the IWA could expect some accommodation from the middle-class reformers in planning workers' tours that they hoped would encourage working class independence and international solidarity, a project somewhat at odds with their benefactors' own aims of fostering national identities and class concili-ation at home through travel abroad.

The International and the Educational Idea

Established in London in 1864, the IWA was committed to several impera-tives, including the support of national independence movements and the development of international labor solidarity. The 1867 Paris exhibition pre-sented the IWA with a number of opportunities for furthering these goals, although the minute books leave the purpose of the Special Committee's travel arrangements for "British workingmen and others" to conjecture.[7] First, presumably, workers tours of the exhibition would advance the IWA's mission (as stated by the Geneva Congress in 1866, and restated at the Brussels Congress in 1867) to "function as a common centre of action" for an international proletariat seeking "their complete emancipation from the domination of capital." By bringing workers together in a single city, the IWA would help "make the workmen of the different countries not only *feel* but *act* as brethren and comrades in the army of emancipation." At the same time, the exhibition would have also offered the IWA an opportunity, as Marx had suggested in Brussels, to conduct a "statistical inquiry into the situation of the working classes of all countries" carried out "by the working classes themselves" rather than by state bureaucrats. The IWA would establish their own truth claims about foreign and domestic competition, shop floor conditions, and the "moral" well-being and "education" of working people in multiple industrializing nations. "By initiating so great a work," the IWA believed that "workmen will prove their ability to take their own fate into their own hands."[8] Third, by exposing British workers to French culture and craftsmanship, workers' tours of the exhibition would address the IWA's commitment to "the intellectual improvement of the working classes and their children." Thus, the proposed 1867 tour presented the IWA Council with an opportunity to shape British workers' behavior and consciousness at home through their experience of travel abroad – to "not only *feel* but *act* as brethren."[9] Perhaps, then, the council members viewed culture – in this case, travel-as-culture – as an agent of change, much like the rational recreationists viewed travel as an agent of reform. Here, yet again, through the agency of the IWA, the educational idea met up with the travel idea within the exhibitionary complex.

That the IWA voiced the rhetoric of improvement embedded within the statistical idea and the educational idea, reflects its own commitment to a cultural revolution in state formation, one shaped, however, by IWA activists and theorists rather than bourgeois bureaucrats. Its engagement with the language of improvement was to be expected, for this concept had entered the common stream of ideas that comprised the radical, reformist, and progressive climate of the mid-Victorian era. Labor leaders, artisan intellectuals, and middle-class reformers often read many of the same books, mingled at working men's educational institutes and clubs, and occasionally shared memberships at scientific and literary societies. As Patrick Joyce argues, radicals were formed by the same forces as the middle classes; worker intellectuals and leaders drew from the same repertoire of cultural resources as middle-class reformers and state bureaucrats to assemble their vision and practice of education.[10] The IWA, therefore, would have applied many of the same technologies and ascribed much of the same educational value to travel as the middle classes – with the difference, it should be clear, of serving working-class interests rather than those of the liberal state. At the 1866 Geneva conference, for instance, the IWA turned the educational idea on its head in a statement composed by Marx. The Council's instructions to the Geneva Congress stated:

> The working man is no free agent. In too many cases, he is even too ignorant to understand the true interest of his child, or the normal conditions

of human development. However, the more enlightened part of the working class fully understands that the future of its class, and, therefore, of mankind, altogether depends upon the formation of the rising working generation. They know that, before everything else, the children and juvenile workers must be saved from the crushing effects of the present system. This can only be effected by converting *social reason* into *social force*, and, under given circumstances, there exists no other method of doing so, than through *general laws*, enforced by the power of the state. In enforcing such laws, the working class do not fortify governmental power. On the contrary, they transform power, now used against them, into their own agency. They effect by a general act what they would vainly attempt by a multitude of isolated individual efforts.[11]

In this passage, Marx advocates government intervention in mandating a system of education that will prepare working-class youth for their future role in the dictatorship of the proletariat.[12] Seeking to transform "governmental power" into working-class power, the IWA imagined how culture and education could ultimately be used as tools of working-class emancipation from the bourgeois state, just as Cole and other reformers envisioned them as tools of working-class subordination to it. For the IWA, therefore, mass tours of the Paris exhibition would not only promise to stimulate the intellectual engagement of "British workingmen and others" with French culture and craftsmanship, but an identification with working-class causes that extended beyond national borders – an identification that required a multitude rather than individuals to effect change.

Perhaps with the exhibition's utility for meeting these goals in mind, the Council agreed to Dupont's plan, and the IWA's Special Excursion Committee quickly got under way. The committee wrote letters to their French correspondents in the IWA for information that would enable them to offer British workers "travelling, boarding, and lodging at a fixed tariff," and contacted travel agents and railway offices for the best rates on first- and second-class return tickets to Paris of one to two weeks duration.[13] Eventually, however, they turned to the Universal Tourist Company for help with simplifying the dizzying matrix of travel regulations and options. The results proved less than satisfactory.

With a healthy starting capital of £50,000 the Universal Tourist Company, one of the newly licensed tourist agencies to arise in light of the exhibition, had placed advertisements for "Workingmen's Exhibition Excursions" in *The Commonwealth*, *The Bee-Hive*, and other working-class newspapers.[14] For "only" £3 19s, reported *The Bee-Hive*, the Universal Tourist Company offered a package deal that covered transportation, board, lodging, admission to the Exhibition, the use of an interpreter, and accident or death insurance. Furthermore, recognizing that no self-respecting workman would part with such a sum based on the firm's propaganda alone, the managers invited delegates from trade and friendly societies to join them, free of charge, on a pre-excursion Paris tour. Set for March of 1867, the working-class delegates would travel together to assess the quality of the agency's accommodations in Paris and, as an added perk, present the French Emperor with a "memorial."[15] Finding little to fault with this proposal (except, perhaps, the memorial, given radical responses to the fawning petition that crowned the 1861 Whitsuntide excursion), the IWA elected Mr. Jenkins, an organ-builder, to represent the association in Paris.[16] Yet, the much-anticipated pre-excursion tour never came to pass. After two delays and considerable inconvenience to the delegates, the Universal Tourist Company lost the confidence of the IWA, which decided to look elsewhere for assistance.[17]

It is not clear from the record what prevented the Universal Tourist Company from following through with its plans. Perhaps it simply lacked the experience to adequately coordinate package tours. What is certain is that it faced stiff competition. After two-decades in the excursion business, Cook, for example, possessed the connections, the capital, and a well-oiled propaganda machine in *The Excursionist* to undertake mass tours abroad with relative ease. Competitive and, at the same time, protective of the niche he had carved out, Cook annihilated the Universal Tourist Company in the press, attacking the up-start agency as a "fraud" and a pernicious "bubble" scheme run by "incompetents." Ever ready to "promote," as he put it, the "physical and intellectual recreation of thousands" and to "assist in the glorious cause of Peace, Education, and Progress," Cook cautioned his readers to stay the course with his own travel agency, for the "days of dupes is not yet over."[18] With these hardball tactics, Cook no doubt won a significant portion of the excursion commissions. Cook and his agents not only conveyed, fed, lodged, and guided thousands of middle-class families and organizations in Paris, but, continuing with his own brand of commercial philanthropy, organized special savings and excursion clubs for workers in provincial towns and cities. Ultimately, however, it was not Cook's Tours that edged out the Universal Tourist Company.

Cook and the Universal Tourist Company also faced strong competition from a reform network of middle-class industrialists, civil servants, and public intellectuals who banded together under the banner of the Working Men's Club and Institute Union (WMCIU) to give tactical as well as philanthropic support in an excursion project once again presided over by Austin Henry Layard. Committed to the political, social, and cultural imperatives of rational recreation, and guided by philanthropic principles rather than the profit motive, the WMCIU triumphed over the competition. Bringing members of the IWA into the fold, the WMCIU succeeded in taking control of the working men's tours of the 1867 exhibition.

Founded in 1862 by Henry Solly, a Unitarian minister, the WMCIU epitomized the paternalist, middle-class crusade to ameliorate class relations. It projected this liberal reformist identity in its promotional literature, including the final report of the excursion committee, which emphasized the WMCIU's dedication to "Adult [male] Education, Cultivation of the Fine Arts, Recreation, and Provision for the Future."[19] In 1867, *The Bee-Hive* reported that the Working Men's Club and Institute Union consisted of 115 clubs (69 self-supporting) with a total membership of 12,814. Stressing education, the clubs produced lectures and courses on various subjects and collectively possessed 51,436 books in their libraries.[20] The education at the WMCIU, however, deliberately steered away from the scientific or "useful" knowledge to be had at Mechanics' Institutes, and instead sought to provide working men with culturally elevating instruction combined with amusement and relaxation. To support these multiple functions, the clubs generally provided members with not only a library and committee rooms suitable for study and lectures, but a lounge, a bar, and a game room. The range of these facilities and the numbers of club members, Richard Price argues, indicate that the WMCIU was "very clearly a movement *for* the working classes which was accepted *by* the working classes." The club movement appealed to working men because it "fulfilled a need of the working-class community."[21] Working men used the clubs for amusement, to gain a glimmer of a liberal arts education, and also for political discussion and organization. For working-class activists, it also gave them access, though limited, to wealthy, influential, or powerful men with whom to press radical agendas.[22] The trade-off, however, was that if working class members wanted to use these facilities, as George Howell, a trade union activist and IWA member complained, they were forced to endure the "patronizing spirit" that pervaded the clubs – that is, until their democratization in 1889. Solly did not disguise the fact that he and other middle-class patrons condescended to spend time in their midst, stating in an 1867 meeting that the "clubs offered a mutually beneficial interchange of views and cultivation of friendly feeling with persons of higher social positions and culture.[23] For the middle class patrons, therefore, the clubs became a venue for connecting with and understanding the needs, aspirations, and grievances of working men and to "civilize" and "refine" their behavior, beliefs, and opinions in the process. The WMCIU thus institutionalized many of the governmental aims of the 1861 tour organizers.

In the months leading up to the tours, these aims took on even more urgency. During this period, economic depression, severe unemployment, and a cholera epidemic produced significant discontent, and there was a threat of violence in the demonstrations for the franchise in the North and in London itself, led by none other than Lucraft and his "ultra radical" cohorts.[24] Indeed, it was a time, Layard complained to Cowley, when the agitations of the "working classes, pandered to by Disraeli, had taught them [that] they have only to combine & to threaten to get whatever they want."[25] And, it was a time, according to Sir John Bowring, a prominent Liberal and WMCIU council member, "when all classes needed to be on terms of greater friendship and to have only one interest, the interest of their country, at heart." For such men, then, this state of affairs necessitated turning the clubs into "efficient instruments" for shaping working-class politics.[26] The middle-class leadership of the WMCIU thus courted approval for its activities from various working class groups and individuals such as the London Trades Council, Friendly Societies, and IWA committee members.[27] By so doing, both middle class radicals and working class political and trade union leaders had some reason to hope for such a rapprochement, even if lingering working-class mistrust sometimes produced only tentative compromises. Indeed, a palpable tension, evident to all, existed between some IWA members, hard-line trade unionists, and the WMCIU at their first meeting to discuss the 1867 Paris excursion for working men. As the WMCIU secretary noted in the minutes, "the Trade Unionists evince some interest, but are shy and suspicious. Robert Applegarth (secretary, Carpenters and Joiners) is, as usual, hearty and downright in support. But, W.R. Cremer is coy; and Coulson, Allen, and other members of the Junta are at best negatively neutral."[28] Thus, in this moment of conciliation, punctuated by middle class condescension on the one hand, and working-class hostility on the other, the organization of WMCIU's workingmen's tours got under way as an uneasy alliance between capital and labor, and between middle-class reformers and working-class radicals.

The Working Men's Club and Institute Union and its Parisian Playground

The WMCIU would have welcomed the IWA's disappointment with the Universal Tourist Company as an ideal opportunity to strengthen cross-class alliances and to educate as well as cultivate the hearts and minds of working people. Indeed, like the IWA, the WMCIU took advantage of its ideological adversary's weaknesses in order to engage in "mutually beneficial" projects, which ultimately fortified the radical-liberal conciliation of the mid-Victorian era. The WMCIU, for example, exploited internal dissension at the IWA between socialist, communist, and anarchist groups to promote projects that, in tolerating the middle class's incrementalist organizations, appeared to transcend ideological factions and class divisions. Thus, even though the ideological roots of the London IWA stemmed back to late Chartism and aspirations for social democracy, its affiliation with trade unionism tended to dilute its revolutionary legacy as union leaders sought piecemeal pragmatic reforms and were willing, in some instances, to cooperate with the middle classes to get them, as demonstrated by the first meeting between IWA representatives (many of them trade union leaders) and the WMCIU to discuss the terms of their collaboration.[29] The hard-liners, no doubt, surmised that collaboration with the WMCIU effectively negated the original purpose and meaning of the tours. But, perhaps others expected that in maintaining this point of contact with the WMCIU, they could still hope to shape workers' responses to travel abroad.

It was in this context of tenuous cross-class cooperation, then, that the WMCIU began organizing the tours in earnest, guided by Solly's successor, Hodgson Pratt, who had joined the organization in 1863. The history of Victorian radicalism and liberal reform takes little note of Pratt, although he had a hand in the successful formation of several political movements before his death in 1907. Pratt's commitment to social reform began as a child when he waved the flag of democracy for Chartist demonstrators in his home town of Bath – a sensibility that he translated into a radical vision of the civilizing mission during his early career in India and afterwards in the imperial metropole.[30] As an education inspector for the Bengal Civil Service, Pratt encouraged greater integration between the educated Bengali and British classes, and advocated government scholarships for deserving youth to study in England. Like many other paternalist reformers, however, charity was neither the beginning nor the end point of his activism. By educating "the able and well born" for "*increased resort to native agency in the civil administration of India* [Pratt's emphasis]," the British Empire, he intimated, could hope to expect consensus over conflict from its subjects on the subcontinent. Indian subjects would eventually welcome imperial rule as well as the colonial logic of liberal ideology. Indeed, Pratt surmised that the people of Lower Bengal were already the least "self- dependent of the Indian populations" and the most appreciative of the "advantages of our rule, in the security which it gives to property, and in the impulse which it gives to trade."[31]

Pratt carried his passion for education and social amelioration, along with his governmental experience and authority, back to the British Isles in 1857. His colonial career, in fact, prepared him, like other Utilitarian reformers before him, for social activism at home in Britain where, he claimed, "self government is the great national principle" and the foundation upon which citizenship was realized.[32] Upon his return, Pratt turned his attention to working men who seemed receptive to pastoral guidance through cross-class sociability. When he arrived in London, he immersed himself in the reformist community: he befriended Fredrick Denison Maurice and other Christian Socialists who had started a working men's college in London; he joined the co-operative movement, which (before its appropriation by the middle classes at mid-century), attempted to devise alternatives to competitive capitalism domestically and internationally; and, he threw himself into the club movement, where he wanted to turn crude workmen into productive citizens by exposing them to practices of "self culture" and the ethos of "self government."

Pratt assumed the presidency of the WMCIU in 1867, just in time to put his energies firmly behind the working men's exhibition tours. This event epitomized the aims and values of the institution's founder, Henry Solly, and allowed Pratt to work with other reformers with similar ambitions to better the condition of working people in service of the greater good. Bowring, like Pratt, for example, had tested methods for imposing "obedience and discipline" on Egyptian soldiers and workers during his colonial career and would have brought this experience to bear on arrangements for managing, through governmental power, workers tours of the Paris exhibition.[33] But, for assistance with coordinating the tours' most basic elements, Pratt turned to Thomas Cook.

In February of 1867, Pratt contacted Cook for help organizing the WMCIU tours. According to Cook, Pratt admitted having "been at work for a long time" on the project, but had run into the usual difficulties that befell novice tour organizers. Consequently, at Pratt's request, according to *The Excursionist*, Cook agreed to coordinate transport, to secure lodgings, and to advertise the WMCIU tours in *The Excursionist* and in the 5000 circulars and over 30,000 handbills he had printed for the 1867 Exhibition.[34] With these arrangements settled, Pratt and other WMCIU officers subsequently embarked on a similar campaign from their main headquarters at 150 Strand.[35] They contacted club members, advertised in the press, arranged weekly savings deposits, and invited "great employers of labour, manufacturers, and others interested in the industrial progress of the country ... to join the committee in raising a guaranteed fund of £3,000."[36]

The WMCIU excursion committee helped garner more support for the project than it might have received otherwise. Layard stood first among the committee members as the President of the WMCIU excursions, but the vice presidents were also crucial to the project's success. They included the Earl of Lichfield, W.F. Cowper, MP, W.E. Forster, MP, G.J. Goschen, and Henry Hoare, each of whom commanded state and public support as government bureaucrats, politicians, or education ministers. Importantly, Henry Cole also participated on the committee. Cole's presence would not only have inspired confidence in the project but would have enabled organizers to infuse new pedagogical technologies into what was becoming an exhibition excursion "system." In his dual role as director of the Art and Science Department at South Kensington and British Executive Commissioner to the Exhibition, Cole's influence with the French authorities probably smoothed the way for Pratt to make special arrangements for the excursionists.

Indeed, Pratt eventually rejected Cook's lodging options (infuriating Cook) and devised a package deal with the French authorities that comprised a means of disciplinary power. Traveling to Paris, Pratt consulted Cole's French counterpart, Frédéric Le Play, a French social scientist and President of the Imperial Commission, over the question of lodgings.[37] Committed to the rational organization of society, they agreed that "a series of wooden houses" would be "specially built for the purpose." As the WMCIU committee described it in their final report, the contractors arranged the working men's lodgings "like a camp within an enclosure, in the open ground facing the Porte Rapp entrance to the Exhibition." The complex (a remodeled military barracks) would be large enough to contain 112 beds in rooms fitted with two to four beds each. Additionally, the WMCIU supplied an "agent" to register the excursionists upon their arrival and to see to their needs during the duration of their stay in Paris.[38]

In their deliberations, Pratt and Le Play had thus devised an architectural means for the containment and discipline of British working-class tourists that replicated the "short-lived artificial city" of a military barracks, a formation that was more than apt for the situation. Foucault writes that the rationally designed military encampment exercised a "seat of a power that must be all the stronger, but also all the more discreet, all the more effective and on the alert in that it is exercised over armed men."[39] While the WMCIU excursionists did not shoulder rifles, they did arrive in France armed with ideas and experience as trade unionists, experiences that French workers lacked, but desired. Crucially, therefore, the workman's lodgings needed to regulate workers and at the same time permit them freedom. One way Pratt and le Play may have achieved this was by making a portion of the Avenue Rapp lodgings exclusive to British nationals, limiting the British workers' interactions with working-class continental Europeans. Precluding late-night fraternal gatherings with potential European subversives, the arrangement likely nurtured British national identities, but did little to promote Cook's ecumenical cosmopolitanism or the IWA's desire to enable workers of the world "to *feel* and *act* as brethren and comrades." Moreover, the encampment, facing the exhibition itself, was essentially part of the exhibition complex. It was as much a spectacle of rational urban organization as the display of the "model working-class cottage" (occupied by a tin-worker and member of the pro-Bonapartist Palais Royal Group) within the gates of the exhibition grounds.[40] On display for all to observe, the organization of the Avenue Rapp lodgings discreetly coerced respectable working men into self-governance and into monitoring and curbing the behavior of others by way of example or censure. Indeed, it functioned as a carceral city, but also as a playground in which WMCIU officers and members of the excursion committee offered their charges guidance and friendship far from home.

This surveillance on the one hand and unobtrusive guidance on the other extended to another "specially built" environment, the Workman's Hall, located in the British section of the exhibition. The Workman's Hall had been built at Pratt's suggestion and funded by the Royal Commission on the Exhibition. Multiple contributors to the Royal Commissions' Report to Parliament, overseen by Henry Cole, praised the conception and utility of the Workman's Hall. C.B. Ewart, of the Royal Engineers, remarked that the Workman's Hall functioned like a club away from home by ensuring that "the British workman, on his arrival, will be no homeless stranger left to fight his own way in a great foreign city." Another contributor to the report, Charles Haussoullier, the manager of the Workman's Hall and former translator in the 1861 Treaty of Commerce between France and England, explained that it offered workers, "without charge, a place of repose, the newspapers of their country, guides and interpreters, information of every kind, and lastly, permissions to visit manufacturing establishments" in Paris and the provinces. The "beneficial results" of the Workman's Hall, Haussoullier predicted, would make such spaces an "indispensable accompaniment in all future exhibitions on those governments who care for the moral and intellectual welfare of their subjects."[41]

The amenities that the Workman's Hall offered, served to keep the excursionists' active and productive. If the organizers had their druthers, however, the workshop visits to industrial manufacturers would top the list of each excursionist's itinerary. Indeed, the overall success of the Paris excursions seemed to rest on the numbers of workers who took advantage of the workshop visits and who wrote reports about their tours. The WMCIU, in conjunction with the Lords of the Committee of Education, the Art and Science Department, and the Royal Commission on Exhibitions, offered cash prizes for the "best reports by artizan excursionists" on the "present condition of industry and fine arts in France." Such reports, Pratt declared, would be "a great value to England" and a "truly national object," by allowing "about 3,000 citizens to improve their taste and add to their industrial knowledge." The reports not only promised to be "of remarkable value both to the employers of labour, and to the skilled industry of the kingdom," they would also add "to the enjoyment and culture of the individual workmen themselves."[42] While the organizers valued these goals, they also valued the tours because they functioned as a counterweight to the competition posed by the IWA and other political and labor organizations for working-class loyalty and identification of interests. Encouraging British workers to examine French workshop conditions and practices, and exhorting them to take notes that could help improve British industry, the Committee on Education sanctioned the collection of new knowledge about international labor by workers themselves. Thus the WMCIU co-opted the IWA's own initiative to construct new knowledge, again defusing the revolutionary potential of workers' travel abroad. Indeed, workers need not even conduct independent research as the Workman's Hall provided them with government statistics and maps, and supported these aids with paid interpreters hired for the occasion. The Workman's Hall and its affable manager thus guided British workers toward learning the correct lessons from the tours, serving its governmental purpose.[43]

In this way, the 1867 WMCIU's working men's tours did not rival the IWA's plans so much as absorb them into their own arrangements. However, although the WMCIU appropriated the original role and identity of the IWA tours, IWA organizers and other radical working class leaders still managed to assert an oppositional identity and influence over the tours and their meanings. Haussoullier and his assistant, Fouché, a carpenter and member of the *Conseil des Prud'hommes* (a French court of arbitration between employers and operatives), offer some insights.[44] Employed by the British government, Haussoullier and Fouché wrote reports that communicated the results of their own surveillance. While the Royal Commission asked Haussoullier to divulge general statistics (5000 Britons took advantage of the Hall's services, 95% of whom arrived under the auspices of the WMCIU), they asked Fouché, whom they had hired to accompany the British workers to French shops and factories, to express his "opinion about the trade unions and also the unionists with whom [he] had intercourse in the Exhibition." Fouché "recollected" speaking with four such men: J. Prior, Robert Applegarth, George Howell, and Thomas Connolly, the latter three of whom were members of the IWA General Council in addition to "unionists." Praising their leadership in trade unions, Fouché described them as:

> Very honest, animated with the best intentions, regarding the employers, and wishing them well, in (sic) the same time they wished their own welfare; unfortunately said they, many of our employers are blind enough not to see that in defending our interests we defend theirs.[45]

Fouché's comments are telling. Evidently, these IWA members had accepted the WMCIU's invitation to use their excursion services, perhaps in the spirit of "cooperation." They likely also lodged at the Avenue Rapp barracks, which had been placed under the managerial authority of William Glazier, a joiner and IWA member. It would have been possible, then, to exert influence by their very presence even if it fell within the governmental sphere of the WMCIU.[46] Indeed, implicit in Fouche's report, was their unwillingness to accept the logic behind the lessons of the excursion endorsed by the WMCIU. Thus collaboration between the advanced middle class and radical working-class leaders also reveal struggle and contestation, a point that revisionist social historians rightly stress in analyzing the Lib–Lab alliance, an alliance that had a profound influence on the organization and promotion of the tours.[47]

The Lib–Lab Alliance and the "ABC of International Life"

Social historians have complicated an older view of the Lib–Lab leadership as "respectable radicals," men who were willing to suppress militant laborism in order to curry favor with high-placed liberals and to implement a gradualist program of social and political reform. Typically representative of this older scholarship is F.M. Leventhal's work on the bricklayer and labor leader, George Howell. Leventhal contends that Howell and other labor leaders who were hungry for professional, financial, and social success succumbed to "the ideal of self-help," which "instilled alike by the forces of Benthamite Radicalism and religious dissent, vitiated the class consciousness of mid-Victorian artisans, fostering accommodations with the existing order rather than rebellion against it."[48] But, as revisionist historians argue, such views that claim either workers' "complete assimilation or complete rejection" of "respectability" and the liberal platform, obscure the complexity of both the relationship between middle-class and working class radicals and "popular liberalism."[49] The activist career of Hodgson Pratt, which overlapped with those of William Cremer, Benjamin Lucraft, and George Jacob Holyoake, – each of whom had a role to play in the working men's exhibition tours – reveals this complexity. Pratt, as noted, dedicated his public life to radical causes.[50] In this commitment, his activities often subordinated working-class leadership to his own, which was a strategy he used to establish and maintain control at the WMCIU. Indeed, while Pratt reached across the class divide in "friendship" and "mutual respect" at the WMCIU, neither he nor other middle class leaders, endorsed social "equality." Pratt, consequently insinuated himself in other working-class organizations and causes where he hoped to exert influence. Shortly after the founding of the Workmen's Peace Association (WPA) in 1870, for example, Pratt petitioned the board to be given an active role in the organization. The board and, presumably, the WPA's founder, William Randal Cremer, seem to have viewed Pratt's request with suspicion, perhaps reflecting Cremer's experience of collaboration with the WMCIU in the working men's excursions to the 1867 Paris exhibition. Yet, after debating the advisability of inviting a bourgeois reformer into their midst, WPA members conferred to him the title, "Honorary International Agent" with the expectation that his facility with languages and experience as a well-traveled civil servant, would stand the WPA in good stead.[51] During his time in the WPA, Pratt attended international congresses where he would have collaborated on some level with Benjamin Lucraft, who held the title of Honorary Treasurer of the WPA until 1872. In subsequent years, Lucraft continued to attend WPA conferences, including a memorable experience at the 1878 Paris Peace Conference, which he recalled as the "one of the most glorious demonstrations he had ever witnessed, and the realization of his twenty years' cherished idea of the union of artisans of all nations, whose rulers constantly pitted them against each other."[52] Lucraft's career overlapped with Pratt's in other ways as well. Although he was an "ultra radical," whose credentials included leadership roles in Chartist activism, the IWA, and the Land and Labour League, which agitated for land nationalization, Lucraft was open to building cross-class understanding, as exampled by his joint chairmanship over a reform conference in 1858, attended by Chartists and middle-class radicals.[53] This overture presaged other collaborations, such as membership on the WMCIU Council in 1874, which brought the total of representative working men to 6 (out of forty), a number that must have irked Lucraft for its blatant paternalism.[54] The pinnacle of Lucraft's Lib–Lab collaboration and projection of working-class respectability, however, came with his election to the London School Board in 1870, a position he held for two decades. Nevertheless, it was there that he campaigned to make state education free, secular, and compulsory. Lacking a single political identity, Lucraft has been defined as a "radical liberal," a moniker that would also suit George Jacob Holyoake, the author of, among many more works, *The Good of Going to Paris to see the Exhibition*, a promotional pamphlet endorsed by the WMCIU, but that curiously conveys an ultra-radical message even as it praises bourgeois paternalism.[55]

Old guard social historians have denounced Holyoake as a "respectable radical," a working-class activist turned opportunist, seduced by money, influence, and fame. No one, in fact, played the game of collaboration better than Holyoake, a man who wore many hats in a life devoted to many public causes. The record shows that even after becoming a liberal politician, he refused to tow the party line when it did not square with his own values and objectives in defending working people from the avarice of industrialists or the discrimination of parliament.[56] Although Holyoake's cooperation with the radical middle classes brought him many material benefits, as Peter Gurney argues, he was a "great nuisance" to them, for he "consistently put issues of democratic reform and participation on the political agenda." The son of a whitesmith, Holyoake began his working life at the age of eight when he followed his father into the foundry in 1825. By his early twenties, however, he had become a career radical. He courageously defended the secularist movement, surviving six months imprisonment for blasphemy; he also endorsed moral force Chartism, refusing to engage in violent protest; and, he professed an enduring belief in Owenite socialism, the foundation for his life-long commitment to the co-operative movement. According to Gurney, the co-operative movement became one of the largest and most important working-class associations of the Victorian era. As one of its chief theorists in the 1860s and 1870s, Holyoake not only played an important role in its formation, but did so in part by emphatically claiming that the movement's function was to set the stage for immanent communism. Liberals had been duly warned, which is why, perhaps, Pratt's career became intertwined, yet again, with another working-class movement, the co-operative movement, and its working-class leadership.

Both Holyoake and Pratt served on the first Board of Co-operators in Britain in 1869, and reportedly maintained friendly relations until Holyoake's death in 1906. Indeed, the co-operative movement like other working-class organizations in the mid Victorian era, sought to legitimate their programs by using public figures, like Pratt, as markers of respectability. Thus, although Holyoake and Pratt shared the co-operative platform, their take on the movement often diverged along the fault lines of class. In the early nineteenth century, Owenite socialists, such as Holyoake, defined co-operation as an alternative to competitive capitalism. As such, the concept of co-operation, Gurney explains, became "interchangeable" with the ideologies of socialism and communism. Democratically run co-operative stores and wholesale societies, as well as labor co-operatives, gave working people an experience of economic production and exchange de-linked from the independent capitalist and from the exploitation of labor and working class consumers. Around mid-century, the movement's rapid growth appeared to threaten the social and economic order. Consequently, capitalists and middle-class reformers, such as Pratt, took notice and deliberately appropriated the meaning and practice of co-operation to serve their agendas. As Gurney demonstrates in a linguistic analysis of the movement, they re-configured the language of co-operation to uphold rather than overturn bourgeois hegemony. Co-operation and the related concepts of "profit sharing" and "co-partnership," came to signify positive relationships between capital and labor, rather than working class economic initiatives divorced from capital. In the bourgeois lexicon, therefore, "co-operation," signified an antidote to socialism, not its fundamental characteristic. It followed then that liberals viewed the International Co-operative Alliance (ICA), a mostly middle-class profit sharing organization founded in the 1880s, as an antidote to international socialism. These blurred meanings have subsequently obscured Holyoake's commitment to socialism and working-class causes. That the ICA included on its rosters not only Pratt and Brassey, but Holyoake and George Howell, only adds to the confusion. However, as Gurney reminds us, yet again, Holyoake often used his position on the boards of paternalist co-operative ventures and other bourgeois organizations, such as the Social Science Association, to shame the middle classes with "unpleasant truths" and scathing critiques. Holyoake's "The Good of Going to Paris," also held this potential.[57]

Holyoake's pamphlet, which bore directly on the "internationalist" implications of combining working-class travel abroad with rational recreation, offered cold comfort to capitalist ideologues.[58] Framed as a homespun dispatch to "Willis Chater, Weaver, of Mytholmroyd" – a provincial Everyman – Holyoake's pamphlet provided potential excursionists with a working-class ideology of travel that also harmonized, in some respects, with the aims of the WMCIU. The "English workingman," Holyoake began, "is an insular creature ... just as though going about the world was not a pleasant thing."[59] Now, however, the WMCIU offered working people an opportunity to develop more cosmopolitan identities – a progressive change in history. Praising the paternalist largesse of the WMCIU, Holyoake explained that "it was always the distinction of a gentleman that he travelled, and it is one of the new and priceless advantages of our time, that Working Men are permitted to do it, encouraged to do it, and that gentlemen afford them the means of doing it." For only "Thirty Shillings," the WMCIU provided everything to ease the mind and comfort of the novice traveler: They "take a man to Paris and bring him back, and lodge him for a week in a Government bed-room with four beds in it, so that he has company if he is dull; people to talk to if he can't sleep; or to console him if he is frightened at being by himself in a new country." But, most importantly, the WMCIU tours promised to enlighten workers with an education quite different to anything that they could experience at home. "There is no education, new or old, from book or teacher, like that of travelling," declared Holyoake. But, one of the most important lessons to be derived from travel, he insisted, was "the ABC of International Life." Using his pamphlet to stump for the first meeting of the "great Conference ... of the Co-operators of all nations" set to take place in Paris during the Exhibition, Holyoake announced that "what is wanted now among the working class is international thought." In this rhetorical shift to a consideration of global economics informed by socialism, Holyoake challenged his readers to consider how modernity – "steam and electricity" – made the world smaller, more interconnected, in which "nothing is remote." On a national level, Holyoake wrote, "we are beginning to understand that every man's welfare is the common interest" in which "the wages paid in the next factory or town may affect those" of another. But, on an international level, Holyoake continued, "if a man is wise enough to see it, there is nothing in this world which does not concern him, and very nearly too; and any one nation is concerned no less in the condition of every other." The education to be gained by the exhibition tours, therefore, did not replicate the education to be gained on a gentleman's "Grand Tour." Instead, the exhibition tours offered a modern education in social, economic and political conditions globally, an education that was crucial for workers' well-being domestically and internationally. Thus, the "ABC of International Life," he concluded, "is an immense subject, fruitful in splendid and, to our insular habits of mind, inconceivable results. This Working Men's Excursion to Paris is the first international introduction to it which has been set on foot: you should go, and persuade all the neighbours and friends you have to go too."[60]

Clearly, Pratt and other WMCIU patrons would have rejected Holyoake's claims. They had hoped to foster national rather than working-class identities through travel and to expose their charges to the realities of economic competition on the continent that confirmed liberal ideology. But, here Holyoake presented travelers with an alternative conception of social relations and global economics. Collaborating with ruling elites in endorsing the tours, he at the same time challenged some of their suppositions. All may desire "peace between nations," as the exhibition propaganda literature proclaimed, but collaboration has its limits. After all, he intimated, international travel has the benefit of educating workers in the rudiments of their collective interests, a point well taken by the French authorities, who refused to host Holyoake's Co-operative Congress at the 1867 Exhibition.[61]

Conclusion

The IWA needed the assistance of the WMCIU to put their plan for working men's excursions into action, and, reciprocally, the WMCIU needed the sanction of labor leaders to make the tours successful. The magnitude of the 1867 Workingmen's Paris Exhibition Tours dictated this necessity. But their size also allowed social reformers to realize their ambitions on a mass scale. Technologies for mass travel and rational recreation, from cheap railway fares to purpose-built environments, such as the Avenue Rapp "barracks" and the Workman's Hall, aided the flow of culture through more extensive capillary systems than perhaps Cole first imagined in devising a system of national museums. Like Stowe's ideal schoolyard, the WMCIU turned Paris into a spectacular playground in which to test governmental power at a distance. In the estimation of reformers, workers would learn to govern themselves while being subjected to the surveillance and direction of their middle-class benefactors even beyond the British Isles. The success of the tours seemed to support this assumption.

As Layard announced in the Excursion Committee's concluding report, the WMCIU viewed both the planning and operation of the 1867 tours as a "great opportunity" to "enable ... men of different ranks of society to work together in friendly cooperation for the attainment of a great public object."[62] Consistent with this public proclamation of "cooperation," Layard confessed in a letter to Cowley that he especially valued the tours as an important means for "learning the opinions of the working classes."[63] Similarly, Cole reported from Paris that the workers had responded positively to the arrangements. First listing some of the sites the tourists had visited, Cole commented that "they seem happy and contented, which is satisfactory & unusual – as I find that generally when you strive to be particularly polite, people upbraid with being a beast!"[64] Both understood, however, that while the working men may have expressed pleasure and even gratitude, many, as the next chapter explains, drew different lessons from Paris than those Cole, Layard, and even Holyoake, had hoped to impart.

3

"The Lessons of Paris": The 1867 Working Men's Exhibition Tours and the Artisan Imagination

On the evening of 8 June 1867, two hundred working men assembled on the platform of London Bridge Station, laughing and joking with "innocent banter" as they waited to climb aboard a Cook's excursion train. The high-spirited travelers comprised the first batch of 3000 workers who would attend the Paris Exhibition between June and October under the aegis of the Working Men's Club and Institute Union (WMCIU) and its special Working Men's Excursion Committee.[1] Presided over by the radical MP, Austen Henry Layard, and manned by other liberal reformers and "earnest" working men, the WMCIU had worked tirelessly since December of 1866, to organize the tours. Preparations included winning subsidies from the Education Department and garnering charitable donations from subscribers; coordinating railway timetables, discount railway fares and advertising; and conducting pre-excursion trips to Paris to attain official permission from the French government and to arrange for the workmen's food, lodging and tourist itineraries. Now, at last, the tours were under way.

As the largest "peaceable invasion" of Paris by British working men, the first tour warranted a grand "bon-voyage," which was sponsored by the metropolitan branch of the excursion committee and held at the home of Sir Henry Hoare in St. James's Square. Writing for *The British Lion*, one participant observer, an artisan identified only by the initials C.B.S., described the festivities: "It was a strange and suggestive sight to see many working men – whose social status was ill-disguised by their Sunday dress – welcomed within the stately portals of a residence, where pride and exclusiveness alone were supposed to dwell." Although these "representatives of labour" entered the mansion "somewhat timidly," they were soon made to feel at home. The guests consumed a "substantial" tea, applauded speeches made by their hosts (who offered sound traveling advice and exhorted their audience to use "their visit for the future good of themselves and their fellows"), and cheered Hoare's daughter who entertained the men with a rendition of the "Banks of Allanwater" on a piano provided by Broadwood and Sons – a firm which in two weeks' time would send their own employees to Paris with the WMCIU. Much gratified by the attention, the excursionists were "touched with emotion, proving that humanity is found in all, and that the rudest natures readily submit to the potent influence of kindness and beauty."[2] Evidently, as C.B.S. suggests, workers' contact with the respectable upper classes could bring them within the pale of civilization, as the WMCIU had hoped.

The WMCIU's overarching aims in carrying out the work men's tours were, first, to bring cross-class learning and fellowship to a new social space – France – and the exhibition itself. By orchestrating the way that workers came in contact with the continent, organizers hoped to influence how British workers defined their interests both at home and abroad. No doubt the WMCIU wished to take this task in hand rather than leave it to autonomous workers' organizations such as the International Workingmen's Association (IWA), especially given the IWA's influence over the new model unions and the growing allure of international working-class solidarity. Second, the WMCIU expected the tours to promote "peace between nations" and the "advancement of science." By uniting British and French workers on the WMCIU's terms, organizers hoped that the tours would encourage workers to assess their comparative craft and industrial skills, and cement their mutual interest in the economic survival of their respective countries through free trade and even international "co-operation" (as middle-class opinion understood the term). It was a tall order, but the WMCIU believed that the tours would be of "remarkable value both to the employers of labour and to the skilled industry of the kingdom, as well as to the enjoyment and culture of the individual workman themselves."[3]

Demonstrating his commitment to these goals, Layard accompanied the first group across the Channel and continued to oversee their itinerary in Paris. The following day, for instance, he guided 200 of the working men through the Louvre and its galleries where, like a "cicerone," he explained the lessons they held for civilization. To crown the event, he then arranged to introduce the WMCIU tourists to the Emperor. According to Layard, "my working men," were "very much delighted with all they have seen, and ... well satisfied with the accommodation we have been able to provide for them."[4]

Layard's testimony rings true, but it is superficial and incomplete. Even though he claimed to speak for his "working men," they had better representatives among themselves. What did the excursionists convey about their experiences and reveal about their subjectivities? Given their testimony, did the WMCIU achieve its goals? To answer these questions, this chapter explores what the working men themselves thought of the tours and how they occupied their time abroad. C.B.S., for one, wrote that the tours represented a "desirable progress significant of almost limitless expansion." At the 1851 London exhibition "it was mostly the opulent and well-to-do who came to see and admire." But, in 1867 the demographics had changed. "In the modern temple improvised in Paris on the Champs de Mars," C.B.S.

triumphantly announced, "multitudes of the labouring populations are also invited to behold, to learn, and to excel" and were "emphatically answering this call." Indeed, like the workers feted at St. James's Square, thousands more would purchase WMCIU tickets and board Cook's excursion trains that would then speed them away towards their first "lessons of Paris."[5] Many workers shared C.B.S.'s enthusiasm for the exhibition and were as committed students of French life and customs as the organizers could have wished. In absorbing the "lessons of Paris," the WMCIU tourists entered into a dialectical realm of identity construction – a learning process, according to Holyoake, of inestimable value. Finding similarities and differences with their French hosts, workers' cross-cultural encounters could challenge or reinforce their political, social, and cultural identities, and turn their tours into personally transformative experiences. For some, their experiences would translate into articulating resistance to elite rule, the capitalist order, and social-control technologies; for others, into articulating a liberal vision of social democracy that anticipated the welfare state. In their various prescriptions for change, all demanded recognition of their humanity and the dignity that came with social equality – a demand that they saw as a perfect complement to the political equality that they were coming to claim at home. The workers' reports thus reveal a complex relationship not only with the French Other, but with the British ruling-class Other – a formative experience in identity construction that committed working people neither to total acceptance nor dismissal of radical-middle-class – or, for that matter, radical-working-class – values and objectives.

Working Men Excursionists and Artisan Reporters

Reconstructing workers' impressions of their tours is a challenging task. Some scattered commentary can be found in local papers or in the archives of various manufacturers, such as the testimonial signed by employees for Broadwood and Sons thanking the firm for the "very grand treat."[6] More detailed narratives, however, have proved elusive. Yet, the reports of a special group of 84 "artisan reporters" who visited Paris under the auspices of the Society of Arts (SA), offer some insight into these touristic experiences. Because middle-class sponsors supported both groups' tours, and because both groups shared the same class and craft backgrounds, the experience of the SA's artisan reporters can be seen as broadly representative of those of the WMCIU excursionists.[7]

The SA constituted a quasi-governmental institution comprised of civic-minded aristocrats, civil servants, industrialists, and academics, whose mission was to promote British arts, manufacturing, and commerce. High on the SA's agenda during the Victorian period was finding solutions to structural impediments to progress. This mission included improvements to working-class education that would enhance the quality and competitiveness of

British industry and, concomitantly, finding solutions to conflicts between capital and labor. Like the WMCIU, therefore, the SA sought ways to build cross-class alliances that fostered a sense of shared interests and defused the potential for class conflict. Convinced that sending selected artisans to report on the Paris Exhibition would serve this purpose, the SA collected financial contributions from civic organizations and wealthy individuals, augmented by a matching grant from the Lords of Council on Education. With these funds, the SA offered the artisan reporters free travel and lodging in Paris with the WMCIU excursionists, and an additional £3 stipend for writing their reports.[8]

The SA's fundamental objective in subsidizing the reporters was to enable Britain's most skilled artisans to evaluate Britain's strengths and weaknesses in light of continental nations' advances in craft and industrial production, social and labor relations, and working class-education. Although, in the SA's estimation, the artisan reporters were unlikely to discover new truths that other writers from "different stations" had not already observed and published, they still wanted reports that a working-class audience would likely read and trust to be true.[9] To foster this trust, the SA underscored their political and ideological impartiality both in selecting the artisan reporters and in editing their reports. The SA stated that they chose the artisan reporters based on their superior skills, which were "judged of by the recommendations they brought, either from their employers or fellow-workmen."[10] Additionally, the SA promised unadulterated testimony, claiming that they made only the "most unimportant corrections" to the reporters' manuscripts. No matter how militant the reporters' beliefs or how fearful some of the subscribers may have been about "statements made by the men"[11] the SA maintained that they would respect the "integrity" of the reports.[12] True to their word, trade union and political activists such as Benjamin Lucraft, Thomas Connolly, Herman Jung, and George Howell (who were skilled not only at their trades but also in shaping working-class opinion), filled the ranks of artisan reporters, as did other individuals who, rejecting an identification with organized labor, promised an alternative perspective.[13]

Given the SA's selection process, the artisan reports reflected a wide spectrum of working-class attitudes towards contemporary social, labor, and, economic questions, and, therefore, shared the wide range of expectations and meanings that workers on the WMCIU tours gave to their experiences in Paris. Indeed, the artisan reporters and WMCIU tourists shared much in common beginning with their strong resolve to attend the exhibition. Both groups acquired permission from their employers to take time away from work, and those not subsidized by the SA or by their employers produced, themselves, the necessary funds for their tours.[14] According to John Randall, an artisan reporter and china painter from Shropshire, such planning and saving proved a daunting task for many would-be-tourists. Although large manufacturers established saving clubs and provided their workers with excursion "incentives," "thousands, with convictions of the benefits to be derived from the Paris exhibition, fritter[ed] away means which, by a slight embargo on accustomed indulgences for a few weeks, would take them there."[15] The "thousands" who overcame these obstacles to join the WMCIU tours were thus as committed to attending the exhibition and to reaping its "benefits" as the SA's artisan reporters.

Another similarity between the two groups is that most men traveled alone, leaving their wives and family at home. While the WMCIU had secured lodging for married couples, few women, married or single, surmounted the economic considerations, family responsibilities, or gender norms, which would have prevented most from attending the exhibition. Indeed, the WMCIU probably used middle-class taboos against un-chaperoned single women to reject multiple requests for inclusion in the tours. In the WMCIU's final report, the Corresponding Secretary of the WMCIU Paris Excursion Committee explained, with "regret," that they could not accommodate women excursionists, as too many "difficulties" stood in the way. The secretary left the precise nature of these "difficulties" to the imagination, but made it poignantly clear that women passionately wished to join the excursion. He writes:

So often and so eagerly were requests made and repeated, to allow women to proceed in small parties – so willing were they to submit to any little inconvenience – and so apparently genuine were sometimes the applications and ground upon which they were based, that the most delicate and ungrateful part of my duty consisted in saying No![16]

The secretary's emphatic "No" silenced most women's demands, but some still managed to make the journey on their own, such as the young domestic servant who, the WMCIU's secretary reports, had "contrived" to meet her fiancé at the exhibition, but was forced to return early due to an "emergency."[17] It is possible, therefore, that more working women attended the exhibition than the existing record suggests. Women workers, however, may also have been discouraged from taking part in the tours by their fathers, husbands, or, for that matter, "fiancés." While some artisan reporters referred to their Paris tour as a "holiday," the excursions in no way resembled middle-class leisure tours in which whole families traveled together. Rather, they mirrored fraternal trade society conventions which, based on male group solidarities, combined pleasure with labor and vocational learning. Indeed, the exclusion of women from the tours was consistent with their exclusion at the time from most trade unions.[18] The presence of wives, therefore, would have feminized the overall masculine tenor of the tours, which were often depicted in military terms as "troops" or "deployments." Although advertised as "peaceful invasions," they clearly stood for Britain's prowess on the field of international industrial competition. Needless to say, the SA overlooked skilled women workers in selecting their artisan reporters.

Because the artisan reporters traveled and lodged with the WMCIU excursionists, they also shared core touristic experiences, from purchasing their travel tickets to assuming new identities as travelers. The initial leg of Thomas Connolly's journey, in which he became "a foreigner for once in my life," provides some insights. Connolly, an Irish stonemason and London radical, wrote that immediately after learning that he had been accepted by the SA as an "artisan reporter," he walked to the offices of the WMCIU and bought a round-trip ticket for 31 shillings. The ticket (which was more like an all-inclusive voucher) covered the cost of transport and one week's accommodations at the WMCIU lodgings on the Avenue Rapp. The next day, he boarded a train for the Channel, and looking around him, discovered that he had "plenty of company of the third class like myself – many of them fine, stalwart men from the north – bound for Paris and the Exhibition."[19]

Connolly and his fellow travelers also discovered that they had some adjustments to make in adapting to their new roles as tourists. Symbolically, the transition from mere workmen to cosmopolites began when the excursionists first exchanged their British sovereigns for French francs at the Newhaven port station and began their rite of passage: the "dreadful ordeal" of the Channel crossing. The excursionists were given two choices in the type of vessel that would see them through to the coast of France: a first- and second-class "paddle," or for a shilling less, a worn-out "screw," "as the lives of the third class," Connolly caustically remarked, "were not so precious." Considering that "even if I went to the bottom, I should be more at home with my own order," Connolly boarded the suspicious craft and set sail with his new companions across the Channel. Bouts of seasickness tested the travelers' mettle, but, as Connolly assured his readers, bracing swigs of brandy and rum and hearty refrains of "Britannia Rules the Waves" gave them courage enough to withstand the ocean tumults until they disembarked at the port of Dieppe.

Two hours later, Connolly at last set foot upon French soil and, looking around him, discovered that "everything" seemed "strange." There was so much to take in at once: "the quaint old town, with its picturesque streets and stone buildings ... the people all speaking in an unknown tongue"; and, not least, "the quiet-looking gens-d'armes, who never appear absent from your sight while you stay in France." Hungry after the grueling journey, Connolly, with "the aid of sundry signs – for my tongue was now of little use to me," found his seafaring friends at the Hôtel Chemin de Fer, and sat down to a hearty English breakfast reasonably priced at 2fr. The men then decided to take in the sights before boarding the train that would carry them on the final stretch of their journey to Paris. Most memorable to Connolly was the church of St. Jacques, "a fine specimen of flamboyant Gothic." Climbing the 216 steps to the top of the tower, which gave a view of the Channel and the countryside below, the excursionists felt that it was "well worth the labour."

Once they commenced with the rest of their journey, settling into the "rough" but "comfortable" third-class compartments of the French train, the men admitted feeling anxious about visiting Paris. Not only was it a large city, but the language barrier seemed to portend unknown dangers. But, as Connolly disclosed, their experience en route (which included a stop in Rouen, the "Manchester of France," and more sightseeing) cured most of their apprehensions. If any lingering doubts did remain, they vanished when the men spotted a "young lad in Highland costume" waiting to greet them on the platform of the Paris train station. "How agreeable is the sight of a national costume when away from home," Connolly commented, "you feel that you can rely on the wearer for advice or protection." Their guide shepherded the men into covered wagons, which conveyed the excursionists from the station to their lodgings, offering them their first visual engagement with Paris along the way. No "finer" vision, Connolly declared, could be found "on this side of Paradise."[20]

Pulling up to the portal of the Avenue Rapp lodgings, where a "guard from the Mexican expedition" stood sentry, the travelers stepped down from the wagon and were "immediately surrounded" by earlier excursionists who "obliged" the new arrivals "to answer many anxious inquiries relative to the old land." After assuring the crowd that "the Queen was still upon the throne," and that "there still was traffic in Fleet Street," the excursionists met the resident manager, William Glazier, the English joiner and union member employed by the WMCIU. Entering the excursionists' names in a logbook, Glazier divided the men into groups of four and gave each a key to their quarters in a "series of clean, well-ventilated, one-story, temporary buildings, separated into blocks by nicely gravelled walks." Left to their own devices the travelers stowed away their belongings, refreshed themselves with "a good wash" and, with their metamorphosis into respectable British tourists completed, lit out for Paris's "splendid" boulevards. When they retired for the night to their "well-ventilated" quarters, Connolly noted the narrow, uninviting beds that, like military cots, discouraged loitering in slumber. "When you think of turning" he commented, "it is time to get up. The Committee had this in mind, no doubt, when they furnished those places ... desirous that we should not waste our time in bed."[21]

On their first full day in Paris, Connolly and many more of the WMCIU excursionists found their way to the British Commission's Workman's Hall located on the exhibition grounds. The Workman's Hall, just as Ewart predicted, acclimated British workers to their new surroundings and facilitated the learning process by offering a central hub in an otherwise strange city. At the hall, workers obtained a free "Pocket Interpreter" of French phrases and purchased local maps. They also met up with other artisans and formed tourist groups led by bilingual guides to visit government buildings, shops, and manufacturers related to their trades in the city and environs. For those with spare time in the early morning or late afternoon, the hall's billiard and reading rooms beckoned.

Tantalizing options also beckoned on the fairgrounds that schooled visitors in their civilizational and imperial heritage. Many workers chose to explore "exotic" temples and restaurants in the immediate vicinity of the Hall, which G. Berry, an engraver, described as "the most instructive parts of the exhibition": "You can walk from one nation to another ... from the summer palace of the Viceroy of Egypt ... [to] tents of the more uncivilized inhabitants of the Earth ... – Arabs."[22] Berry and others, such as John Randall, a china painter, seem to have learned this lesson well. Neither used their reports to question the march of civilization reflected in the hierarchical display of nations that led from humble dwellings to majestic palaces.[23] The exhibition's imperial contexts, in fact, are not significantly remarked upon in their reports. Perhaps this absence reflects the empire's ubiquitous presence in the imperial metropole, warranting little commentary despite its Parisian context; or, perhaps, this absence was a function of the reports themselves, which were to weigh the merits of industrialized nations against their own. Either way, artisan reporters only occasionally expressed imperial identities based on the authority of their craft knowledge. James Plampin, a "working Jeweller" from Birmingham admired Indian silver filigree, the "delicacy" of which was "unequaled," and noted a very "un-Indian" piece that was remarkable for its simplicity rather than, as usual, vulgar showiness.[24] More substantively, William Bourne, the foreman of an indiarubber factory, opened his report by establishing the importance of the empire in everyday life, noting how rubber had become a staple in English households and concluded his report listing the quality and prices of rubber in far-flung parts of the world, including in East India, Honduras, Borneo, and Africa.[25]

Before they could begin to gather such information, however, the SA required its artisan reporters to present their credentials to the manager of the Workman's Hall soon after their arrival. Connolly, "like a dutiful servant," was one of the first in his travelling party to walk through the open exhibition gates in the early morning and to have been "received" by Haussoullier with "distinguished consideration."[26] At the Workman's Hall, Connolly would have met up with other artisan reporters and workers who traveled to the exhibition on WMCIU's tickets. Attendance at the Workman's Hall was strictly voluntary for the WMCIU excursionists, but Glazier, the Avenue Rapp manager and IWA member, made it his calling to round up willing recruits. In a letter to the SA in 1868, seeking a similar appointment, Glazier explained that he not only ran the lodgings with military efficiency and attended to the men's physical welfare in Paris (knowing the "helplessness men feel if taken ill in a strange country"), but, accommodating the aims of the WMCIU (if only rhetorically in what amounted to a job application), took it upon himself to direct his lodgers towards the Workmen's Hall. "It is not sufficient merely to say 'Here are the means, use them,'" he enthused, "but that it is necessary there should be an active energetic spirit constantly pushing and promoting the object in view."[27]

This, then, was how many of the SA's artisan reporters and WMCIU excursionists began their journeys. Presumably, there were other experiences that the two groups shared. Conceivably, they would have conferred similar meanings to their tours based on lives of struggle and hardship in dialogue with religious, gender, or other salient identities. Few, for instance, probably gave the tours such a politically robust interpretation as Connolly, who remarked that, like his betters, he felt entitled to a holiday after laboring long and hard to get the Second Reform Bill passed.[28] But many others likely identified with the pathos expressed by Charles Hooper, a cabinetmaker and freethinker, who, having "known little else than toil from ... boyhood, working at a bench not less than ten hours a day," conveyed his gratitude to the SA for the "first and only fortnight's holiday I ever had in my life."[29] While the uniformity of the workers' subjective feelings must be left, in the end, to speculation, more concrete links between the WMCIU's excursionists and the SA's artisan reporters can be observed by examining how organizers encouraged both groups to develop critical perspectives during their travels abroad.

Britain, France and the Idea of "Complementarity"

The WMCIU's excursionists and the SA's artisan reporters arrived in Paris well equipped to tackle their jobs as tourists and reporters. First, they packed into their traveling bags *Black's Guide to Paris and the International Exhibition*, a general handbook issued to the WMCIU excursionists and artisan reporters that offered tips on how to travel economically and that identified the most "important" tourist sights to visit.[30] Second, they brought with them a mental map that charted out how they should survey the foreign landscape. This mental map, in part, reflected the WMCIU's suggestions and the SA's instructions to compare France with Britain and to think critically about the differences between the two nations from their own perspectives as British working men.[31] One goal of this exercise was to enable workers to ascertain for themselves, as Connolly put it, "what truth was in the cry that all the nations on earth were beating us, and that the trade of England was leaving it."[32] More generally, however, radical discourses surrounding the idea of "complementarity" encouraged such comparisons for the good of the nation and, in broader terms, civilization. Writing on Victorian political thought, Georgios Varouxakis observes that many theorists believed that advanced nations and peoples could improve their own "distinctive" characteristics by appropriating the best qualities of others. Identifying national characteristics and drawing comparisons, therefore, was a matter of practical utility.[33] This philosophy, which Varouxakis terms "complementarity," did not sit well with many nationalists, especially Francophobes who refused to concede French superiority over any aspect of British political, social, or cultural life. As Linda Colley has argued, negative stereotypes that historically defined France as Britain's depraved antithesis contributed to the formation of a British national identity. Therefore, even countervailing narratives about the French, such as those promoted by free trade activists who constructed a more moderate discourse of the French as pacific economic partners, or workers who subscribed to French socialist ideas, did little to dislodge negative stereotypes of France from the popular imagination.[34] Nevertheless, proponents of complementarity persisted in challenging this conceptual framework by asking Britons to view themselves in a more critical light. For example, the liberal theorist John Stuart Mill condemned Whig "smugness" over Britain's "political adaptiveness and constitutional continuity" and argued that the economic and constitutional experiment of the 1848–49 French Republic offered "the encouraging lesson about the possibilities of popular government."[35] Similarly, the cultural critic Matthew Arnold returned from a continental tour in 1859 vilifying the "barbarous" culture of Britain's middle classes and lauding France's centralized state that had not only produced superior educational institutions but a superior culture to match. An enlightened democracy, Arnold insisted, required a national system of education based on the French model, a prescription that *laissez-faire* purists were loath to countenance, but one that positivists, and certainly many working-class radicals were coming to favor, notwithstanding the despotism of Napoleon III.

In contrasting British faults with French virtues, however, these critics, as Stefan Collini explains, also tended to "trade in stereotypes, and especially to homogenize [British] culture in order to produce a liberatingly uncomplicated target" for criticism, earning the contempt of conservative intellectuals who questioned their patriotism.[36] Additionally, their remarks understandably distressed Orleanist liberals in France who were opposed to the Second Empire. As one baffled representative of the Orleanist party enquired, how could his movement use Britain as a model of liberal freedoms in its struggle against Napoleon III's autocratic rule, if Arnold and others appeared to approve of the state's heavy hand? Yet Arnold defended his stance, arguing that "his Anglo-French comparisons were aimed not at convincing the English to imitate their French counterparts, but rather at producing a better breed than either the existing French or the existing English middle classes."[37] Indeed, well aware of France's faults, these critics refused to repeat the common cant of "British superiority."

Varouxakis restricts his analysis of "complementarity" to public intellectuals, yet the idea circulated more widely than his study would suggest. In holding their ground, elite critics of British triumphalism found support with many liberals, such as members of the SA and the WMCIU, who found continental industrial advancements an increasingly menacing threat to British economic prosperity. Many, for instance, had begun to argue that

Britain would have to adopt continental methods of technical training to educate its own industrial workforce, and suggested, like Arnold, that state intervention on the French model would be necessary to make these improvements possible. Nor should it be overlooked that working-class radicals would have found the idea of "complementarity" with the French ideals of 1789 and 1848 neither novel nor threatening, but welcome.

The idea of complementarity, therefore, was part of Britain's cultural climate, and informed workers' approach to their Paris tours even if some were unaware of the formal arguments surrounding the concept. In the specific context of their tours, they encountered these ideas in George Holyoake's pamphlet, *The Good of Going to Paris* (1867).[38] In it, Holyoake not only endorsed the co-operative movement, but offered his readers instructions for sightseeing and travel writing that incorporated the idea of complementarity.[39]

Tourism, Holyoake cautioned, is "not so plain and easy as it seems." Describing a plan of action more akin to work than recreation, Holyoake suggested that the WMCIU tourists rest well before embarking on each day's excursion, and cautioned them to visit the most important sites first lest fatigue overcome them before reaching the end of their itineraries. For those with "a taste for reporting," Holyoake offered a few words on how they should make sense of all that they saw – a project that required developing a critical perspective.

"We get all our knowledge by comparing one thing with another," Holyoake instructed, adding: "A man who has been abroad sees things and understands things at home when he comes back which he never observed before." What they could expect to see in Paris, Holyoake disclosed, was "a wealth of foreign thought" that will make "you learn to respect other nations and think modestly of your own." According to Holyoake, the French outdid the British on any number of fronts, from their tasteful dress and manners to their "inventive power and skill." But, the point in all this, Holyoake emphasized, was to understand that "no man can know one thing well unless he knows many others. You cannot tell what a thing is until you see what it is not." Travel provided this perspective. By assessing the comparative merits of one country over another, one could then make improvements at home based on this knowledge.[40] Not all of the WMCIU excursionists would have agreed with Holyoake's assessment of France and its merits. However, as the artisan reports reveal, working people approached the lessons of travel by thinking in comparative terms that, like Mill and Arnold, would help produce a better Britain, one that could perhaps even realize the French ideals of liberty, equality, and brotherhood.

Identity, the Artisan "Flâneur," and Textual Production

The SA's arrangements for the artisan reporters in Paris reflected its commitment to facilitating the reporters' ability to think critically about social and industrial questions swirling at the center of contemporary public debates. The Workman's Hall provided the artisan reporters with maps, phrase books, and interpreters, which gave them access to the city and enabled contact with French artisans in the places where they worked and spent their leisure hours. The organizers also offered the reporters a moral safety net in the ideology of complementarity that allowed them to critique Britain, if they chose, in constructive ways that served a patriotic purpose. Additionally, the SA gave the reporters a set of categories to help them organize the information they collected including "style and quality of work," "materials," "wages and hours of labour," "education," "habits of life and amusements," and "trades' associations." What the SA could not provide, however, was a template for the narrative construction of their reports.

When the artisans returned home from their travels and prepared to compose their reports, they could not turn to a standard model for imitation. For the few artisans who could read French, the French artisan reports of the British 1862 exhibition might have served as models.[41] Not one artisan reporter, however, refers to them in their own reports. Another potential model would have been the government jury reports from previous exhibitions or current competitions published in the London papers. Yet, such polished, highly specialized texts were also inadequate. Instead, a close reading of the reports reveal that the artisans turned to the popular medium of urban journalism for imaginative help not only with constructing their narratives, but also for conducting their investigations.

Although no two reports are identical in form or content, taken together they duplicate many of the stylistic features that journalists – often social reformers – used to tell their tales of urban vice and squalor. In an important synthetic analysis of this genre, Judith Walkowitz explains that journalists surveyed city landscapes on two levels. As "rationalists" they were confident that "through reason and its 'science'" they could establish "a reliable and universal knowledge of 'man' and his world." Complicating this "rationalist sensibility," Walkowitz suggests, was the urban spectator's "propensity for fantasy."[42] Henry Mayhew's interviews with London workers for the *Morning Chronicle* (1849–1850), and ten years later for his *London Labour and the London Poor* (last volume, 1861), for instance, offered readers statistical information on wages and working conditions, but also narratives that dramatized his subjects' lives through vivid dialogue and description.[43] Moralists added other dimensions to this genre. Many journalists divided the city into zones of good and evil, while others made more ethically ambiguous statements by "juxtaposing a West End of glittering leisure and consumption and national spectacle to an East End of obscure density, indigence, sinister foreign aliens, and potential crime."[44] Imperial rhetoric also seeped into these narratives when journalists constructed London slums as unmapped territories, which they courageously penetrated, undaunted by the danger that lurked within. Journalists combined these elements with the added sensation of dramatizing their own lives as they went "in search of strangers and secrets." Sometimes disguised as lowly indigents, at other times accompanied by the local police, they gathered "good copy and anecdote" that would garner a high price from publishers in the popular press.[45] Incorporating, therefore a "mixture of fact and fancy" the exploration literature surrounding urban investigations constituted a "melange" of imaginative, sensationalist, and disciplining discourses. The practical and literary result was "a range of disparate texts and heterogeneous practices which emerge in the nineteenth-century city – tourism, exploration/discovery, social investigation, social policy." As critiques of contemporary society in support of reform – as critiques that blended "fact and fancy" in a journalistic style – the artisans' reports belong to this odd mix of "disparate texts."[46]

With the imaginative flair of popular journalists, the artisan reporters wrote inward-looking or politically-strident narratives that meshed descriptive travel commentary with more quantitative technical and trade information and statistics. To do so, many entered Paris much like the upper-classes entered the East End – with a sense of entitlement – a sensation that only the most political among them had come to feel in their own cities, as the recent Hyde Park riots had proved. As Walkowitz further explains, it was generally the upper classes who "established a right to the city – a right not traditionally available to, often not even part of, the imaginative repertoire of the less advantaged."[47] As privileged males, urban explorers, or in Baudelaire's term, *flâneurs*, were entitled to engage the metropolis, speculatively and experientially, in its entirety – to not only traverse the ordered boulevards of high society by day, but to cross over into the chaos of outcast London, Paris, or New York by night. In contrast, few British working people imagined that they had a "right" to their cities, and instead conceptualized their world from a "localized perspective" or "a vision largely restricted to the neighborhood." Material and structural conditions reinforced this perspective. "Without respectable attire, working men ran the risk of arbitrary arrest and conviction for nuisance activities if they ventured out of their own locale." [48] The artisan reporters, however, could roam freely, Deemed capable of self government, and entrusted by the SA with the responsibility of reporting on the industry and social conditions of their Parisian counterparts, they established their right to the city as artisan flâneurs and transferred this right into their writing. Their reports thus document a wide range of identities put in motion by their investigations as they wrestled to adequately represent both the French "other" and themselves.

In attempting to convey to their readers the alien world of Paris, the artisan reporters enhanced the narrative power of their reports with anecdotes, dialogue, and statistics. To this end, some artisans constructed elaborate ruses to acquire information. Two carpenters, T.W. Hughes and John D. Prior, for instance, conducted an informal survey of French literacy rates by "accosting" the poorest of the population that they encountered in walking

Paris' boulevards to "test their capabilities." Feigning to have lost their way, the reporters "solicited" assistance from passersby and asked their subjects to read a set of directions, deliberately scribbled in a "far from legible hand." Their imposture proved that even the lowliest among the poor could read with "perfect" comprehension, a significantly different result, they left their readers to surmise, than could be expected had they conducted the same experiment in London.[49]

The Birmingham glassmaker, T.J. Wilkinson, added intrigue to his report with information acquired through industrial espionage. "Fully expecting to have free admission into the glass works in and around Paris," Wilkinson instead found himself "doomed to disappointment." Not even Haussoullier at the Workman's Hall could secure permission for him to visit shops related to his trade. Wilkinson, therefore, decided to take the matter into his own hands, and "resolved, if the discourtesy of the employés was determined to keep me out, that I would try what my own perseverance would do to get me in." As Wilkinson explained, it took "three days spent in dodging about, my labour being double on account of my not being able to speak the French language. But, eventually I succeeded, and found myself inside a glass works, expecting every moment to be turned out for not having a permit." Successful in his mission, Wilkinson took his readers on a tour of a vast, well-ventilated shed that contained four large furnaces and hummed with the work of boys and men "like so many bees in a hive."[50]

Unlike Wilkinson, the ill-fated joiner, Alexander Kay, freely visited several joinery workshops and openly engaged workers in lively conversations, sometimes trading information on craft techniques. When first meeting a staircase builder, Theodore Canrouget, at his bench, for example, Kay brashly appraised his work: "The interpreter told him that I considered the workmanship not good. He got quite offended, and told the interpreter that he would defy any man to make a better job." Adopting a more diplomatic posture, Kay attempted to sooth away the insult. "I had then to explain to him that his hand-work was good, but the system he adopted was expensive ... which seemed to take him by surprise." In the interest of friendly exchange, Kay demonstrated how Canrouget could use an alternative system employed in London. Being "a very intelligent, industrious workman," Canrouget, Kay smugly noted, was "quite open to adopt any improvement." Later, the two treated each other (and the interpreter) to wine at a local café, whereupon Kay asked his friend if the men at the shop "would object to me coming to work ... if I learned the French language." Canrouget responded that "they would be happy to welcome me, as from the questions I had asked and answered, he was sure I was a practical joiner."[51] Although Wilkinson could only observe French workers by stealth, Kay and other reporters reveled in their cross-cultural encounters. Through their interactions they sometimes developed identities as superior craftsmen, but they also shared trade identities with their French hosts, and pride in good craftsmanship.

Economic comparisons through statistics also inspired cross-cultural identities. Lending scientific weight to their findings, most reports contained statistical information. The artisans gathered this information primarily from French government reports that were provided and perhaps translated by Haussoullier at the Workman's Hall and (when writing on specific displays at the exhibition), from the exhibition catalogue. Reporting on cutlery, John Wilson crafted a learned and sweeping history of his trade that charted technological advances through the periods of the ancient Middle East, to the Norman Conquest, and on to the age of Chaucer and Rabelais. Reaching the industrial period of the nineteenth century, literary references to technical progress gave way to statistical data about the social and economic conditions of workers that showed change within decades rather than epochs.[52] Wilkinson also fleshed-out his report with statistics compiled by the government on the "morals and habits" of Paris's 649 glassmakers. Perhaps an oblique critique of the *livret* system, which required workers to carry a passport describing their conduct and work from one employer to another – a practice openly disparaged in other reports – Wilkinson disclosed that "629 have good characters; 14 doubtful; and 6 bad."[53] Reflecting the significance of these statistics to the artisans' reports, George Howell, a bricklayer and secretary of the Reform League, found it necessary to obtain more figures after he had returned home. Writing to Haussoullier, Howell requested the "average prices" for 1000 bricks in Paris.[54] Such statistics naturally led to comparative critiques of wage differentials, especially when the reporters' earnings failed to match or surpass those of their French counterparts. In listing these differences, the radical tailor, R. Sinclair, stated that he would "advise English tailors to go over" to Paris. Not only would they be paid better than at home, but would command more respect from employers.[55]

In their new roles as urban explorers, the artisan reporters traversed Paris's boulevards with a determination to understand the French Other that rebuked what Holyoake had termed the "insular character" of the provincial British working man. The narration of their experiences, however, posed a number of discursive challenges. Apologizing for their inexperience in writing reports, most of the artisan reporters expressed little confidence in the stylistic quality, and occasionally, the qualitative content of their reports. "This being the first time I have had to report anything," wrote Sinclair, "I find it very difficult, but I hope you will bear with me if it is not so concise and orderly as it should be."[56] P.A. Rasmussen, a silversmith, similarly asked for the Council's "indulgence ... for any imperfection in language or expressions, which, no doubt, will be found in this report, the preparation of which has of course been to me a task of a novel kind."[57] Others, such as Aaron Green, a porcelain decorator, attributed his unease with writing to an inadequate education. "Disclaiming all pretension to learning," Green declared, "I write, as a working man, on the executive or manipulative part of decoration only, leaving schools and styles of art to be treated by writers of far higher attainments."[58] Wilkinson similarly lamented his writing skills. "In presenting this Report," he began, "I do so with a certain amount of diffidence. In the first place, because I have not had the honour of writing a Report before on any subject; and secondly ... [because] I was compelled to begin work at the early age of seven years ... my stock of learning is but small, and not calculated to enable me to write a very good Report."[59]

Some artisans not only apologized for their prose, but also their ability to report adequately on each of the categories requested by the SA. These artisans, at times, offered tentative assessments, or felt compelled to qualify their truth claims, suggesting that their observations were more impressionistic than empirical. "To do justice to our subject," wrote carpenters T.W. Hughes and John D. Prior, "we should require a much more intimate acquaintance with the French workmen than could possibly be acquired during a short visit."[60] Likewise, Francis Kirchoff, a glassmaker, feared that some of his observations "may have been but an erroneous impression received by a Cockney on his first visit to Paris, and so I should not generalise from one or two instances."[61] Compounding the problem of time and experience, others, such as Frederick Thompson, a "practical" foreman of a saddlery workshop in Birmingham, complained that despite the availability of interpreters, language was a "great bar to getting information I should otherwise have obtained."[62] Hard pressed to acquire substantive information and daunted with the task of textual production, some artisan reporters understandably expressed disappointment with the results of their efforts. Kirchhoff, for instance, closed his report by calling it "weak."[63] Similarly, William Bramhall, a Sheffield saw-maker, reproached himself for having "very inadequately performed his duty."[64]

While these self-effacing and qualifying statements may have reflected the artisans' genuine self-perceptions, they may have also served a pragmatic rhetorical purpose in their texts. First, by recognizing their literary limitations and phrasing some of their findings in a tentative manner, some artisan reporters likely intended to disarm prospective critics, a defensive strategy that literary critic Sara Mills argues other marginalized authors, such as women travel writers, employed.[65] Working-class intellectuals and activists, for example, were well aware that critics often trivialized their literary outpourings and political ideas as childish or amateurish. Even elite champions of the working classes belittled workers' attempts to have their opinions heard fairly and with dignity. Layard, in his role as MP for Southwark, for instance, publicly disparaged his radical constituency, commenting in a parliamentary debate that the men (Benjamin Lucraft among them) rousing the crowds during the 1866 Hyde Park demonstrations merely delivered "foolish speeches" that lacked serious import.[66] If any of the artisan reporters suspected that their reports might be trivialized in a like manner, their intuition was justified. After the reports' publication, Thomas Cook recommended them to the readers of *The Excursionist*, not only because they contained some useful "facts," but because of their entertainment value. As Cook patronizingly explained, "the extreme naïveté with which [the artisan reporters] describe their experiences is as interesting as it is quaint and amusing."[67]

Secondly, and perhaps more representative of the artisans as a whole, this defensive strategy might have served, in the reporters' eyes, to deflect readers' attention away from their literary limitations, to focus not on style, but on the more important content of their reports. Based on empirical observation and personal experience, and framed in terms of national contrasts or complementary practices, the artisan reporters insisted that they grounded their reports in objective truth. Connolly, for instance, noted that while writing reports was not "so easy a task as some persons think – more especially to one who has been brought up the greater part of his life to chiseling stone," he stressed that "however imperfect a summary, [his report] will be the result of my own observation and inquiries."[68] Wilkinson likewise concluded that his "object" in pointing out his failings was to "request those who read and those who hear it read to look kindly upon all deficiencies, while this may be relied upon, that I shall here state only my own honest convictions without prejudice of any kind."[69] Bramhall similarly requested readers to accept his "honesty of purpose, having no ulterior view but such as a truthseeker always has – the truth in itself alone."[70]

In underscoring their objectivity, many artisan reporters emphasized selective "truths" about France to solicit support for political, economic, and social reform at home. Radical workers had long used cultural resources to respond to economic changes with class-based analyses, as E.P. Thompson's work on the London Corresponding Society illustrates, as does Margot Finn's analysis of Chartist poetry and fiction.[71] The reports offered a congenial medium to carry this rhetorical tradition further. A recurrent theme in the artisan reports, for instance, was the industrial degradation of their crafts. David Sarjeant attacked the mass production of papier-mâché goods, and placed the blame on British manufacturers who, like the Belgians (and unlike the French), jettisoned quality for quantity, by catering to and profiting from the "depraved and vulgar taste" of an untutored public.[72] The watchmaker and political activist, Hermann Jung, critiqued industrialization by decrying the division of labor which "exert[ed] a deadening influence upon the imaginative and designing faculties of the workman." A "drudge" who repeats the same mechanical task each day, Jung stated, "neither works for honour nor beauty."[73] James Mackie, a London wood-carver, also concerned with quality production, compared French and British workshop culture, education, and wages. Well paid for his labor, the French carver, Mackie reported, used his leisure time to "enlarge his store of knowledge" and to develop "that interest and pleasure in his labour" that accounts for French "success." Moreover, Mackie continued, the "liberty of the workshop" in France "is considerable, for the iron hand is not upon the men; neither is the employer or foreman regarded as a warder of a model prison whose duty it is to keep men silent and at their labour." Without this "liberty" in wages, leisure, and workshop culture, Britain, Mackie intimated, was doomed to reproduce a "class of dull workmen, who will never give us good art."[74]

As workmen in the artistic trades, the reporters also addressed the break-down of the apprenticeship system and the absence of technical institutions to take its place in training British youths to become viable competitors with better-educated French workers. Most cautioned their readers that if Britain persisted in neglecting the artistic and technical education of workmen – and the taste of the general public – it could expect to lose its lead over France in manufacturing and trade. Connolly warned that "it is impossible to estimate the loss which is entailed upon England through the neglect of art culture. ... Through it we are reduced to mere hewers of wood and drawers of water for other nations."[75] Thomas Jacob, a cabinet draughtsman, seconded Connolly's opinion, commenting sarcastically that anyone who had been to Paris should "feel quite contented to be beaten by a people whose government does every-thing for artistic improvement." France not only nurtured workers' ingenuity, energy, and competitiveness through proper training from youth to adult-hood, he wrote, but also fostered "a taste for the beautiful ... amongst the [French] people" simply by virtue of their surroundings.[76] Unlike London's filthy streets, pedestrian buildings and indifferent storefronts, everything in Paris was calculated to dazzle, please, and train the eye so that the city itself constituted a veritable "school of art." A jeweler named James Pamplin echoed these observations. "Place our artisans under equal conditions," he wrote "and we believe they will produce equal results, and England will not long be threatened with the danger of having industries which supply her millions with bread taken away from her by foreign superiority." Suggesting state intervention on the French model to "avert ... this danger," Pamplin, like many of his fellow reporters, underscored that technical education could not be "left to art societies with insufficient grants, inadequately supple-mented by private liberality; but, to quote the words of an able orator upon a totally different theme, 'It is a question for the Crown, for Parliament when it meets, and for the whole nation, whose honour and interest are at stake.'"[77]

The artisans also used their reports to address economic grievances in the context of women's work. Their comments reveal on the one hand, a bias for the "honour and interest" of the respectable artisan male breadwinner, but also, on the other hand, a willingness to look at the different patterns of French female labor and domesticity in complementary terms. Gender critiques predictably drew on working-class rhetoric that defined "the norm of the male breadwinner, the ideal of a family wage, and notions of working class domesticity for women."[78] This separate spheres ideology stemmed, as Anna Clark has shown, from artisans' struggles to win the franchise by defining masculinity in middle-class terms. Thus, citizens with a political stake in the nation conducted themselves as respectable husbands and fathers and as disciplined breadwinners.[79] This ideology, however, did not mesh with working-class reality because respectability also required a family wage that allowed working-class wives to assume their "natural" sphere and duties in the home, a crucial economic component that, for most workers, was impossible to realize. Employers undercut male wages by drawing on a growing pool of poorly paid women and child laborers, producing tensions between the rhetoric and the reality of masculine respectability and domestic ideology, and fostering antagonism between male and female workers. The unfamiliar setting of France and the command to evaluate the French Other in terms of complementarity, encouraged the artisan reporters to explore alternative constructions of masculinity and femininity.

Artisan reporters recognized female industrial labor as a fact of life in France. Not one report suggests that French women should be, or even could be, relegated to the home and excluded from the workplace. One reason for this may be that the reporters did not encounter (or chose to omit from their reports) the kind of gender antagonism in France that existed in Britain. Most of their references to women's industrial production consisted of government statistics that listed the subdivision of manufacturing processes and relative wages. According to their reports, French male workers generally received higher wages than their British counterparts, and women workers received wages that the reporters deemed appropriate to the auxiliary jobs they performed. Jacob, who identified himself as an "advocate for the better employment and remuneration of women," for example, appreciated the division of labor in France into properly gendered spheres. In the carpentry trade, women worked at "French polishing," a task that required little "skill or thought," while the men labored at design, carving, or engraving – jobs that required the "use of their mental powers." In Britain, however, men were too often employed in work more suitable to women, such as French polishing, which "absolutely wasted" their "faculties." Moreover, the rational distribution of jobs and wages in France, they noted, also seemed to contribute to the general well-being of French women workers. The tailor, Sinclair, for instance, wrote that in his trade "the French female worker does not look care-worn as her English sister, and is never seen drunk or in rags."[80]

While these contrasts served to critique industrial capitalism in Britain, they also served to critique British women workers in unfavorable terms. In describing French gender relations, the artisan reporters devoted considerable space to contrasting French and British women's dress and manners. Kay and Jacob, for example, both painted a pastoral narrative (in an urban setting) of "mechanics' wives, &c." walking home from market in the early morning. "A sight worth going to see," they described the women dressed in their typical "white crimped caps," and trim, neat dresses, hems decorously set just above the ankle, holding baskets on their arms that contained the day's "provisions," as they purposefully set about the day's tasks.[81] An iconic figure in the artisan reports, these white-hatted women, who, Jacob wrote, had the "appearance of our country girls, though they lived in the town," symbolized a kind of fresh-faced modesty and thrift missing from the culture and comportment of British women workers, seduced by the finery displayed in shop windows. Seemingly chagrined by the new consumer culture that had captured the imagination, savings, and dubious tastes of British working-class women, Jacob "thought what a pity it was that our young women, who so much wish to follow the fashions of Paris, cannot often go there ... and see for themselves what are the fashions generally in use among people of their class in that city." Indeed, a trip to France would show them that French women were "quite content to dress according to their means." In France, "instead of seeing a long trawling dress, draggled with mud, a gorgeous head-dress, and miserable boots (I hope I am not too severe), they would see all, from the poorest, particularly clean and very neatly dressed."[82] Jacob offered his critique in the voice of a kindly paternalist, but it betrayed an underlying hostility towards women's wage-earning status.[83] Indeed, Jacob drew on nineteenth-century "scientific" and moralist rhetoric that saw love of "finery" as one step up the ladder toward prostitution.[84] Praising the modest and fiscally prudent French female worker as the ideal model of womanhood, Jacob used the concept of complementarity to discipline his own country-women and to assert his own identity of masculine respectability.[85]

Jacob and other reporters similarly demonstrate an ambivalent process at work in defining women's domestic roles. Some artisan reporters, for instance, were quite receptive to French domestic arrangements, particularly reproductive and childcare practices, which facilitated French women's greater productivity at home and in the workplace. As Kay noted, one "evil the Frenchman avoids" was a large family: "It is a very rare occurrence for a French lady to have more than a couple of children, and these she sends to the country, to be reared until they become able to do for themselves." Liberated from the usual domestic cares, "French ladies," Kay noted, "are all interested in some business, or other mode of industry, whereby they add greatly to the comforts of home, and the health and pleasure of all around them."[86]

Another domestic advantage that French workers enjoyed was family sociability outside their small apartments. "What an Englishman considers, and is proud to call a 'home,'" wrote Jacob, "I believe scarcely exists in Paris." As he and most of the artisan reporters were startled to discover, family conviviality took place not by the hearth, but in cafés. Rather than condemning café domesticity, however, Jacob and most of the artisan reporters recognized that this form of family life suited working peoples' lives in Paris where a critical housing shortage, like that in London, deprived them of customary domestic comforts. After the day's work, Jacob observed, "wife, children, and all," gathered at the café, "drinking their wines or coffee; perhaps playing dominoes, cards, billiards, or reading the papers ... all very respectable ... all very quiet and orderly."[87] This mixed-sex sphere of leisure contrasted favorably with the sexually divided social world at home in Britain. As such, it allowed the artisan reporters to articulate a more sympathetic attitude towards women and leisure, and also to define a different kind of feminine respectability and identity in public spaces that ultimately idealized family relations.

In praising these aspects of French gender norms, the artisan reporters held France up as a model for British emulation. But, clearly, the artisan reporters left much unsaid. Paris, like London, employed its share of social investigators who explored the city's mean streets beyond the "masquerade" of the Grand Boulevards. But the artisan reporters chose to ignore the slums located directly behind the uniform buildings, glitzy cafes, and public gardens that characterized the modern city in Napoleon III's Paris.[88] Indeed, because many of the reports flattered the French, and, on occasion, Napoleon himself, the French government wished to have them translated for the instruction of their own working classes.[89] Such a prospect must have disheartened the Paris chapter of the IWA, just as Arnold's comments about the virtues of continental statism had distressed the Orleanist Party. Yet, perhaps some of the artisan reporters, again like Arnold, viewed this rhetoric in pragmatic terms as a means of encouraging improvement at home, even if it came at the expense of their French compatriots.

The reporters' pragmatism may have left other stones unturned as well. Although Bramhall felt at liberty to write with little "fear from the publication of the truth," others may have felt more reticent about disclosing negative observations, reflecting extra-textual constraints on the writing process.[90] Some artisans, for example, may have considered what impression their reports would have on their employers, many of whom helped subsidize their tours. Did they view their appointments in terms of patronage that would have required some form of reciprocity? Even the more militant among them seemed to have engaged in self-censorship. IWA members, Howell, Connolly, and Lucraft most likely made contact with the members of Parisian chapter of their organization. Yet the IWA is absent from their reports. Moreover, Lucraft, who with other Chartists despised Napoleon III, expressed not one word of insult for his host, but instead focused his strongest critique on the ideology of free trade. Similarly, Howell's report rarely diverges from the aesthetics and techniques of bricklaying, and uses government statistics to support his conclusions. Even Connolly's report which begins and ends ridiculing class distinctions, contained humor as well as rancor. Perhaps, then, the generally noncombative tone of the artisan reports reflected the growing rapprochement between labor and liberal leaders, an alliance that was beginning to produce results, as the Reform Bill indicated. After all, working-class radicals possessed other forums in which to articulate more militant views.[91] Moreover, they had begun to garner significant financial and social support from liberal patrons, such as Samuel Morley, an SA council member.[92] Thus, while the artisan reporters were free to write what they wished, for some, prudence may have dictated restraint.

Not every artisan reporter, to be sure, felt such restraints. In finding little to admire about France, some projected conservative identities. They reacted negatively to Sunday work and recreation, for example, and asserted Protestant values in denigrating French Catholicism and the Bonapartist regime. Thus, John Evans, a mechanical engineer and one of the few foremen the SA accepted as an artisan reporter, offers a distinct contrast to the views of reporters with political or trade union affiliations. Writing "without favour or prejudice," Evans refused to examine France uncritically, reflecting his position of power on the shop floor and an identity of interests with his employers.[93] A sabbatarian, he disapproved of the "Continental Sunday" which permitted both work and play on the Sabbath. The crime of a Continental Sunday, he moralized, was that it deprived workers of at least one free day a week for rest and spiritual renewal. He also characterized French workers as sullen and lethargic. Obviously, they could not compete with British workers who, he claimed, joyfully and energetically went about their tasks. In the convoluted logic of management, even at the level of foreman, Evans attributed these differences to the greater hours French workers applied to recreation. "If my observations on this point are correct," he argued, "it would seem that the English workmen have the advantage over the French, for working hours are more than the hours for relaxation, therefore those men are best off who take the greatest interest in, and enjoy their lives most while at work."[94] Consequently, Evans found that while "there are many things which we might with advantage learn from the French ... I cannot join with those who see nothing but what is admirable abroad, and underestimate the advantages we enjoy at home."[95]

Other artisan reporters objected to the Continental Sunday, but emphasized the state's sinister role in enforcing cultural practices they deemed inimical to human freedom. Appalled at the intervention of the French state in so many aspects of citizens' everyday life, Bramhall, for instance, remarked that "in England the government is the servant of the people; in France it is their master." Recording his disgust, he listed such offenses as compulsory military conscription and the lack of free speech, the cornerstone of universal suffrage. Seeing Britain for the first time "from a distance," he had come to appreciate "John Bull" more than ever before, concluding that "it is not only with feelings of regret that I have to report upon the inferior condition of our continental fellow-labourers, but that of deep thankfulness that 'we are not as other men are.'"[96]

T.W. Hughes and John D. Prior could only agree. In their joint report on carpentry and joiners' work, they excoriated the French government's intrusiveness and infantilization of the population, describing Paris as a nightmarish world of bread and circuses:

Take an English artisan, any one of the many who work hard, who spend their few leisure minutes ... in active endeavours to ameliorate the moral, political, and social condition of their class; take one of these, and place him in Paris, among Parisian workmen; compel him to lead the life they lead; and we venture to predict that, at the end of six months, life will have become to him a burden, or he will have been rendered unfit for any useful, practical purpose in life.

Hughes and Prior attributed this disintegration to two sources: the government's "capricious and arbitrary treatment of the people," and, in turn, the people's "vain and frivolous pursuits." While Hughes and Prior recognized that "oppression may rankle in the breast" of a few worthy men, they believed that France's arbitrary rule and fantastic spectacles had produced a hegemonic effect on ordinary citizens. Given to pursuits no more noble than "emptying a wine-bottle or skipping about a dancing-room," and unable to discern "the true purposes of life," the French were "bound by trammels which they must cast aside ere they can hope to rise to the dignity of a free and independent nation." What the French could learn from the British, therefore, was that "to spend a life in the service of liberty is even more noble than to die for it" – a declaration supporting the British propensity for gradualism (and by implication, rising Lib–Labism), over the French impulse for revolution.[97]

Although the reports offered readers multiple perspectives on the French people and their government, most reporters found common ground in praising the French predilection for social equality. Indeed, social equality seemed a palpable reality in France, but only a vision for the future in Britain. For, if the French lacked the liberties that every "freeborn" Englishman enjoyed, Britain had something to learn about "equality." According to the artisan reports, social equality in France existed on three levels: between "masters and men" on the shop floor, between the upper and lower classes in public spaces, and in workers' access to elevating, healthful recreation and education. Connolly noted, for instance, that "on the whole, the Frenchmen take their work easy, and appear to be very little frightened of their foreman or employer."[98] Sinclair put this relationship in blunter terms: "Like the English master, [the French master] roars and finds fault with your work, but you are allowed to pay him back in that respect, and he does not complain." In Britain, on the other hand, "to answer back a West-End foreman or master, whilst he is gratuitously dealing out insulting language to you – just answer them, and you are immediately discharged – a pretty state of things, in the 19th century, between employer and employed."[99] In France's public spaces, politeness also prevailed between the classes. William Elliott, a die-sinker, observed that the "French workman has the opportunity of spending his leisure hours in so many pleasant places, where it is not considered derogatory to sit alongside of a blouse [the traditional uniform of the workman], or hold converse with the wearer." "Such things," he concluded, "must tend to harmonise the social strata of society."[100] Even

Hughes and Prior concurred, finding that "class prejudice does not appear to be so prevalent in France as in England." In their investigation of Paris, they "saw no signs of that arrogant assumption on the one hand, and cringing servility on the other, which are too frequently to be met with in this country."[101] Similarly, but also with some ambiguity, as if Solly and Pratt had taken hold of their pens, the lace-makers Edward Smith, Joseph Bird, and George Dexter appreciated French workers' "perfect freedom of access to the picture galleries." With a word of advice to British readers, they implied that social equality, or at the very least, "mutual respect" existed for those capable of cultivating good taste and manners, commenting that "the closer and more constantly the minds of a people can be brought into contact with a higher standard than their own particular class furnishes, must prove a powerful means in their elevation, in all matters of taste, and a great lever in a nation's progress."[102]

The artisan reporters thus essentialized different aspects of both French and British politics, culture, and society in asserting their truth claims. Yet, at the same time, these generalizations could lead in different directions and toward different conclusions, reflecting how relations of power between capital and labor, and between middle-class reformers and working-class radicals, structured their tours and influenced the subjective rendering of their experiences. Despite the artisans' varied perspectives on France's virtues and failings, however, they seemed to agree that French social equality complemented British liberty and could set it ever more firmly along the path to "progress." Nowhere is this view better articulated than in Charles Hooper's report on decorative carpentry, a report that devotes very few words to his trade. Instead, Hooper sustains an argument on the question of social equality in a 25-page discourse on France and its relevance as a model for Britain, a land where, as even Connolly's humor failed to disguise, class injuries were visible around every bend of the road.

"We Claim the Right, as in France": Charles Hooper's French Lessons

Arriving in Paris in the early evening, the cabinetmaker, Hooper, and a group of new acquaintances he had met on the train, immediately assumed their new roles as flâneurs. Traversing the city's boulevards, they "couldn't believe [their] senses." Summoning up all his literary power, Hooper recounted the magic of this first nocturnal ramble:

> It is dark. The Boulevard is crowded. The splendid shops, the grand cafés, the magnificent buildings, the brilliant illuminations, the long lines of trees and lamps, the people sitting in the open air, at neat little marble tables, taking their wine, smoking cigars, or sipping their coffee, under the trees, the handsome French waiters, with their clean napkins and their polite

attentions, the orderly conduct of the French people, the soldiers in their gay costumes, the women in their neat dresses and pretty white caps. To us, it is fairyland.[103]

For Hooper, Paris was everything London was not. Placing working people squarely in the center of the metropolis, Hooper described an alternative urban cosmology that, he believed, should serve Britain as a model of rational social organization. Indeed, Hooper's report set out to prove that Britain had much to gain by emulating French people, customs, and manners. Persuaded by the idea of complementarity, Hooper stated "that in all countries, among all peoples, and in all religions, is to be found somewhat of the good, the beautiful, and the true." While he was "not so foolish as to suppose that all is perfection in Paris, and the reverse in London," he was yet "bound to assert that we are very far behind in many most important things necessary to us as a civilised nation, and which we ought to be only too happy to learn, when the opportunity is afforded us to do so."[104] Hooper, therefore, approached Paris resolute to "represent the truth naked and bare, and without reserve."[105] Hooper's "truth," which his report embodied, was an amalgamation of radical middle- and working-class thought. Fraught with contradictions, it promoted an interventionist state crowned by social control mechanisms; and, yet, denied power to unrestricted competition and the reproduction of the capitalist order. Indeed, Hooper's imagined reality found points of contact and contestation with both middle-class reformers and working-class radicals in projecting a vision of social democracy that, however imperfectly, anticipated the welfare state. Committed to writing "only the truth" and "anxious to relate facts, without exaggeration," Hooper presented his report as the product of unremitting empirical research and rational analysis.[106] To Hooper's mind, a number of factors supported his claim to objectivity. First, he announced that he was not a member of any political, social, or religious body, and thus spoke for himself alone, "independent" and "free." Secondly, as a "Free Thinker," he was committed not only to free speech and the freedom of conscience, but to questioning the dominant discourse about France, just as he had come to question organized religion.[107] All his life, Hooper recalled, he had been told of

the wickedness, immorality, and dirtiness of the French people, their indifference to decency and moral habits, their irreligion and impiety, and lastly, their want of freedom, the tyranny exercised over them, and how very thankful I ought to feel, born in England in a Christian land!

He went to Paris, therefore, "with a determination to explore, as far as possible in the time allotted ... the habits and customs of the people."[108] However, he also had a larger object in mind. Other voices (such as Hughes and Prior) chose to emphasize France's authoritarian regime over its egalitarian social environment, shoring-up the hard-won, if still slim, political gains of the Chartist legacy. Hooper, on the other hand, deliberately painted an encouraging portrait of Paris, articulating a view that affirmed reformers' governmental and Positivist aspirations for an orderly and rational society, one that promoted industrial progress, but that jettisoned the classically liberal emphasis on individual self-interest.[109] To do so, Hooper constructed his report using the rationalist persona of the urban social investigator and journalist. This literary guise lent legitimacy to his vision, and allowed him to create Paris as a unified whole, where moralists would be hard-pressed to draw zones of good and evil or a binary world of ostentatious wealth and unconscionable depravation.

Although this was Hooper's first visit to Paris, he assured his audience that he had come to know it well. With unfettered access to all that Paris had to offer, Hooper devised an itinerary that did more than satisfy Holyoake's criteria for educational travel experiences. "Having come over to Paris with a determination to make myself as fully acquainted as possible in the time with Parisian life," Hooper explained, "I rose early, and got to bed in time enough to snatch a few hours' rest." Indeed, he "devoted every day to some fresh pursuit, and so managed not to waste time."[110] True to his word, Hooper records a staggering number of touristic feats. Following the SA's directions, he visited a number of carpentry shops with other artisan reporters and exchanged "good will" with his French "brethren," taking note of R. Racault et Compagnie's carpentry firm on the Rue du Faubourg St. Antoine, which the guide explained, was a site of special significance because of the workers' revolt that had taken place there, igniting the fires of the 1848 Revolution.[111] Additionally, he visited "nearly all the public buildings and places of interest," took "bus rides through all the principal boulevards and streets," and boarded the "steam-boat from the Exposition to the Jardin des Plantes" to take in the "gardens, menagerie, and wine-market." Even the city morgue, a modern and popular tourist destination, commanded his attention, but feeling a "sickening sensation" as he studied a "fine, strong-looking man ... lying there to be owned," he soon "turned away."[112]

In this way, Hooper quickly became acquainted with Paris, but always with an eye for sites of elucidation and epiphany. During his rambles he sought solutions to the problems plaguing urban society in modern industrial Britain. Referring to the recent "agitation" in London for "respectable" and clean dining halls, Hooper discovered that Parisians built their restaurants and cafés much "like a palace, light, cheerful, and airy" where "you could dine in state and fancy yourself a lord, for one shilling!"[113] He also admired Paris' consumer cooperative stores, and reflected on how "co-operation" between capital and labor should operate on the same principles – a view of co-operation that played into the hands of middle-class industrialists who intended to usurp the growing power of trade unions. Hooper, however, may have regarded these measures, much like Holyoake, as necessary steps to achieving social democracy. Indeed, in anticipating the unequal and undemocratic "profit sharing" schemes of welfare capitalists in the last quarter of the century, Hooper mused that at least with an economic stake in a company "the toiler may get some share of the golden fruit his skill has produced, and, in his old age, instead of dying of starvation, which the machine is nearly worn out and become so shaky as to be no longer fit for use, he may not end his days in a 'course house'."[114] Paris even offered Britain lessons on managing prostitution, a subject that Jacob and other reporters neglected to mention in their idealization of the white-hatted market women. Although Hooper had "respectfully" declined "invitations ... to visit very questionable places," he managed to acquire enough information to make some judgments on the great "social evil," determining that the licensing and containment of prostitution to certain areas was the only viable solution to a recurrent "social problem."[115]

Nor did France's clean, affordable, and spacious workmen's dwellings escape his notice. Recalling the all-too-common experience when in London, "through unforeseen circumstances," he had been forced to leave one residence for another, Hooper complained that although he would inquire at up to fifty places a day, he was inevitably turned away. Either the "lady of the house" refused to rent a room to his family of seven, or looked at him as if he "were some monster in human form who dare expect to live in a decent house, and proclaim myself a father of a family." This "great evil" Hooper explained "only the wage class themselves can know." Acknowledging that reformers were making "great efforts" in London to "remedy" the problem of urban housing, Hooper emphasized that in France, the government, much to Napoleon III's "honour," had "devoted much time and attention to this subject." It was little wonder then, Hooper insisted, that the Emperor's "great popularity among the workmen is through his anxious endeavours to improve their moral and social condition."[116]

Hooper's praise of France's municipal institutions, its laws, and its Emperor worked rhetorically to condemn Britain for its failure to institute similarly progressive and humanitarian programs. But a key component of Hooper's critique, one that is carried throughout the text, is the idea that common perceptions of working people in Britain, perceptions that constructed the working classes as "monsters," were not wholly undeserved when British workers were compared to French workers. The difference between the two working classes, Hooper argued, lay in the "training of the people" for civility. The French emphasis on manners, dress, and taste he insisted, made rational social organization possible. The governmental emphasis on culture not only educated people to appreciate orderly public conduct, but produced a respect for the principle of social equality that conferred dignity to each individual no matter their station in life. Much of Hooper's investigation, therefore, dwelt on the relationship between civility and social equality that made Paris a magical metropolis in contrast to dystopic London. He demonstrated these truths by weaving his own history into the fabric of his report.

When Hooper first arrived in Paris, he had elbowed his way "John Bull like" through the crowds, but, a "few hours' experience" he wrote, "soon made me ashamed of my boorish manners, and I felt that I had entered a school where I had everything to learn over again."[117] In this school of manners, Hooper learned to raise his hat when entering a room, to take a numbered ticket, to stand in a queue before boarding an omnibus or entering a public building, and to drink coffee "out of a basin with a tablespoon." These customs, he observed, not only made public interactions pleasant and orderly, but also inculcated a sense of self-respect, one based on accepted French norms of social behavior.

It did not take long, for example, for Hooper to notice that the personal dignity of working people resided, in large part, in the care they took with their appearance – the cultural expression, to his mind, of an evolved civilization. Surveying the city one day while riding atop an omnibus, Hooper remarked how "strange everything looked to me." From his elevated perch he spied "two women with barrows ... crying 'fruit!' ... their heads bound in handkerchiefs, but they are clean, and wear strong shoes, and their clothes, though poor and patched, are not in rags." The next scene that played out on the street below was of soldiers mounted on horseback or strolling in pairs. "How smart they look," he commented, "and how important, with their hands in their baggy trousers and showy coats; they walk so easy, as though they felt it an honour and not a disgrace to be a military man." Hooper concluded that while "we talk in England a good deal about the dirty foreigners – to my surprise, the whole time I was in Paris, I scarcely ever met with a dirty face, a ragged dress, or bare feet; what a contrast to what we are accustomed to every day in the streets of London."[118]

More impressive still was the effect egalitarian dress had on labor relations. During visits to Parisian workshops, Hooper noted that the apparel of skilled workers indicated "more freedom, more equality in manners between men and foreman and their employers," than could be found in England. At home, Hooper explained "we have foremen and overlookers who wear fine cloth, and decorate their persons with jewellery, and to whom we are expected to look up to as to some one very superior to our selves, because they carry a pen behind their ear." In Paris, however "the foreman appeared in the same garb as the men – the blue blouse common to both; each one treated the other with proper respect, as became the office he fulfilled." Most satisfyingly, Hooper commented with relief, "you were not disgusted with either the pride of the one or the degrading servility of the other; each man knew his place and kept it. Oh! I many times while in Paris blushed for my countrymen!"[119]

The French reverence for equality, albeit a reverence that failed to dismantle social hierarchies, held a powerful place in his imagination, for it not only preserved individual dignity in labor relations, but gave working people access to public spaces generally reserved for the well-to-do in England. He returned to the workmen's blue blouse to illustrate this point: "Our London workman (myself included) would feel ashamed to go into society unless he could wear a suit similar in appearance to his employer, and flash a little jewelry to correspond." In Paris, however, workers "would be attired in a good pair of black trousers and vest, with a watch in his pocket, over this a clean blouse, and a cap, or 'wide-a-wake,' evidently proud to own himself one of the wage class." As a consequence, Hooper concluded, "there is not that difficulty with them to keep up a certain appearance, as in our country, where outward show is everything, and manners and good breeding a very little consequence."[120] Perhaps uncomfortable with the growing "swell" persona adopted by some of the more affluent workers in London, he preferred the transparent, and eminently respectable, working-class identities that, he argued, were acceptable in all parts of Parisian society.

Hooper had an occasion to experience this "unity of all classes" himself when, during his first full day in Paris, he and his "friend," Lucraft, found themselves in the presence of the empress in one of the exhibition's furniture galleries. Quick learners, they raised their hats as she and her entourage passed by, smiling and bowing to her well-wishers along the way. Even the empress's own attire, Hooper intimated, broke down the social barriers he was accustomed to in London. "I must here notice," he wrote, "that Her Majesty was dressed plain and neat, in black silk and lace. Had we not heard it whispered by our side that it was the Empress, we should not have known her from any other private lady." But, most importantly, while "agreeably surprised to find myself so close to Her Majesty" he noted that the "admirable conduct of the visitors in the building" made such encounters possible. There was, he wrote, "no pushing, no crowding, no policeman to drive us back, no shouting to clear the way – though there were plenty of officials in all parts of the building – everyone quietly stood and formed a passage."[121]

Paris's salubrious environment, Hooper argued even dissolved barriers between Britons of different social classes. The city, it seemed, offered ample opportunity for the high and low of British society to occupy the same public spaces and to engage in friendly exchanges. In Paris, Hooper lodged in the "British working men's" quarters at the Avenue Rapp "barracks," a site which had experienced some class mixing, perhaps deliberately orchestrated by Pratt in order to maintain surveillance over the excursionists and artisan reporters.[122] He also records his excitement and self-satisfaction in having strolled through the "charming" Bois de Boulogne with a British "lady" who, in conversing with him, confirmed his own identity as a "respectable British mechanic."[123] Most remarkably, according to Hooper, he enlisted a member of the SA to act as a guide his second night in Paris, inverting the class-based roles of explorer/interlocutor common to urban journalism. Hooper had seen the unnamed "gentleman" once before at the offices of the SA's committee responsible for the artisan tours, and so approached him to convey his gratitude for allowing him to "realise a dream of years." Pleased, the gentleman suggested that he accompany Hooper and several acquaintances through the exhibition grounds and across the Pont de Jena into the city proper: "It being a very fine night we walked on, inquiring and talking, getting as much information as possible of the wonders of Paris ... the gentleman very kindly pointing out and explaining everything of interest by the way."

Not content to stroll along the boulevards, Hooper, his companions, and their gentleman guide, decided to experience various restaurants and cafés. At the "handsome" Café Delta, for instance, Hooper describes how a hostess ushered them into a large, elegant billiard room tastefully decorated with large bouquets of flowers. Sitting down at a table and leaning comfortably into a velvet-covered settee, they ordered coffee and brandy, lit their cigars, and "at [their] ease, watch[ed] the company." Looking around them they observed "workmen in blouses playing at billiards with gentlemen in black coats" and others "sitting with wives and companions, at the tables, taking coffee and playing dominoes." Inevitably, Hooper found striking contrasts between French and English leisure and marriage:

> In Paris, the workman does not spend his whole evening sitting in a dirty tap-room, leaving his wife and family at home to do the best they can. No! In Paris the workman can enjoy his game of billiards ... in company with gentlemen of education and refined manners, and his wife can sit in the same place, taking a cup of coffee, play an innocent game of dominoes, or chat with a friend, and then go home sober, none the worse for the evening's entertainment.

With this "insight into much of French life and manners," an insight that had been reinforced by his own interactions with a "gentleman" of "education and refined manners," Hooper returned to the Avenue Rapp "highly gratified," but also puzzled.[124]

"How was it," he wanted to know, "that in Paris a workman in his blouse could sit with and enjoy the society even of the upper class, who were not ashamed to take wine or coffee with him ... in a grand café"? Not only did they occupy the same public spaces, but they interacted with one another in recreational settings. Hooper reflected that in his own experience, "there were men of my own class, in my own trade, whom I found it impossible to associate with out of the shop; how much more were they separated from the educated and refined."[125] But as Hooper could see from his rambles through the city, Parisians built social equality upon more than good manners and egalitarian dress.

The other component of civility was an appreciation for rational recreation that not only "lightened" workers' workweek and "improved their health," but elevated their habits and tastes. In France, parks, galleries, museums, lecture halls, and cafés entertained and enlightened the working class throughout the week, including the Sabbath. At Versailles, for instance, Hooper admired the Parisian families, sweethearts, and young artists, who spent their Sundays clustered around the "Great Masters," sharing a "taste and love of art." Similarly, at the regular fête in the park at Saint Cloud, Hooper watched children running and jumping with youthful enthusiasm as they played "touch about," adults taking "quiet walks down the shady groves," and people of all ages dancing the quadrille to the strains of a grand orchestra. Peering into "almost every nook and corner of the fair," Hooper could not detect "riotous conduct ... drunkenness, impudence ... fighting, quarrelling, or indecent behaviour of any kind."[126] Asking his readers to contrast this scene with a London Sunday, he suggested that England left much to be desired. While the working classes might have access to open churches or dusty, dark, and smoked-filled coffee houses, generally "dirty men, and ragged, slovenly women, and shoeless children, spent their last copper" at "great glaring pothouses" to "drown care in burning gin."[127]

These contrasts between the conduct of French and British working people, Hooper declared, lay squarely on the shoulders of Britain's sabbatarians. In his most impassioned demand for social equality, Hooper charged sabbatarians with a "tyranny, injustice, and utter absence of all Christian and benevolent principles" for denying working people the freedom to pursue healthful, enjoyable, and elevating recreation on Sunday. "Confined the whole week in a workshop, labouring for the benefit, comfort, and luxury of the wealthier class," workers, he wrote, "have no other opportunity, except by suffering loss, from visiting the national institutions, which those who have leisure and little care have every opportunity of enjoying." Indignant, Hooper demanded, "what right have they to claim the opening of their own places on that day, and dare to keep closed those we wish to enter?" Indeed, if working people could command the laws, he imagined that "everyone would have perfect liberty to go to his church or chapel, his meeting or lecture hall, and to visit, if so disposed, a picture gallery, a museum, a menagerie, or a public garden." Hooper thus declared, "We claim the right, as in France; and I believe that it will not be long ere we shall enjoy the pleasure of it."[128]

Given all that he had seen and heard in Paris, Hooper stated that he could no longer countenance the falsehoods with which "preachers and teachers" maligned France. "We, the working class of Great Britain," Hooper stated,

> have always had France shown us as some fearful monster, not as a pattern for us to copy, but the reverse. Horrible representations have been invented, and diabolical doings have been placed before us of what we should come to if we took for a model our neighbours across the Channel.

What was more, "Paris has been held up to view as a shocking picture, something dreadful to be shunned, and, finally, an awful warning to the unenlightened, uninstructed, and inexperienced workpeople of England!" But such misrepresentations, Hooper decided, had been circulated by those who had failed to "thoroughly examine and make proper inquiry," or who had failed to "look at things from a French point of view, setting aside their English prejudices." An interview with an English-speaking French mechanic whom Hooper had met on an omnibus, brought this point home:

> I inquired about the liberties and freedom of the people in France. I was laughed at, and told that in my country we had plenty of liberty to work, and toil, and grumble, and drag up our families as best we could, and have scarcely any recreation; but in France they had no need to grumble, everything was done to make the life of the workman happy, and he was respected and honoured as such. He could visit all the public buildings, gardens, and places of instruction and interest on Sundays and holidays ... and was not confined to dirty, miserable, unhealthy quarters, as in London, shunned and despised because he is a workman. In Paris all society acknowledged him. So, said my French companion, "don't laugh at or pity us; we are content to enjoy all the good things we find here for our use while you in your country and grumbling and workings, and craving for those same things (and don't get them). ... In conclusion," said he, "we have laws, and you and every country have laws, to be obeyed for the benefit of the whole community; if we do what is right, and live in peace and harmony, what more do we want?"[129]

The burning issue, therefore, was how to convince Britons that working people's lives could be improved in ways that, based on the French model, promoted civility and its corollary – social equality. Although Hooper was not "unmindful" of the "gigantic efforts" the working class had made "to improve themselves and their condition," he argued that there was much more work to be done, and who knew that better than the British working-classes themselves? The "hundreds of intelligent, sober-minded toilers ... the rational, temperate, thoughtful, and refined, practical experimentalists" knew what it was "to suffer and to bear the hardships of our position, which the theorist whose bread is buttered for him can never understand."[130] What was wanted, then, was a radical prescription for change, one with which Hooper was happy to oblige his readers. Laying out his plan for reform, Hooper stated:

> We want in our country a system of "national education" free from all sectarianism, and entirely secular, leaving everyone to exercise his own judgment in religion. ... Let us have free access Sundays and weekdays, to all the national institutions. Let there be no restraint put on rational, healthful, innocent recreation, and let us have this always encouraged. ... On Sunday, our leisure day, let us have not only churches and chapels

open free to all … but let us have lecture halls as freely open, where we can be educated in the arts and sciences, the history of men and nations, and the wonders of creation; where the mind can be elevated, improved, refined; where we can learn how to train our children in knowledge and wisdom, and teach ourselves how to behave in a becoming manner to each other, and where we might practice affability, courtesy, and polite conversation.[131]

With these freedoms, however, Hooper also advised restraints. Suggesting a gradualist program of social improvement, Hooper decided that only "when the nation has been properly schooled and trained … would [he] add music and dancing, and dramatic entertainments which when properly conducted, are of an elevating and refining nature." This ideal environment for national self-improvement also required the positive intervention of the state. "Let government restrictions be put upon, and strongly enforced against, every thing and every place of a vicious, or, degrading nature." Appreciative of France's ubiquitous "gendarmes" who discouraged "rough, vulgar, unmannerly conduct and conversation," Hooper also recommended "the presence of Government officials in all public places, who should enforce well-ordered conduct and proper behaviour for the benefit of the whole community."[132]

Finding a certain comfort in Paris's orderly society that allowed the "greatest good" to exist between the state and society, between the working classes and the upper classes, and between capital and labor, Hooper based his vision of social equality on positive freedoms that, to his mind, liberated rather than enslaved humanity. For Hooper, therefore, unlike other artisan reporters (but not unlike the rogue petitioners of 1861), even Napoleon's state apparatus offered a useful model for Britain. But these contradictions over the relevance of Paris as a model of social equality and educational opportunity should not be surprising. Hooper's report and those of the other artisan reporters articulated a range of political and social beliefs and values, as well as national, gender, religious, and class identities. These workers' Paris tours had thus shown them an alternative reality to what they knew in Britain, or better still, a new authoritative language in which to express their desire for reform. The contradictory ways they chose to interpret the French landscape, however, indicates that there was no clear consensus on how to construct a Britain that could achieve a balance between liberty and social justice, and between government intervention and personal freedom.

Conclusion

At the end of the day (and their tours), the question still remained: how could British working people achieve social equality that best complemented Britain's constitutional liberties and working people's growing political power? Hooper's portrait of Paris as a totemic model for modern liberalism, one that in Britain would tie gradualism to reform and the "new Liberalism," perhaps resonated with some working-class readers of the artisan reports. Clearly, it would have satisfied organizers' aims in producing the exhibition tours, for Hooper's report affirmed many of the tenets of liberal governmentality. Without question, therefore, the tour organizers had achieved a measure of success. As Hooper recognized, both middle-class reformers and radical artisans desired progress: better relations between capital and labor, better schools for their children and technical training for youths and adults, and access to high art and culture on Sundays and every other day of the week. Yet, despite this convergence, Hooper perhaps imagined a more authoritative role and place in the nation for rational, industrious working men – men, again, like himself – than most middle-class radicals, such as Pratt, were then willing to grant. Connolly and Lucraft knew that there was a battle still to be won, even if their reports lacked a strident political message of class conflict over consensus. Nevertheless, Hooper, many of his fellow reporters, and perhaps the thousands of other working-class excursionists, felt that in going to Paris they had gained a valuable education – one that would be a benefit to Britain, to themselves and to their class, just as the IWA and the WMCIU had hoped, albeit for different, if sometimes overlapping goals and visions of the future.

Figure 1 Cook's excursionists at the Gare du Nord, Paris, 1861. *Illustrated London News* (1861) (Courtesy of Thomas Cook Archive)

Figure 2 Cook's excursionists on the Champs Elysees, Paris, 1861. *Illustrated London News* (1861)

Figure 3 "A Sudden Opening for a Young Man" *The Daily Graphic* (1873). The caption illustrates class assumptions surrounding travel and tourism. (Courtesy of Thomas Cook Archives)

Figure 4 "Visit of the Working Men's Club and Institute Union to the Alexandra Palace" (n.d.)

Figure 5 "Deputation to France (1867)": Mr. L.S. Booth and J. Gutteridge, (Weavers); and Mr. J. Gregory and J. Stringer (Watchmakers). The four "artisan reporters" are on route to the 1867 Paris Exhibition. The image is derived from Joseph Gutteridge's autobiography, *Lights and Shadows in the Life of an Artisan* (1893). (Courtesy of the Coventry History Centre)

MR. HOGG AT FORT COLLINS, COLORADO, IN 1886, WITH SOME INSTITUTE MEMBERS WHO HAD SETTLED THERE.

Figure 6 "Mr. Hogg at Fort Collins, Colorado, in 1886, with some Institute Members Who Had Settled There." (Courtesy of University of Westminster Archive)

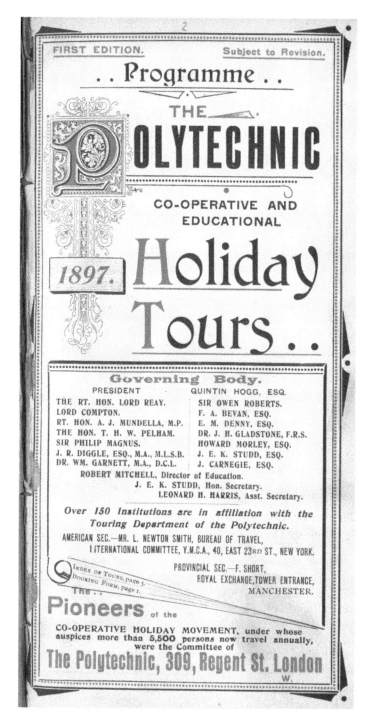

Figure 7 "Programme: The Polytechnic Co-operative and Educational Holiday Tours (1897)." (Courtesy of Thomas Cook Company Archives)

4

"High Attainments": The Artisan Exhibition Tours and the Campaign for Technical Education, 1867–1889

At the Fourth Ordinary Meeting of the Society of Arts in December 1867, the Chairman of the Council, William Hawes, remarked that the recent artisan exhibition tours had been so successful that the SA intended to repeat the "experiment" in the years ahead. The object would be to "send workmen to other seats of industry abroad, so as to bring them into contact with foreign workmen, [and] to give them additional opportunities to ascertain in what particular points they excelled."[1] As good as their word, the following year the SA sent artisans to Brussels to study "foreign industry" and the educational and social conditions of Belgian workers.[2] In addition, Hawes also specified that the selection of artisan reporters would be based on clearly verifiable credentials. With these measures, Hawes hoped "to select such men from among those who have either taken prizes at our examinations or from among those art-workmen who receive prizes at our annual competition."[3]

SA member and master coachmaker, George Hooper (not to be confused with the cabinetmaker Charles Hooper), also praised the utility of the artisan tours and advocated workers' educational travel throughout his professional life. Hooper first articulated his views on educational travel in 1868, in response to an SA questionnaire that had asked members to comment on "Workmen's Holidays."[4] "Much good would result," Hooper suggested, if "travelling scholarships," which would be "highly esteemed by the artisan class" were made available to "working men of intelligence above their fellows."[5] Three components comprised his plan. First, visits to foreign countries would be conducted on a regular basis, and would be "paid for partly by [the artisan scholar's] own savings and partly as a grant from some public body, as a reward for talent and good conduct." Second, to take "full advantage" of their tours, Artisan Scholars would not only absorb the cultural benefits of foreign travel, but with the aid of British embassies and officials abroad, would visit "celebrated" manufacturers to study how other countries conducted their crafts and industries. And, third, travelling scholars would be chosen among those who had won SA art prizes and examination awards. This form of recognition, Hooper asserted, would "encourage these young men, after they have become workmen, to look forward to such further distinction."[6] Hooper clearly linked his sketch of working men's holidays to governmental technologies and the educational idea. Not only would such scholarships "reward talent and good conduct," but they would teach young workers the value of thrift. In saving their wages and applying for travel-subsidies to help fund study-abroad, workers would understand that "there is a certain sweetness in enjoying leisure and change of scene [through] the fruits of one's industry and frugality." But the lessons to be derived from such activities concerned more than self government. They concerned the economic vibrancy of the nation. Indeed, Hooper argued that economic development required new knowledge and skills that could only be acquired through travel, rather than stasis. Thus, Hooper envisioned artisan leisure travel in ways that tightly bound it to continuing study in foreign countries, ideally with some form of "public" assistance, and, importantly, to academic qualifications.[7]

The connections that Hawes and Hooper made between national prosperity, artisan travel, and academic qualification are important to understanding the development of study abroad and the SA's own role in the process. In the second half of the nineteenth century, the SA set out to bureaucratize and systematize technical education in Britain. The spurs to this initiative were the reports of education experts warning that competitor nations possessed superior educational methods and had begun to train advanced industrial workforces. They advised, therefore, that if Britain expected to maintain its economic superiority, it must improve educational provisions for skilled workers. In response to these warnings, the SA devised a national system of testing, certifying, and rewarding "high attainments," as one proponent of adult education described it in the *Bethnal Green Times*. In a letter to the editor, the correspondent promoted the SA's examination system by inviting a group of East London workers, the Spitalfields Weavers, to test their knowledge from among five subjects: cotton, paper, silk, steel, and carriages. The rewards included "certificates of merit and prizes" and, presumably, greater personal – and national – prosperity. "The requirements may seem rather high," the writer cautioned, "but, where competition with the whole world is involved, high attainments are indispensable to success."[8, 9]

The call to "high attainments," then, was emblematic of this broader movement for educational reform and another manifestation of the "educational idea." And, yet, many workers, employers, and state bureaucrats rejected the SA's examination services and, for that matter, rejected the argument predicting the decline of British economic and industrial superiority. As a consequence, the 1867 artisan exhibition tours and the subsequent publication of the artisan reports, many of which criticized employers and the state for neglecting education, became one of several strategies that the SA devised to publicize Britain's crisis in technical education and to win converts to reform.[10] Indeed, Peter le Neve Foster, the SA's secretary, explained that the combination of artisan travel, study, and written reports would not only "exercise a beneficial influence upon the men themselves, but also upon the progress of industry."[11] Likewise, Hawes argued that the tours would prove to be the SA's most significant effort yet to stimulate interest in technical education in its century long history.[12] Although they could not know the long term outcome of the tours, the SA's confidence in the project was well founded. The 1867 artisan tours not only led to subsequent tours that also promoted technical education, but ultimately contributed to the passage of the triumphant (if limited) 1889 Technical Instruction Act.[13]

This chapter examines the technical education movement to further explore the merging of travel with the educational idea. To do so, it revisits the Society of Arts (SA) and the artisan tours of the 1867 Paris exhibition, and also embarks on three subsequent artisan exhibition tours: the 1873 Vienna tour, organized by two Midlands societies; the 1878 Paris tour, managed by the SA; and the final artisan tours to Paris in 1889, organized by a Mansion House committee of the City of London. These tours not only supported the technical education movement, but became another motive for expanding working-class travel. The chapter begins, therefore, by examining the historical context for the artisan exhibition tours, emphasizing the SA's role in the technical education reform movement. It analyzes the formation of the tours, from their sources of funding and means of advertisement to the selection of artisan reporters. It then assesses the artisans' responses to both the technical education movement and reformers' attempts to rationalize adult education, including the qualifications for the post of artisan reporter.

Both middle-class reformers and certain sectors of the working class committed themselves to developing technical education, hoping to bolster Britain's economic supremacy and, in the case of the workers, to boost wages and occupational prestige. Ultimately, one outcome of these ambitions was to deepen the divides between skilled and unskilled workers. Even though the SA promoted the tours in terms of patriotism and the common good, it is during this period that travel itself came to be seen as an important advantage to students or apprentices seeking expertise in new technologies – not to mention employers and the state, which would profit from an advanced industrial workforce. The selection process reflected this perception by privileging a minority, and played a part in opening fissures that would further stratify the working class in the wake of the educational reform movement. Thus, the purpose of this chapter is to examine the ways in which travel, by way of the artisan tours, became incorporated into the technical education movement and its implications for social relations and identities during this period of working-class activism, trade unionism, and liberal reform.

Government, Society, and the Genesis of the Educated Worker

The call to "high attainments" had its primary origins in the Great Exhibition of 1851 when Britain stood at the pinnacle of its industrial power. The Society of Arts and the Royal Commission organized the exhibition as a nationalist celebration of British manufactures and of Britain itself, which was presented as a model of economic enterprise, good government and social stability. Behind the scenes, however, the Great Exhibition also offered a venue in which British industrial specialists could compare domestic and foreign industry and thus "identify and rectify" Britain's "manufacturing deficiencies."[14] In this capacity, it revealed serious impediments to Britain's future prosperity. The root of the problem, these specialists discerned, was Britain's failure to educate its artisan classes.

Reformers had argued for many years that Britain's education system needed to be responsive to the changing technical and commercial needs of industry.[15] Early in the century, voluntary associations had established mechanics' institutes for the training of artisans in the scientific principles of their trades, but by mid-century most had become centers of rational recreation for the middling classes. The state had also funded Schools of Design to help British manufacturers better compete with the aesthetically and functionally superior products of continental industries. However, these institutions were limited in number and poorly funded.[16] The Great Exhibition, therefore, became the catalyst for a new education crusade, one that proponents framed as a question of national defense.

Sounding the alarm for a national system of technical and scientific education in Britain, was Lyon Playfair, an industrial chemist, member of the Society of Arts, and high-level administrator of the Great Exhibition. In 1852, Playfair visited European educational institutions to gage their influence on the development of continental industries. In a well-publicized lecture made upon his return, Playfair confirmed the impression made by the 1851 Exhibition, stating conclusively that industrial education on the continent posed a serious threat to British commerce.[17] Hoping to call forth the same sense of urgency that he had come to feel since 1851, Playfair phrased the problem in proto-Darwinian terms as a struggle for survival. "The competition in industry" he stated, "is year by year becoming more and more a competition of intellect." "The nation," he continued, "which most quickly promotes the intellectual development of its artisans must, by an inevitable law of nature, advance, while the country which neglects its industrial education must, by the same law, inevitably recede." The only solution, Playfair determined, was to beat continental nations at their own game.[18]

This disclosure and, later, the dismal result of the 1867 Paris Exhibition, in which Britain won a mere ten prizes out of the ninety classes available, helped fuel education debates and government policy initiatives for the next quarter-century.[19] Royal Commissions and subcommittees inquired into art, technical, and scientific instruction, while public intellectuals issued books and tracts on the subject, and delivered lectures reiterating the common theme of decline.[20] Samuel Smiles's cautionary yet inspirational speech delivered at the annual soirée of the Huddersfield Mechanics' Institute in 1867 drew on Playfair's reports to insist upon an interventionist plan of action. Smiles, the nineteenth-century guru of self-help, characteristically intoned that "workers must be helped to help themselves." But, in endorsing state intervention, he also qualified the statement. Helping workers to help themselves, he argued, could "only effectually be done after a well-devised plan and system, which it is the business of society, acting through its organized instrument – the Government – to arrange and settle." Without government intervention into technical (and elementary) education, declared Smiles, Britain "must fall behind in the race of competition with the world."[21]

Reformers, therefore, cast their mission as the "patriotic duty of all classes," and a battle that must be fought for Britain's very survival.[22] As one educator put it, in order for Britain to maintain its industrial supremacy it must, like continental nations, create "ordered legions of trained workers equipped with intellectual weapons, and clothed with sound science." To ignore this urgent call, he counseled, would "doom" Britain in the "great struggle for existence" between competing nations.[23] These calls for "high attainments" thus eventually led to new schools and examination systems that reformers anticipated would turn British artisans, such as the Spitalfields Weavers, into an advanced industrial workforce. Implementing educational reforms, however, would prove an arduous process that required the cooperation not only of government and society, but, as Smiles suggested, workers as well.

Reformers identified diverse areas in Britain's educational arena in need of change, and advocated equally diverse solutions to rectify Britain's educational dilemmas. Yet, most reformers concurred that Britain's education system required improvements in three basic areas. First, they believed that Britain must develop a national system of compulsory elementary education and adult remedial courses (sometimes described by contemporaries as "industrial education") for those who already lacked such schooling. Only with this rudimentary foundation could artisans and mechanics fully understand the more complex principles of their trades. Second, they stressed that Britain must create technical (and teacher training) schools to compensate for the inexorable breakdown of the apprenticeship system that had traditionally turned inexperienced youths into skilled masters, but which now required a different training system to teach the specialized skills necessary to operate modern industrial machinery. Finally, they encouraged the founding of more government-sponsored schools of design (first implemented in 1837) to improve British standards of artistic taste. This objective, they argued, included augmenting existing curricula with the creation of museums as well as mobile exhibitions that would circulate through the provinces, providing workers with "illustrative examples of the applications of principles in both science and art."[24] While reformers achieved much of the first objective with the 1870 Elementary Education Act, the latter two goals took much longer to be even partially realized. The first substantive gain, however, came in 1853 with the creation of the Department of Science and Art.

In response to the revelations of 1851, Prince Albert, a formidable ally of the education movement, established the Department of Science and Art (DSA) as a division of the Board of Trade – a reflection, perhaps, of the interests of capital in industrial education. Overseen by both Henry Cole, the superintendent of the former School of Design, and Lyon Playfair, its objective was to promote instruction nationally in technology and design, also referred to as "practical art."[25] Both Cole and Playfair had worked together as members of the Royal Commission to bring the 1851 Exhibition to fruition, and now set out to encourage the growth of new schools across Great Britain for the benefit of the "industrial classes." Inhibiting their progress, however, were limited government funds, recalcitrant laissez-faire liberals, and a growing hostility towards powerful state bureaucrats who presumed to dictate reason and reform. Opponents of the DSA, for example, not only viewed state intervention and centralization with suspicion, but as Peter Hoffenberg shows, reviled Cole, Playfair, and other reformist state bureaucrats for having presumed to act as de facto "cultural experts ... responsible for cultivating ideas, maintaining intellectual life, forging a national culture and generally connecting the arts, professions and the people."[26] Given such impediments, schools that did arise through the DSA's efforts were largely self-supporting, endowed through charitable donation, and managed on the day-to-day level by local boards of trustees. As a consequence, a piecemeal national system of technical education arose over several decades, in which the DSA functioned mostly as a central organizing body, supplying school inspectors, helping to pay teacher salaries, and administering examinations.[27]

The DSA thus not only encouraged the creation of new educational venues, but interacted with established educational bodies, such as the SA. The SA had promoted education since its inception in the late eighteenth century, promoting "industrial" as well as technological (and later commercial) instruction. Like the DSA, the SA also functioned as a central organizing office for what became known as its "Institutes in Union," a national and colonial association of educational affiliates, such as literary, scientific, and mechanics' institutions. In this capacity, the SA provided the Institutes in Union with a number of services, including a venue for annual conferences and educational exhibitions, an institutional journal in which to share news and disseminate new knowledge, and a system of industrial examinations and certificates, which the SA first developed in 1856.[28]

The SA's system of examinations may have been its most important contribution to adult education. The SA's system preceded the DSA's own exams by three years, presenting the "upper part of the lower class" at affiliated institutes with graded certificates upon completion of a course that attested to the level of their competence in a given subject.[29] Initially, students could select courses and take exams in English literature, as well as "geometry, mechanical drawing, building construction, physics, chemistry, natural history, Latin, French, and mathematics." The more ambitious could also advance to qualifying exams in the principles of art and science in relation to their trade.

Although the SA and the DSA operated separately, they nevertheless complemented one another in several ways. First, the Department's top officials – Playfair, Cole, and the latter's successor, John Donnelly – also served on the SA's councils. Additionally, they shared a number of school inspectors and examiners. Eventually, the two institutions managed to coordinate their programs and ministered to a wider, national constituency of British students than each alone might have otherwise achieved. Thus by 1859, two institutions – one, a government body, the other, a voluntary association – had furthered a nascent liberal and national agenda to improve technical education.

Yet, for all these advances, the technical education movement produced only limited results during the 1850s. It would take the particularly miserable showing of British workmanship at the 1867 Paris Exhibition before technical education became a serious subject of deliberation among government ministers and still more time would elapse before trade processes (rather than "principles" alone) would be taught with examinations to match.[30] Moreover, manufacturers and artisans, the supposed beneficiaries of these improvements, impeded more determined growth. Many employers rejected reformers' contention that poorly educated workmen gravely threatened British industry and commerce. Rather, to their minds, the menace to national prosperity lay in trade barriers erected against British exports and, worse, the avarice of trade unions.[31] Furthermore, cautious employers feared that trade secrets would be revealed in the classroom and lost to the open market when men came together to "discuss matters in which trade secrets were involved." Preferring the workshop apprenticeship system, however antiquated, to technical or scientific training in institutions unaffiliated with their firms, many employers discouraged employees from attending courses and at times even penalized those who did.[32]

Workers' negative responses to technical education and the examination system varied as much as their employers. Many workers, for example, were often too poor or too exhausted to attend evening classes.[33] Others, having experienced little formal education, chose to ignore the "principles" of their trades rather than face the alien setting of a classroom and the intimidating oral and written examination process.[34] Others simply desired to acquire practical experience, dismissing the "scientific principles" of their trade altogether.[35] Still other artisans, as C.T. Millis, an iron molder, explained before a Technical Instruction Commission in 1884, were dissuaded from seeking technical training because they could not find employment to match their new skills. Overqualified, such workers found themselves reduced to teaching rather than actively practicing their crafts.[36] Finally, many skilled workers suspected that technical education would lead to the demise of the apprenticeship system and subsequently the loss of workplace control.[37] Indeed, the prospect of systematic technical training in a school environment may have signaled to some workers another pedagogical incursion into their lives that might very well invalidate their knowledge and compromise their autonomy. Certainly, as Foucault observes, the emergence of examination systems "superimposed power relations onto knowledge relations." It gave reforming elites not only the power to determine what constituted "useful" knowledge, but to "define the aptitude of each individual, situate his level and abilities, [and] indicate the possible use that might be made of them."[38]

From the very start, therefore, the SA faced significant resistance to its efforts at educational reform. In fact, lack of student interest had forced it to cancel its first scheduled examination in 1855 when only a lone chimney sweep, a Mr. Medcraft, arrived at the society's chambers to face examiners in mathematics on the appointed day.[39] But the SA would not concede defeat. After the debacle of the first examination session, the society decided to reevaluate their program, sending questionnaires to various firms and trade societies that might shed light on the lackluster response to their educational enterprise. The solution, they learned, hinged on the "value" of the SA's examination certificates. To make the certificates worth a student's time, trouble, and expense, they had to be made serviceable to employers. In other words, employers wanted certificates to guarantee superior workmanship and talent, and the students wanted preferential treatment from employers, including wage increases. The SA's pragmatic response to this information was to draw up a "form of declaration" signed by 400 "leading firms" stating that the SA's certificates would be viewed as "testimonials worthy of credit." The immediate result was 52 new students willing to take examinations in 1856.[40]

While the SA claimed to have administered approximately 9000 exams by 1868 (and the DSA nearly three times that number), reformers were little satisfied.[41] Compared to the growing need for technically trained artisans and mechanics in trades that had undergone important innovations since mid-century – such as "navigation, building construction, agriculture, chemists' and druggists' work," – the limited success of the course and examination system was readily apparent.[42] More would have to be done to win significant support for the cause of reform. This support would ultimately come from workers themselves, largely in the form of trade unionism, but also through various other practices, such as a growing "prize culture" fostered by the SA that linked workers' educational improvement not only with national defense, but with artisans' collective and individual self-interest.

Technical Education and the "Superior Class of Workman"

Working people pursued education for any number of reasons. Some hoped to acquire basic literacy and upward mobility, while others aspired to a "full" knowledge of the world through literature, science, history or politics.[43] In defining educational agendas between 1850 and 1870, however, working class leaders, such as trade unionists, looked to serve broader interests. First, they aimed to strengthen the collective power of trade unions and other "enterprises of self-help," such as friendly societies and cooperative movements, through education, believing that only educated members of such societies could effectively represent workers in the expanding arena of British politics.[44] To strengthen British industry and economic security, and thus improve workers' livelihoods, they also advocated reforming the moribund apprenticeship system and improving educational provisions to match or surpass those of continental workers.[45] Critically, they also aimed to transform, and yet maintain control over, the symbolic markers of "skill" that traditionally defined male labor and status but that were eroding under industrialization. This was a particular concern of the so called labor aristocracy: artisans and mechanics whose superior skill and education defined them as respectable working men. Indeed, occupational skill and education were two important characteristics that workers used to define themselves against – or in relation to – others as they struggled for status, power, and resources within their workplace and community.[46] Many trade unions discerned, therefore, that technical education certificates from the SA or the DSA could very well garner higher wages and better jobs for members, and help secure their superior position in relation to semi-or-unskilled labor. During this period, therefore, trade societies encouraged improvement through education, sharing middle-class reformers' vision of a national system of technical and scientific education.[47]

In attempting to maintain or assert authority over the shop floor and the meaning of artisanal or industrial skill, trade unionists contributed to new education practices and debates.[48] Trade union officials organized their own meetings and committees to discuss educational reform, and funded schools for members and their children.[49] They also entered into wider debates in providing testimony to various governmental and public organizations, from the Royal Commission on Scientific Instruction and the Advancement of Science, overseen by the Devonshire Commission in 1869, to the National Education League, a liberal pressure group that advocated government-sponsored and compulsory education. Robert Applegarth, the General Secretary of the Amalgamated Society of Carpenters and Joinery (ASCJ), contributed to these and many more committees, groups, and institutions, including the SA. In an 1868 letter to the SA praising its dedication to educational reform, Applegarth expressed his commitment to fostering the technical education of union members. Applegarth stressed that his union's first priority was to gain legal legitimacy in the eyes of the state, but assured the SA that once this agenda had been achieved, technical education would become "one of the fundamental principles of their societies." Indeed, reflecting their members' "zeal to better qualify them to compete with the continental workmen by a higher state of education," the union had already established two schools, one in Manchester and the other in London "almost ready for opening for teaching."[50]

Technical education and examination certificates offered one more testament to the labor aristocracy's exclusive status and "respectable" union identity.[51] Applegarth, for example, made no bones about the fact that his "society men" stood head and shoulders above ordinary workers. In speaking before the Royal Commission on Trade Unions in 1867, Applegarth stated that members "as a rule consist ... of the superior class of workmen [many of whom] hold positions of responsibility as foremen and managers, ... and however much we regret to leave a man behind who is not up to our mark, we do it."[52] This exclusivity carried over to the union's education grants. In 1875, the ASCJ negotiated with the DSA and the SA to include joinery and carpentry on their list of examinations, promising annual scholarships of £100 to the best examination candidate – provided, that is, that the candidate was a union member.[53]

With this union support of technical education, certification through the SA and the DSA became another mark of distinction and respectability, valued by skilled artisans as well as workers who either aspired to union membership or simply upward mobility. The story of a Sheffield joiner, Richard Bastow, is a case in point. Bastow wrote to Le Neve Foster in March of 1873, to inquire about the "Technological examinations" advertised in *The British Mechanic*. At the age of 33, Bastow had decided that he "want[ed] to be judged and examined by cleverer men than myself." Even though he had "studied [his] business closely," had "attended the School of Art in Sheffield and Durham whilst serving [his] time [as an apprentice]," and had "always" received "the highest wages," he "remain[ed] in the regular rank and file of common workmen." A Society of Arts examination, he hoped, would allow him to command the respect his institutional learning and experience demanded. "I fancy possessing a certificate of my abilities would be one round up the ladder amongst my fellow workmen, and thus give honour and preference to those to whom it is due," he explained. "As things are, the Society of Joiners acknowledges all men equal, non-society men are at a discount. I am a non-society man, [and] therefore by their standard worse than a common workman." Fed-up with his marginal status, Bastow appealed to the SA and its certification system for legitimation.[54]

As acceptance for the examination system grew enterprising workers could hope to achieve occupational advancement from attending courses and completing exams. One benefit Bastow derived, for example, was his appointment as an artisan reporter to the 1873 Vienna Exhibition, a post that required exceptional skill and learning. As the introduction to the Vienna collection of artisan reports stated, the organizers hoped that workmen "will learn from [reading the *Artisan Reports*] the fact that intelligence, education, and technical skill does meet with reward."[55] Bastow may or may not have gained an entrée into the ASCJ with his "certificate of ... abilities," but there is little question that technological examinations became one way that he and other workers came to define their identity and occupational worth. Union qualifications for membership in part added to this growing appeal of technological exams in the 1870s. But acceptance came from a two-pronged attack on older value systems and practices surrounding artisanal skill and education, because the SA also nurtured workers' desire for skilled status in the early 1860s by developing a prize system that incorporated the artisan exhibition tours as a promotional venue for educational reform.

Prize Cultures and the Pursuit of "Fame"

Since its founding in the late eighteenth century, the Society of Arts promoted innovations in the arts and sciences by awarding gold and silver medals to British inventors and artists. In 1863, the society became "equally anxious," as the chairman put it, "to reward those whose labour, though in a less exalted field" deserved recognition.[56] This anxiety stemmed from the unsatisfactory enrollments for their examinations. The society therefore hoped to inspire more confidence in their educational programs by offering workers cash prizes and scholarship awards for exceptional examination records and for art-workmanship in "original" and "prescribed" design of ceramics, iron, and hand or machine woodworking crafts.[57] Yet, like the responses to the society's examinations, workers displayed, at best, a tepid enthusiasm for the SA's prizes. Indeed, as late as the fifth annual Art-Workmen's Prize Competition held in February of 1867, the society distributed less than half the prize monies available from a purse of over £600.[58]

What precluded more worker interest in the SA's competitions? A journalist and former mechanic, Robert Coningsby, claimed to know the answer and, more than that, a solution. He unveiled both at an SA council meeting in 1866.[59] A man of working-class origins and inestimable energy and ambition, Coningsby felt more than qualified to diagnose the SA's prize problem and to offer advice on how to elicit more interest in their programs. As a young apprentice in the 1850s, Coningsby had minded the furnace of an engravers shop. But, in the early 1860s, he exchanged his mechanic's cap for the journalist's quill, having become a war correspondent for *The Times*. Coningsby's meteoric rise, according to his friend, Richard Whiteing, also a former mechanic and a fellow journalist, came about as a deliberate process of self-fashioning. Whiteing described Coningsby as a "pure artisan in manners and customs," and at the same time, "a miniature Disraeli." An astute self-promoter, Coningsby was "determined to arrive" and possessed the talent, imagination, and nerve to cause a commotion and draw a crowd. These qualities came to the fore in a sensational letter to *The Times*, in which Coningsby effectively renounced his radical associations, past and present, by denigrating the Reform League's call for the extension of the franchise, proclaiming: "we will have no king but Caesar."[60]

With these words, Coningsby became the darling of conservative elites and the scourge of labor leaders. The IWA, in fact, devoted a long discussion to Coningsby's defection on 30 May, 1865, with reference to his position as secretary to an Anglo-French Workingmen's Exhibition to take place at the Crystal Palace in the fall. The IWA had already come to feel that the proliferation of "national and international" exhibitions were, in part, a conspiracy by "the wealthy classes" to "divert the attention of the working classes from the nobler aim of the political enfranchisement of their class." That Coningsby had been appointed secretary and had claimed to represent British workmen participating in the exhibition, only intensified their suspicions. Indeed, Coningsby's position, they felt, would surely (and deliberately) "alienate from the Committee the sympathies of British Democrats." Given these grievances, they resolved to denounce Coningsby. They informed the exhibition's French committee that Coningsby had become the "avowed enemy of the working classes of Great Britain, and, consequently, the common enemy of the working classes of Europe." Furthermore, they resolved to announce Coningsby's enemy status to the world by translating their resolution into four languages and printing them for wide distribution.[61]

Blacklisted by the IWA, Coningsby now stood before the SA claiming to know what working men wanted. Deliberately courting a more powerful elite than the IWA by asserting his new identity as a conservative working man, Coningsby had succeeded in clawing his way out of the furnaces and into the professional class of the new journalism. In the aftermath of his denouncement, *The Times* editor invited him to join the staff, and William Hawes, the Chairman of the Council of the SA, appears to have championed his career with special assignments, such as reporting on the 1867 Paris exhibition and subsidizing a tour of the United States, where he reportedly met with the American president, Andrew Johnson.[62] Coningsby's engagement with the SA reveals the tenuous nature of cross-class cooperation and the flexibility of the SA (and other middle-class reform groups) in reaching out to more radical or more conservative allies as necessity dictated and the political climate allowed. Thus, Coningsby, seemingly without a care for the IWA's sanction, and with a journalist's flair for drama, offered the SA advice on how to stimulate workers' enthusiasm for their programs.

In presenting his solution to the Society's dilemma over examinations, Coningsby's speech focused on the 1865 Anglo-French Workingmen's Exhibition that he and Whiteing had organized and that had so angered members of the IWA. Launching the exhibition during the year of the

British and French "Jubilee of Peace," they billed the event as the "first skilled" and "first international Industrial Exhibition," conducted by and for "self-reliant" workingmen.[63] Although they had failed to keep expenditures in the black, Coningsby assured the SA that, given his experience with skilled artisans at the exhibition, he could help make the SA's courses, examinations, and competitions the talk of every working man's pub, shop floor, and union meeting.[64]

Few of the "highest class of workmen," Coningsby reminded the audience, bothered to participate in the SA's competitions. The reasons for this were twofold. First, artisans of negligible talents, "incapables," received prizes at the SA's competitions, and nothing, Coningsby stated, was more pernicious to the success of the society's program. When a "notoriously unskilled workman gains a prize," Coningsby warned, it "does more to damage the *éclat* attending your distribution, and breeds more indifference to your inducements, than people unacquainted with the tone of art-workmen's society would suppose."[65] Second, Coningsby confided to the SA, "I happen to know, that several art-workmen think that one reason for the non-success in this branch of your operations is, that, for the present day, you are not sensational enough." How then might the society gain *éclat* and produce a sensation? Coningsby made his prescription plain: only permit highly skilled artisans to compete for prizes that would bring them "fame," and "in a word," make "your" competitions "international."[66]

Referring to the Anglo-French Workingmen's Exhibition as an example, Coningsby informed the council that he and the other organizers had two goals in mind when they devised their plan for an international exhibition. First, they intended to discover whether an exhibition devoted solely to the products of skilled craftsmen could succeed in drawing participants and audiences at a time when "amateur productions" had infiltrated industrial exhibitions around the country – including, it seemed, the Society of Arts' competitions. Second, they wanted to learn whether French artisans would be "sufficiently friendly towards their English brethren to co-operate ... in a public work." They, according to Coningsby, met with an affirmative answer on both counts.[67] Sending a delegation of workman headed by Whiteing to Paris to promote their plan, they managed to secure on "very short notice" 70 displays from French firms and individual artisans and, in the process, learned a third "moral." "Fame," more than any other "inducement," had prompted workers to participate in the first Anglo-French Workingmen's Exhibition. Without the lure of monetary awards, both French and British skilled workers had taken the trouble to arrange for their works to be exhibited, each with their names (rather than the names of their employers' firms as was usual in most exhibitions) prominently displayed on the items. Given this response, Coningsby recommended that if the society wanted "to encourage art-workmen," and thus "to encourage commerce," they must "look favourab[ly] upon the intercommunication of peoples."[68] They must, therefore, take over where the workers' committee of the Anglo-French Workingmen's Exhibition had left off in 1865.

Coningsby suggested that under the sponsorship of the Society of Arts and an Anglo-French Association, the Workingmen's International Exhibition could become "a succession of annually-recurring [workers'] fêtes ... of the highest productions of two most skillful nations." With this agenda, he added, workers would be stimulated into "active competition" and the society could put the debacles of past award ceremonies behind them. And what better time to put this "movement" into action and to create a "stir," Coningsby pointed out, than with the upcoming 1867 Paris Exhibition? Envisioning a special pavilion where the works of individual British and French artisans could be displayed side by side "in friendly rivalry," Coningsby asked the society to stretch their imaginations even further to grasp all the possibilities. Imagine, he said, "monster" excursion trains that would carry even the lowliest worker across the Channel to reap the educational benefits of an international exhibition that celebrated workers' contributions to industry around the world. "Instead of 'eight hours at the sea side,'" Coningsby exclaimed, "let the cry be 'eight days with our friends the French.'" In this way, British artisans would be encouraged to develop their skills and aspire to the "honor" and international "fame" of having their works displayed at a special pavilion dedicated collectively to workers' skills, and to their own and their nation's glory.[69]

Intrigued by Coningsby's suggestion, Hawes later inquired into the logistics of constructing an art-workmen's pavilion for the 1867 Paris Exhibition, but learned that the classification system precluded placing British and French works side by side on one site.[70] Nevertheless, Hawes and others incorporated the spirit of Coningsby's ideas into the formation of the artisan exhibition tours. Arising in part out of workers' dissatisfaction with the SA's examination and prize system, the artisan tours were designed to win the "higher class of artisan" a measure of distinction. The tours thus accomplished a number of the society's goals: they became events that offered the most highly skilled and most promising artisan intellectuals the opportunity to travel and study abroad; they manufactured an aura of "honour," "fame," and celebrity "sensationalism" in the society's competitions; and they became a vehicle for promoting technical education – transforming resistance – organizers hoped – into acceptance or, at the very least, compromise.

While the first artisan tour in 1867 began as a novelty, the three that followed established something of a tradition. Indeed, over the course of two decades, the tours' organization and promotion became somewhat ritualized, as did the selection of artisans and the publication of their reports This ritualization process, however, still allowed for change, which can be attributed to workers' growing political influence and impact on the technical education movement. Thus, how reformers and workers imagined and experienced the artisan tours of 1867, 1873, 1878, and 1889, reflected, in large measure, how they related to one another within and, increasingly, beyond the Lib–Lab alliance; and, how they came to perceive technical education and travel abroad in the context of state formation.

A common feature of all four tours, for example, was the organizational and ideological support they received from the Society of Arts. While the society directly managed only the 1867 and 1878 Paris exhibition tours, they lent their expertise to the remaining two tours: the 1873 Vienna exhibition tour, jointly organized by the Manchester Society for the Promotion of Scientific Industry (MSPSI) and the Birmingham Chamber of Commerce (BCC); and, the 1889 Paris exhibition tour, organized by the Lord Mayor's Mansion House Committee in association with the London Guilds. Ensuring continuity, the 1873 and 1889 tour organizers drew liberally upon the organizational models established by the SA in 1867 that provided a blueprint for acquiring funding and securing cheap transport, lodgings, interpreters, and advertising. They also obtained the advice and support of SA officials who had either participated in previous SA artisan exhibition tours or who were connected to the British Commission on Exhibitions. The chief organizer of the 1873 Vienna exhibition tour, W.C. Aitken, for example, was a Birmingham booster, a vocal proponent of educational reform, and a veteran of the organizational committee of the 1867 SA tour of the Paris exhibition. Aitken thus used his considerable experience and influence to help manage the 1873 artisan tours to Vienna. Capitalizing on his acquaintance with Philip Cunliffe Owen, a member of the SA and Secretary of the British Commission for the British Section at the Vienna Exhibition, he acquired introductions for the artisan reporters to meet with Viennese dignitaries, and arranged for reasonably priced lodgings near the exhibition grounds. Similarly, the Mansion House Committee for the 1889 Tours also maintained strong links with the SA by gaining the advice of Henry Trueman Wood, who at that time was SA secretary and the Commissioner Delegate of the "unofficial" British Section of the Exhibition.[71] Having had experience organizing the SA's 1878 artisan tours, Wood lent his expertise to the Mansion House Committee, again ensuring a significant level of continuity with earlier exhibition tours.[72]

This continuity across all four tours was also facilitated by the primarily liberal ethos of the individual tour committees, whose members, from John Stuart Mill and Joseph Chamberlain to Charles Dickens and Thomas Hughes, read like a *Who's Who* of Victorian middle-class radicalism and reforming interests. Public administrators and educationists including Leon Playfair, Henry Cole and J.P. Kay-Shuttleworth, offered their names, their time, and their purses to the cause, as did education ministers W.E. Forster and Anthony Mundella. Model employers such as Titus Salt and Samuel Morley, MP, also contributed substantial sums and served as committee members. Equally committed to educational reform, however, were labor leaders who served on the 1889 Committee, such as Randal Cremer (MP),

George Howell (MP), and the ultra radical trade unionist and London School Board member, Benjamin Lucraft. Howell and Lucraft brought ideological continuity (from the labor perspective) to the 1889 Paris tour having had significant first-hand experience as artisan reporters during the 1867 Paris exhibition.[73]

The means for funding the tours also provided institutional continuity. The political, social, or financial stature of committee members ensured that the artisan exhibition tours received some state funding from municipalities and from Westminster, as well as financial support from individuals, private firms, and civic bodies. The SA, for example, funded the 1867 and 1878 Artisan Exhibition Tours to Paris, with a matching grant from the British Commission on Exhibitions. This grant placed government funds at the society's disposal on the recommendation of the Lords of the Committee on the Council of Education, underscoring the educational attributes of the tours as well as the powerful interests at play in ensuring their success. With financial backing from the state, the SA called upon artisans from across the United Kingdom to apply for posts as artisan reporters, turning the 1867 and 1878 artisan exhibition tours into national endeavors.[74]

In contrast, the 1873 Vienna artisan exhibition tour and the 1889 Paris tour operated without direct government assistance. Drawing funds solely from voluntary subscription, organizers confined artisan recruitment to smaller geographic areas. The Manchester Society for the Promotion of Scientific Industry (MSPSI), for example, worked collaboratively with the Birmingham Chamber of Commerce (BCC) to send only midland artisans to the Vienna Exhibition. Such limitations rankled the organizers. In his "Introductory Report" to the 1873 *Artisans' Reports*, Aitken bluntly criticized "Her Majesty's Government" for endorsing a "parsimonious policy" towards the tour that made state aid "an impossibility." Aitken declared that given the lack of state support, "it became evident [that] ... if valuable lessons were to be read [at the exhibition], and artisan reporters were to be sent, they could only be through such means as those the ... [BCC] adopted and carried out in connection with the [MSPSI]."[75] Nevertheless, whether regional or national in scope, all tours required an advertising apparatus to recruit charitable donations and artisan reporters.

Promotion for the tours took different forms to enlist financial sponsors and to encourage workers to apply for the post of "artisan reporter." In soliciting voluntary donations for the 1867 and 1878 Tours, the SA sent out circulars to trade associations, unions and guilds, as well as to business firms, chambers of commerce, mayors' offices, and educational institutes, each including a supportive testimonial from the society's president, the Prince of Wales, who had subscribed £50 from his own household treasury.[76] The society's members also conducted meetings at these sites to recruit individuals and organizations for participation in the tours. Aitken, for instance, won the Birmingham Chamber of Commerce over by appealing to their sense of national honor. Indeed, he shamed his audience into sponsoring the tours by reminding them that other countries, being "more alive to progress than our own," had sent their own artisans to report on each of Britain's international exhibitions since 1851.[77] Inspiring individuals and organizations to set up their own committees, the SA managed to elicit support from across the British Isles. For example, the Special Exhibition Committee of the Dublin Mayor's office made the educational function of the 1878 exhibition the central selling point of its circular. In it, the Mayor's Office expressed its confidence that "the manufacturers and employers in this city ... will afford their ... support towards a movement having so laudable an object in view as the enlightenment of the working classes in this country, and the advancement of the education of Skilled Labour."[78]

"Advanced" firms also needed little prodding from the SA to encourage their own employees to participate in the tours or to donate subscription funds. The SA's records show that corporate sponsors – including Guinness & Co., brewers; Broadwood & Sons, piano makers; and Woollam's paper factory – generously participated in the 1867 and 1878 tours, while other firms conducted their own tours, perhaps galvanized by the "sensation" surrounding the exhibition tours. J. Pullar & Sons Dye Works informed the SA that they were "so satisfied of the important educational value of the Exposition" that they had shouldered the cost to send 16 of their "managers, foremen, and skilled-men" to the exhibition. Having asked their employees to write reports, Pullar & Sons offered them as possible contributions to the SA's own volume of *Artisan Reports*.[79]

Although the SA's correspondence shows significant support for the tours, some firms vigorously rejected the idea of sending artisans abroad, much like the pockets of resistance that flared up against the technical reform movement. Consequently, James Samuelson, Deputy Chairman of the Liverpool Town Hall Exhibition Committee, experienced the dual "pleasure" and "regret" of informing the SA in 1878 that while the Town Hall had received grants from trade societies, they had "not been well supported by the Employers – in fact many are very much opposed to it."[80] Despite such drawbacks, sources of support came from all corners of industry. Some firms hoped to turn a profit or to increase their commercial visibility from the artisan exhibition tours. In response to receiving an SA circular for the 1878 exhibition tour, J. Knight, general manager of the Brighton & South Coast Railway, agreed to support the tours as long as his company enjoyed free publicity from the SA organizers, responding with an offer of £10 for the "Artizan's Trip" on condition that the SA mention the railway in their advertising. "Although the numbers which may be going are small," Knight wrote, "I fear that the absence of any allusion to our route may be calculated to prejudice us with the working classes, and it is therefore not so much a question of this traffic in itself, as the mention of the Company's line in your announcements."[81]

Organizers also distributed tour advertisements wherever prospective artisan reporters were likely to congregate or to leaf through a newspaper. Promoters distributed circulars for publication in popular and trade journals and for posting on the walls of educational institutes, union houses, and working men's clubs.[82] Additionally, national and regional papers such as *The Bee-Hive, The Star, The Daily News,* and *The London Times* printed stories featuring local organizers and firms which supported the tours and, sometimes listed the names and occupations of men selected as artisan reporters.[83] Like the print media, word of mouth also played a part in circulating news of the tours. In a letter to the SA postmarked 2 March 1879, W. Loveday, a gold refiner, wrote to say that he had learned from a friend in the jewelry trade that the SA sent reporters to exhibitions. Perhaps hoping to beat the competition, he offered his "services" for the Sydney Exhibition that was to take place over a year later.[84] Evidently, the artisan exhibition tours had caused "a stir" in artisan communities.

While advertising and trade gossip served the organizers' immediate purpose of spreading information, news of the tours did not begin and end with the exhibition itself. *The Bee-Hive* announced in October of 1867, that Charles Hooper, cabinetmaker, intended to turn his report into a pamphlet and to present it as a lecture to London audiences.[85] Over a decade later, Hugh Findlay traveled "the circuit" presenting his lecture "Artisan Reporters at the Paris Exhibition" to Edinburgh crowds. Enlivening his tale with anecdotes about his own experience as an artisan reporter in 1878, he added historical complexity to the story by drawing on the adventures and observations of the first generation of artisan reporters in 1867.[86] Artisan reporters also recounted their experiences in regional and national papers. The prolific John Randall, FGS, a renowned china painter, geologist, and chronicler of Madeley lore, not only submitted his report to local papers in Shrewsbury, Wolverhampton "and other places," but also enlightened *Times* readers with a view of the 1867 Paris Exhibition from below.[87] Finally, the artisans' reports themselves proved an enduring mode of advertisement. Printed in single volumes, separate tracts, or fitted for publication in various trade magazines, the artisans' reports populated the shelves of public and private libraries, workers' shop floors, and the railway bookstalls of W.H. Smith & Son.

The circulation of the artisans' reports was, of course, critical to the SA's reforming agenda. The reports advertised the fact that the middle-class organizers helped workers to collect information that was of "use" to themselves and to their nation, and encouraged other working-class travelers to pursue the same goals. Furthermore, the *Artisan Reports* articulated the theme of educational reform. As part of reformers' attempt to create a capillary system within which knowledge and culture flowed through the nation as broadly as possible, the *Artisan Reports* achieved their maximum utility by reaching the hands of other workers. Digested as either textbook forms of knowledge, as travel narratives, or simply as propaganda for educational reform, they "multiplied culture's utility." Like-minded employers and municipal officials shared the SA's objectives in assuring the wide distribution of the artisan reports. As Charles Saunderson, coachmaster, communicated to Henry Trueman Wood in 1879: "I have sent presentation copies [of coachmaking reports] to the leading builders in the United Kingdom, and had thanks for so valuable and useful a publication – but if thrown on a shelf and not sent into the workshop – its object is lost and frustrated."[88] Given how critical the dissemination of these reports were to employers, it was imperative that the artisan reports be readable, useful, and written by credible sources among the working class. No part of arranging the artisan tours, therefore, could have been more crucial than the careful selection of the workers who would produce these invaluable tracts.

An equally enduring trait of the artisan tours was the organizers' selection of artisan reporters based on their skill and, after 1867, their academic credentials as well. These qualifications constituted the primary educational underpinning of the tours, particularly the growing prize culture associated with the examination system. With each successive tour, however, organizers refined the selection process, eventually allowing workers themselves to take a part in choosing the artisan reporters – a process that, by 1889, would become entirely dominated by the workers and the growing power of trade unions that they represented. This course of action reflected the growing radicalization of tour organizers, which paralleled the trend toward liberal accommodation to social democratic themes in the political sphere. Just as labor politics changed the character of the Liberal Party, workers' participation in the selection process altered the character of the artisan tours.

Much as Coningsby had suggested, tour organizers made the post of artisan reporter highly competitive. In 1867, for instance, committee members sorted through a mass of inquiries and applications that flooded the SA's office seeking "intelligent," literate artisans, recognized as the "best" in their trades whose reports would likely "command the attention" of workmen and manufacturers alike. Often relying upon employer recommendations and "fellow worker" testimonials that attested to the applicants' "fitness to undertake the task assigned him," they eventually settled on 85 candidates.[89] The competition had been stiff. Of the 81 applications received at the Birmingham Committee office alone, only 25 workmen passed inspection.[90]

Especially rigorous was the selection process for the 1873 Vienna exhibition created by the Manchester Society for the Promotion of Scientific Industry and the Birmingham Chamber of Commerce. Of the 320 applicants who applied to the MSPSI and BCC, only 90 made it through the weeding process's examinations and interviews.[91] In the introduction to the Manchester section of the *Artisan Reports*, William Larkins, Secretary of the MSPSI, explained that in addition to the general qualifications established in 1867, the committee had also determined that only "bona fide" workmen who earned their living through their trades and who had "risen to be fore-men, or to positions of trust" would qualify. Workmen of the "lower grade" Larkins cautioned, need not apply.[92] To further ensure suitability for the task, the committee also required applicants to take oral and written examinations to determine "practical proof of ... fitness, before selection."[93] Offering some insight into the qualifying and selection process, Aitken explained in the "Introductory Report" of the *Artisan Reports* (Part Two: Birmingham Artisans' Reports) how he had applied the "strictest test as to the knowledge possessed by the candidates in the trade to be reported upon." Aitken forwarded to each applicant an examination (which he duplicated in his "Introductory Report," and that is replicated here in the following quotation) that would assess the candidate's talent for narrative description.

Visit of Birmingham Artisans to the Vienna Exhibition

Your application has been received. You will observe that *experience and ability determine selection.* A *report* has to be *written.* As a proof of your descriptive power, express in as *few words* and as *clearly* as you can (on foolscap paper, written on one side only), the description of

[*Here was inserted description of construction, or rationale of process used in trade, &c., of the applicant*]

The description is to be made from practical experience and observation. No book description is to be copied. Your description will be tested by reference to an experienced authority in your trade. Your name will not be disclosed.[94]

Less than half of the original 88 Birmingham applicants returned Aitken's "test," but those who did make the effort, submitted "elaborate" and "well written" papers, some of which were accompanied by illustrations when applicable. However, only 10 of the 40 Birmingham finalists qualified to become artisan reporters.[95]

In planning the 1878 artisan tours of the Paris exhibition, the SA gave working men a stronger say in nominating artisan reporters than in previous exhibition tours, and in so doing acknowledged the trade unions' power and importance for furthering educational reform. However, in the 1878 Paris tour as in 1867 (but not in the 1873 Vienna tour, in which individual SA members served in an advisory capacity only), the SA organizers continued to exercise overarching control over the selection process. For instance, in 1878 the SA asked workers to contribute to the selection of artisan reporters in two ways. First, the SA's Selection Committee appointed a subcommittee responsible for garnering advice from both workmen and employers across Great Britain on how best to select candidates to become artisan reporters.

Additionally, a "select" group of London workers comprised of top labor leaders and artisan intellectuals met with the subcommittee during the month of July to draw up a list of suitable candidates from the London area. Committee members included Thomas Patterson, a carpenter and secretary of the Workingmen's Club and Institute Union; Joseph Leicester, a skilled craftsmen and union organizer for the Flint Glassmakers; and Benjamin Lucraft. Additionally, letters to the SA from George Potter, the militant editor of the *Industrial Review* (formerly, *The Bee-Hive*), suggest that he may have also served on the committee.[96] However, while the SA had accepted the committee's selection of 30 candidates, Le Neve Foster apparently refused to abdicate the entire selection process to men whose class and political affiliations made their abilities as arbiters of "character" and "fitness" for the job suspect.[97] Behind the scenes, he directed his assistant, Henry Trueman Wood, to verify the character of each nominee with their employers: "Could you not get printed a short letter to employers marked confidential asking if 'so and so' when selected from the men's lists is a suitable man and enclose [a] stamped and addressed envelope for reply?"[98]

Such lingering mistrust of the politicized labor aristocracy played little part in the selection process of the 1889 tours. With the passing of the Third Reform Bill and mounting working-class political activism in the 1880s, the 1889 selection committee took a bolder egalitarian turn. More democratic than previous Artisan Exhibition Tour organizations, the Mansion House Committee included the usual middle-class reformers, model employers, academics and educationists, but also labor leaders such as George Howell, MP; W.R. Cremer, MP; Benjamin Lucraft, and George Shipton, Secretary of the London Trades Council. Reflecting the Committee's strong labor representation and social-democratic sensibilities, they left it to workmen to "handpick" candidates as their "representatives" after which the Committee then handed the list of nominees to the trade unions and societies to determine "wherever practicable" the final selection.[99]

Although workers exercised more control over the selection process, the qualifications remained much the same as previous competitions for the post of artisan reporter. In 1889, the Mansion House Committee directed the "trades" to choose only those with "exceptional qualifications." They therefore selected artisans whose "intelligence and knowledge were such that the reports in their respective industries would not only be good, but be of public value, and command the attention and respect of their fellow workmen and the public generally."[100] This meant, just as it did in post-1867 artisan exhibition tours, that artisan reporters not only possessed proven craft or mechanical/engineering skills, but also academic credentials, including prizes for high examination scores in subjects from blow-pipe analysis to draftsmanship. Consequently, such qualifications remained a central organizing feature of the tours, making Conigsby's and Hawes vision an enduring reality. A glance at the 1867 and 1878 applicants illustrates the degree to which the prize culture surrounding technical education not only became an integral feature of the artisan tours, but began to formalize the structure of study abroad for educated British workers.

In selecting candidates for the 1878 artisan tours, Le Neve Foster and Wood would have sifted through stacks of letters that had made their way to the SA's office on John Adams Street. Perhaps hoping to increase their chance of a favorable response, many applicants emphasized their formal technical training. Writing to Foster in late July, Benjamin Askew inquired whether workmen who had passed the SA's technical exams (in his case, gas manufacture) "will have the privilege of becoming one of the artisan reporters." Receiving an affirmative reply, Askew duly submitted his application.[101] Thomas Duckworth, a Liverpool mechanical engineer and student, confidently presented impeccable credentials, writing that Foster need only check the SA's records to learn that he had not only passed the SA's examinations in steel manufacture, winning first prize, but was also a Whitworth Scholar.[102] William Cross also presented exemplary academic credentials, introducing himself as a 22-year-old mechanical engineer and a student at the Royal School of Mines who had won multiple prizes for his scholarship. "The Summer vacation being now on, "he wrote, "I am free until Oct. 1st."[103] Joseph Leicester, the flint glass maker and union secretary, also applied for the post, informing the SA that he had "taken 2 first class honours for art work [from the SA's prize competitions] over the heads of all competitors" and had "made every article or nearly so which was first in [the] 1867 Exhibition" for his employers at the Powell Glass Works. Making a patriotic pitch, Leicester boasted: "Should your society require a *fit* person to represent and to report on our beautiful art of glass making, I think I can honestly lay claim to be a proper person for the work," adding, "I am vain enough to think we shall beat all the *Foreigners* this time."[104]

As to be expected, the committee received a number of letters from anxious applicants. Leicester, for instance, still waited for a response five months after submitting his application. "As time is fast fleeting into future," he reminded the committee, "I should like to know how I stand and if to go when."[105] In fact, there may have been some hesitation over Leicester's application given that the French authorities initially denied him permission to attend the 1867 Paris Exhibition on account of his "revolutionary activities." Paris officials relented only upon receiving word from his employers assuring them that Leicester was a man of "irreproachable character and exceptional fitness for the work." Askew, the student of gas manufacture, also could not bear wait. After posting three probing communiqués within the space of a month, Askew finally requested that the SA inform him when they had made their selection "as I would prefer to know my fate in this matter rather than remain in expectation (*un*blissful ignorance!) after the affair is 'un fait accompli.'"[106] Others urged the committee's decision in order to make all the necessary arrangements with employers. Edwin

Robins, inquired whether "I may call myself as one of the Artisan workmen reporters." If the answer was affirmative (it was), Robins wished to know "the latest date you intend to send any as I wish to prepare accordingly in consideration of work I have in hand."[107] Samuel R. Dermot also took the "liberty" to inquire "whether your Committee has been pleased to elect your humble servant as one of the artisan reporters," given that "circumstances compel me to ascertain whether I am to hold myself in readiness."[108] Another aspirant, W.J. Fleming, a "negative retoucher" in the photographic trade, wrote on 9 August 1878 to learn the status of his application, which he had submitted two weeks prior to this date. Seemingly desperate to get to Paris, but with no "means" of his own, he vowed that should his application, references, or his own experience appear insufficient, he was quite capable of producing a useful report, particularly since he would be assisted by two French photojournalists who had "kindly proffered to give every assistance to visitors at Paris & give them any information & advice they possibly can." A man on the go, Fleming wished to leave for Paris in little more than a week and urgently requested Foster's immediate response. "I waited expecting a letter from you the latter end of last week to say whether I was going to be sent to Paris or not; & have waited up to now & received no reply at all." Enclosing two stamps, Fleming asked that Foster telegraph his answer.[109]

It is impossible to determine the final selection of artisan reporters in 1878. The SA did not accept all reports submitted for publication, and the only extant list of known reporters is the contents page of the book itself. Yet, there is little doubt that the results of these inquiries would have disappointed many artisans who held out the hope for an appointment. Letters preserved in the SA's archive show how their responses to rejection varied. J. Murray merely wished his letters of recommendation returned "as they are likely to be of service to me."[110] Thomas Warsop, however, refused to be deterred by a mere rejection slip. Assiduously pleading his case, Warsop attempted to strike a deal. "As I have not been fortunate enough to be selected, at present" he bargained, "I beg to offer my services to you, at a reduced rate, *viz* £6.10.0 that in place of receiving £3.0.0. on presenting my reports, it should be reduced to £1.10.0 and, I would do my best to make my report second to none, of the Artisans you kindly send to the Exhibition."[111] Collective pleas also found their way to Foster's desk. John Rogers, an "engine fetter", wrote on behalf of himself and four other artisan "Science Teachers" (two shipwrights, a joiner, and a turner) to request that Foster reconsider their applications on the grounds that the committee had erroneously disqualified them from the competition.[112] The glitch may be attributable to the Department of Science and Arts' stipulations regarding scholarships, which stated that recipients "must not be the teacher, pupil teacher, or other paid servant of a school."[113] Given that the tours were funded in part by government grant, these stipulations ambiguously applied even to artisan instructors. Yet, Rogers assured Foster that although they instructed students in "various Mechanical branches of Science" during winter evenings, they were not teachers by trade, but "bona-fide Artizans" who practiced their crafts year round. Additionally, their experience as both workers and teachers, Roger stated (underscoring one of the core objects of the tours), made them especially qualified "to widely spread such important advanced information as is obtainable at the Exhibition."[114]

These letters reveal some of the candidates' expectations and anxieties in 1878, indicating not only workers' desire to visit the continent, but the cultural and economic capital associated with the title "artisan reporter." Autobiographical information contained in workers' correspondence, memoirs, and reports, also reveal common characteristics that appealed to selection committees. Organizers selected artisan reporters through nomination, personal application, oral interviews, and written examinations. Given this process, the reporters largely represented Britain's artisan elite: literate, industrious, and respectable. Generationally and occupationally, however, they represented two broad groups: seasoned craftsmen, primarily "artworkmen" and "mechanics" who, with little formal education, took an interest in understanding the principles of their trades, and the new vanguard of technically and scientifically schooled industrial operatives who bridged the gap between the older craft tradition of apprenticeship training and formal instruction.

Emblematic of the labor aristocracy, many of these artisans' lives in the first group spanned the "pre-1850 ultra-radical movement, the advanced labourism of the 1860s, and the Lib–Lab alliance in the late 1860s and 1870s."[115] As such, many were Chartists, trade unionists, members of the International Workingmen's Association and the Reform League, and a few eventually stood for parliament. Despite these achievements, the majority of these artisan reporters could claim, at best, only a smattering of formal instruction at dame, charity, and Sunday schools. In educating themselves, these artisans had joined mutual improvement societies, provincial Young Men's Christian Associations, and mechanics' institutes, saving precious pennies to pay for membership dues, to build personal libraries and geological collections, to visit museums and local exhibitions, or to buy materials for experiments and inventions.[116]

Known for their superior skill in a particular trade and often their encyclopedic knowledge, several artisan reporters claimed celebrity status in their villages, towns and, occasionally, the nation as "exceptional" men. Joseph Gutteridge, a Coventry weaver of silk ribbons and artisan reporter for the 1878 Paris exhibition tour, was also a naturalist who built expertly designed telescopes. His views were as varied as his talents and the people with whom he socialized. An atheist, Owenite socialist, and, as Eugenio Biagini emphasizes, a free trade advocate, Gutteridge moved comfortably within different circles.[117] He entertained "men of all ranks" in his small weaver's cottage, sharing with his visitors a mutual fascination with electricity, geological formations, medical technology, spiritualism, and even the art of violin making.[118] John Randall, a Coalport china painter and a Fellow of the Geological Society, also commanded the respect of his fellow citizens. The SA invited Randall to read a paper at a conference dedicated to working men's views of technical education in 1868, and published his paper in their journal. It constituted merely one among a score of works he wrote and published during his lifetime on education, geology, local folklore and history.[119] At the age of 99, Randall, the "grand old man" of Madeley, was honored in a town ceremony with the "freedom of the Borough of Wenlock."[120]

The biography of Harry Hems, an Exeter ecclesiastical and architectural sculptor who began his working life as a cutter at the age of 14, parallels the celebrity Gutteridge and Randall achieved in their lives. Traveling to Italy to study the "old masters" in his early twenties, Hems was imprisoned as a Garibaldi conspirator. Eventually, he gained his freedom and "walked home" to begin a successful career which included not only production in his craft, but writing for trade and popular journals on subjects ranging from travel to technology. In 1905, *The Decorator* described Hems as "perhaps the best known private individual in the country."[121]

The second group of artisan reporters, primarily young engineers who had achieved exceptional test scores or who had won prestigious prizes, were just as well known to the SA. Separated by a generation or two from many of the art workmen, their lives of scholarship and labor had been documented by the normalizing technologies of the examination system. To know any of these individuals, the SA merely consulted educational records that measured and recorded each individual's failures, triumphs, and abilities in assessing their productive capacities. Edmond Mondy, for example, "a very clever young man" from Oldham, reported on shipbuilding at the 1867 Paris Exhibition at the age of 19.[122] A year later Mondy won a Whitworth exhibition prize and became a Whitworth Scholar in 1871, receiving £300 over a three-year period while he studied at the Royal School of Mines. Working towards becoming a civil engineer, generally a closed road for anyone without middle-class assets or connections, Mondy became "fully acquainted with the path of success through the society's examinations." Sitting for exams at both the SA and the DSA, Mondy studied the "Principles of Mechanics, Practical Mechanics, Trigonometry, [and] Bookkeeping," and "Electricity & Magnetism, Higher and Elementary Mathematics, Theoretical and Applied Mechanics, Machine Drawing, [and] Naval Architecture and Steam."[123] Fred H. Millington, another Whitworth Scholar from Worsley, Manchester, reported on general machinery at the 1873 Vienna Exhibition. By the age of 21 he had already spent six years in apprentice work, and had "taken a considerable interest in the manufacture of steel." Likewise, John Heywood an artisan reporter in 1878, had won several prizes and awards in courses ranging from chemistry, machine and geometrical drawing to Latin, French and German. A diligent student, he won a scholarship to the Royal

School of Mines to pursue studies in engineering – a long process, he wrote in a letter to Foster, of exams, qualifying courses, and deadlines designed "to make students suffer."[124]

Ambitious, civic-minded and, over the years, progressively educated in new technologies related to their trades, the artisan reporters epitomized the value of modern education in maintaining Britain's industrial supremacy. As such, they functioned as quasi-official delegates to continental exhibitions. On the one hand, they became mobile exhibition displays representing Britain's advanced corps of skilled artisans and industrial operatives. By way of example, they taught other workmen the values of hard work, intellectual and trade skills, and respectability. On the other hand, they represented the nation's most ardent spokesmen for educational reform and, lamenting their own lack of formal education, also represented Britain's civilizational shortcomings. Articulating and circulating the goals of the educational reform movement in their reports, they sustained a two-decades-long polemic against a class system that neglected workers' intellectual, cultural and vocational development – the failure of a liberal state that, they argued, boded ill for the economic and social stability of Britain's future.

The *Artisan Reports*: A Genre and a Discourse

Bell & Daldy, book publishers, presented the public with the first volume of reports by artisans in December 1867. It was an ideal firm for the job. Specializing in educational titles since 1839, the retail bookseller and publisher projected confidence in the ethos of improvement. Its catalogue included university texts, child and adult literary classics, and titles in art, architecture, and archeology which, reportedly, had first attracted Henry Cole's patronage. It even produced a popular series of travel guides.[125] It is difficult to imagine a publisher more suited to the task, and no doubt Cole and the artisan reporters praised the results. One outcome they may not have anticipated, however, was the creation of a new genre and discourse of travel and exhibition literature that collectively marked an expanding tradition of artisan scholarship, reporting, and travel on the continent. Since the publication of the first volume in 1867, the *Artisan Reports* reflected a distinctly working-class literary inventiveness and sensibility, one that communicated a class critique of Britain by comparing continental values and practices with those of home. This continuity in part stemmed from the organizers' mandate to the artisan reporters to write on continental industries, educational institutions, and workers' social and economic conditions. The development of this uniquely working-class genre and discourse, however, also stemmed from the multiple realities of the artisans' trips abroad: their sense of themselves as "tourists" with unusual tales to tell of foreign climes, their sense of themselves as students with something to learn from their tours abroad, and their sense of themselves as working-class reporters invested with a moral imperative to evaluate the similarities and differences between industrialized nations.

The first volume of *Artisan Reports* had set the ideal for a distinct brand of working-class travel narrativity, one that combined the pleasures of sight-seeing with urban exploration and industrial reporting. In subsequent volumes, however, editors often mediated the terms between this ideal and the reality of the finished product, frequently thwarting reporters' narrative ambitions. Aitken "regretted," for example, that the "want of space" required "delet[ing] many paragraphs from the [1873] Reports which quaintly, gracefully, in some instances elegantly, told of incidents which occurred, habits observed, buildings seen, museums visited, and scenery passed through."[126] The 1878 and 1889 artisan reports fared little better – a point of contention for one artisan reporter, R. Frances, a carver and guilder, who in 1889 complained that "brevity, terseness, and conclusiveness, were recommended by the Lord Mayor to the Delegation in the preparation of their reports." Given these stipulations, Frances sarcastically suggested that readers "follow me with such forbearance as they can summon to what I fear will, at the best, be a wearisome task ... [as he] strained the quality of brevity to its utmost tension."[127] Another artisan reporter of the 1889 tour, a carpenter by the name of T. Vest, began his report in perfectly touristic fashion, marveling at Paris's wide boulevards, ubiquitous statuary, and exciting nightlife. Like Frances, however, he ultimately felt compelled to keep his report on point. Reminded of his task, Vest wistfully remarked that while he wanted to mention several more notable features of his tour, "I must not do so – as I am encroaching on the space allotted."[128] Others, fortunately, felt no such compunction.

In the breezily conversational manner of a professional journalist, W.H. Edmunds, a bookbinder, described the minute details of his journey including the adventure and thrill of dining at the Café Alsace et Lorraine on the first floor of the Eiffel Tower, still under construction for the 1889 Exhibition. Following a champagne toast to Queen Victoria, the artisans climbed "even" higher to the second floor ("about the height of St. Paul's Cathedral"), where they visited the printing office of *Le Figaro* and favored the French paper with an interview. With so much activity to stimulate the senses, but with a report still to write, Edmunds "resolved to tear myself away from the seductions of Paris at all hazards; – that is, at the end of a fortnight."[129] Other reporters maintained the urban exploration narrative style of the 1867 reports. F. S. Knowles, for instance, described his "déjeuner" at an "ordinary eating house" with a group of French hatters as if it was as extraordinary an event as a visit to a Parisian dance hall. After consuming a "small plate (five inches across) of 'rosbif,' with three marble-sized potatoes ... two spoonfuls of green peas ... a dish of stewed prunes ... a glass of black coffee ... [and] a thimbleful of cognac," his Parisian companions spent the next two hours playing cards while "arguing and gesticulating over a bottle of wine" before returning to work.[130]

Each volume also sustained the 1867 reports' consideration of the host country's political environment and its implications for working people. Artisan reporters to the 1873 Vienna Exhibition, for instance, likened Austria to a barracks society, while the 1878 reporters described France as a police state which they experienced first-hand when they arrived in the capital and were escorted to their lodgings by government gendarmes. A new kind of optimism, however, surfaced in the 1889 reports, many of which favorably reviewed France's republican government and articulated an intensely internationalist vision. This new optimism owed much to the French government's lifting of some restrictions against trade unions in the early 1880s, and the revival of socialism which, by 1886, had become embodied in a definable (if sectarian) group in the Chamber of Deputies opposed to the "radical" (conservative) bourgeoisie.[131] Thus, while Leicester pitied unionless and impoverished French glass-makers in 1878, a decade later artisan reporters documented a palpable shift in the political atmosphere of the French capital, particularly with regard to trade unions.[132] For example, in contrast to the artisan reporters' steely reception in 1878, delegates from Paris's Municipal Council and the (predominantly socialist) labor exchange, the *Bourses du Travail*, warmly greeted the 1889 artisan reporters at the station and whisked their guests off to a banquet in their honor.

Politics, in fact, permeated the air of the 1889 Paris Exhibition Tours. Indeed, the Exhibition celebrated the centennial anniversary of the French Revolution, an anniversary that suited socialists for the founding of the Second International in Paris. T.D. Wright, a clockmaker, recorded that immediately after shaking hands with the welcome committee from the *Bourses du Travail* their hosts expected to exchange political ideas. They would be "disappointed," Wright wryly noted, "for our captain informed them at a very early stage that whatever our individual political opinions might be – and they probably differed very much – we were strictly a non-political body."[133] Despite the artisan reporters' "non-political" mission, however, they seemed to encounter French politics everywhere they turned. Lavishly feted their first evening by the municipal council and the labor exchange, they joined their hosts in toasts to the "workers of the world," which disgusted some in their party and delighted others.[134] Wright, for instance, simply endured their speeches and disparagingly commented that "as we listened to one speaker enthusiastically asserting that capital and labour were natural enemies, and that labour would not get its rights until the capitalist was crushed, we got impatient."[135] Others, however, were intrigued by the political vivacity of their hosts, although not one – perhaps intentionally maintaining the "non-political" character of the tours – mentioned the Second International. G. Summers, who reported on machinery associated with baking trades, discovered that "a trade question in Paris is a political question, and a Frenchman must not attempt to sever one from the other."[136] Indeed, Summers felt compelled to wear his politics on his sleeve in order to win an interview with French workers. "Unless I let the French operative baker see that my heart and soul was with him, and led him to believe that my trade ideas were in accord with strong political principles," Summers reported, "they treated me with a great amount of coolness; but when once they understood that I sought the redemption of the workers, it was all smooth sailing."[137]

Taking a complementary view of French institutions, Summers and other artisan reporters also found much to commend in the Municipal Council and its support of the labor exchange. In the late 1880s, Republican municipalities encouraged and helped fund the *Bourses du Travail* (BT), which provided trade unions with meeting halls and unemployed workers with lists of job opportunities.[138] Politically savvy, Summers understood that the ruling establishment intended to control and educate labor through such institutions. However, while "the [municipal] Council may have had ulterior political reasons [for supporting the BT]," wrote Summers, "the institution satisfies a very long-felt want, and it would do the London County Council credit to establish such an institution for the workers."[139]

The Municipal Council also earned the artisans' respect not only for their warm welcome, banquets, and parties, but for providing them with access to "places of interest" from technical schools to the city sewers. D. Toomey, a metal worker, noted that "the impression this treatment forcibly made upon my mind was that it was evidently their desire to establish the most cordial relations between the workers of both countries, as well as to lay the foundation of the most kindly feelings between the workmen of all nations."[140] Other artisan reporters followed suit. Commending the internationalist spirit of the Parisian government, C. Kinggate, a coachbuilder, reported that:

> If our visit has not resulted in benefiting the various industries we represented, it certainly has been the means of engendering a good feeling between the workers; and for the peace and progress of the world, nothing is more necessary than that a bond of sympathy should exist between the workers of all countries.[141]

Given their hearty welcome by the French, many artisan reporters likely joined Vest in "hoping that, instead of simply going during the time of an exhibition, in the future to pay [Paris] a visit at intermediate periods."[142]

The most striking similarity in each volume of the reports since 1867, however, was their sustained attack on British educational provisions for working people, which they articulated within a nationalist framework. In 1873, Malcolm MacLeod remarked on Germany's compulsory elementary education, "excellent trade schools," and the "important work" of Vienna's "Working Man's Education Union."[143] "Armed with education," German workers, MacLeod warned, posed a serious threat to British industry.[144] In 1878, James Hopps, a mechanical engineer, praised French laws that "compelled" masters to allow apprentices evenings off to attend one of the city's many free night schools, science classes, or public libraries to advance their "theoretical knowledge."[145] Such provisions for education, Hopps asserted, "promise[d] to exert a great effect on the engineering industry of France in the future." Unless British "masters are willing to allow their apprentices to sacrifice their time in the workroom in order to obtain instruction out of the office," Hopps concluded, Britain faced inevitable "decline."[146] Likewise, William H. Howard, a wood carver, patriotically placed the still unrelieved hunger for "greater facilities ... for art workmen to study art" within a narrowly nationalist cash nexus. "It is a national question," Howard observed, "because if a class be improved the nation generally shares the benefit, money being then spent at home which would otherwise go abroad."[147]

Such critiques maintained their currency through to the 1889 tours, indicating reformers' limited success in rectifying Britain's crisis in industrial education. More than two decades after the first artisan exhibition tours, J. Brooke, a specialist in tile and mosaics, clung to the familiar refrain decrying the want of British "taste" in design, lamenting that there was "no use shutting our eyes to long-standing abuses, and allowing our neighbours to have it all their own way."[148] The 1889 artisan reporters also applauded France's technical schools. K.M. M'Crae, a boot- and shoemaker, admired how French institutions provided young men and women with "excellent preparatory instruction ... to enable them the better to do battle in this world of keen competition," but felt "uneasy" when he compared these provisions to the antiquated apprenticeship system in Britain. Cautioning readers that France's schools for workers put the future of British "supremacy" in "doubt," he scorned Britain's "half-hearted measures" to provide technical classes and institutions through charitable or voluntary sources.[149] Edmunds also joined the fray, complaining that London had scandalously "shut out [the poor] from the benefits of [educational] endowments intended for them while the rich scramble into their places."[150] Only a free and national system of education, Edmunds argued, could possibly remedy Britain's resistance to educational improvement.[151]

Conclusion

Sustaining the themes of an earlier discourse, the artisan reporters endorsed a stronger role for the state in providing educational opportunities for workers, and underscored the importance of educational travel. France, Edmunds stated, set a "grand example for us to follow." Remarking on the School of Apprentices and its "travelling scholarships" for deserving youth, Edmunds reported that "seventeen of the most promising students ... are taken for twenty-five days' travel to the best shops in France, or sometimes even Belgium or elsewhere, to give them an insight into the workshops where they must eventually complete their trade education." Such systematic provisions for technical education, Edmunds concluded, should be emulated by the British rather than maintaining "the slop fashion [of apprenticeship training] which obtains at present."[152] T. Vest also remarked on educational travel. Perhaps referring to the School of Apprentices, or perhaps reflecting on his own experience as an artisan reporter, Vest declared that in order for young British workers "to acquire a better knowledge of artistic design" travel was of utmost importance:

> I know of no better way than, if possible in connection with some of our technical institutes, to grant travelling scholarships, when students who earn these scholarships under the Society of Arts, or the Royal Institute of British Architects, might travel together, and so exchange each others' ideas, which would be of mutual benefit to both.[153]

That Vest and other reporters made this connection between apprenticeship training, technical education, and travel makes sense, because they imbricated the older and familiar "journeymen's tramp" (the "workingman's grand tour") with Britain's growing appreciation for "systematic" technical education, the SA's scholarship and prize system, and their own experiences as educational travelers.[154] In making these connections, the artisan reporters contributed to the discourse of educational travel and educational reform that had inspired the first artisan exhibition tours in 1867.

The SA had initiated the tours as a way of alerting the nation to Europe's growing industrial power and of promoting educational reform as one solution to the challenge from abroad. Eliciting the support of skilled artisans and mechanics who attended continental exhibitions to study and compare British and European industry, social relations, and educational provisions, the SA drove this point home to working-class readers of the *Artisan Reports*. The rituals surrounding the tours – the propaganda, the selection process, and the reports themselves – created a "sensation" and a "stir" drawing attention to the implicit message of the tours. First, in order to maintain the health and wealth of the nation, workers would need to accept the bureaucratization of their trades through a systematic and standardized system of technical education. They, thus, must accept new relations of power surrounding the production of knowledge, relations that labor leaders hoped to control even as they were taken out of the shop floor and into the classroom. Furthermore, employers and the state would need to provide the means and the encouragement to see that Britain's "legions" were properly manned with "intellectual weapons" and "sound science." Only, through this joint effort, as M'Crae stated, could Britain hope to win the battle for economic "supremacy."

The strategic importance of the artisan exhibition tours to the educational reform movement also helped make working-class travel itself a branch of educational reform. As the Mansion House declared in 1889, "the educational effect of [its] system of reporting, in inducing workmen to study the requirements of other countries, and to profit by the knowledge of some ways in which they manage things better in France, is likely to be widespread."[155] Combining systematic study and reporting with the recreational aspects of a tour, this form of working-class travel encapsulated the tenets of the educational idea. Certainly, Vest's and Edmund's comments above suggest that the idea of travelling scholarships for skilled workers had caught on. But, would study abroad become a desired component of working-class education once reformers realized some of the objectives in their technical education campaign? In 1889, the Mansion House Committee had optimistically, and quite correctly, predicted that their system of artisan reporting and travel would be taken up by any number of civic and trade associations.[156] What the committee failed to predict, however, was that mass tours organized for artisan reporting on European exhibitions would soon lose their imperative with the passage of the 1889 Technical Instruction Act.[157]

The 1889 Act ushered in what has been described as "the golden age" of technical education, by providing state and municipal funds for technical schools. After nearly four decades of agitation, academic lobbies had at last succeeded in getting tax monies funneled to local county councils to support technical education committees and to fund new and existing technical schools for the artisan classes.[158] These institutions offered elementary education in addition to practical workshop training and courses in the fundamental principles of the skilled trades. Thus the Technical Instruction Act largely satisfied reformers' arguments for improving technical education, which the artisan exhibition tours had helped to provoke.

Despite the provisions made by the Technical Instruction Act, however, technical education remained the neglected stepchild of the British education system. By 1889, the higher branches of theoretical, pure, and applied science, as well as engineering, had made significant inroads into secondary, public, and university curriculums. To be sure, the classical liberal curriculum still dominated institutions of higher learning, but a grudging acceptance of scientific studies had been made during this period which recognized that specialists were needed to create new knowledge and to aid industrial progress if Britain was to compete economically with modern industrialized nations.[159] Yet, on the level of technical education government support was neither systematic nor comprehensive. Even with the helpful boost of government rates and a governing body (now under the direction of the London City and Guilds Institute), the state marginalized technical education and forced it to rely largely on charitable subscriptions and voluntary supervision for its everyday operations.[160] Associated with physical rather than with mental labor, and hostile to theoretical knowledge, technical education became "normatively part-time and institutionally marooned between the workplace and mainstream education."[161] Given technical education's low status and still less than adequate rates of provision, government support of working-class educational travel merited little consideration. For this reason, voluntary associations continued to organize different venues for educational travel, often maintaining the key values and aims of the earlier tours.

Reformist segments of civil society had supported working-class educational travel during the period of the artisan exhibition tours and continued to do so. Thomas Cook and the officers of the WMCIU had adopted the governmental imperatives of the educational idea that sought to control, contain, and neutralize working-class discontent through travel. In devising new travel opportunities for working people, these and other quasi-philanthropic groups also added to their programs the artisan exhibition tours' emphasis on technical education. Indeed, each successive artisan exhibition tour put these ideas of travel's utility back into circulation, propelling other workers' tours with similar ambitions. In 1870, Cook, for example, attempted to capitalize on the technical education movement in *The Excursionist*, combining his expanding travel enterprise with Britain's industrial predominance and workers' vocational training. Comparing himself to "a good general," Cook sought to muster troops of tourists for the summer season, assuring the "rank and file," that "no one need be left behind – or fail to experience the 'gratification' of travel." Speaking directly to workers, Cook continued:

> Even the factory operative might often, if he so pleased, share the enjoyments, to which the past generation were utter strangers. We have clubs for many purposes; why should we not have holiday clubs. A few pence saved weekly would enable a body of intelligent workmen to visit the principal cities of France, Belgium, and Holland, and perhaps Italy, where they would become acquainted with what their Continental rivals were doing, their modes of labour, and habits of life. Such practical experience as this could not fail to prove beneficial to our artisans, both individually and collectively. We must no longer glory in our isolation. If we are to maintain our industrial supremacy we must not affect to disregard what our continental brethren are doing.

Evidently, Cook was willing to subordinate his ecumenical philosophy to the rhetoric of industrial competition in order to attract working-class clients.[162] Later in the century, paternalist employers also maintained these themes in organizing tours (and holiday savings clubs) for their workers, much as Broadwood and Sons, piano manufacturers, had in 1867. The proliferation of company excursions for workers, from those of Cadbury Brothers (chocolate manufacturers), to those of Bass, Ratcliff, and Greeton, Ltd. (brewers), as one article on the subject noted, gave "poor people," at last, opportunities to "benefit" from travel, as few travel agents had attended to their "needs." On such tours, workers behaved with exemplary self "discipline," whether their employers accompanied them or not.[163] Lever Brothers (later Unilever), a paternalist soap manufacturer, offered a variety of travel and learning opportunities to its workers that predictably sought to win hearts and minds. For example, Lever Brothers treated 200 of its Port Sunlight workers with an all-expense-paid, one-day excursion to the 1900 Paris exhibition. In French police reports, surveillance operatives complemented the workers orderly public comportment and expressed astonishment at their employer's generosity. Reminiscent of the artisan tours, Lever Brothers also offered its employees cash awards for the best reports written about company holidays in Brussels. These visits to Lever's overseas factory in Brussels encouraged workers to identify leisure and learning with their service to the company.[164] Educational and social institutions for workers also integrated travel into their programs, such as the Working Men's College, which arranged summer excursions for its students, and the Toynbee Settlement House, which subsidized two travel clubs for its working-and lower-middle-class members.[165] Thus civil society maintained British culture's civilizing mission by seeking to create governable and self-governing workers and citizens through travel even after the artisan tours were rendered obsolete by the 1889 Technical Instruction Act and the technical schools that it helped to support, such as the Regent Street Polytechnic. As heir to the artisan tours, the Regent Street Polytechnic, in fact, made travel a core component of its educational programs and institutional ethos. Indeed, one legacy of the artisan tours was the reinvention of the grand tour for the modern, industrial context.

Like the aristocratic grand tour, the artisan tours made the continent the primary site of new learning experiences. But, with roots in the age of industrial capitalism, the artisan tours veered from the aristocratic path of the classical past on to a new path that privileged science and technology as the font of learning and the engine of progress. In this way, the artisan tours also anticipated twentieth-century modes of study abroad, with their vocational component, their public and private sources of funding, and their intersection with the state's evolving education system. Much like travel scholarships today, tour organizers selected artisan reporters through a competitive process based on skill, academic qualifications, and employer recommendations. Financed through state subsidies, philanthropic endowments, business or corporate grants, and private subscriptions, the artisan reporters also furthered the private and public interests of subscribers through their learning experiences abroad. Moreover, the artisan tours emerged out of a liberal educational reform movement surrounding technical and scientific instruction that was closely tied to the exigencies of international economic competition – a precursor to today's globalized education economy. In short, the artisan exhibition tours (and modern study abroad practices) were the outcome of industrialization and the attendant conditions of an emergent mass society, the professionalization (and eventual specialization) of science and industry, and international economic forces that preceded the "information" or "service" economies of post-industrial nations. The artisan tours thus contributed to study abroad practices that today equip students with the skills, academic qualifications, cultural backgrounds, and worldview necessary to develop national economies within a globalized market place. As the next chapter demonstrates, the Polytechnic continued to develop these characteristics in its own travel practices that included holiday learning tours, foreign language programs, and what amounts to vocational "work-study" courses abroad. In the process, however, the Polytechnic reproduced the class and gender exclusions typical of wider society. Ultimately, these exclusions limited travel's democratizing potential as a vehicle for personal transformation and citizenship.

5

Class Trips and the Meaning of British Citizenship: The Regent Street Polytechnic at Home and Abroad, 1871–1903

At the launch of the tourist season in the spring of 1895, John Cook, the director of one of Britain's largest commercial travel agencies, Thomas Cook & Son, sent a series of missives to the Education Department demanding redress. In the letters, Cook accused Quintin Hogg, the founder of the London Regent Street Polytechnic and Young Men's Christian Institute (YMCI), of using – perhaps even misappropriating – government educational grants to fund the Polytechnic Touring Association (PTA) and its "educational and co-operative tours." "Pray do not misunderstand me," Cook advised in one communiqué, "I am willing to admit that travelling is an important feature of education, but at the same time, I maintain that Thos. Cook & Son have done, and are doing more toward that particular line of education than anybody else in the Kingdom." Thus, Cook reasoned, "if the Polytechnic is entitled to a Government allowance, then I must ask, what is Thomas Cook & Son entitled to?"[1]

Had the Polytechnic, in fact, been misappropriating government grants to fund its own travel agency, Cook would have had a legitimate complaint. The Polytechnic originally developed educational tours for its students and members: young artisans, mechanics, and clerks. But, according to Cook, when the Polytechnic extended its travel services to the general public at bargain prices, it used the same government grants allocated for the education of its students to turn a profit. As Cook shrewdly pointed out, not only was the Polytechnic taking the government for a ride, but government taxes obliged him to supply the Polytechnic, albeit indirectly, with capital – the very ammunition it needed to compete with his own firm.

Cook's grievance found little purchase with government officials. In the inquiry that followed, Hogg – as uncompromising as Cook (but better connected) – satisfied the Education Department that Cook's complaint amounted to no more than a mean-spirited ploy to discredit the competition. Moreover, the inquiry revealed that Hogg had subsidized the tours himself.[2] Yet, there is more to this story than the rivalry of two travel titans for market shares.

Cook's tongue-in-cheek claim that his firm deserved a government sub-sidy for its own "educational" tours was not as far-fetched as it first appears. The late nineteenth century continued to witness considerable debate about both the role of government in secondary and adult education and the appropriate curriculum to train technical and clerical workers. Educational travel, broadly defined, was part of the conversation. Moreover, Cook initi-ated his case against Hogg at a political juncture at which conservative reac-tion threatened not only the democratizing ambitions of the school boards but also over two decades of educational innovation often subsidized, at least in part, by the state.[3] Wittingly or unwittingly, Cook plunged into the debate and, pulling the Polytechnic along with him, implicitly challenged the state to define the purpose of educational travel, to identify who would have access to it, and to explain the government's own role in facilitating it. Cook's dispute with Hogg, in other words, goaded the state into confer-ring on educational travel either the status of a "right" or a "privilege." As such, the dispute marks a crossroads of sorts in the institutional formation of educational travel.

This chapter retraces the steps leading to this crossroads. Entering into the world of the Polytechnic, the analysis examines how tensions surrounding the nature of citizenship influenced the Polytechnic's travel practices and their meanings. Celebrated in its own day as a progressive social institute and technical school for thousands of London's wage-earning youth, the Polytechnic connected mobility to the teaching of citizenship and to the fulfillment of its promise. The Polytechnic therefore has a story to tell about educational travel, its ideological foundations, and the students and administrators who contributed to its formation. This analysis will show, however, that the pressures stemming from mass society in Britain and from international economic competition in Europe and the United States created the conditions for what was truly modern about educational travel: that is, the mobilization of ordinary youth, rather than elites alone, to acquire personal growth and new skills around the world.[4] The mobilization of a young and, in a sense, cosmopolitan working class – one that was bilin-gual, open to learning from diverse cultures, and at ease occupying foreign spaces – hinged, in part, upon the creation of new travel practices designed to educate future voters for citizenship, a project in which the Polytechnic had a role to play.[5]

Nineteenth-century social reformers, as this book has shown, had long used travel (and culture more generally) as a pedagogical tool with which to regulate, elevate, and instruct working people in the middle-class values of respectability and self-governance. John Cook's father, Thomas Cook, for one, had viewed mass travel as a "true agent of civilisation." Although John Cook eventually steered his father's agency toward a more affluent, even royal clientele, other philanthropists, such as Hogg, stepped in to fill the gap.[6] Thus, in the 1880s – in another period characterized by elite fears of mass democracy as well as the failures of classical liberalism – the Polytechnic expanded travel opportunities for London youth and aligned them to its educational and social agenda.

Embedded in the progressive movements of the time, particularly within the "new liberal" imaginary that sought to reconcile capitalist production with social welfare, the Polytechnic's overriding goal was to integrate its working- and lower- middle-class students into the nation as active citizens and moral beings. The Polytechnic shared the political convictions of the Oxford idealists, for example, in recognizing the necessity of an interventionist state, one that would enable working people, through education, to realize their human potential; and it shared with other youth-oriented philanthropies the ambition to teach students their reciprocal obligations to the "common good."[7] Reformers anticipated, therefore, that student experiences of these rights and duties within the Polytechnic community would ultimately serve as an antidote to the class divisiveness and alienation of modern mass society. The Polytechnic thus viewed its travel practices, much like Thomas Cook four decades earlier, as agents of reform.

Since its founding as the Young Men's Christian Institute in 1871, the Polytechnic had fostered an institutional ethos that encouraged students to travel, and dignified their experiences abroad as a duty. The Polytechnic created its own labor bureau that facilitated students' emigration and work overseas. To assist this process, it also developed informal networks between the Polytechnic in the metropole and its far-flung students in its self-described "Poly colonies." And, presaging study abroad programs today, it launched its own travel agency to organize holidays and educational tours that enabled self-improving students to cultivate their talents as individuals within group contexts. In the aggregate, these collective practices fostered students' corporate identity as "Poly boys" and underscored the importance of travel as a responsibility to engage the world as British citizens and in service to the empire, a facet of social imperialism that incorporated ordinary people into the imperial collectivity and that subordinated diverse class identities to racial and ethnic identities.[8] The Polytechnic's travel culture thus became a basis for "cultural citizenship," a "process of self-making and of being made within webs of power linked to the nation state and civil society."[9]

As a facilitator of mobility, the Polytechnic attracted urban and skilled working- and lower-middle-class youth who associated it less with disciplinary power than with positive change and innovation that, for them, defined modernity and fueled their ambitions.[10] Yet, as the dispute between Cook and Hogg illustrates, the Polytechnic was also a source of conflict, one that suggests the limits to student agency within the new liberal project and of educational travel itself. This chapter thus analyzes the Polytechnic and its travel practices as a case study in modern mobility. It examines the new opportunities for advancement that the Polytechnic courses and clubs promoted. However, it also examines enduring economic and cultural obstacles that students experienced in seeking to improve their lives.[11] In so doing, the analysis ranges widely to explore the links between travel and citizenship "discursively and experientially" in the life of the Polytechnic at home and around the world.[12]

All but hidden from history, the Polytechnic barely registers in the historiography of the era despite its influence on multiple generations of London youth. This analysis, therefore, takes a different path. The first leg of this journey begins with an introduction to the institute's diverse student population, its leaders, and its educational courses and social clubs. The analysis pays particular attention to how the Polytechnic bears the stamp of Quintin Hogg's individual personality and vision. It explores the ideological foundations of his philanthropy, which reflected his evangelicalism and sense of civic duty, and it examines his personal "theology of love" that connects him to a fraternal community of reformers in London. The analysis then broadens to trace the Polytechnic's travel ethos in its institutional literature and travel brochures and in its classrooms and clubrooms. Further afield, the analysis continues with students' long-term emigration and employment over- seas that the Polytechnic's social and educational programs encouraged and that were fundamental to the formation of study abroad. The journey concludes, however, with conflict and contestation. Arriving once again at the crossroads illuminated by Cook and Hogg's dispute, the analysis examines class feuds and sex wars, in which students' individual and collective experiences of travel and citizenship reveal how social boundaries were established, manipulated, or challenged within the Polytechnic community and, by extension, British society.

The Polytechnic: A Door to Opportunity

Bill Surrey, who carted freight to and from the London rails by day and attended the Polytechnic by night, wanted out. With "twenty pounds odd" saved and more to come, Surrey pictured himself owning a "bit of land" in the United States and "see[ing] the world." How he traveled, however, mattered as much to Surrey as what he would see. "It's all nonsense," he declared, "pretending to see things without money." He would travel, therefore, with good clothes on his back and cash in his pocket – never as a "tramp." The occasion for this disclosure was a chance encounter near Paddington Station in the late 1880s with Charles Finger, the son of a former employer. Inviting Finger to his small room that overlooked a canal off Harrow Road, Surrey shared a plain meal with his guest. They reminisced about the past and plotted out their futures.[13]

The material circumstances of Finger's life stood in stark contrast to Surrey's own. In his autobiography, Finger explained that he first met Surrey in the Mayfair home of his parents, a well-to-do German tailor and his Irish wife, where he knew his old acquaintance as the kitchen "knife boy."[14] Finger's parents, however, had since fallen on hard times and had migrated to the United States. Although Finger had opted to stay behind and to make his way alone in the city, he, like Surrey, also imagined a future enriched by travel, and eventually spent several years roughing it through the wilds and frontier towns of South and North America. The Polytechnic helped set him on this path.[15]

Surrey introduced Finger to the Polytechnic that very night. Finger recalls that when he first entered through the Polytechnic's doors and into a hallway "crowded with young men and lads" from "varied walks of life," he was instantly drawn into the "buoyant companionship" that the institute offered. Preferring friendship over isolation, Finger joined the Polytechnic and became particularly active in its social, literary, and political clubs. However, in 1890 Finger's club activities came to an end when he launched his travel adventures (and a literary career) with three other Poly boys, who were also bound for South America. Thus, for Surrey and Finger, one a member of the struggling but upwardly mobile working class and the other a member of the artisan aristocracy threatened by downward mobility, the Polytechnic, as Finger writes, became a "door to opportunity," one that inspired "ambitious young men" to envision "new horizons" in "trades and professions" that no longer seemed quite so out of reach to them.[16]

Multiple interests with a stake in educational and social reform expanded these horizons by contributing to the Polytechnic's development. Education boards, chambers of commerce, trade unions, popular ministries, and public moralists supplied the Polytechnic with state and charitable funds, supervised course content, organized religious services, and publicized the Polytechnic's many social activities and philanthropic virtues. Hogg's friends and family also donated time and money to the institute, as did their wives and children. The cricketer and evangelical Kynaston Studd served as the Polytechnic's unpaid secretary for 19 years before becoming its president after Hogg's death in 1903. Studd's son, R. G. Studd, followed in his father's footsteps, becoming the managing director of the PTA in 1922.[17] Further down the social scale, students often became Polytechnic teachers and administrators, as well as the institute's most generous and consistent benefactors. Robert Mitchell, the son of a police detective and a skilled metal worker by trade, joined the institute at the age of 16. Mitchell eventually became the brilliant director of the Polytechnic's education department and with his wife "pioneered" the Polytechnic's "co-operative educational travel" program.[18] The example of Studd, Mitchell, and others at the Polytechnic encouraged young men like Surrey and Finger to forge new identities as they prepared for the future in the classrooms and social clubs of the Polytechnic. Even so, it was Hogg who, according to many accounts, held the "most influence" over the institute and its students.[19]

Hogg adopted several identities and roles throughout his life that would have a direct impact on the Polytechnic, its students, and its travel programs. The seventh son of Sir James Weir Hogg, twice chairman of the East India Company, Hogg (1845–1903) attended Eton, where he developed a charismatic personality as a star footballer and campus evangelical, an asset he used to draw support for his later philanthropic endeavors. After Eton, Hogg carved out his own fortune in Demerara sugar, becoming a wealthy City merchant with colonial interests and financial investments across the globe. Hogg's wealth and stature thus gave him a commanding say in municipal politics. Serving as a liberal alderman to the London County Council (LCC) from 1889 to 1895, Hogg was especially active in progressive educational reform, which was strengthened by his commitment to "practical" Christianity, the basis of his social activism and philanthropy.[20]

With little tolerance for zealotry or literal interpretations of the Bible, Hogg took religion itself to mean "brotherly love" and "fellowship."[21] Hogg's daughter and biographer, Ethel Wood, explains that he first translated this belief into action at the age of 18 when he started a "ragged school" for indigent children. Joining forces with other London philanthropists, and assisted by like-minded Eton alumni, Hogg was determined to turn "wretched little chaps" into "God- fearing, respectable citizens." He taught them to read, steered them toward a trade, and helped many more emigrate.[22] Eventually, however, Hogg shifted his attention to creating a secondary school for "better-class boys" in the wage-earning sector.[23] Hogg envisioned, as he believed "Christ" would want, a free and compulsory secondary school system in Britain that would see as its duty the development of each student's "capacity as an individual and as a member of a community."[24] For Hogg, this meant educating the "whole man," his motto for nurturing students' spiritual, intellectual, physical, and vocational "talents."[25] Hogg, therefore, viewed state intervention in educational reform as a moral necessity and a national imperative. Hogg united both of these ambitions in founding the Young Men's Christian Institute (YMCI) for young apprentices at Long Acre in 1871. When demand exceeded available space in 1882, Hogg moved the institute to the Polytechnic on Regent Street. Previously a venue for popular entertainment and scientific demonstrations, the Polytechnic was ideally suited for the expansion of the institute's "experimental" educational programs and Hogg's vision of reform.[26]

During the day, the Polytechnic offered secondary schooling and vocational training to students between the ages of 8 and 17, while at night, artisans, mechanics, and clerks between the ages of 16 and 22 (later extended to 26) attended classes in technical, science, and commercial subjects. Students and nonstudents who paid a small "membership" fee also had access to the institute's vast sports grounds and recreational facilities, as well as to evening concerts and popular lectures, the largest (reportedly) mock parliament in Britain, social and language clubs, and a variety of travel programs. Regardless of one's status as a "student," a "member," or a "student-member," Polytechnic administrators encouraged one and all to regard themselves as "Poly boys." By 1894, the Polytechnic's numbers had grown to 14,000, and its educational facilities were augmented by local taxes and government grants that also subsidized the founding of 13 new Polytechnics based on the Regent Street model. These funds lifted much of the financial burden off of Hogg's shoulders, but they also made the Polytechnic accountable to the state – which was the opening Cook had used to challenge the PTA's legitimacy as a commercial or public agency.[27]

By this time, too, Hogg and his wife, Alice Graham Hogg, had founded the Young Women's Christian Institute (YWCI) for "working girls" in trades ranging from domestic service to typing. In the 1890s, the Polytechnic opened some of its courses and facilities to the YWCI, training scores of young women to enter the workforce. The dominant gender discourse at the Polytechnic, however, defined ideal womanhood in terms of marriage and child rearing. This conventional view of British womanhood was, in part, defensive, reflecting conservative fears over women's growing emancipation from the domestic sphere, such as race degeneration and the feminization of the work place; but, it also reflected the Polytechnic's prevailing homosocial environment, which was par for the course in youth rescue work.[28]

Although students occupied social strata far above the indigent children of Hogg's early philanthropy, reformers expected the Polytechnic to transform potential "delinquents" into "men of the future," who would thus form a positive identification with the authority of the institute, the city, and the state.[29] The Polytechnic, in other words, was expected to produce not only "good workers" but also civic-minded individuals committed to the "common good" rather than to narrow class interests.[30] The prescription for this intervention was the same at the Polytechnic as it was at boys' clubs. Based on the public school model, it delivered moral guidance through group activities that shaped corporate and civic identities and that tested manly vigor and character with a strong dose of muscular Christianity.[31] Central to this guidance and key to the Polytechnic's success, Hogg averred, was the "personal touch."

Hogg, faculty, and associates made themselves exceedingly accessible to students in seeking to create a nurturing environment at the institute. In making the Polytechnic a "home" and the source of "true friendship," they exercised what Lauren M. E. Goodlad terms "pastoral charity," a variant of the "pastoral pedagogy" that Ian Hunter identifies with modern bureaucracy and the construction of self-regulating citizens in service to the state. Like Hunter, Goodlad draws on Foucault's concept of pastoral governance. However, Goodlad de-emphasizes the unequal or coercive nature of cross-class relationships underpinned by governmental power, charitable, or otherwise. Reformers and philanthropists, Goodlad shows, imagined civic life as a symbolic extension of home, as a personal realm in which to foster "intersubjective" relationships between the middle and working classes. In this realm, responsive working-class subjects assumed a moral, if not an economic or social, equality with their benefactors, much like the relationship between Hogg and the young metal worker, Robert Mitchell, who began his Polytechnic career as the institute's first (elected) secretary. For Hogg, the "personal touch" was a basis both for pastoral guidance in educating the "whole man" and for cross-class cohesion. According to his daughter, Hogg willingly "sacrificed" his own "identity" to achieve this end.[32]

In the many interviews Hogg granted reporters, he conveyed his dedication to the institute and his intense connection to "my boys" – a term of endearment he used for young students as well as aging alumni. Hogg awed reporters, for instance, by knowing the names and personal stories of each of the Day School boys. And in another familiar anecdote, reporters noted that Hogg's family residence adjoined the Polytechnic. More than a metaphor for pastoral care, home life and civic duty literally merged when Hogg connected the two buildings with a passage that led from his study into the Polytechnic gymnasium.[33] Hogg's identification with students and, as Lunn recalls, his "detachment" from his "own people" and his "own class," thus links him to a coterie of reformers who, as Seth Koven has sensitively described, found their flights across the class divide sources of "personal liberation and self- realization – social, spiritual, and sexual."[34]

The crucible of Hogg's self-realization was the Polytechnic. His daughter writes that "the Polytechnic had indeed become his sole purpose in life, his very reason for existence."[35] At the Polytechnic, Hogg made common cause with students' aspirations and, in exchange, earned their devotion in life-long relationships that seem to have been based on mutual trust and respect. "Nothing," Hogg wrote in a letter to a former student in Colorado, "has sustained and helped me so much, as far as earthly things go, as the love and sympathy of my boys."[36] Reprinted in Hogg's biography, this letter and others expressed his "theology of love" and active pastoral guidance. It also, however, may suggest a form of sexual "liberation" that would have been impossible to express openly.

When Hogg died in his bath of carbon-monoxide poisoning in 1903, George Ives, an older Polytechnic student and early activist for "homogenic" rights, speculated in his diary that Hogg not only took his own life but "destroyed himself" in order to avoid imminent criminal prosecution for homosexuality.[37] If so, it was not only a tragic end to the life of a revered philanthropist but complicates the Polytechnic narrative by introducing a homoerotic, but by no means religiously irreconcilable, dimension to Hogg's commitment to "brotherly love." Merely one among many "fraternal ideologies" circulating in what Koven identifies as a distinctive male reformist community, Hogg's "theology of love" shared in common with these ideologies a fervent belief in the "healing power of brotherhood" and similarly wove within its language homoerotic and evangelical overtones that charged fraternal friendships with a current of sexual energy.[38] The Polytechnic would thus have presented some students (and perhaps Hogg himself) a space in which to express same-sex love, even if it was couched, consciously or unconsciously, in the language of Christian brotherhood, a cross-class fraternity, or more perilously, as Ives also notes in his diary, in the coupling of "working class men" in the changing booths of the Polytechnic's "baths."[39]

The Polytechnic's homosexual subculture is a strong reminder of the complex motivations driving not only individuals within the reform community but students as well, who had their own uses for the institute. The aims of reformers, therefore, should not obscure the dynamic character of the Polytechnic's educational and social programs, which owed their development to an ongoing partnership, and at times a negotiation, between students, Hogg, faculty, and associates.[40] Unlike the children of the club movement, most students were old enough and independent enough to act as agents in their own lives and to contribute to the institute and its culture in meaningful ways. Student councils and club officers influenced administrative decisions from building plans to the PTA's travel itineraries. Student pressure groups lobbied for new programs, such as elocution classes, the Polytechnic parliament, and the founding of the YWCI for their "sisters."[41] And student journalists cut their teeth in the profession with contributions to weekly editions of the *Polytechnic Magazine*, which both chronicled and critiqued the life of the institute.[42]

Thus, in this liberal, liminal environment that respected public opinion and courted popular consent, students felt encouraged to identify as citizens within a Polytechnic polity.

Experimental and progressive, metropolitan and imperial, the Polytechnic provided students with not only a homosocial and cross-class (and to a certain extent, mixed-sex) contact zone but also a fluid and transient space of identity formation and exchange that brought the metropolis into the Polytechnic and the Polytechnic into the world. The Polytechnic's evolving travel culture embodied these traits. In providing an institutional structure for nurturing the "whole man," the Polytechnic offered students, as Henry Lunn, its Sunday evening preacher declared, a sphere for social learning in the rights and duties of individuals within a collectivity that "encircles the globe."[43]

The Spirit of Travel

The essence of mobility and modernity at the Polytechnic was the "spirit of travel," the theme of an 1894 "occasional paper" published in the *Polytechnic Magazine*. In the paper, the author, a "Good Englishman," "claimed that his countrymen held "a first position as the most traveled people of modern times." To the "Good Englishman," the English penchant for travel constituted a national trait and its actuation a fundamentally patriotic act. "Nothing," he argued, "is as certain to make us love our own country."[44] What it meant to "love one's country," was, of course, open to debate at the institute, and the *Polytechnic Magazine* duly records multiple political perspectives on the subject.[45] For his part the "Good Englishman" defined patriotism in somewhat cosmopolitan terms, echoing notions of "complementarity" expressed in *The Good of Going to Paris* in 1867, but without Holyoake's enthusiasm for international co-operation. The author did not advocate dismantling the nation state or salute the universal brotherhood of man, but he did argue that the path to progress required the adoption, rather than rejection as alien or unnatural, of the best qualities of other nations. The primary "advantage" of travel, he explained, is that one is able to appreciate the merits of one's own country in contrast with other countries and, at the same time, learn "some new good" from "every town that can be utilized at home." In fact, many of Britain's virtues, he argued, are owed to encounters with foreign others. Thus, "just as our language is a collection of the good points of many languages, and our people the result of the intermingling of many races, so is our commercial position throughout the world the result of the spirit of travel that has impelled England's sons to trot over the globe whenever opportunities arise."[46] Few students, however, seem to have put the "Good Englishman's" views to useful effect. Comparisons in the *Polytechnic Magazine* that faulted Britain's education system, for example, usually examined German and French pedagogical advances with a jaundiced eye, always mindful of economic competition and imperial tensions.[47]

Even members of the French club denigrated France when opportunities arose to compare it with Britain – a show of bad manners that earned them a "dressing down" by the club's secretary.[48] Nevertheless, few students would have denied the importance of travel in the "Good Englishman's" rhetoric. The "spirit of travel" strengthened their collective identity as "Poly boys," and they often linked their affection for the Polytechnic with the pride they shared as active participants in the nation's prosperity and imperial destiny.

The "spirit of travel" permeated almost every aspect of the Polytechnic's work. In the Polytechnic's reading room, students had access to hundreds of travel- themed memoirs, journals, and novels, as well as maps that administrators periodically refreshed to reflect new territory brought under the British flag.[49] To help students understand the practical implications of their studies, the Polytechnic also invited speakers to discuss global commercial conditions, such as the assistant secretary of the London Chamber of Commerce, who lectured on the "Markets of the World."[50] Thrilling wider audiences, celebrity explorers, war correspondents, and missionaries entertained and informed students with inspirational and hair- raising stories of imperial battles, scientific discovery, and conversion.[51] This trade in sensational tales complemented what the Polytechnic described as its "cosmopolitan character." From time to time, the *Polytechnic Magazine* boasted that students from China, Russia, Poland, Greece, Germany, Spain, and France had made the Polytechnic their "home away from home," including two

"Coreans," a Mr. Yee and a Mr. Yer.[52] Further helping students to become accustomed to the movement of people, ideas, and British power globally, indigenous representatives from the colonies visited the Polytechnic, some of whom participated in its parliament, such as John Ojijatekha Brant-Sero, the Mohawk civil-rights activist. The *Polytechnic Magazine* reported that Brant-Sero's motion for "'removing all disabilities which at present prevent the greater proportion of the Empire's population from following a civil or military career,'" would likely be seconded by a "Hindoo friend," also present at the debate.[53]

Not least, the Polytechnic's commitment to teaching foreign languages, such as German and Hindustani, gave added impetus to the "spirit of travel," preparing students to compete with Britain's imperial and industrial rivals abroad.[54] The *Polytechnic Magazine* continually plugged these courses as well as the Polytechnic's language clubs, citing the urgent threat of international competition. Guest speakers reinforced this discourse. In a speech to the carriage-building class on becoming "smart voters and intelligent workmen," George Hooper, the London carriage maker who had contributed to educational debates and to the discourse of educational travel since the 1867 Artisan Tours, emphasized the value of language and travel specifically for British artisans.[55] "Up to very recent times" Hooper explained, "every young German artisan must of necessity work for three years in foreign countries, to improve his skill, gain experience, and acquire knowledge of foreign languages." This form of educational travel, Hooper argued, had made Germany "a nation." The lesson could not be plainer. The opportunities for advancement that the Polytechnic offered, Hooper insisted, "should be made use of for your own personal advantage, as well as for being individuals forming parts of a great nation."[56]

Encouraging stories in the *Polytechnic Magazine* about students living and working abroad advertised the success of the institute's language campaigns. One member of the French club, for example, was chosen to represent his firm during the Brussels Exhibition of 1897. There he put his Polytechnic patois to good use in attracting new business for the firm. The rewards of this success, he gloated, included a continental trip three to four times a year and the "patriotic satisfaction of knowing that every penny he earns comes out of the Continent to England." "Such instances as these," the *Polytechnic Magazine* declared, "are encouraging and useful examples to others," especially given the "pertinacity of the German clerk." Nationalistic and imperialistic, the Polytechnic clearly defined the duty of citizenship in terms of language, labor, and travel abroad.[57]

Hogg himself modeled the Polytechnic's travel ethos for his "boys." In long letters posted during holiday and business trips abroad, Hogg regaled students with stories of indolent "natives" and Britain's civilizing mission. Just as important, Hogg encouraged students to engage for themselves "Greater Britain beyond the seas."[58] Many obliged. After students struck out on their own, they often returned the favor of Hogg's letters with their own correspondence. Writing from all corners of the globe, they reported joining "Poly colonies" headed by "Poly consuls" who populated the world as emigrants, entrepreneurs, missionaries, soldiers, engineers, and clerks.[59] Some "colonies" originated as deliberate collectivities when students tied their fortunes together, such as 30 tailors by trade, who worked a homestead in Colorado, initially subsidized by Hogg.[60] Other "colonies" emerged as organic clusters when former students met up at sites with high emigration rates of British nationals. Either way, informal "colonies" gave rise to a network of Polytechnic alumni with ties to each other, to Britain, and to the empire. Reflecting Britain's "spirit of travel" the Polytechnic's student networks facilitated the identity of a global collectivity. As the *Polytechnic Magazine* enthused, the institute "has done a truly national, nay, an international work, for the lusty growth of the Regent Street Polytechnic is sending forth its branches like a mighty oak."[61] Finger, whose "roving spirit" had landed him for a time in Argentina as a horse trader, knew this firsthand. Stumbling on an "old Polyite" in the shanty town of Lacuna Grande, he declared, "it is a fine brotherhood, after all – the Poly."[62]

"The Death of the Grand Tour"

The Polytechnic gave the "spirit of travel" more concrete form when it began organizing specific "holiday" tours for its students. Prior to the formal organization of the Polytechnic's travel programs, students took short holidays with Hogg or on their own. In the early 1870s, Hogg founded, for example, "special holiday homes," in which up to 70 boys at a time lodged in the country or at the seaside with Hogg and his family. In 1877, Hogg ventured further afield, taking nearly a hundred students to the Paris Exhibition.[63] At the same time, students organized their own holidays, making their mark on the Polytechnic's evolving travel culture.[64] Some traveled solo and afterward posted reviews of their trips to assist fellow students plan their own holidays.[65] Other students traveled in groups, organizing short tours over Easter and bank holidays. Meeting up with former "Polyites" living and working abroad, especially in the "Poly colonies" of Paris, they described how their friends acted as "cicerones," whisking them from one tourist site to another.[66]

Tapping into students' informal demand for holidays, the Polytechnic began arranging formal tours of its own in the 1880s that contained strong educational and collectivist components. The institute's first official "educational tour" in 1888 has been described as the "first school journey on record."[67] Accompanied by three teachers and a doctor, 51 boys of the Day School enjoyed an "extended geography lesson" in Switzerland.[68] Committed to the idea that a trip abroad constituted an "essential development in practical education," Hogg and Mitchell organized more excursions, such as cheap eight-day tours of the 1889 Paris exhibition intended to improve students' vocational skills. A total of 2100 young men and 400 young women participated in the tours, which took place between mid-June and late September. To facilitate the travel arrangements and to encourage collective identities, the Polytechnic organized each tour group according to students' membership in a particular club, occupation, or, in the case of the sister institute, a sex.[69] Thus, the plumbing school students occupied the same railway car on their way to the French capital and, after arriving, lodged and took in the sights together. In a report "The Plumbers' Week in Paris," penned by the pseudonym "one of them," the author (hoping not to replicate information gathered in the Mansion House "Artisan Reports") described how they managed to combine leisure and learning on their trip. Their first lesson on the road was an ad hoc inspection of the toilets at the Rouen station, which they immediately pronounced "unsanitary." When they reached their destination, however, they found more to praise. Guided by a former "Poly boy," who had become a master plumber in Paris, students not only visited the exhibition but took an excursion through the city's famous sewers and visited a sewage farm at Gennvillies, where they sipped its crystal-clear water and sampled its produce. The tour, according to the guide, had successfully infused their holiday with "actual instruction."[70] With this success, the Polytechnic continued to offer tours each year, developing a sophisticated program of study abroad opportunities by the turn of the century that encouraged educational and collective experiences, from language "holiday courses" for "commercial students" at Grenoble University to a tour of Vienna for the Polytechnic's architecture and building classes.[71] Becoming an essential feature of a modern education, the Polytechnic's tours, as one pamphlet stated, had bridged the gap from traditional artisanal training to the educational requirements of an emerging technological class. While apprentices "in the old days" had concluded their shop-floor training with travels through the "provinces" on the "journeyman's tramp," Polytechnic students supplemented their training with the PTA's "holiday trips" – the "workmen's only means of getting the education that travel alone imparts."[72]

The Polytechnic's vocationally driven tours satisfied the educational needs of specific niches at the institute, but for the healthful recreation and cultural elevation of general holiday travelers, the Polytechnic also bought and developed a cluster of Swiss chalets to operate as a holiday camp and launched its "co-operative and educational tours," both of which received considerable notice in the progressive press. In 1892, the *Review of Reviews*, William Stead's monthly journal, featured the Polytechnic in an article on cooperative travel organizations that conducted tours for the benefit of their members rather than profit alone. What was vitally important about this new leisure movement, Stead reported, was that it gave the "hard working many" the experience of "intelligent foreign travel" and, just as critically, destroyed the "barrier of reserve and isolation between individual members which militate so strongly against corporate life in great towns." Stead's reference to "corporate life" signified an organic common culture and community that dissolved the fissures of modern mass society. The hardship of traveling long distances en masse, he emphasized, required "mutual respect and reliance," which in turn produced "a public-spirited unselfishness." As such, cooperative tours presented Victorians with a new social space and pedagogic field for relating to one another as members of a voluntary collectivity (the tour group) and as British citizens in developing a "deeper and wider comprehension of historical and human solidarity." Praising the Polytechnic's cooperative and educational tours to Switzerland, Norway, and Chicago, Stead validated its ambition to achieve the progressive ideal of rational recreation and corporate integration.[73]

With this encouragement, the Polytechnic expanded its operations still further by opening its cooperative tours to the public in 1894, when it inaugurated the Polytechnic Touring Association as a tourist agency with its own office next to the main entrance of the institute. Charging only a small increase over the cut-rate prices arranged for students, Hogg channeled the profits back into the Polytechnic and claimed that the tours constituted a part of its "educational work."[74] The PTA's brochures soon boasted that it had assisted thousands of "limited means" to get "the best value for the money paid" for their holidays.[75]

For progressive boosters like Stead, the PTA's success would have been celebrated as an important achievement. But for wealthy travelers at odds with mass culture, commercial appeals to "value" symbolized the degradation of a formerly elite cultural practice. Indeed, much like the anti-tourist vitriol that Cook's early excursionists endured, Studd writes that in 1891, one magazine turned PTA tourists into the butt of a joke, warning "swells" to avoid Norway on their holidays because it had been overrun by "dreadful Polytechnic people."[76] PTA tourists, however, read lofty sentiments into the term "value." The PTA stressed that its tours were not only more affordable than any of its competitors (namely, Thomas Cook & Son), but that the nation's leading education experts had endorsed their educational qualities. Customer testimonials backed these claims. Ignoring elite condemnation of "dreadful" Polytechnic tourists, they described how they found their brief time on the road profoundly meaningful.[77]

Looking back on the foundation of the P.T.A. and its significance to participants, Studd explained that in the beginning one "didn't go for a holiday to the continent. You went on an expedition. And you didn't go alone but with a party, a mob, a carefully selected mob that you could trust, that trusted you, in which respectability was reciprocal." Claiming the road as their own, Polytechnic tourists, therefore, reveled in their sociability and reportedly dismissed the individuated travel experiences of their social superiors, as their boisterous reunions at the Polytechnic, some drawing more than a thousand participants, attest. The Polytechnic's tours thus offered reformers a venue in which to imagine, create, and test their desires for an orderly, educated, and skilled electorate, and they offered tourists opportunities to participate in an experience that symbolized all that modernity and mobility promised Britons at the turn of the century. As Studd, with a populist's flourish, declared, the elite "Grand Tour" became a "corpse" when the first "apprentice mechanic" crossed the Swiss Alps on a "Polytechnic educational and co- operative tour."[78]

Travel Writing and the Poly Boy Romance

Teeming with multiple possibilities for engaging the world, the Polytechnic produced a variety of travel texts that conveyed the "spirit of travel" and the institute's collective identity in reports, program itineraries, posters, and advertisements. Students living and working abroad, for instance, inundated the *Polytechnic Magazine* with their letters, warranting regular columns that headlined the Polytechnic's connection to empire in "From over the Water," "Colonial and Imperial," "Empire Building," and "Our Foreign Legion." Over time their letters shared discursive properties that helped extend the webs of the Polytechnic community in networks of mutual assistance around the globe. Students understood, for instance, that it was an "unwritten law," as George Wiles teased in a letter scratched out in the goldfields of Western Australia, to list job prospects for others at "home" contemplating emigration.[79] Other correspondents offered to hold a hand out to new arrivals and gratefully publicized the help they had received from students who had preceded them. Perhaps less consciously, most refrained from being too down- in-the-mouth when frontier life got "jolly" tough, as Hogg sometimes put it, although reports of "bad luck" filtered through.[80] Early on, in fact, Hogg cautioned students to take glowing reports of emigrant life with a grain of salt, as "men do not print the records of their failures."[81] Indeed, most letters, especially those of the younger Day School boys, produced a Polytechnic version of the public school spirit that was standard fare in juvenile periodicals, such as *The Boy's Own Paper*, or replicated the homosocial environments and homoerotic imagery found in the adventure romances of Robert Louis Stevenson and Rider Haggard. Expressing all the same manly courage and dedication to empire as their public school rivals, they depicted a playfully masculine rough-and-tumble world largely bereft of women.[82] Collectively, they underscored a belief in Britain's civilizing mission and the continuing importance of civic duty and corporate life as "Poly boys" and as British subjects at home and in the world.[83]

Characteristic of this genre are the letters of Don Homfray, a "Day School boy." Addressed to Hogg and printed in the *Polytechnic Magazine*, Homfray's letters chart his ocean journey from England to South Africa in 1899, where he was to join the Natal Mounted Police. In a voice redolent of Stevenson's

Jim Hawkins, the youthful hero of *Treasure Island*, Homfray conveyed the thrill of ocean travel, marveling at sharks and "monster" jellyfish spied from the ship's bow. But he also hinted at dangers lurking below deck. Asserting his identity as a respectable youth, Homfray reported that he could not "bear to mix with some of the rough people" on the ship and more ominously still "dread[ed] when the time comes to turn in at night." Sensing, perhaps, sexual danger, Homfray resourcefully found a secret berth above-deck in which to lay his head. There, in his solitude, he thought about his "old Poly friends" and pondered "the land" that would become his new "home." Still musing from his hiding place, Homfray concluded his letter with a melancholy sigh, writing that "Every now and then the cool evening breeze carries the sound of voices and merry laughter to me," while "far below the engine gently throbs, and I feel the soft, light rolling of the ship as it rides the Atlantic swell, leaving behind it a long white foaming train. We are now 5,000 miles from you."[84]

Predictably, Homfray's subsequent letters lost their thoughtful sensitivity to the new experience of travel. Expressing crude confidence in the imperial mission, Homfray narrated his successful integration into the police force, which allowed him to live like a "gentleman." True to form, Homfray also encouraged students to try their fortunes in South Africa as opportunities awaited those who could speak "Dutch, Kaffir, [or] Hindustani," as well as for volunteers to fight a war that promised to be "glorious."[85] Homfray's letters, in essence, narrated the Poly- boy romance, a story that countless others articulated with equal attention to form and content. Frederick Slade, a military engineer in Bangalore, India offers another example. Soon after his arrival in 1893, he experienced a rapid rise in rank, becoming a "full-blown sergeant" in less than a year. Wondering at his good fortune, he wrote to the Polytechnic that "I should scarcely be full corporal if I had remained in England." His studies at the Polytechnic, however, had paid off. As a non-commissioned officer in India, he was entitled to "live like a lord," with two household servants and holidays spent in the jungle stalking tigers. But, these privileges did not deter him from flying "the Poly colors" and keeping "up the reputation of the good ole Poly." In 1895 he became determined to turn his regiment into "whole" men and to inculcate the moral manliness and Christian fellowship that was the core of the Polytechnic's mission. Although Slade's students lacked the "manners and intellect" of the "Poly Boys" in London, they enthusiastically followed his dictates.. Slade thus predicted that if every garrison town supported such "clubs," the "morality of both soldiers and civilians would go up, and the march of civilisation would be accelerated." Reproducing Hogg's pastoral role in Bangalore, Slade had taken it upon himself to nurture "a feeling of brotherliness" among them, extending the Poly boy romance to colonials.[86] A powerful narrative of identity and fellowship, the Poly Boy romance not only sustained, but reproduced the Polytechnic community. Thus even in the Polytechnic's darker moments, when reports came through of students who had met their deaths far from home, the *Polytechnic Magazine* highlighted those who had drawn their last breath while nursed by the "loving hands" of a "Poly boy." In the Poly boy romance that made the British world its stage, a Poly boy need not die alone.[87] Such gripping, as well as more mundane, tales of students in the world made the *Polytechnic Magazine* an anchor of identity that alumni prized. As many former students who kept up subscriptions testified, it had become their "favourite magazine" because it kept them connected "to the dear old place" and to each other.[88] Contributing to the immediacy of the Polytechnic over space and time, their letters rejected the valorization of the heroic individual typical of adventure romances, affirming instead a heroic collectivity comprised of peripatetic "Poly boys."

Students who vacationed together replicated the collective ethos of the Poly- boy romance in their holiday narratives. "Under the aegis of the Poly flag," students wrote of forming "troops" that "stormed," "marched," "bivouacked," "invaded," and "occupied" the continent, peppering their travel narratives with patriotic cheers for the Union Jack, roast beef, and English tea.[89] Although the *Polytechnic Magazine* records occasional objections to students' exuberant nationalism or jingoistic outbursts, their identification with British imperialism and sense of national superiority was difficult to contain.[90] Thus, with a growing sense of entitlement to occupy foreign spaces and to consume tourist sights, students tended to express a cheeky confidence in Britain's imperial power and prestige. They expressed this confidence from a position of strength derived in part from their identity with and incorporation into the Polytechnic community.

Crafted by pseudonymous authors and unidentified collaborators, anonymous travel narratives in the magazine underscored the Polytechnic's collective identity.[91] In some representations of group experiences, the collectivity assumed the mantle of narrating hero.[92] In other representations, one actor narrated the experience for the heroic whole. Thus, "Falcon" spoke for a "small party" of Poly boys who took their three-day bank holiday to visit Boulogne-sur-Mer. In a narrative that began with an excited salute to other Poly boys who, serendipitously, had taken the same vessel, Falcon described a punishing itinerary that led his tour group from one site to another on their one full day in the historic city. By the end of the day, one member had added his name to the graffiti prone pillars of La Barbière, while others had shopped for souvenirs before returning to the boat where they encountered still more Poly boys, an event that led to three enthusiastic "cheers for the Poly."[93]

The PTA's promotional literature also conveyed the message of corporate cohesion and welcomed tourists to share in the Polytechnic's collective identity. Ordinarily guide books and travel brochures presented readers with what David Chirico identifies as a "template for an unlimited number of single acts of travel," one that allowed potential travelers to project themselves onto a landscape unencumbered by the author's subjective experiences, as in a travel narrative.[94] But, rather than "single acts of travel," the PTA's holiday programs encouraged readers to imagine themselves in group contexts, where, enveloped in the Polytechnic's identity and unfettered by the "barrier of class," they, too, could experience "good fellowship" with "our party" and "our fellows."[95] The centrality of travel and tourism at the Polytechnic, therefore, not only produced institutional, civic, national, and imperial identities but appeared to realize the progressive ideal of an organic common culture and community. For some students, however, the Polytechnic's travel programs represented an exclusion that put these identities into question.

The "Upward Pressure": Excursions, Exclusions, and Citizenship

Like directors of study abroad offices today, Hogg reminded students time and again that it was never too early to start planning for the summer holidays. "As each year comes round," Hogg advised in a spring issue of the *Polytechnic Magazine*, "I keep on impressing upon all who can get away the great desirability of their endeavouring to take a trip abroad." Not only was travel "very important as a means of education," it was especially important for "anyone engaged in the commercial world." For these reasons, Hogg continued, the Polytechnic was doing everything in its power to arrange tours to "suit the financial convenience of everyone who can take a holiday at all."[96] Regular readers of the magazine were accustomed to these exhortations, and most would have granted travel's importance as an educational experience. But, there were others who had come to loathe the privileging of "commercial" students in Hogg's rhetoric and who scoffed at the presumption that the Polytechnic's tours met the "financial convenience" of most students.

Belying the liberal progressive ideal, travel practices at the Polytechnic could be a source of conflict as well as cohesion. The roots of this conflict can be found in structural inequalities at the institute, the origins of which paralleled inequalities and exclusions in wider British society. Class divisions, for example, threatened the social harmony of the institute as far back as 1881. At a council meeting held in the institute's first location at Long Acre, council members debated qualifications for membership of the institute, basing their criteria on occupational identities and status. In their deliberations, the artisans and mechanics on the council voted to limit the number of clerks, defined as "those engaged in office work," to the institute's membership rolls. As it was, they argued, clerks enjoyed exclusive access to the Young Men's Christian Association (YMCA), which routinely turned away ordinary working men, like themselves, from its doors. Why should clerks, then, monopolize the few spaces available to new candidates at the institute? Moreover, if the Polytechnic allowed clerks to increase their numbers, they would inevitably hold "undue influence" over the character of the institute. Hogg, sitting as chairman, attempted to steer the debate toward a different resolution. Hogg reminded the council that the institute was founded on "brotherly love" and existed to promote the "improvement of the neighbourhood generally, and not of any one class in particular." To exclude anyone – an artisan, mechanic, or clerk – would "cause disunion and disloyalty." Some council members concurred, acknowledging that social qualifications could very well compromise the integrity of the "community" and their goal of working toward a "common good."[97] But the dissenters got it right. A decade later the institute had changed. By 1891, the lower-middle class, designated as "clerks and others" in the Polytechnic's record books, comprised the institute's dominant occupational group.[98]

The seeds of this transformation may have had as much to do with the institute's relocation to the West End as it did to the initial invasion of young, black-coated workers at Long Acre. When Hogg moved the YMCI to Regent Street, he planted the institute squarely in the "centre of fashion," a residential, leisure, and commercial district characterized by architecturally distinctive homes, fine shops, and milling crowds of upper-class consumers.[99] This was a brash incursion into an elite sanctuary – a form of reverse slumming unlike other types of charitable uplift in the East End, where settlement reformers imagined themselves working in colonial outposts, surrounded by the barbarism of the urban jungle. In contrast, the Polytechnic encouraged rough, young men, such as the former "knife boy" Bill Surrey, to inhabit the environs of Regent Street and to interact with the institute's more well-to-do students. To a certain degree, this achieved Hogg's goal of class mixing. But, the Polytechnic's High Street address did not guarantee class amelioration. The Polytechnic's Day School, for instance, catered especially to the sons (and eventually daughters) of the petite bourgeoisie, primarily West End shop owners, which further strained social relations at the institute.[100]

By no means middle class, Day School children attended the Polytechnic only as long as their parents could pay the fee or until they acquired apprenticeships or jobs in low-level clerical and technical work; or, far less frequently, until they passed examinations for low-grade civil service positions or university courses. Although most of the Day School boys left the institute by the age of 12, the extension of their education beyond elementary school was an advantage for which night-school students longed for themselves. Furthermore, even though Hogg wanted to eliminate status differentials between clerical and technical work, the culture of the Day School created new distinctions that the evening students found difficult to accept, even though they would have encountered similar distinctions outside the Polytechnic between the artisan aristocracy and unskilled workers, much like in the selection of artisan reporters in 1867.[101] Animosity bubbled to the surface, for example, when Hogg formed the Old Quintinian Club for the Day School alumni in 1891. With its own club room and special privileges afforded to the "Old Day Boys," the Old Quintinian Club provoked some "envy" among the "orthodox" Poly boys, who, as one Old Day Boy later remarked, "resented" this "rival claim to the Polytechnic's resources."[102] Other encroachments increased the tension. Some students felt that the growing popularity of the Polytechnic as a social club had contributed to the degradation of the "orthodox" Poly boy community, so much so that they had become "strangers" in their own institute.[103] As the "Inquisitor," a frequent correspondent, complained in 1902, the institute had become a "West-end lounge for millionaires – a trifle passé in regard to decoration and the buffet arrangements, but convenient for the theaters and the whirl of society outside the Poly." Obviously, he continued, "the poor boy earning his ten or twelve shillings a week is an outsider – he would blush to do what I did in the years gone by; bring my own bread and butter, and spend a penny on a cup of tea to wash it down.[104]

The Polytechnic's travel business fanned the flames of alienation, intensifying some students' sense of "outsider" status. While the Polytechnic harped on the importance of a trip abroad as a "means of education," not every student possessed the means to participate in what had become a core feature of its institutional culture.[105] Complaints about the Polytechnic's tours, like the early misgivings over clerks or the Day School, punctuated the usually good-natured "Letters to the Editor" section of the *Polytechnic Magazine*. The "Inquisitor," once again championing economically marginal "Poly boys," claimed that the Polytechnic's original holiday homes, founded as charitable vacation destinations for students, had been mostly abandoned by the institute. In lieu of having students take their vacations at one of these homes, the Polytechnic steered students toward a "week's holiday among strangers" on one of the PTA's many tours. Such "trips," the Inquisitor wrote, "are very good in their way, and I would not wish it to be inferred that I grumble at them – they enable some of us to see places which would otherwise be as sealed books, but my point is that it is more than a pity – it is a blunder – that the distinctive 'Poly Home' has been abandoned, and our younger and least wealthy members are left to shift for themselves."[106] Others protested that the Polytechnic's tours did not fall at the time of year when employers permitted workers and clerks to take their holidays, leaving them "out in the cold."[107] And still others resented that the Polytechnic's tours excluded many more through prohibitive costs. "Every year," one student complained, "a great number of our members are thrown upon their own resources, instead of being catered for by the Institute, whereas to the outsider who can spend more heavily, every facility is given in many trips from June to October."[108] Another unhappy student dismissed the value of the Polytechnic tours altogether, declaring that the Polytechnic's travel business, as well as its growing focus on educational programs, had robbed the Polytechnic of its "sociability," that is, its "value as a social club and institute for mechanics, artisans, clerks, etc."[109]

Hogg tackled many of these complaints in the *Polytechnic Magazine* himself, sometimes with the good humor of an indulgent patriarch and at other times with acerbic dispatch. In one 1896 exchange that addressed the entire gambit of students' concerns, Hogg baited the "Inquisitor" and his fellow malcontents with a slur to their masculinity. Poor "Cinderella," he mocked, is left behind "while her more fortunate sisters are petted at her expense." Warmed to the fight, Hogg defended the institute's travel agency. "More members attend our trips than used to be the case," he argued, "and the facilities offered are greater." Moreover, the tours brought in "revenue" and served as an "effective advertisement" for the Polytechnic, which had allowed it to expand its educational facilities. This was significant, Hogg insisted, because the institute was much more than a social club. It had a "duty" to "equip" students "for life's struggle." To Hogg's mind, benefits included the cross-class relationships to be had at the Polytechnic. "I can honestly say that I have never seen a place – the world over –" he stated, "where all classes mix so freely and readily as they do with us."[110] Thus, what the alienated few required was "unselfish thought for the comfort and feelings of others, or, in other words, a truer Christian brotherhood."[111] The *Polytechnic Magazine* neglects to record whether the "Inquisitor" or his cohorts accepted Hogg's defense of the institute and its travel programs. But what is clear is that fissures in the Polytechnic community reflected inequalities that precluded full access to the Polytechnic's common culture and its corollary, citizenship. No group understood this better, perhaps, than the students of the "sister institute." Some "sisters" in fact had expressed resentment over their marginal status soon after the institute's founding in 1888. Turning underlying gender tensions into a war between the sexes, they challenged the sanctity of the Polytechnic "brotherhood."

Although the *Polytechnic Magazine* praised the institute's female students who had achieved scholarly or professional distinction, the validation of their accomplishments conflicted with the Polytechnic's ideology of separate spheres, which one reporter approvingly noted sought to transform London's "working girls" into "worthy English wives and mothers."[112] Such remarks failed to take into account "Poly sisters," who defined themselves as "New Women" and who, inspired by the election of women to the county councils and school boards, campaigned for equal access to the Polytechnic's courses, clubs, and facilities. The Polytechnic parliament, for example, became a special target for their activism in 1892; but, in a frustrating parallel to the suffragist movement outside the institute, the majority of Poly-boy-parliamentarians trounced their sisters' petitions for entry into the "full duties of citizenship" as MPs.[113] These exclusions stung. As one "Sister" queried "is no girl a member of the Poly, but only a cipher?"[114] The marginalization of "Poly sisters" in the Polytechnic polity migrated to the realm of travel. As the *Review of Reviews* pointedly remarked, the Polytechnic's excursions "afford considerably greater facilities to men than to women; the latter in some cases not being admitted to an excursion at all."[115] Occasionally, "Poly sisters" contributed short travel reports in the limited space afforded to the YWCI in the *Polytechnic Magazine*. In them, one representative usually spoke for the group, but few conveyed the collective romance typical of Poly-boy travel texts. Similarly, occasional references to Poly sisters' travel and work in the empire filtered through. A "Miss Milligan," for example, had accepted a secretarial position at the Cape. Yet, nothing more is heard from Milligan either aboard ship or within a Poly colony, unlike Homfray and the many other Poly boys featured in the *Polytechnic Magazine*. Thus, even as the Polytechnic sought to produce collectivities through travel, and through collectivities achieve the goals of good citizenship, the Polytechnic's travel ethos produced its own exclusions.[116]

Perhaps such exclusions were to be expected at an institution as large and as socially diverse as the Polytechnic became, even as it strived to be, for the most part, inclusive. In terms of social hierarchies alone, the Polytechnic produced an inescapable consciousness of class by virtue of its very function as an institute of upward mobility, one that nagged at students to study hard and to forge ahead in order to attain secure futures and more satisfying identities.[117] And yet students and reformers alike still maintained that they were witness to a momentous era of social change and that they and the Polytechnic led the vanguard.

The Polytechnic's role as an agent of change was an important theme in its institutional narrative. It expressed reformers' and student-members' ambitions for the future and emphasized their contributions to modernity, be they innovations in motor car engineering or, as one forward-thinking Poly boy wrote in defense of women clerks, in changes to "the old order of things." The Polytechnic, he remarked with pride, had enabled women to "raise themselves in the world" like their brothers.[118] In an 1896 address delivered at the Society of Arts, Hogg placed this narrative in a civic context, congratulating the city's elite for its growing commitment to technical education. But he also reminded his audience that what had been achieved thus far was "merely a promise of better things to come." The Polytechnic, he announced, was leading the way toward that promise by becoming "a home, a smaller university and public school, to help our poorer fellow citizens to privileges [sic] which have not had in the past."[119] Although Hogg's rhetoric fell short of asserting such "privileges" as rights, students felt empowered to make these claims themselves. Encouraged by the Polytechnic's environment of educational experimentation, some students had come to feel that social change was not only possible but imminent. Thus, in 1893, the "Radical Ministry" of the Polytechnic parliament vowed to use its platform to "wage war against all privilege and class distinction," a vow that the institute's suffragists echoed in their own demands for equality.[120] In critiquing the state of social relations at the Polytechnic, students made positive claims upon Britain's future. C. J. Peer, a vocal socialist in the Polytechnic parliament, anointed the institute as a "pioneer to the possibilities of the new era." "Alone among the Institutions of modern England," he asserted, the Polytechnic had produced a formidable "army" of students capable, by virtue of its numbers and training, to lead Britain to social "justice."[121] The liberal reformist and Polytechnic enthusiast, Walter Besant, agreed. Bringing the Polytechnic narrative to an even wider public, he turned "Poly boys" into the heroes of a futuristic tale, projecting their collective optimism into the twentieth century.

Although Besant had witnessed the dismal failure of his own pet project, the People's Palace in Whitechapel, a site of rational recreation that seemed to repel rather than attract working people, he fully expected the Polytechnic and similar educational centers for "the People" to spur a "social revolution."[122] How it would unfold is explained in "The Upward Pressure." First published in 1893, the work proposed to look back on the Polytechnic from the 1930s, illustrating the far-reaching and positive implications of democratizing education. Prior to the twentieth century, Besant writes, money, connections, and time conspired against even the most talented students from entering the upper levels of the professions, the church, and the military, and thus from any position of significant authority. But, armed with new knowledge attained at the Polytechnic, students no longer accepted the social hierarchy as "natural." Instead they began to apply enough public pressure, utilizing their skills in the new journalism (the only profession, Besant points out, that was open to their class) to effect change. Consequently, by the early decades of the twentieth century, not only were the professions open to all based on merit alone – by an Act of Parliament, no less – but the House of Lords had been rendered obsolete, completely overturning traditional rule.[123]

Besant's vision, it hardly bears telling, lacked prescience. Instead of spearheading a social revolution, the Polytechnic, financially marginalized by the state, could do little to change the status quo. Besant himself observes that government administrators "reproached" the polytechnics (prior to their imagined twentieth-century transformation) for exposing students to higher learning, when their purpose was to "bring boys together for common discipline and orderly recreation, and to train them in their crafts."[124] That the Technical Education Board debated the minutest dispensation of funds to ensure that expenditures did not become "too extravagant for a rough and ready school" bore this out.[125] The future, it seems, did not bode well for the democratization of education, or for the Polytechnic's travel programs.

By the late Victorian era, travel had become a compelling symbol of national identity, so much so that elementary school primers, such as the ubiquitous and long-lived *Citizen Reader*, taught working-class children that the "duties of the English citizen" extend beyond the British Isles and lauded the "boy" who "crosses the sea" and "travels abroad."[126] In higher education, Whitehall turned this rhetoric into a reality for some students by instituting

British teaching assistantships in French and German classrooms across the channel. Furthermore, state and privately funded "travelling scholarships" steadily became a requirement for students who would soon comprise a new class of university trained professionals, such as teachers, civil engineers, and scientists, some of whom would have had their start at a Polytechnic. Study abroad thus became an important requirement and, it should be emphasized, an entitlement of higher learning institutions. Indeed, study abroad amounted to a "privilege" that the affluent classes shared with only a limited number of state (or quasi-governmental) financed scholarship students, much like today.[127] Civil society also produced scholarship opportunities for deserving working-class youth, but their limited number teased rather than satisfied working people's desire for cultural experiences abroad or the economic necessity of academically or vocationally driven study abroad experiences. In its conception, the Hodgson Pratt Memorial Travelling Scholarship, for example, would "enable workers of either sex to become acquainted with technical and social development in foreign countries or the colonies."[128] But, such limited provisions for educational travel failed as a democratic solution to educational inequalities and were inadequate to carry forward Hogg's ambition to educate "the whole man."[129] Students, consequently, inhabited a number of paradoxes at the Polytechnic that put into question the inclusivity of its corporate identity and the equality implied, but not met, by its travel practices. Indeed, these paradoxes were the outcome of new liberalism's own internal contradictions that could not deliver on the democratic promise of equality and communal belonging within a predominantly capitalist system. In light of students' social and economic disabilities and, in the case of the YWCI, gender discrimination, it can be seen that the Polytechnic's travel culture precluded full citizenship. Instead, the Polytechnic's travel ideologies and practices highlighted differences rather than commonalities, and contestation over social cohesion.[130]

Conclusion

This then is the story behind the dispute between Cook and Hogg. Standing at a crossroads between state and voluntary funding, and between stasis and change, the Polytechnic demonstrates how new conceptions of liberalism in an age characterized not only by anxiety over mass democracy and international economic competition, but also by optimism over technological and social innovation, had made it possible for reformers to imagine, and in Cook's case to presume, a national curriculum that included travel opportunities for working-class and lower-middle-class students and that would serve, ideally, as both an education in and an obligation of citizenship.

Unsurprisingly, the impetus for this ideal was difficult to sustain after Hogg's death. Although the LCC continued to finance the Polytechnic, Studd explains that it was "unwilling" to fund the PTA[131] As a consequence, the PTA became a private limited company in 1911. Continuing as a commercial enterprise, it developed an extensive organizational structure, one in which the "pleasures of the tourist gaze," as John Urry writes of modern leisure travel, came to be experienced as a "right" rather than a "privilege," an interpretation of "rights" that workers had come to associate, across-the-board, with commercial leisure and entertainment by the 1900s.[132] Enlarging ordinary people's sphere of citizenship, the PTA thus contributed to the emergence of the modern consumerist mode of travel and tourism.

What the history of the Polytechnic also reveals, however, is that the significance of travel in modern life was, and continues to be, more than the fulfillment of consumer desires as an individual right. In mobilizing ordinary youth, the Polytechnic responded to students' own demands for opportunities to enhance their skills and to contribute to the "common good."[133] Out of these expectations, the "spirit of travel" articulated the institute's collective identity that students used to improve their economic and social circumstances at home and around the world, and to assert their own claims for citizenship.

Yet, with limited resources afforded to the Polytechnic, the promise of the future that was inscribed in educational travel led students down a path that terminated in a relatively static social order. Indeed, what this chapter has sought to expose as a fundamental conceit is the idea that travel constitutes a democratic vehicle for either social mobility or active citizenship. Thus, as one education official blithely remarked in a parliamentary report nearly two decades after Besant's Poly boy heroes stormed the barricades of class privilege, "the Polytechnics were intended to be institutions to make the rank and file the most capable rank and file in the world," while the universities were intended to "train those who would lead them."[134]

Study-abroad visionaries in the early twentieth century replicated this perspective in seeking to make foreign travel a standard feature of university curriculums. Indeed, universities rather than the polytechnics became the locus of educational travel programs in Britain. Henry W. Crees, Honorary Secretary of the Association for the International Interchange of Students (AIIS), argued in 1910, that "leaders and citizens" are defined not only by their academic degrees in a particular field of study, but by their experience in the "world" and the "Empire." The AIIS proposed, therefore, to send select university students abroad. The AIIS described its ideal candidate as a university "man" who was not only academically gifted and physically fit, but was an "all round man," that is "a man of character, and popular with his fellows." In other words, the AIIS wanted to recruit university men (and "women," as Crees also notes) who possessed ambassadorial qualities.[135] Scholarship recipients would thus be worthy representatives of their respective nations and eminently qualified to meet with the political, academic, and industry leaders of "all countries and nations." Such travel,

Crees emphasized, would not be undertaken as a leisure activity, but would constitute "part of their university training."[136]

Although universities, needless to say, had fostered student mobility prior to the AIIS, its emergence at the turn of the century and on the eve of the Great War underscores how new travel technologies as well as international tensions had produced some effort between universities and government agencies, domestically and internationally, to collaborate in developing study abroad opportunities.[137] These early twentieth century programs served many overlapping interests and aims. They sought, for example, to assist foreign students to attain higher education credentials abroad. They also sought to support the financial interests of the host country and its institutions of higher learning. And, they sought to assuage international tensions by orchestrating points of contact between peoples and thus opportunities for mutual understanding. Both Cambridge University and the London School of Economics, for example, began offering summer and short-term courses, respectively, to accommodate the schedules of non-resident student travelers and, at the same time, bring in revenues.[138] It was at this time, too, that arrangements for student exchanges began to be coordinated by voluntary and government organizations. The trust for the Rhodes Scholarships, which the AIIS looked to as a model for their own grants, was founded in 1902 and intended to foster "good understanding" between Britain, its colonies, Germany, and the USA, which Rhodes felt was necessary to "secure the peace of the world." Believing that "educational relations form the strongest tie," scholarship recipients – academic high-achievers who were "successful" in "manly outdoor sports," of sound "moral" character, and public spirited, natural "leaders" – were invited to take postgraduate degrees at Oxford University. In the congenial environment of Rhodes's alma mater, they would form lasting bonds with other Rhodes Scholars that would transcend the petty rivalries of nations.[139]

The Rhodes scholarship excluded women until the late twentieth century, but there were other educational venues were women could play a role – if still limited – on the world stage. At the level of the professional middle classes, the growing interest in modern languages spurred the Education Department to facilitate student exchange programs in France and Germany. Beginning in the late 1890s, government scholarships enabled accredited teachers and university "pupil teachers" of both sexes to teach at secondary schools in Paris or Jena. In turn, their French or German counterparts would be placed in British secondary schools for the same purpose of attaining greater language competency and professional teaching experience. According to Miss Williams, President of the Franco-English Guild, Paris, and Lecturer at the Ecole Normale Supérieure at Fontenay-aux-Roses, the ideal female candidate was not only "well read" and competent in French, but "endowed with common sense, tact, suppleness, [and] the power of adapting herself to a new environment." If bereft of these "moral" qualities, failure loomed for the student abroad---and---for the nation. Indeed, Williams cautioned female students at French teacher training colleges to "remember" that, in the eyes of French students and acquaintances, "the reputation of English women, perhaps even of the whole British nation ... rests with her."[140] Student exchanges thus took place at the professional level in the training of teachers, and at the loftier heights of interpersonal relations between the future leaders of industry, science, culture, and politics. In either instance, such exchanges were regarded by higher education professionals as crucial to domestic security and international relations.

The twentieth century imperative for international cooperation and exchange in higher education was never more apparent than during the interwar years. In 1919, the USA's Institute of International Education (IIE) set out to coordinate government policies with college and university programs for the education of foreign students and, concomitantly, for sending American students abroad. In 1934, the United Kingdom followed suit with the founding of the British Council. Such organizations inched towards the creation of an international infrastructure for study abroad in higher education with the positive promise to "promote international understanding through international education," and perhaps more pragmatically to extend their sphere of influence internationally.[141] The importance of these objectives would have been difficult to deny during the unfolding of World War II and, afterwards, the Cold War, in which international economic and military competition once again accelerated.[142] Consequently, in 1945, UNESCO, the United Nation's Educational, Scientific, and Cultural Organization, as William Hoffa writes, "legitimized international educational exchange on a worldwide basis," while a year later the USA's federal Fulbright Program, created scholarships for student and faculty exchanges with debtor nations.[143] Many of these debtor nations soon formed the European Communities, which gave rise to ERASMUS (European Action Scheme for the Mobility of University Students). Founded in 1987, the aim of this organization was to coordinate student (and faculty) exchanges within the European Communities (and later the European Union within newer programs, SOCRATES I and II, and currently the Life Long Learning Programme), an aim that was to strengthen pan-European identities and economy.[144]

These programs (and many more) for study abroad in higher education during the twentieth century, emerged, therefore, in response to the geopolitical and economic contexts of postwar Europe and North America. In Britain, however, one economic trend of note has been the emphasis on recruiting fee paying students from abroad. Hans De Witt writes that universities in the United Kingdom during Tony Blair's Labour government, turned international education in Britain into a "fee paying" "export commodity," a practice that initially alienated EU countries that were integrated into the student exchange system initiated through ERASMUS, but which have since entered the race for market shares, not unlike Cook and Hogg a century earlier. In Britain, the revenues from student fees and tourism have assisted capital flows and funded higher education programs. However, de Witt also notes (but does not explain), that these revenues do not necessarily support study abroad for UK students, who, it appears, are "reluctant" to participate in exchange programs on the Continent.[145] Indeed, as the conclusion to this book argues, the postwar expansion of university education in the United Kingdom did not meet with a correlating expansion of opportunities for international education. John Cook, whose agency had proudly catered to wealthy, university-educated, and titled "travelers," perhaps won his case after all.

Conclusion: Goody, Gordon, and Shilpa Shetty "Poppadom": The Politics of Study Abroad from the New Liberalism to New Labour

When Jade Goody, the working-class "reality" TV star of Britain's *Big Brother* (BB) and *Celebrity Big Brother* (CBB), attempted to rehabilitate her career in 2008, she made two trips to India that her publicists spun as educational tours. At the invitation of the Indian government, she visited Delhi, where she marveled at its beautiful temples and gardens, and, after spending a heartrending day at a rescue center for orphaned street children, donated £100,000 of her own fortune to the institution. Six months later at the invitation of *Big Boss*, the Indian version of *Celebrity Big Brother* in Mumbai, she joined the "house" as a contestant. This would be the third and last time that she would enter the Endemol matrix. Endemol, the broadcasting corporation that had launched her to celebrity stardom in 2001, would also be her undoing.[1]

The poorly educated, "mixed-race" daughter of petty thieves and drug addicts, Goody made a bold impression when she first entered the BB house a little over a decade ago with (as many observers noted) her ready smile, zest for fun, and loud, guileless chatter. Growing up on a Bermondsey council estate, where she had survived abusive boyfriends, had cared for her disabled and drug-addled mother, and had barely scraped together an education, Goody, was excited to make her debut on a nationally televised show. She imagined that her time in the house would be like living in a blissful "holiday camp" where she could escape the harsh realities of her day-to-day life.[2] Instead, *Big Brother* took this "ordinary" Briton, and put her on display, not once, but three times, in the human zoo of the "here and now," Arjun Appadurai's term for understanding how the tools and processes of globalization, such as mass media and mass migration, have altered how we experience the world. Collapsing time and space with live feeds that still circulate in YouTube's virtual archive, Endemol's "Big Brother" brand not only gave Goody an opportunity to explore her own subjectivity and refashion her image over and over again in a "reality TV" environment, but encouraged the mass media and a global public, from London to Mumbai, to do the same, creating polarized "communities of sentiment" at home and abroad.[3]

161

As it turned out, Goody's class status made her fair game for media abuse from the very start.[4] "Thick," "Pig," "Slag," "Pikey" (a derogatory term for a "gypsy traveller") and the all-purpose "Chav" (a supposed acronym for "council house and violent") topped the list of insults that the tabloids used to denigrate Goody's intelligence, appearance, speech, and culture.[5] The British media, in fact, demonized her in ways that, as Owen Jones writes in *Chavs*, his brilliant exposé on social class in contemporary Britain, would not be tolerated if the vitriol reflected race hatred or sex discrimination.[6] But, in the neoliberal environment of the post Thatcher era, the demonization and dehumanization of the working class has become normalized, so that working people are openly "despised" as "scum of the earth," a perception that hearkens back to the Othering of the working class as "pests" and a race apart during the Victorian era.[7] Thus when Goody exited the Big Brother house during her first stint on the reality show, she confronted hostile jeers from many Big Brother fans in the crowd who, with impunity, chanted "Kill the Pig."[8]

Despite ridicule from the press, Goody won an army of fans who recognized her as one of their own. She, as one reporter notes, had a go-getter attitude to life that Samuel Smiles, not to mention, Margaret Thatcher, would have applauded. Never out of work, Goody (of necessity, since childhood) was a self-reliant self-improver. Her fans understood that and admired her for it. Consequently, the tabloid press changed its tune after realizing that positive stories about this British "everywoman" sold more papers and television news clips than stories berating her. Since that time, Goody had amassed over 8 million pounds in lucrative TV promotions, two autobiographies, exercise DVDs, and her own perfume "Shhh!," which rivaled other High Street scents with the fragrant promise that ordinary women like her could also live the good life.

The reason for her invitations to India – the event that had plunged Goody's career into a downward spiral in 2007 – was a televised altercation in the Celebrity Big Brother house between Goody and the regal (by contrast) Bollywood actress, Shilpa Shetty. In a dispute over a grocery list, Goody lambasted Shetty as a snob, a "fake," and a "liar," and criticized Shetty's sheltered upbringing among servants: "Take a walk in the slums of your own backyard," Goody yelled, and "see how real people live!" Although they mended their rift, most troubling for her career was that Goody referred to Shetty in conversations with other contestants as "Shilpa Poppadom" and "Shilpa Fuckawalla" – monikers that Goody later glibly explained were attributable to her limited Indian vocabulary derived from restaurant menus.[9] In the cocoon of the CBB house, neither Goody nor Shetty could have imagined the media frenzy their altercations would ignite. Shetty's fans in India took to the streets, burning CBB executives in effigy; India's ruling Congress Party demanded that Britain restore Shetty's "honor"; and India's Information and Broadcasting minister wanted Shetty to testify before the

Indian High Commission in London. Downing Street also weighed in on the affair: "What clearly is to be regretted and countered," Prime Minister Tony Blair's spokesman stated, "is any perception abroad that in any way we tolerate racism in this county."[10] As for Goody, the tabloids maligned her again as an ignorant "chav," and excoriated her as a bully and a racist. When the two contestants finally emerged from their reality television quasi-panopticon, Britain had crowned Shetty the winner, while Goody met with the stony rebuke of producers and the disdain of the public. Although Shetty firmly absolved Goody of racist "intent" or "discrimination" and instead put their conflicts down to "class" and "cultural differences," the public refused to relent.[11] Genuinely contrite and mortified by her conduct, Goody apologized profusely in multiple media venues and, after a severe bout of depression that led to a short stint at the Priory – an upscale, celebrity asylum – eagerly embarked on her "goodwill" tours to India.[12]

Cast in the press as belated educational tours, the opportunities for cross-cultural exchanges that the visits facilitated would school Goody (and, it was presumed, the wider British public) in racial and ethnic tolerance. Indeed, in Goody's first Big Brother appearance, her sketchy educational background had been essential to the entertainment value of the show. In the house, she had assumed that Rio de Janeiro was a person, that Portugal was in Spain, and, closer to home, that Cambridge was a London borough. Most infamously, she confused East Anglia ("East Angular" in "Jade speak") with a foreign country. The tabloid press mocked the "imbecile" and her "Jadisms," and echoed her TV housemate's incredulous query, "Jade, did you take a stupid pill again?" Reportedly, airlines were so taken aback by Goody's appalling lack of geographic knowledge that they offered to help school her in the subject by flying her gratis to foreign destinations.[13]

Unlike their nineteenth-century predecessors, however, the twenty-first-century British travel industry and media mouthpieces of middle-class ideology did not spout visions of a domestic civilizing mission realized through international travel. Although contemporary British elites have come to view study abroad as a prerequisite to "global" citizenship, the British working class has become more deprived of access to education – much less educational travel – than ever before, as the recent protests and riots over cuts in the Education Maintenance Allowance (EMA) and university tuition attest.[14] The intellectual and cultural self-actualization of working Britons – viewed as vital to social welfare by Victorian reformers – appears wholly detached from British elites' contemporary education discourse. The intersection of the Jade Goody affair with the career fortunes of one New Labour politician provides a case in point.

In the first instance, the public and political outrage over the racist bullying served up as light entertainment on CBB coincided with Chancellor Gordon Brown's first state visit to India, which was to help establish his foreign policy credentials in a bid for the position of Prime Minister. During his visit, many of the topics on the table for discussion, such as economic globalization and, not least, student exchanges, were inseparable from his proposed domestic agenda. A dominant theme in Brown's domestic platform was to meet the challenges of globalization head on – especially the economic threat posed by China and India and their increasingly skilled and educated workforces (the France and Germany of their day).[15] Brown's first priority therefore was to make British education "world class." Sounding like a modern-day, Lyon Playfair, he stressed that Britain needed to understand that education and skills had become an "economic necessity, and not just a social goal."[16]

The political fallout over CBB upstaged the gravitas of Brown's visit to India. As Sunder Katwala, the *Guardian* columnist, commented, Jade Goody presented Brown with a vital "reality check." Symbolizing "the historic weakness of British education, which combines excellence at the top with indifference to what happens to less able children," Jade had left school at the age of 16 in 1997, joining the legions of demoralized youth between the ages of 16 and 24 classified as "NEETs" (not in education, employment, or training). In 2007 the proportion of this age group fitting this category was 13.1%, and it had climbed to 17.1% by 2011.[17] Despite the radical roots of the Labour Party, its contemporary incarnation as "New Labour" (along with its New Coalition successors under the Cameron government) not only presided over a deepening social crisis for working Britons, but developed a vision for British "global" education that left, practically speaking, no viable place for an educated and upwardly mobile working class. In fact, the degradation of educational provisions for higher learning has strengthened the conditions for the development of a migrant, subaltern class and sub-proletariat that, Immanuel Wallerstein, referencing Marx and Engels, has described as the "fourth specter" haunting capital (the multinationals and the elite cosmopolitan ruling class).[18] Brown's call for a "world class" British education system thus depends on study abroad experiences totally inaccessible to most Britons. The new "global citizenship" appears to be nothing more than elite citizenship. Indeed, in his post-Downing-Street career, Brown has accepted new roles that center on education and global citizenship, such as New York University's first "distinguished global leader in residence." In this post, in which he serves NYU's "ambitious global mission" to integrate a network of global education programs and study abroad campuses, Brown spends "two weeks a year at the university's New York campus, as well as a week in Abu Dhabi and a week at one of 12 study-abroad sites." The former Prime Minister explained his enthusiasm for his new work, stating that "The idea of a global network university where barriers are broken down and people can use modern technology to debate and educate each other is incredibly appealing … .N.Y.U. is setting the pace that others will follow."[19]

As Brown's new life at elite institutions of higher learning and global governance might imply, only students from affluent backgrounds will have access to his vision of global education. Such exclusions, of course, replicate well established patterns in state education. As historian J. F. Donnelly has argued, and as the artisan tours and the Polytechnic have demonstrated, "class stratification is associated with qualitatively distinct curricula in schools and colleges, including the fields of science and technology." Indeed, "the historical origins and present-day practice of public education," he writes, "are based on the impetus to produce a fragmented, disciplined and hierarchical workforce" in the service of capital.[20] Study abroad practices today reflect this stratification. A recent report underscores the inequalities in British education and educational travel. Students at state schools are less affluent and more ethnically diverse, and a far lower percentage of these students study abroad than students at British public schools. Indeed, by and large, students at state schools do not study abroad without scholarship aid, whereas lack of scholarships does not make educational travel cost-prohibitive for students at public schools because their parents can generally afford to pay. Furthermore, not only are the privileged students at Britain's elite schools able to study abroad, but they study abroad at elite foreign institutions.[21] Although the same education business researchers whose work exposes these inequalities argue that Britain must send more of its students abroad to assure the future vitality of the British economy and avoid isolating Britain in an increasingly globalized world, these concerns have not translated into policies opening study abroad to wide segments of the British student population.[22] As Johanna Waters and Rachel Brooks argue in another study that confirms the obvious, study abroad is an elite privilege that merely serves to "facilitate the reproduction of their privilege."[23] The rhetoric of global citizenship (much like imperial citizenship at the Polytechnic), similarly serves this process by creating distinctions and exclusions through travel, the singular means for acquiring what educators term "global citizenship competency."

The message in the education rhetoric surrounding globalization insists that study abroad is the prerequisite for "global citizenship," a phrase of indeterminate meaning. In an important analysis that attempts to make sense of this rhetoric, Lynette Shultz identifies two dominant discourses. Economic actors, she writes, whose activities forge a single global market are the heroes, the "global citizens," of neoliberal ideology, while activists who defend the weak and marginalized – the individuals and regions impoverished by multinationals and finance capital – are the heroes, the "global citizens," of radical ideology. As a corrective to these dichotomous perspectives, Shultz suggests a new educational approach to global citizenship, which she terms "the Transformationalist Global Citizen," in which education facilitates an understanding of a "common humanity" though a "shared environment" and "shared interests and activities."[24] Nevertheless, no matter how "global citizenship" is defined, its present usage as an educational goal clearly masks the harsh legacy of liberalism's educational reforms.

Educational travel has long functioned as a mark of personal distinction and means of national advancement. Although in today's "globalized marketplace" the purpose of "global" advancement has been coupled with the nineteenth-century liberal vision of national prosperity, study abroad perpetuates the Victorian structures of a class-stratified society. The upper classes can lay claim to privileges of "global citizenship" that the working class, under the current system and its nineteenth-century liberal ethos, cannot hope to attain.[25]

The practical exclusion of working people from this new rhetoric of "global citizenship" is not lost on Britain's working class.[26] British "everywoman" Jade Goody, who, back in her Bermondsey days, fleetingly attended a technical school successor of the nineteenth-century Polytechnics, journeyed to India for what was widely interpreted as much needed instruction in racial harmony and respect for cultural and ethnic difference. Compelled to return home to Britain after it was revealed on the Indian reality spin-off *Big Boss* that she was dying of cervical cancer, Jade Goody proved to be more worldly-wise than some Britons had supposed. Astutely observing what privileges and opportunities were necessary to become a "global citizen" with a "world class" education, Goody announced her deathbed wish to the nation: that her two sons continue to be educated at a private school "until they are 18," where they would get "the very best chance in life," even if it seemed to mean that she was "betraying" her "roots."[27] Moreover, she wanted her sons to enjoy many "holidays and travels," just as she had, and, at the same time, wanted her sons to visit "Third World" countries to better understand their own privileged status.[28] Like Alexander Kay and her "Poly sisters" of yesteryear, Goody was all too aware of the structural inequalities that precluded full citizenship. Although poorly educated and still publicly derided as a "chav" and, now, as a class bounder as well, Goody shrewdly recognized that her sons' future success depended on the education and travel experiences that British elites deemed essential to their self-aggrandizing claims of distinction through "global citizenship." This "everywoman," it turned out, was just as discerning as her working-class supporters always knew her to be.

Notes

Introduction: Grand Tours and Workers' Tours: Rethinking Victorian Travel and Education

1. Alexander Kay to Peter Le Neve Foster, November 5, 1878, A/RSA/28/L-V, 1878/ Box 2/RSA Archive 15. A/RSA/28/L/33. Royal Society of Arts Archive, London, hereafter (RSA). Kay narrates his predicament with reference to the novels of Wilkie Collins. Kay's confinement also resembles the highly publicized court case of Georgina Weldon in 1878. Weldon waged a battle for her freedom against her husband (and the medical authorities) who wanted to commit her to a private asylum. Kay's case is an important reminder that "lunacy" threatened the autonomy of working-class malcontents as well as eccentric or disposable middle-class women. Kay rotated in and out of several institutions, escaped and was recaptured, and continued to voice his discontent in a number of forums, even becoming the subject of parliamentary debate. See, Sir Herbert Maxwell and Sir William Harcourt, "Lunacy Acts: Alexander Kay, An Alleged Lunatic," Hansard, HC Deb March 10, 1884 vol. 285 cc1036–7, 1036 and 1037, in http://hansard. millbanksystems.com/commons/1884/mar/10/lunacy-acts-alexander-kay-an-alleged (accessed August 17, 2013). In the debate, Maxwell remarks that Kay's personal narrative of persecution and wrongful confinement can also be found in *The Westminster and Lambeth Gazette* (November 16, 1883) and (December 16, 1883). For Collins and Weldon, see Judith Walkowitz, *City of Dreadful Delight: Narratives of Sexual Danger in Late-Victorian London* (Chicago: Chicago University Press, 1992), 171–189. For more on Collins and the subject of lunacy see, Fiona Subotsky, "Armadale (1866), Wilkie Collins – Psychiatrists in 19th-century Fiction," *The British Journal of Psychiatry* 194 (2009): 445.

2. The symbolic association of British Royalty with "whales," precedes Kay's biblical effusions. As Herman Melville noted in 1851, "by old English statutory law, the whale is declared a royal fish (121)," and sperm whale oil is used for coronations. See Melville, *Moby Dick or The Whale* (New York: Penguin Books, 1992), 121, 123. However, this association also appears to have become a radical working-class trope later in the century. As George Tremlett notes, "The Political Secretary of the West Marylebone United Club observed in the Journal: 'A schoolfellow of his wrote the name of the prince of Wales as the prince of Whales; although laughing at the time, he had since considered that his companion was not, perhaps, so far wrong, after all inasmuch as Royalty is very fishy, and, although princes may not be whales, they certainly are sharks.' " See Tremlett, *Clubmen: the History of the Working Men's Club and Institute Union* (London: Secker & Warburg, 1987), 71.

3. Alexander Kay to Peter Le Neve Foster, November 5, 1878, A/RSA/28/L-V, 1878/ Box 2/RSA Archive 15. A/RSA/28/L/33. Austin Henry Layard, the MP for Southwark and president of the Workingmen's Club and Institute Union's committee for the workingmen's tours of the 1867 Paris exhibition, was also celebrated for having discovered Nineveh, where Yahweh, according to Biblical legend, sent Jonah (transported in the belly of the Whale) to convert the gentiles. Layard may therefore also play a part in Kay's biblical allusion. In Biblical typology, Jonah

prefigured the crucifixion and resurrection of Jesus Christ; the "whale"— hell. Anticipating Christ on the cross, Kay expressed his feelings of anger and the pain of betrayal; and, with the resurrection, his righteousness and personal renewal (or rehabilitation) outside of Peckham. For an analysis of Biblical typology with reference to Jonah and the Whale, see, Rebecca Lemon *et al.*, *The Blackwell Companion to the Bible in English Literature* (Oxford: Wiley-Blackwell, 2009), 103, 231–232.

4. See letters from Kay to Peter Le Neve Foster for the years 1867–1878 at the RSA.
5. E.P. Thompson, *The Making of the English Working Class* (New York: Vintage Books, 1966), 12.
6. Education for the professions evolved in tandem with the interest in technical education for workers. Study at German universities was a necessity for both British and American middle-class students interested in science and engineering. See, Joan Elias Gore's discussion of American's mid-nineteenth century study at German universities in *Dominant Beliefs and Alternative Voices: Discourse, Belief, and Gender in American Study Abroad* (New York: Routledge, 2005), 35–36. Peter Le Neve Foster's son, Ernest Le Neve Foster, exemplifies the new professional elite emerging with the growth of science and engineering. After taking a degree from the London Royal School of Mines, he took another year abroad in 1868, at the School of Mines in Freiberg, Germany, before taking up work and residence in Colorado. See, Wilbur Fiske Stone, ed., "Biographical Sketches: Ernst le Neve Foster," *History of Colorado*, Vol. II (Chicago: S.J. Clarke, 1918), 704–705, paraphrased in http://www.coloscisoc.org/history/Presidents/Foster. html (accessed August 17, 2013).
7. See Margaret Shennan, "Education Beyond the Classroom," in *Teaching About Europe* (London: Cassell Educational Limited, 1991), 153–171; Katherine M. Kalinowski and Betty Weiler, "Educational Travel," in *Special Interest Tourism*, eds. Betty Weiler and Colin Michael Hall (London: Belhaven Press, 1992), 17. Scholarship in English on the history of modern educational travel or "study abroad" is limited and emphasizes American travelers to Europe in the nineteenth and twentieth centuries. Some examples are, Joan Gore, *Dominant Beliefs and Alternative Voices: Discourse, Belief, and Gender in American Study Abroad* (Routledge, 2005); William Hoffa, "A History of US Study Abroad: Beginnings to 1965," Special Issue of *Frontiers: The Interdisciplinary Journal of Study Abroad* (Carlisle: Dickenson College, 2007); Sandra L. Singer, *Adventures Abroad: North American Women at German Speaking Universities, 1868–1915* (Westport, CT: Praeger, 2003); Whitney Walton, *Internationalism, National Identities, and Study Abroad: France and the United States 1890–1970* (Stanford, CA: Stanford University Press, 2010).
8. Central Bureau for Educational Visits and Exchanges, *Survey of British Organizations Concerned in Furthering Educational Travel*. London: Hamilton House, July 1949. British Library.
9. Maura O'Connor, *The Romance of Italy and the English Political Imagination* (New York: St Martin's Press, 1998), 14. For specific scholarship on the educational underpinnings of the Grand Tour see, George C. Brauer, *The Education of a Gentleman: Theories of Gentlemanly Education in England, 1660–1775* (New York: Bookman, 1959); Kenneth Charlton, *Education in Renaissance England* (London: Routledge and Kegan Paul, 1965); K.S. Dent, "Travel as Education: The English Landed Classes in the Eighteenth Century," *Educational Studies* 1 (1975): 171–180.
10. Black, *The British and the Grand Tour* (London: Croom Helm, 1985); John Towner, "The Grand Tour: A Key Phase in the History of Tourism," *Annals of Tourism Research* 12 (1985): 297–333. F.M.L. Thompson, *The Rise of Respectable Society: A Social History of Victorian Britain, 1830–1900* (Cambridge, MA: Harvard

University Press, 1988), 290–291. For the (largely European) workers' "Grand Tour" see Judith Adler, "Youth on the Road: Reflections on the History of Tramping," *Annals of Tourism Research* 12 (1985): 335–354.

11. Józef Böröcz, "Travel-Capitalism: The Structure of Europe and the Advent of the Tourist," *Comparative Studies in Society and History* 34 (1992): 712–713.

12. Dean MacCannell's now classic ethnographic exploration of the role of the tourist in modern society, for instance, specifically targets how modern tourism "comprises an essential component" of middle-class identity. See MacCannell, *The Tourist; A New Theory of the Leisure Class* (New York: Schocken Books, 1976), 13. See also John Urry, *The Tourist Gaze: Leisure Travel in Contemporary Societies* (London: Sage Publications, 1990); Chris Rojek and John Urry, eds., *Touring Cultures: Transformations of Travel and Theory* (London: Routledge, 1997).

13. David Engerman, "Research Agenda for the History of Tourism: Towards an International Social History," *American Studies International* 32 (1994): 15.

14. James Clifford, *Routes: Travel and Translation in the Late Twentieth Century* (Cambridge, MA: Harvard University Press, 1997), 34–36.

15. In 2005, John K. Walton declared that the field still lacked a substantive investigation into British tourism and labor history. See, Walton, "Introduction," *Histories of Tourism: Representation, Identity, and Conflict* (Clevedon: Channel View Publications, 2005), 14. In that same year, Susan Barton made an inroad with *Working-Class Organisations and Popular Tourism, 1840–1970* (Manchester: Manchester University, 2005). She addresses working-class international travel primarily in the post-1945 context. Another recent contribution is Susan Dawson, *Holiday Camps in Twentieth-Century Britain* (Manchester: Manchester University Press, 2011). Walton, helped define the field of working-class leisure travel with, "The Demand for Working-Class Seaside Holidays in Victorian England," *Economic History Review [Great Britain]* 34 (1981): 249–265. See also, C. Ward and D. Hardy, *Goodnight Campers! The History of the British Holiday Camp* (London: Mansell, 1986); and Peter Bailey's important contribution to leisure history and theory, *Leisure and Class in Victorian England: Rational Recreation and the Contest for Control, 1830–1885* (London: Routledge & Kegan Paul, 1978).

16. F.M.L. Thompson, *The Rise of Respectable Society: A Social History of Victorian Britain, 1830–1900* (Cambridge, MA: Harvard University Press, 1988), 291.

17. John Benson, *The Rise of Consumer Society in Britain, 1880–1980* (London: Longman, 1994), 99.

18. Peter Bailey, "A Role Analysis of Working-Class Respectability: 'Will the real Bill Banks please stand up?,'" in *Popular Culture and Performance in the Victorian City* (Cambridge: Cambridge University Press, 1998). 30–46.

19. Patrick Joyce, *Work, Society and Politics. The Culture of the Factory in Later Victorian England* (New Brunswick, NJ: Rutgers University Press, 1980); Gareth Stedman Jones, "Working-class culture and working-class politics in London, 1870–1900: Notes on the remaking of a working class," in *Languages of Class: Studies in English Working Class History, 1832–1982* (Cambridge: Cambridge University Press, 1983), 179–238. For a cogent reevaluation of the "culture of consolation" thesis, see Andrew August, "A Culture of Consolation? Rethinking Politics in Working Class London, 1870–1914," *Historical Research* 74, no. 184 (May, 2001): 193–219. See also Brad Bevan, *Leisure, Citizenship and Working-Class Men in Britain, 1850–1945* (Manchester: Manchester University Press, 2005) 4.

20. Jonathan Rose, *The Intellectual Life of the British Working Classes* (New Haven, CT: Yale University Press, 2001). The "Toynbee Travellers" included the bookbinder turned publisher, J.M. Dent, the founder of *Everyman's Library*, and Thomas Okey,

a former basket-weaver who later became a professor of Italian at Cambridge. See Dent's impressions of the Toynbee Travellers' Club and their first trip to Italy in 1888, in Joseph Malaby Dent and Hugh Railton Dent, *The Memoirs of J.M. Dent, 1849–1926* (London: J.M. Dent and Sons, 1928), 51–53.

21. Susan Thorne contributes to this revisionist strand in, *Congregational Missions and the Making of an Imperial Culture in 19th Century England* (Stanford, CA: Stanford University Press, 1999); Eugene Biagini, *Liberty, Retrenchment, and Reform: Popular Liberalism in the Age of Gladstone, 1869–1880* (Cambridge: Cambridge University Press, 1992); Margot Finn, *After Chartism: Class and Nation in English Radical Politics, 1848–1874* (Cambridge: Cambridge University Press, 1993). Bernard Porter takes issue with the "revisionists" and argues that the British, and especially the British working classes, were little conscious of Britain's imperial contexts and certainly did not contribute to the formation of an "imperial society." See, Porter, *The Absent-Minded Imperialists: What the British Really Thought About Empire* (Oxford: Oxford University Press, 2004). Porter draws on Jonathan Rose's research in *The Intellectual Life of the British Working Classes* (2001), to help support his claims, but he has not had the last word on the matter. See, Andrew Thompson, *The Empire Strikes Back? The Impact of Imperialism on Britain From the Mid-Nineteenth Century* (Harlow: Pearson, 2005); and, Catherine Hall and Sonya O. Rose, eds., *At Home with the Empire: Metropolitan Culture and the Imperial World* (Cambridge: Cambridge University Press, 2006), 16–17. In the context of travel and tourism, the literature that refutes British parochialism is more abundant with regard to the middle classes. Maura O'Connor, for instance, argues that middle-class travel in Italy reveals the formation of class, national, and imperial identities in *The Romance of Italy and the English Political Imagination* (New York: St Martin's Press, 1998), 17–18; Margaret Hunt similarly analyzes questions of identity and the late eighteenth-century jingoism of English-business travelers to the European continent in, "Racism, Imperialism, and the Traveler's Gaze," *Journal of British Studies* 32 (October 1993): 333–357. Suggestive of these works is Marjorie Morgan's *National Identities and Travel in Victorian Britain* (Basingstoke: Palgrave, 2001), which examines Victorian middle-class travelers' texts and the process of identity and nation building in the European context. Morgan's study, however, replicates the class exclusions of most travel scholarship. Even though Morgan uses the travel diary of a household maid, Alison Cunningham, to illuminate the quotidian aspects of a travel journey, she uses these revelations to add context to the middle-class experience, rather than that of a British servant abroad.

22. Katherine M. Kalinowski and Betty Weiler, "Educational Travel" in Betty Weiler and Colin Michael Hall, eds. *Special Interest Tourism* (London: Belhaven Press, 1992), 17.

23. Philip Corrigan and Derek Sayer, *The Great Arch: English State Formation as Cultural Revolution* (Oxford: Basil Blackwell, 1985), 129, 141.

24. Michel Foucault, *Discipline and Punish: The Birth of the Prison*, trans. Alan Sheridan (New York: Vintage Books, 1979); Foucault, "Governmentality," in Graham Burchell, Colin Gordon and Peter Miller, eds., *The Foucault Effect: Studies in Governmentality* (Chicago: University of Chicago Press, 1991), 87–104. Ian Hunter, *Rethinking the School: Subjectivity, Bureaucracy, Criticism* (New York: St Martin's Press, 1994), 75–76. My analysis of travel and tourism as a governmental technology also derives much of its analytical insights from Tony Bennett, *Culture, A Reformer's Science* (London: Sage Publications, 1998). Critical and comparative analyses of modern education systems have aided this work including Andy Green's Gramscian analysis, *Education and State Formation: The Rise of Education Systems in England, France and the USA* (New York: St Martin's Press, 1990).

25. Aihwa Ong, "Cultural Citizenship as Subject-Making: Immigrants Negotiate Racial and Cultural Boundaries in the United States," *Anthropology* 37, no. 5 (December 1996); 737–62, esp. 738.

26. Seth Koven, *Slumming: Sexual and Social Politics in Victorian London* (Princeton, NJ: Princeton University Press, 2004); Lauren M. E. Goodlad, *Victorian Literature and the Victorian State: Character and Governance in a Liberal Society* (Baltimore, 2003). Cultural and social historians today are not as quick as in the past to condemn individual reformers, social workers, and philanthropists for their lack of self-awareness in perpetuating inequalities despite good intensions. Instead, like Koven and Goodlad, they explore the complex motives that compelled individuals to devote part or most of their adult lives to the working class and the poor. For this empathetic approach see, also, Ellen Ross, *Slum Travelers: Ladies and London Poverty, 1860–1920* (Berkeley: University of California Press, 2007). While such studies are by no means exculpatory, Corrigan and Sayer's *The Great Arch*, is a good reminder of the harsh reality behind many coercive practices imposed from above.

27. Geoff Eley, "Rethinking the Political: Social History and Political Culture in Eighteenth and Nineteenth Century Britain," *Archiv für Sozialgeschichte* 21 (1981) 438–457. See also, Keith Flett, *Chartism after 1848: the Working Class and the Politics of Radical Education* (Monmouth: Merlin Press, 2006).

28. Margot Finn, *After Chartism: Class and Nation in English Radical Politics, 1848–1874* (Cambridge: Cambridge University Press, 1993). John Belchem unravels the multiple political alliances and ideologies of this period in *Popular Radicalism in Nineteenth Century Britain* (New York: St Martin's Press, 1996). For a lucid account of classical liberalism and the reinterpretation of liberal principles that becomes known as the "new liberalism," see Ian Bradley, *The Strange Rebirth of Liberal Britain* (London: Chatto and Windus, 1985). For the transition from classical to "new" liberal principles, see Avital Simhony and David Weinstein, eds., *The New liberalism: Reconciling Liberty and Community* (Cambridge: Cambridge University Press, 2001); Stuart Hall and Bill Schwartz, *Crisis in the British State, 1880–1930* (London: Hutchinson, 1985).

29. It is therefore imperative to avoid retrospectively imposing uniform categories of politicized class consciousness on nineteenth-century Britons who did not view their position in Victorian society in that way, as recent studies on working-class conservatism attest. The "working class" was by no means homogenous and consisted of unskilled laborers as well as the highly skilled craftsmen of the "artisan aristocracy," who would not have regarded themselves as belonging in the same class category. Similarly, while the civil society facilitating the Lib/Lab rapprochement was predominantly composed of middle-class Britons, the reformist "middle class" included aristocrats who were persuaded by the merits of liberal economic theory or of liberal governance. In short, "working-class" and "middle-class" correlated with "radical" and "reformist" or "liberal," but this correlation must not be mistaken for congruence. For the multiplicity of working-class political identities see, Andrew August, *The British Working Class, 1832–1940* (Harlow: Pearson Longman, 2007), 79, 93, 154–55, 234–5; and Alex Windscheffel, *Popular Conservatism in Imperial London, 1868–1906* (Woodbridge: Boydell Press, 2007).

30. Piers Brendon's *Thomas Cook: 150 Years of Popular Tourism* (London: Secker & Warburg, 1991), is the most reliable analysis of the firm and briefly examines some of Cook's initial tours for workers. See also Susan Barton, *Working-Class Organizations and Popular Tourism, 1840–1970* for an analysis of other entrepreneurs (in addition to Cook) of early railway travel and tourism.

31. Richard Price, "The Working Men's Club Movement and Victorian Social Reform Ideology," *Victorian Studies* 15 (1971): 117–147. See also, Peter Bailey, "Rational Recreation in Action: The Working Men's Club Movement," chapter 5 in *Leisure and Class in Victorian England: Rational Recreation and the Contest for Control, 1830–1885* (London: Routledge and & Kegan Paul, 1978); and, George Tremlott, *Clubmen: The History of the Working Men's Club and Institute Union* (London: Secker & Warburg, 1987).

32. Anthony David Edwards, *The Role of International Exhibitions in Britain, 1850–1910: Perceptions of Economic Decline and the Technical Education Issue* (Amherst, MA: Cambria Press, 2008). Lara Kriegel, examines how industrial design museums emerged in response to this educational deficit and analyzes the contestations between artisans, manufacturers, and government bureaucrats over the "education of taste" in the mid-Victorian era in, *Grand Designs: Labor, Empire, and the Museum in Victorian Culture* (Durham, NC: Duke University Press, 2007).

33. In analyzing the travel experiences of workers on the artisan and working men's tours, it is necessary to acknowledge the ambiguity surrounding the terms "artisans" and "working men." Artisans should not be confused with semi-skilled workers, much less unskilled laborers. Artisans can be defined as skilled, male wage-workers in traditionally specialized trades such as tailoring, cabinetmaking, and carpentry. They can also be defined as male workers in the new, mechanized trades involving iron and high-powered machines, which sometimes earned them the additional designation of "engineer." "Artisans" and "working men" were sometimes used as interchangeable terms, but, although all artisans were working men, not all working men were artisans. Some semi-skilled or unskilled male workers (working men but not artisans) did participate in the tours, as did some married women workers (some of them female artisans) but only in accompanying their husbands. Nevertheless, these definitions of highly trained, male artisans represent most of the travelers on the artisan tours. See, Iorwerth Prothero, *Radical Artisans in England and France, 1830–1870* (Cambridge: Cambridge University Press, 1997) 2–3. In a nuanced analysis, Anne B. Rodrick shows that skilled artisans – as working men and self-improvers – also rejected the monikers of "mechanic" and "worker" which failed to connote their aspirational identity and culture as active citizens and members of improvement societies. See Rodrick, *Self Help and Civic Culture: Citizenship in Victorian Birmingham* (Aldershot: Ashgate, 2004), 114–115.

34. For the 1851 Great Exhibition and its varied meanings over time, see Jeffrey Auerbach, *The Great Exhibition of 1851: A Nation on Display* (New Haven, CT: Yale University Press, 1999), 228–231.

35. Bennett, "The Exhibitionary Complex."

36. Paul Greenhalgh, *Ephemeral Vistas: The Expositions Universelles, Great Exhibitions, and World's Fairs, 1851–1939* (Manchester: Manchester University Press, 1988). Pieter Van Wesemael documents the multiple sites of pedagogical technologies at exhibitions in, *Architecture of Instruction and Delight: A Socio-Historical Analysis of World Exhibitions as a Didactic Phenomenon (1798–1851–1970)* (Rotterdam: 010 Publishers, 2001).

37. Peter Hoffenberg examines the gaze of colonial subjects and white colonial settlers as well as Britons to show how the exhibitions allowed these groups to imagine themselves as part of a united imperial identity. See, Hoffenberg, *An Empire on Display: Indian and Australian Exhibitions from the Crystal Palace to the Great War*. Berkley: California University Press, 2001.

38. Susan Barton, "'Why Should Working Men Visit the Exhibition?': Workers and the Great Exhibition and the Ethos of Industrialism," in *The Golden Age: Essays in*

British Social and Economic History, 1850–1870, ed. Ian Inkster (Aldershot: Ashgate, 2000), 146–163; Susan Barton, *Working-Class Organisations and Popular Tourism, 1840–1970*. Jeffrey Auerbach also accounts for the working-class experience in *The Great Exhibition of 1851: A Nation on Display*.

39. Representative works are Michael Sanderson, "French Influences on Technical and Managerial Education in England, 1870–1940," in *Management and Business in Britain and France: The Age of Corporate Economy*, ed. Youssef Cassis *et al.* (Oxford: Clarendon Press, 1995); and Edwards, *The Role of International Exhibitions in Britain, 1850–1910*. Both works consult the artisan reports for their analyses.

40. My analysis of working-class identity, subjectivity, and narrativity draws on the insights of literary critics and historians. See, Reginia Gagnier, *Subjectivities; A History of Self-Representation in Britain, 1832–1920* (New York: Oxford University Press, 1991); Carolyn Steedman, *The Radical Soldier's Tale* (London: Routledge, 1988); and, especially with regard to placing the production of the artisan reports (marginalized in the past, as well as today) within a travel context has been Sara Mills, *Discourses of Difference: An Analysis of Women's Travel Writing and Colonialism* (London: Routledge, 1991). Useful for thinking about middle-class expectations in tension with the reality of working-class subjectivities is Seth Koven, "The Whitechapel Picture Exhibitions and the Politics of Seeing," in *Museum Culture: Histories, Discourses, Spectacles*, ed. Daniel J. Sherman and Irit Rogoff (Minneapolis: University of Minnesota Press, 1994), 22–48. For the "dialectical" process of identity construction in the context of travel, see Lloyd Kramer, "Victor Jacquemont and Flora Tristan: Travel, Identity and the French Generation of 1820," *History of European Ideas* 14 (1992): 789–816; and, Kramer, *Lafayette in Two Worlds: Public Cultures and Personal Identities in an Age of Revolutions* (Chapel Hill: The University of North Carolina Press, 1996), 12–15.

1   "A True Agent of Civilisation": Travel and the "Educational Idea," 1841–1861

1. Thomas Cook, "Excursions! Excursions!" *The Excursionist*, June 9, 1870, 7–8.
2. For an introduction to these "ideas" and their utilitarian links to national improvement, see Corrigan and Sayer, *The Great Arch*; Bennett, "The Multiplication of Culture's Utility," 107–134.
3. Foucault, *Discipline and Punish*, 307.
4. This analysis draws on the insights of Ian Hunter, *Rethinking the School: Subjectivity, Bureaucracy, Criticism* (New York: St Martin's Press, 1994); and Tony Bennett, "Cultural studies: The Foucault Effect," in *Culture, A Reformer's Science*, 74–77.
5. Hunter, *Rethinking the School*, 63–64.
6. Quoted in Ian Hunter, *Rethinking the School*, 10–11.
7. Ian Hunter, *Rethinking the School*, 72–73.
8. *Ibid.*, 68–69, 73; Corrigan and Sayer, *The Great Arch*, 115–165.
9. Foucault, *Discipline and Punish*, 298–299.
10. Peter Bailey, *Leisure and Class in Victorian England: Rational Recreation and the Contest for Control, 1830–1885* (London: Routledge & Keegan, 1978), 56–57.
11. *Ibid.*, 64. See also Peter Bailey, *Popular Culture and Performance in the Victorian City*, 19; Leonore Davidoff and Catherine Hall, "Prologue" in *Family Fortunes: Men and Women of the English Middle Class, 1780–1850* (Chicago: University of Chicago Press, 1987), 13–35.

12. Bailey, *Popular Culture*, 19.
13. Bennett, "The Multiplication of Culture's Utility," 107–134, 115.
14. Bennett, "The Exhibitionary Complex," 338.
15. Bennett, "The Multiplication of Culture's Utility," 107–134: 107, 115. For the 1845 Museum Bill, see Bennett, "The Exhibitionary Complex," 344. For the Library Acts, see Thomas Kelly, *The History of Public Libraries in Great Britain, 1845–1965* (London: Library Association, 1973).
16. Quoted in Bennett, "The Multiplication of Culture's Utility, 122.
17. *Ibid.*, 118, 122–123.
18. *Ibid.* See also Seth Koven, "The Whitechapel Picture Exhibitions and the Politics of Seeing," in *Museum Culture: Histories, Discourses, Spectacles,* eds., Daniel J. Sherman and Irit Rogoff (Minneapolis: University of Minnesota Press, 1994, 22–48. Raymond Williams, *The Long Revolution: An Analysis of the Democratic, Industrial, and Cultural Changes Transforming our Society* (New York: Columbia University Press, 1961), 56–58, 125–127.
19. Bennett, "The Multiplication of Culture's Utility," 124–125.
20. Piers Brendon, *Thomas Cook: 150 Years of Popular Tourism*, 2.
21. Two popular studies of Thomas Cook & Son that are frequently, and often uncritically, referenced in the history of travel and tourism are John Pudney, *The Thomas Cook Story* (London: Michael Joseph, 1953); and Edmund Swinglehurst, *The Romantic Journey: The Story of Thomas Cook and Victorian Travel* (New York: Harper & Row, 1974). The authoritative text is Piers Brendon's *Thomas Cook: 150 Years of Popular Tourism*. Brendon's work provides the context for my analysis of Cook's interest in educational travel.
22. Quoted in Brendon, *Thomas Cook*, 7–8.
23. Thomas Cook, "How to Keep a Tourist Note Book," in *The Excursionist*, April 1, 1868. The name of Cook's advertising newspaper, *The Excursionist,* varied over time. All subsequent cites will refer to the paper as *The Excursionist*.
24. Brendon, *Thomas Cook*, 18.
25. "Arrangements in Paris," *The Excursionist*, April 27, 1861, 1–4.
26. Ibid., 15. Although it has come to my attention too late to incorporate into my analysis, see the fascinating study on the "mob" as it relates to railway travel in Susan Major, " 'The Million go Forth': Early Railway Excursion Crowds, 1840–1860" (Ph.D. dissertation, University of York, 2012).
27. Quoted in James Buzard, *The Beaten Track: European Tourism, Literature, and the Ways to 'Culture': 1800–1918* (Oxford: Oxford University Press, 1993), 30.
28. James Buzard describes this rhetoric as "anti-tourist" discourse. See *ibid.*
29. Thomas Cook, "Pleasure Trips Defended," *The Excursionist*, June 1854, 2.
30. *Ibid.*
31. Cook, "Our First Trip to the Continent," *The Excursionist*, August 6, 1855, 3. Brendon, *Thomas Cook*, 63–65.
32. Cook, "The Anti-Excursion Press of London, and the Continued and Increased Popularity of Cook's Swiss and Italian Tickets," *The Excursionist*, September 18, 1865, 4.
33. Hugh Cunningham, *Leisure in the Industrial Revolution, c. 1780–c.1880* (London: Croom Helm, 1980), 157.
34. "Hints and Suggestions by a Working Man," *The Excursionist*, June 21, 1851, 5; "Why Should Working Men Visit the Exhibition?" *The Excursionist*, May 1851, 2.
35. Jeffrey A. Auerbach argues that the Great Exhibition would later help to provide unity and coherence to the Liberal Party. See Auerbach, *The Great Exhibition of 1851: A Nation on Display*, 31.

36. John R. Davis, "The Great Exhibition and the German States," in *Britain, the Empire, and the World at the Great Exhibition of 1851*, ed. Jeffrey A. Auerbach and Peter A. Hoffenberg (Aldershot: Ashgate, 2008), 147–172; 150.
37. Bennett, "The Exhibitionary Complex," 345.
38. Susan Barton, " 'Why Should Working Men Visit the Exhibition?'", 146–147.
39. Quoted in Thomas Cook, "The Harmonizing & Ennobling Influence of the Great Exhibition" in *The Excursionist*, June 21, 1851, 2–3.
40. Susan Barton, "'Why Should Working Men Visit the Exhibition?'"146–163.
41. *Ibid.*, 150.
42. Brendon, *Thomas Cook*, 64.
43. "Exaggerations," *The Excursionist*, June 6, 1863, 2; "Working Men's Excursion Clubs For Paris," *The Excursionist*, July 21, 1863, 1. Cook praises the "active and philanthropic men" of a "Birmingham Excursion Club," which he assisted in arranging a "Special Train" for Paris, August 10, 1863. Cook is likely referring to a Birmingham working men's excursion to Paris that took place on the same date and was recounted in the press by one of the middle-class organizers. Although no mention is made of Cook, it reflects the growing numbers of workers traveling abroad with the assistance of middle-class philanthropists for the purpose of rational recreation. See "Another Trip to Paris," *The Excursionist*, 6 August, 1863, 1; and Frederick Hine, *A Week in Paris: Reminiscences of 1863* (Birmingham: Billing Brothers and Whitmore, 1867), Bodleian Library, Oxford.
44. Prothero, *Radical Artisans in England and France, 1830–1870*, 113.
45. "International Working Men's Congress at Brussels, September 7th," *The Excursionist*, August 1, 1868, 2.
46. "The European Labour Congress at Lausanne," *The Bee-Hive*, September 7, 1867, 1.
47. "The Tourist Season of 1861," *The Excursionist*, October 19, 1861.
48. Brendon, *Thomas Cook*, 44, 58, 73–75.
49. Brendon, *Thomas Cook*, 65.
50. "Arrangements in Paris," *The Excursionist*, April 27, 1861, 1–4.
51. *Ibid.* Cook advertised the tour as a "national" event. However, the railways to the far north and west of England declined to reduce their fairs or provide special trains. This left excursionists from Manchester, Liverpool, Birmingham, and Bristol to find their own way to the departure sites in London. Most excursionists, therefore, resided in the Midlands, although a reportedly small number of Londoners also took advantage of Cook's arrangements. See Brendon, *Thomas Cook*, 73–74.
52. *Ibid.*
53. Thomas Cook, "The Great International Excursion to Paris," *The Excursionist*, April 27, 1861, 1.
54. According to the corps' captain, Kloutz Rowsell, the venture had the implicit sanction of the British minister of war, and the explicit favor of the Emperor Napoleon as a way of maintaining cordial relations between France and England. See J. Klotz-Rowsell, letter to the editor "M. Rowsell and the Volunteers," *The Times*, November 12, 1860, 8.
55. "The Great International Excursion to Paris," *The Excursionist*, April 27, 1861, 1–8.
56. Both Lucraft and Merriman were to become founding members of the International Workingmen's Association and serve in numerous radical causes. In addition to the Chartist movement and the International, Lucraft chaired the Workingmen's Peace Society, participated in the Workingmen's Club and Institute Union, protested against the Contagious Diseases Act, and served on the London School Board. For more on Josiah J. Merriman, see Ann Pottinger Saab, *Reluctant Icon: Gladstone,*

Bulgaria, and the Working Classes (Cambridge: Harvard University Press, 1991), 105–112. Cook explains this network of connections in "The Great International Excursion to Paris," 144, 1. By 1861, Cook and Paxton had collaborated on many philanthropic projects over the preceding twenty years. Early in Cook's career, Paxton had assisted with Cook's temperance excursions to the stately grounds of Chatsworth owned by the Duke of Devonshire, Paxton's employer at the time. They likely viewed this new venture as one that would put their rational recreation schemes on a grander national and international level, and, it should be added, one that would promote new consumer incentives for railway travel with which they both had vested interests (Paxton had financial ties to the railways). See Brendon, *Thomas Cook*, 44, 58, 73.

57. "British Workmen in Paris" *The London Review*, reprinted in *Reynolds's Newspaper*, June 1, 1861.

58. Thomas Cook, "The Great International Excursion to Paris, *The Excursionist* (April 27, 1861), 1–2.

59. Margot C. Finn, *After Chartism: Class and Nation in English Radical Politics, 1848–1874* (Cambridge: Cambridge University Press, 1993), 192. See also Royden Harrison, "The Setting," in *Before the Socialists: Studies in Labour and Politics, 1861–1881* (London: Routledge & Kegan Paul, 1965), 1–39.

60. Finn, After Chartism, 193.

61. *Ibid.*, 139–44.

62. *Ibid.*, 193–195, 216–217. For additional analysis on the communication between British and French workers see Prothero, *Radical Artisans in England and France, 1830–1870*.

63. Finn, *After Chartism*, 198–202.

64. "British Workmen in Paris," *The London Review*, reprinted in *Reynolds's Newspaper*, June 2, 1861.

65. For more on labor's responses to economic liberalism during this period, see Finn, *After Chartism*, 196.

66. Sir A. Henry Layard, *Autobiography and Letters* (London: John Murray, 1903), Vol. 2: 234.

67. See for example, Layard's dismissive comments concerning working-class speakers in Hyde Park for the 1867 reform bill in his parliamentary speech in *Hansard's Parliamentary Debates*, Ser. 3, V. 182, 1400–1403.

68. *The National Book Union, For the Dissemination of Sound Literature Among the Working Classes*, 1860 [?] Circular, Layard Papers, 38995 Vol. LXV (ff.432) 1868. Bound Volume. British Library Manuscript Collection.

69. Quoted in Gordon Waterfield, *Layard of Nineveh* (New York: Frederick A. Praeger, 1968), 292–293.

70. See A.H. Layard to Henry Richard Charles Wellesley, 2nd Lord and 1st Earl Cowley, March 1861, Public Record Office: FO 519/195 ff 1–234. 54–56, 57–59, 61. For quote, see 57. The dates of each day are illegible. The page numbers refer to archival notations.

71. *Ibid.*, 55.

72. *Ibid.*, 57.

73. "Working Men's Proposed Excursion to Paris," *Reynolds's Newspaper*, May 12, 1861, 5. Merriman, Blanchard, and Cook also gave speeches, as did the peace activist and philanthropist John Passmore Edwards. Representing the original "body of working men," Lucraft was also present on the platform.

74. For Layard's speech, see "Working Men's Excursion to Paris," *Lloyds Weekly Newspaper*, May 12, 1861, 5. Radical republicans in the crowd did not share

Layard's positive perspective about the lessons to be learned in Paris, as the tone of one report suggests. See, *Reynolds's Newspaper*, "Working Men's Proposed Excursion to Paris," May 12, 1861, 5. For an analysis of governmentality and the "liberal city," see Patrick Joyce, "City Past and City Present: Building the Liberal City," chapter 4 in *The Rule of Freedom* (London: Verso, 2003), esp. 148–149.

75. A.H. Layard to Cowley, March 1861, Cowley Papers, letter un-numbered.

76. *Ibid.*, 57–59. See also Cook's detailed explanation of the arrangements in "The Tourist Season of 1861," *The Excursionist*, October 19, 1861, 1.

77. Thomas Cook, "The Great International Excursion to Paris," *The Excursionist*, April 27, 1861, 1–4.

78. "The Whitsuntide Trip to Paris," *The Illustrated London News*, June 8, 1861.

79. *Ibid.*

80. For the history and politics of the paper see "Reynolds's Newspaper," http:// newspapers11.bl.uk/blcs/ReynoldssNewspaper.htm (accessed August 17, 2013). For the editorial that condemned the petition, see "The English Excursionists to France, and the French Empire," *Reynolds's Newspaper* (June 2, 1861). Benjamin Lucraft, wrote to say that none of the working men from the London committee had signed the document. See, Lucraft, "To the Editor: The English Excursionists and Louis Napoleon," *Reynolds's Newspaper* (June 9, 1861). With regard to the tour generally, see excerpts from various papers reprinted in *Reynolds's Newspaper*, June 2, 1861.

81. "The Emperor and the English Excursionists," *The Daily Telegraph*, reprinted in *Reynolds's Newspaper*, June 2, 1861.

82. "English Workmen in Paris," *The London Review*, reprinted in Reynolds's *Newspaper*, June 16, 1861.

83. Cook, "Annual Whitsuntide Trip to Paris," *The Excursionist*, May 7, 1863, 1; Cook, "'Pecuniary Profit' and 'An Honourable Livelihood,'" *The Excursionist*, February 1, 1868, 8.

84. Cook used his business to promote rational recreation and the democratization of travel, and, at the same time, drew profits from the expansion of the tourist industry. Brendon, *Thomas Cook*, 63.

85. "The Whitsuntide Trip to Paris," *The Illustrated London News*, June 8 1861. See also excerpts on the tours from various papers re-printed in *Reynolds's Newspaper*, June 2, 1861.

2 Turning the Educational Idea on Its Head: The Lib–Lab Alliance and the Organization of the Working Men's 1867 Exhibition Tours

1. *Minutes of the International Workingmen's Association*, October 2, 1866, 13–14; October 28, 1866, 22. Bishopsgate Institution and Library, London.

2. Lucraft served on a committee for the 1861 workingmen's tour of Paris. See Chapter One and "The English Excursionists and Louis Napoleon," *Reynolds's Newspaper*, June 9, 1861.

3. Dupont's suggestion is recorded in *Minutes of the International Workingmen's Association*, October 2, 1866, 13–14; October 28, 1866, 22. Bishopsgate Institution and Library, London.

4. See for example, David Fernbach, "Introduction," in Karl Marx, *The First International and After: Political Writings: Volume 3*, edited by David Fernbach (New York: Penguin Classics, 1992), 16; Royden Harrison, "E. S. Beesly and Karl Marx," *International*

Review of Social History 4 (1959): 208–238. The Soviets contributed to this perception. See, *Great Soviet Encyclopedia.* 3rd Edition. Eds. A. M. Prokhorov and M. Waxman (New York: Macmillan, 1973), s.v. "Eugene Dupont," in http://encyclopedia2. thefreedictionary.com/Eugene+Dupont (accessed August 17, 2012).

5. Reference to the French workers' tour of the 1862 London Universal Exhibition, and Dupont's 1871 letter are noted in a contemporary book review essay, see "The Commune of Paris," *The Edinburgh Review or Critical Journal* (American Edition. New York: Leonard Scott Publishing Company, 1871) CXXXIV(July–October, 1871): 263–290, 263, 271.The Open Library. http://ia600305.us.archive.org/22/ items/edinburghreview45coxgoog/edinburghreview45coxgoog.pdf (accessed September 22, 2013).

6. Belchem, *Popular Radicalism in Nineteenth-Century Britain*, 112–115. Henry Collins analyzes the overlap of interests between some middle-class reformers, trade union leaders, and radicals. In an interesting reversal, Marx made concessions to the large but politically moderate English trade unionists by toning down his rhetoric. See, Collins, "Karl Marx, the International and the British Trade Union Movement," *Science & Society* 26, No. 4 (Fall, 1962): 415; Keith Flett further explores these overlapping interests, contradictory ideologies, and Marx's rhetorical and linguistic compromises in *Chartism after 1848*, 127–129 and *passim*. Marx's pragmatic compromises also explain, in part, his membership in the Society of Arts between 1869 and 1871. His candidacy, as per the society's bylaws, was proposed by three members, after which the majority vote approved his candidature. Marx then accepted Foster's formal invitation to join a society that, historian D.G.C. Allan remarks, "however well- intentioned towards the proletariat" represented, as Marx would have seen it, the interests of capital. See, Allan, "The 'Red Doctor' Amongst the Virtuosi: Karl Marx and the Society," *Journal of the Royal Society of Arts* 129, No. 5297, Part 1 (March, 1981): 259–261; Part 2 (April, 1981): 309–311.

7. The minute books do not state the goals of the tours, but the IWA's objectives outlined at two Congress meetings that bookend the exhibition are suggestive. See, *Minutes of the General Council of the First International 1866–1868, Explanatory Notes* http://www.marxists.org/archive/marx/iwma/documents/minutes/footnotes1. htm (accessed August 17, 2013).

8. The IWA council made these recommendations at the Geneva Congress of 1866 and again at the Brussels Congress of 1867. See, Karl Marx, *The First International and After*, 86–88; "The European Labour Congress at Lausanne," *The Bee-Hive*, September 7, 1867. The literature on statistics and governmentality is extensive. See Corrigan and Sayer, *The Great Arch*; and, Patrick Joyce, *The Rule of Freedom*. While statistical knowledge was used to assert disciplinary power by making populations knowable domestically and imperially, Benedict Anderson shows the unintended consequences of this knowledge in producing new political subjectivities – the "imagined communities" of anti-colonial liberation movements. See Anderson, *Imagined Communities: Reflections on the Origin and Spread of Nationalism* (London: Verso, 1983).

9. Margot Finn's definition of "class consciousness" informs this analysis. While Finn accepts the material basis of class identities, she argues that class-consciousness required a "heroic act of imagination." Because class did not "spring magically" from the shared experience of economic exploitation, workers deliberately found ways to efface differences among them by creating common platforms. See Finn, *After Chartism*, 11–12. See also Flett's concise historiographical discussion of class analysis in *Chartism after 1848*, 11–15.

10. Patrick Joyce, *Democratic Subjects: The Self and the Social in Nineteenth-Century England* (Cambridge: Cambridge University Press, 1994), 86–87. Ian Hunter, for instance, writes that in the 1830s the "education Chartist," William Lovett, articulated ambitions for mass, working-class education that echoed the disciplinary and policing functions of Stow's pauper schools, *Rethinking the School: Subjectivity, Bureaucracy, Criticism* (New York: St Martin's Press, 1994), xiv, xii, xvi–xvii. Radical agendas continued to shape working class education and the propagation of "really useful knowledge and more" long after the demise of Chartism. See Flett, *Chartism after 1848*.

11. Karl Marx, *The First International and After*, 89.

12. For further analysis see, Robin Small, *Marx and Education* (Aldershot: Ashgate, 2005), 146–147.

13. *Minutes Book of the International Workingmen's Association*, October 28, 1866, 22; November 6, 1867, 31. Bishopsgate Institution and Library, London.

14. Universal Tourist Company Records, Public Record Office, BT 31/1335/3499.

15. "The English Working Classes and the French Exhibition," *The Bee-Hive*, January 2, 1867, 1.

16. "Working Men's Association," *The Bee-Hive*, January 12, 1867, 1.

17. Universal Tourist Company Records, Public Record Office, BT 31/13335/3499. The company folded ten months later. The records do not reveal the long or short term vision of investors.

18. "Police Court Revelations," *The Excursionist*, October 1, 1867. "Bubble Excursion Schemes," *The Excursionist*, April 17, 1867, 4.

19. *Report of the Paris Excursion Committee* (1868), Exhibition Foreign and Colonial Paris, 1866–1870. Victoria & Albert Museum Archive, Blythe House.

20. *The Bee-Hive*, June 22, 1867.

21. Richard Price, "The Working Men's Club Movement and Victorian Social Reform Ideology," *Victorian Studies* 15 (1971): 125.

22. Tremlett, *Clubmen*, 74–75, 31.

23. For quote see "5th Annual Meeting" in *Working Men's Club Reports*, Vol. 1. (18 June, 1867), The Working Men's Club and Institute Union Archive, London.

24. Harrison, *Before the Socialists*, 85; Belchem, *Popular Radicalism in Nineteenth-Century Britain*, 117–118.

25. Layard to Cowley, May 29, 1867, PRO FO 519/195 Part 4 of 4. ff 580–829; and *ibid.*, April 16, 1867. See also Layard to Cowley: April 16, 1867; February 9, 1867; June 17, 1867; June 20, 1867; May 29, 1867. Ff 580–829. FO 519/195 Part 4 of 4, Public Record Office, London.

26. See "5th Annual Meeting" in *Working Men's Club Reports*, Vol. 1. (June 18, 1867) 17, The Working Men's Club and Institute Union Archive, London.

27. *Ibid.*, 7. Industrialists held this instrumentalist view of the WMCIU long after its founding. See Richard Price, "The Working Men's Club Movement and Victorian Social Reform Ideology," *Victorian Studies*, 141.

28. For the secretary's comments on the meeting see, Tremlott, *Clubmen*, 33. For more on cross-class tensions, concessions and alliances and their impact on the content and character of liberalism in the later decades of the nineteenth century, see Finn, *After Chartism*, especially; Introduction, 9, 189, 239–240, and 316; and Flett, *Chartism after 1848*.

29. Flett, *Chartism after 1848*, 142; Belchem, "Radicalism, Liberalism, and Reformism, 1850–75," chapter 6 in *Popular Radicalism in Nineteenth Century Britain*.

30. These movements included educational reform for the working classes at home and for indigenous populations in India, the national expansion of the WMCIU,

the Peace Movement, and the Cooperative Movement. Pratt's cross-class sensibilities accommodated mixed-sex associations by the end of the century. He defined patriotism, for example, in terms of international rather than nationalist (or masculinist) identity during his tenure as chairman of the politically inclusive International Arbitration and Peace Association. See, Heloise Brown, *'The Truest Form of Patriotism': Pacifist Feminism in Britain, 1870–1902* (Manchester: Manchester University Press, 2003), 120–121. See also, Arthur Eyffinger, *The 1899 Hague Peace Conference: 'The Parliament of Man, the Federation of the World'* (The Hague: Kleuwer Law International, Martinus Nijhoff Publishers, 1999), 59, 58, 63. Writing for Edward Hale's progressive *American Journal* in 1897, Pratt reflected on his early radicalism, commitment to the cooperative movement and the collectivism of new liberalism (without, however, holding much faith in the state to exact justice, peace, or progress), and his enduring belief in the power of the WMCIU to nurture respectable individuals and informed citizens. See, Hodgson Pratt, "The Working Men's Club and Institute Union," *Lend a Hand: Record of Progress* XVIII, no. 1 (January 1897): 30–40, chapter in http://books.google.com/books?id=K7FCAQA AIAAJ&pg=PA30&dq=Hodgson+Pratt&hl=en&sa=X&ei=e4yUT_HkMsiigwefqLjZB A&ved=0CGUQ6AEwCDgK#v=onepage&q=Hodgson%20Pratt&f=false (accessed August 17, 2013).

Pratt's life work is memorialized in J.J. Dent, *Hodgson Pratt and His Memorial* (London: Hodgson Pratt Memorial Ltd, 1918). Richard Price, on the other hand, puts a damper on the hagiographic glow of Pratt "memorials," emphasizing how social control technologies pervaded club practices and ideologies. Despite his liberal humanism, Pratt related to the working class as subordinates. Indeed, Pratt refused to relinquish the Presidency of the WMCIU, assuming that workingmen's legitimate claim to full citizenship as responsible, autonomous adults, was still only a distant possibility. Not surprisingly, when workers obtained full leadership of the national office, as Price notes, they rarely trumpeted the call for class conciliation in the WMCIU's literature. See, Richard Price, "The Working Men's Club Movement and Victorian Social Reform Ideology," *Victorian Studies* 15 (1971):146, 131,194. See, also, T.S. Peppin, *Club-Land of the Toiler: Exemplified by the Workmen's Club and Institute Union* (London: J.M. Dent & Co.), 1895.

31. Guari Viswanation shows how methods for disciplining indigenous populations in India came to be used for disciplining subordinate populations in Britain, in "Raymond Williams and British Colonialism," *The Yale Journal of Criticism* Vol. 4, no. 2 (1991): 47–66; See also, Eric Stokes, *The English Utilitarians and India* (1959; reprint, Oxford: Oxford University Press, 1989). For Pratt's views on Indian education and colonial relations see Pratt's pamphlet, *University Education in England for Natives of India, Considered with a View to Qualify them for the Learned Professions or the Public Service and to create a Class who shall mediate between the Indian People and their English Rulers* (London: James Ridgeway, 1860). In the opposite trajectory, working men's clubs began to pepper the colonial landscape after Pratt took over the presidency, but were not sustained. Nevertheless, WMCIU members would have felt connected to Empire through the exhibitions, but also in their encounters with colonial populations in the metropole such as the visit of Mr Sasipada Bannerjea from Pratts' former sphere of colonial influence in West Bengal. A Hindu social reformer, Bannerjea had attended the 1871, WMCIU General Meeting held in London, where he had received a "hearty welcome." This experience, the WMCIU reported, had "bore fruit" with the formation of the first Bengal Workingmen's Club, where he and other upper caste progressives held "out a hand to workmen of low caste to promote their educational and

social elevation." Triumphantly documented in the WMCIU's Annual Reports, was the fourth year anniversary celebration of the Baranagore Working Men's Club at Barrackpore Park, in which fifty of the members assembled "with reverence" at the monument of Lady Canning, lauded the good governance of her husband, the Viceroy, Lord Canning, and praised, with song, the Queen's benevolent rule and her government's support of education. Bannerjea, as an intermediary for colonial governmentality, clearly adopted the pastoral role in seeking to produce self-regulating, moral beings divided, in this context, by caste, but also collectively divided from the metropole, by race. Colonial governmentality, as Patrick Joyce writes, measures itself against an "other." While the 1867 Reform bill may have rewarded "respectable" male artisans, India was still in its minority. See, Joyce, *The Rule of Freedom*, 250–254. WMCIU *Annual Reports and Appendix*, Vol. II, 1873–1874: 10–11, 26–27; WMCIU *Annual Reports* 1877–78.

32. Pratt, Hodgson. "The Working Men's Club and Institute Union."

33. Timothy Mitchell, *Colonizing Egypt* (Berkeley: University of California Press, 1988), 40, 42, 46.

34. See *The Excursionist*, February 1, 1868.

35. For accounts of the working men's excursions to Paris organized by Layard, Pratt, and the WMCIU see "Notice: Layard Papers April, 1867 38995 Vol. LXV (ff.432) 1868 Paris Excursion Committee of the Metropolitan District Association of Working Men's Clubs and Institutions, British Library Manuscript Collection; Layard to Cowley: April 16, 1867; February 9, 1867; June 17, 1867; June 20, 1867; May 29, 1867. Ff 580–829. FO 519/195 Part 4 of 4, Public Record Office. See, also, "First Visit of English Workmen (By one of themselves)," *The British Lion*, June 29, 1867, 12, British Library, Colindale, and Layard Papers British Library Manuscript collection 38995 Vol. LXV (ff.432) 1868, 49–50; *The Bee-Hive*, 1867–1868 *passim*. The savings system is described in W.O. Pocklington, "Excursions for Working Men to the Paris Exhibition," Letters to the Editor, *The Daily Telegraph*, March 13, 1867, Newspaper Cuttings: Paris Exhibition 1867. July 1863–July 1867. II. Pp 167 Victoria & Albert Museum Archive, Blythe House.

36. *The Bee-Hive*, May 11, 1867.

37. Cook and Pratt had a falling out midway through the Exhibition season and both used the popular press to accuse the other for failing to uphold their promises. Cook, for instance, insinuated that the WMCIU tours and Pratt, himself, were "lamentable failures." See *The Excursionist*, February 1, 1868. For Le Play and his role in the Imperial Commission see, Michael Z. Brooke, *Le Play: Engineer and Social Scientist* (New Brunswick, NJ: Transaction Publishers, 1998), 59–76; Van Wesemael, *Architecture of Instruction and Delight*.

38. *Report of the Paris Excursion Committee* (1868).

39. The "military encampment" became a model for all urban developments (from working-class housing estates to prisons) that allowed "embedding" or "hierarchical surveillance." See Foucault, *Discipline and Punish*, 170–172.

40. M. Chaboud, a tin worker and prolific writer of pro-Bonapartist propaganda inhabited the model "cottage." For a description of Chaboud and the display see "Visit of English Workmen to Paris," *The Bee-Hive*, June 15, 1867; for Chaboud's connection to the Palais Royal Group see David I. Kulstein, *Napoleon III and the Working Class: A Study of Government Propaganda Under the Second Empire* (Los Angeles: The California State Colleges, 1969), 126–128.

41. W.C. Aitken, "Artizans' Visit to Paris," *Journal of the Society of Arts* 15 (September 13, 1867), 668; Henry Cole, "Mr. Cole's Report Appendix P," in *Reports on the Paris Universal Exhibition, 1867 Volume 1 Containing the Report by the Executive*

Commissioner, and Appendices Presented to Both Houses of Parliament by Command of Her Majesty (1867), RSA/SC/EX/1/25, 1867.

42. *The Bee-Hive*, May 11, 1867; July 20, 1867; September 28, 1867.
43. *Report of the Paris Excursion Committee* (1868); Dean MacCannell suggests that tourists' visits to "work displays" in the second half of the nineteenth century were emblematic of modern modes of tourism and constituted a form of "alienated leisure." The working men's tours analyzed here and in later chapters, suggest alternative readings of such "work displays." See MacCannell, *The Tourist: A New Theory of the Leisure Class* (New York: Schocken Books Inc., 1989), 57.
44. "Artisans' Visits to the Paris Exhibition," *The Bee-Hive*, May 4, 1867.
45. Henry Cole, "Mr. Cole's Report Appendix P," in *Reports on the Paris Universal Exhibition, 1867, Volume 1, Containing the Report by the Executive Commissioner, and Appendices Presented to Both Houses of Parliament by Command of Her Majesty* (1867), RSA/SC/EX/1/25, 1867.
46. *The Bee-Hive* notes that Glazier attended a "special" general meeting of the Working Men's Association where he moved for a resolution on the extension of the franchise. See *The Bee-Hive*, January 12, 1867, 1.
47. Peter Gurney, *Co-operative Culture and the Politics of Consumption in England, 1870–1930* (Manchester: Manchester University Press, 1996), 161.
48. F.M. Leventhal, *Respectable Radical: George Howell and Victorian Working Class Politics* (London: Weidenfeld and Nicolson, 1971), xiv.
49. Gurney, *Co-operative Culture*, 122–123. See also Finn, *After Chartism* (1993); Belchem, *Popular Radicalism* (1996); Collins, "Karl Marx" (1962); and Flett, *Chartism after 1848* (2006), which contains a lucid explanation of the ideological contradictions in the beliefs and actions of prominent radical activists.
50. See fn 30.
51. On Pratt and the question of "equality" see Price, "The Working Men's Club Movement," 140, n.58. In 1883, Pratt accepted the Chairmanship of the middle class International Arbitration and Peace Association. See, Martin Ceadel, *Semi-Detached Idealists: The British Peace Movement and International Relations, 1854–1945* (Oxford: Oxford University Press, 2000), 91; Brown, *"The Truest Form of Patriotism"*, 115–116.
52. Ceadel, *Semi-Detached Idealists*, 91; George Dyer, "Benjamin Lucraft," in *Six Men of the People: Biographical Sketches with Portraits*, by Dyer and William Catchpool (London: Dyer Brothers, 1882), 8.
53. Flett, *Chartism after 1848*, 176.
54. B. T. Hall, *Our Fifty Years: The Story of the Working Men's Club and Institute Union: Together with Brief impressions of the Men of the Movement* (London: Working Men's Club and Institute Union, 1912), 45.
55. Flett describes Lucraft as a radical liberal – especially given his election to the London School Board in 1870, the only viable political option for effecting change within the established system prior to the formation of the Independent Labour Party and the Social Democratic Federation in the 1880s. Thus Lucraft championed free, compulsory, and secular, state education for all, and used his office to ferret out elite malfeasance in the re-distribution of charitable funds intended for working-class education. See, Flett, *Chartism after 1848*, 174–176, 187–190, 152; George Holyoake, *The Good of Going to Paris to See the Exhibition: A Letter to Willis Chater, Weaver, of Mytholmroyd* (London: London Book Store, 1867). Holyoake actively supported middle-class radical parliamentary candidates and acted as a go-between for working-and middle-class radical leaders. In exchange, Holyoake enjoyed loans, gifts, and patronage from liberal grandees. See, Finn, *After Chartism*, 189–190, 210.

56. Flett, *Chartism after 1848*, 143; Gurney, *Co-operative Culture*, 10
57. Peter Gurney, "The Middle-Class Embrace: Language, Representation, and the Contest Over Co-operative Forms in Britain, c. 1860-1914," *Victorian Studies* 37, No. 2 (Winter, 1994), 253-286, esp. 254, 257, 262-263, 266, 269, 270. See also, *Report of the First International Co-operative Congress held in the hall of the Society of Arts, on 19th, 20th, 22nd, and 23rd August 1895*, (London: P.S. King & Son, 1896). http://books.google.com/books?id=HzkKAQAAMAAJ&printsec=frontcover&source=gbs_ge_summary_r&cad=0#v=onepage&q&f=false (accessed September 22, 2013).
58. Edward Royle, "George Jacob Holyoake," in *Religion, Radicalism, and Freethought in Victorian & Edwardian Britain: Selected Pamphlets by G.J. Holyoake, 1841–1904*, ed. by Edward Royle (East Ardsley: EP Microform Ltd., n.d.) 5.
59. Holyoake, *The Good of Going to Paris to See the Exhibition*.
60. *Ibid.*
61. "History of the Prohibition of the Co-operative Congress of Paris," *The Social Economist, Industrial Partnerships Record & Co-operative Review* (1867), 129–30. http://books.google.com/books?id=X3UOAAAAQAAJ&pg=PA26-IA7&lpg=PA26-IA7&dq=history+of+the+prohibition+of+the+Co-operative+congress+in+paris&source=bl&ots=yWWM7BvTEg&sig=bVAFcygmSFYDFZNRbegLZFqDsqo&hl=en&sa=X&ei=X8Y_UsCqDO_eyQGdzIHQBw&ved=0CC4Q6AEwAA#v=onepage&q=history%20of%20the%20prohibition%20of%20the%20Co-operative%20congress%20in%20paris&f=false (accessed August 17, 2013).
62. *Report of the Paris Excursion Committee.* This report is also included in the appendix to Working Men's Club and Institute Union, Paris Excursion Committee, *Modern Industries: A Series of Reports on Industry and Manufactures as Represented in the Paris Exposition in 1867, by Twelve British Workmen, Visiting Paris under the Auspices of the Paris Excursion Committee* (London: MacMillan and Co, 1868).
63. Layard to Cowley, May 29, 1867, Ff 580–829. FO 519/195 Part 4 of 4, Public Record Office; Bruce William Layard, *Autobiography and Letters*, reprinted letter to Mrs. Austen June 13, 1867 in *Sir Henry Layard: Autobiography and Letters*. Vol. 2 (London: John Murray, 1903).
64. Henry Cole to Austin Henry Layard, July 22, 1867, Layard Papers, Add 38994 Vol. LXIV, British Library Manuscript Collection.

3   "The Lessons of Paris": The 1867 Working Men's Exhibition Tours and the Artisan Imagination

1. "First Visit of English Workmen to Paris (By one of themselves)," *The British Lion*, June 29, 1867, 12, British Library Colindale, and Clipping in Layard Papers, 38995 Vol. LXV (ff.432) 1868, 49–50.
2. *Ibid.*
3. Working Men's Institute and Club Reports, 1867–1868, 18. The Working Men's Club and Institute Union Archive, London.
4. Austen Henry Layard, *Autobiography and Letters from his Childhood until his Appointment as H.M. Ambassador at Madrid*, Vol. 2 (London: John Murray, 1903), 235.
5. "First Visit of English Workmen to Paris (By one of themselves)," 12; Clipping in Layard Papers, 38995 Vol. LXV (ff.432) 1868, 49–50.
6. See Broadwood and Sons, "Paris Exhibition, Return Thanks to the Men," August 16, 1867, Surrey History Centre, 2185/JB/.

7. The WMCIU also promoted, published, and awarded prizes for artisan reports. Many of the reports were near duplicates of the SA reports, having been written by the same artisans. See the circular listing the prize-winners and the titles of their reports in "Prize Reports by British Workmen," A/RSA/18/K-Z 1868/Box 2/ (M-Z) Royal Society of Arts Archive 50, hereafter RSA. For the funding of the prizes and complications with a matching grant from the Lords of the Committee of Council on Education, see Hodgson Pratt to Henry Cole, March 20, 1868, in Exhibition Foreign and Colonial Paris 1866–1870, Victoria & Albert Museum Archive, Blythe House. For the published reports, see, Working Men's Club and Institute Union, Paris Excursion Committee. *Modern Industries: A Series of Reports on Industry and Manufactures as Represented in the Paris Exposition in 1867*, http://books.google.com/books?id=OxZAAAAAYAAJ&dq=inauthor:%22Working+Men's+Club+and+Institute+Union%22&source=gbs_navlinks_s (accessed August 17, 2013).

8. Society of Arts, Preface to *Reports of Artisans to Visit the Paris Universal Exhibition, 1867* (London: Bell and Daldy, 1867), iv–vi.

9. Hawes, "On the Reports of the Artisans Selected to Visit the Paris Universal Exhibition of 1867," *Journal of the Society of Arts* (January 24, 1868): 161–180, 162.

10. *Ibid.*

11. The editor of the Birmingham reports, William Costen Aitken, noted in a letter to the SA's secretary, Peter Le Neve Foster, that members of the Chamber of Commerce appeared "afraid" of what the reports might contain, and assured them that they were not "responsible for anything said by the artizans." See William Costen Aitken to Peter Le Neve Foster, November 1, 1867, RSA 18/A/26.

12. Hawes, "On the Reports of the Artisans", 162.

13. Working class social and trade activists may predominate as artisan reporters on two counts. First, the SA, like the WMCIU, sought to build bridges between the classes. Possibly, Chambers of Commerce members, employers, and the Society's Council favored more powerful artisans over others as a way of offering patronage. Second, working-class activists tended to be highly literate "self-improvers," and thus more capable writers. See David Vincent's comments on working-class militants and literacy in *Bread, Knowledge and Freedom: A Study of Nineteenth-Century Working Class Autobiography* (London: Europa Publications Limited, 1981), 9.

14. Joseph Gutteridge, a ribbon weaver and artisan reporter, noted that it was necessary to obtain the "consent" of his employers before accepting his "commission" from the SA. "As trade was at a low ebb," he remarked, "leave of absence for a month was readily granted." See Gutteridge, *Lights and Shadows in the Life of an Artisan* (Coventry: Curtis and Beamish, 1893), 179.

15. John Randall, "Pottery and Porcelain, With some Notes on Iron Manufacture" in *Reports of Artisans* (1867), 178–179.

16. See J.T. Dexter, Appendix III, pgs. 123–124, in Working Men's Club and Institute Union, Paris Excursion Committee. *Modern Industries: A Series of Reports on Industry and Manufactures as Represented in the Paris Exposition in 1867*.

17. *Ibid.*

18. For unions and the exclusion of women, see Andrew August, *The British Working Class, 1832–1940* (London: Pearson Longman, 2007), 41; Richard Price, *Labour in British Society: An Interpretive History* (London: Routledge, 1986), 83. WMCIU provisions for married couples, however, can also be seen as a progressive nod to the liberal ethos of rational recreation, one that conformed to the middle-class ideal of family sociability.

19. Thomas Connolly, "Masonry, & c." in *Reports of Artisans* (1867), 250.

20. *Ibid.*, 253–254.
21. *Ibid.*, 254.
22. G. Berry, "Engraving" in *Reports of Artisans* (1867), 35.
23. John Randall, "Pottery and Porcelain," *Reports of Artisans* (1867), 179. For the hierarchical organization of the exhibition see Greenhalgh, *Ephemeral Vistas*.
24. James Pamplin, "Jewellery and Gilt Toys," in *Reports of Artisans* (1867), 52. Pamplin's response reflects a mid-Victorian ambivalence towards Indian culture and art in debates of art workmanship, education, and display. Lara Kriegal analyses this "grammar" of Indian arts, and its fullest expression in the establishment of the Indian Collection at the South Kensington Museum, London. See Kriegel, *Grand Designs*, 140–144. In the 1889 reports, T. Smyth, a plasterer, explains the importance of the "Indian Museum" at South Kensington for his work. See, Smyth, "Plastering," in *Reports of Artisans Selected by the Mansion House Committee to Visit the Paris Universal Exhibition, 1889* (London: C.F. Roworth, 1889), 525–526. Smyth notes that the construction of the Indian Palace was conducted by the French and English (all of the plaster work was English and based on models of Indian art housed at the museum). He does not mention their provenance in India. This illustrates Timothy Mitchells' point that representations – in such imperial contexts as the exhibitions – warped metropolitan realities, perceptions, or understandings of the colonial Other. See Mitchell, "Egypt at the Exhibition," in chap. 1, *Colonizing Egypt*, 1–33.
25. William Bourne, "The Manufacture of Caoutchouc," in *Reports of Artisans* (1867), 380–383.
26. Connolly, "Masonry, & c.," 255.
27. William Glazier to Peter Le Neve Foster, July 1, 1873. A/RSA/23/A-H 1873. RSA Archive 13, 23/G/87.
28. Connolly, "Masonry, & c.," 250.
29. Charles Alfred Hooper, "Cabinet Making" in *Reports of Artisans* (1867), 25.
30. The Excursion Committee provided the artisan travelers with *Black's Guide to Paris and the International Exhibition* compiled by D.T. Ansted, which contained "helpful hints on how to be an economical tourist." For reference see A.H. Layard, *Report of the Paris Excursion Committee* (1868) in Exhibition Foreign and Colonial Paris 1866–1870 at Victoria & Albert Museum Archive, Blythe House. Thomas Cook offers a short review of *Black's Guide* in *The Excursionist* April 17, 1867, 2.
31. William Hawes, "On the Reports of the Artisans selected to Visit the Paris Universal Exhibition of 1867," *Journal of the Society of Arts* (January 24, 1868): 161–180, 161.
32. Connolly, "Masonry, &c.," 250.
33. Georgios Varouxakis, *Victorian Political Thought on France and the French* (Basingstoke: Palgrave, 2002), 12.
34. See Linda Colley, *Britons: Forging the Nation 1707–1837* (New Haven, CT: Yale University Press, 1992).
35. Stefan Collini, *English Pasts: Essays in History and Culture* (Oxford: Oxford University Press, 1999), 133.
36. Here, Collini refers specifically to Mill. See *ibid.*, 132.
37. Varouxakis, *Victorian Political Thought*, 16.
38. George Holyoake, *The Good of Going to Paris to See the Exhibition*.
39. Holyoake's pamphlet was typically didactic with regard to the educational value of travel. For didactic travel literature see Margaret Hunt, "Racism, Imperialism, and the Traveler's Gaze in Eighteenth-Century England," *Journal of British Studies* 32 (October 1993): 333–357, especially 346–353; Judith Adler, "Travel

as Performed Art," *American Journal of Sociology* 94, No. 6 (May 1989): 1366–91; Buzard, *The Beaten Track*, 65–79; Marjorie Morgan, "The Meaning and Mechanics of Travel in the Victorian Age," in *National Identities and Travel in Victorian Britain* (Basingstoke: Palgrave, 2001), 9–45.

40. Holyoake, *The Good of Going to Paris to See the Exhibition* (1867).

41. For scholarship on French "Artisan Reports" at the 1862 and other exhibitions, see Kulstein, *Napoleon III and the Working Class*, 125, 136; Leorna Auslander, "Perceptions of Beauty and the Problem of Consciousness: Parisian Furniture Makers" in Lenard R. Berlanstein, ed. *Rethinking Labor History: Essays on Discourse and Class Analysis* (Urbana: University of Illinois Press, 1993), 149–181. Auslander, in part, argues that the French artisans used the reports to level critiques on the aesthetics of art workmanship vs. commercial manufacturing and left political and social questions to their trade union meetings and publications. See also, Auslander, *Taste and Power: Furnishing Modern France* (Berkeley: University of California Press, 1996); Jacques Rancière and Patrick Vauday, "Going to the Expo: the worker, his wife and machines," in Adrian Rifkin and Roger Thomas, eds. *Voices of the People: The Social Life of "La Sociale" at the End of the Second Empire* (London: Routledge & Paul Kegan, 1988), 23–44; Michael Z. Brooke, *Le Play: Engineer and Social Scientist*. German artisans also visited British and Continental exhibitions, but their reports do not appear to have been published, or if published were not meant for wide distribution, see John R. Davis, "Württemberg at the Exhibitions. A Study in the Dissemination of Knowledge and the Role of the State in Industrialisation" (Unpublished Paper, Kingston University); and, Ingeborg Cleve, Dem Fortschritt entgegen. Ausstellungen und Museen im Modernisierungsprozess des Königreichs Württemberg, 1806–1918), in *Historische Anthropometrie* (*Jahrbuch für Wirtschaftsgeschichte* 9/1, 2000/1, 149–169.

42. Judith Walkowitz, *City of Dreadful Delight*, 16.

43. Regenia Gagnier, *Subjectivities: A History of Self-Representation in Britain, 1832–1920* (New York: Oxford University Press, 1991), 65–66.

44. Walkowitz, *City of Dreadful Delight*, 20.

45. *Ibid.*, 16.

46. *Ibid.*,16. For other analyses of London, middle-class men (and women) who ventured into the East End, see Seth Koven, *Slumming: Sexual and Social Politics in Victorian London* (Princeton, NJ: Princeton University Press, 2004); and Ellen Ross, *Slum Travelers: Ladies and London Poverty, 1860–1920* (Berkeley: University of California Press, 2007).

47. Walkowitz, *City of Dreadful Delight*, 16.

48. *Ibid.*, 42. Patrick Joyce briefly discusses the masculine, middle-class flâneur in the context of governmentality in *The Rule of Freedom*, 201. The modern city leading into the turn of the century, owed something to the exhibitions in producing new and spectacular consumer vistas that catered to mass society, rather than to male, middle class flâneurs alone. New spaces for mass consumption allowed those on the margins to blend in the crowd. See Urry, *The Tourist Gaze*, 126–127. Antoinette Burton addresses the issues of public space, tourism and racialized flâneurs in, *At the Heart of the Empire: Indians and the Colonial Encounter in Late-Victorian England* (Berkeley: University of California Press, 1998), 5, 12, 153, 166, 174.

49. T.W. Hughes and John D. Prior, "Carpenters and Joiners' Work," in *Reports of Artisans* (1867), 214. George Howell conducted similar experiments. See George Howell, "Bricklaying," in *Reports of Artisans* (1867), 198.

50. T.J. Wilkinson, "Table and Fancy Glass," in *Reports of Artisans*, Part II (1867), 152–153.

51. Alexander Kay, "Joiners' Work," in *Reports of Artisans* (1867), 234.
52. John Wilson, "Cutlery," 52–54, 61.
53. T.J. Wilkinson, "Table and Fancy Glass," 154. For the *livret* system see Prothero, *Radical Artisans in England and France*, 79.
54. George Howell to Charles Haussoullier, September 12, 1867. Letter No. 37, George Howell Letter Books #12 (4137) ff. 1–494, Bishopsgate Institute, London.
55. R. Sinclair, "Tailors' Work," in *Reports of Artisans* (1867), 369.
56. *Ibid.*, 363.
57. P.A. Rasmussen, "Silverwork," in *Reports of Artisans* (1867), 296.
58. Aaron Green, "Ceramic Decoration," in *Reports of Artisans* (1867), 26.
59. T.J. Wilkinson, "Table and Fancy Glass," 149.
60. Hughes and Prior, "Carpenters and Joiners' Work", 209.
61. Francis Kirchhoff, "Glass Painting," in *Reports of Artisans* (1867), 74.
62. Frederick Thompson "Leather, Harness, Saddlery, Whips, Portmanteaus, Etc." in *Reports of Artisans*, Part II (1867), 28.
63. Francis Kirchhoff, "Glass Painting," in *Reports of Artisans* (1867), 82.
64. William Bramhall, "Saws and Tools," in *Reports of Artisans* (1867), 51.
65. Sara Mills, *Discourses of Difference: An Analysis of Women's Travel Writing and Colonialism* (London: Routledge, 1991), 69, 83.
66. *Hansard's Parliamentary Debates*, Series 3, V. 184, 1866, 1403.
67. Thomas Cook, "Paris and the Parisians Pictured by English Artisans," *The Excursionist* February 1, 1868. For Cook's further commentary on the artisan's reports see *The Excursionist*, April 1, 1868.
68. Connolly, "Masonry, &.c.," 255.
69. Wilkinson, "Table and Fancy Glass," 149.
70. Bramhall, "Saws and Tools," 37.
71. See Thompson, *The Making of the English Working Class*; and, Finn, *After the Chartists*, 110.
72. David Sarjeant, "On Papier Maché," in *Reports of Artisans* (1867), 104–105.
73. Hermann F. Jung, "The Horological Department," in *Reports of Artisans* (1867), 353–354.
74. James Mackie, "Wood-Carving," in *Reports of Artisans* (1867), 98–99, 101.
75. Connolly, "Masonry &c.," 268–269, 263.
76. Thomas Jacob, "Cabinet Work," in *Reports of Artisans* (1867), 107–108.
77. Pamplin, "Jewellery and Gilt Toys," 55.
78. Sonya Rose, *Limited Livelihoods: Gender and Class in Nineteenth-Century England* (Berkeley: University of California Press, 1992), 138.
79. See Anna Clark, *The Struggle for the Breeches; Gender and the Making of the British Working Class* (Berkeley: University of California Press, 1995).
80. Jacob, "Cabinet Work," 114–115; R. Sinclair, "Tailors' Work," in Reports of Artisans (1867), 371.
81. Kay, "Joiners' Work," 240–241.
82. Jacob, "Cabinet Work," 112.
83. *Ibid.*
84. Rose, *Limited Livelihoods*, 136.
85. Jacob, "Cabinet Work," 112.
86. Kay, "Joiners' Work," 241.
87. Jacob, "Cabinet Work," 113–114. For an analysis on café domesticity in Paris, and one that could be less "orderly" than the artisan reporters suggest, see W. Scott Haine, *The World of the Paris Café: Sociability among the French Working Class, 1789–1914* (Baltimore: Johns Hopkins University Press, 1996), 52–54, 57.

88. See S.C. Burchell, *Imperial Masquerade: the Paris of Napoleon III* (New York: Atheneum, 1971), 103–107; Donald Reid, *Paris Sewers and Sewermen: Realities and Representations* (Cambridge, MA: Harvard University Press, 1991); and Matthew Truesdell, *Spectacular Politics: Louis-Napoleon Bonaparte and the Fête Impériale, 1849–1870* (New York: Oxford University Press, 1997).
89. See Charles Haussoullier to Peter Le Neve Foster (November 28, 1867), A/RSA/18/A-J. RSA Archive 58. 18/F/65; (May 13, 1868), A/RSA/18/A-J. RSA Archive 58. 18/F/143; (February 12, 1868), A/RSA/18/A-J. RSA Archive 58. 18/F/154.
90. Bramhall, "Saws and Tools," 51. As Sara Mills writes, quoting Foucault: "'what happened' and 'what was seen to happen' and 'what was written' are entirely dependent on the rules of discursive formations, which allow certain things to be described; hence, there is no question of a 'simple transcription'" of an objective truth. See Mills, *Discourses of Difference*, 85.
91. Leorna Auslander makes this point with regard to French artisan exhibition reports and "speech communities." See Auslander, "Perceptions of Beauty and the Problem of Consciousness," 161.
92. See Margot Finn on Samuel Morley's patronage of working-class causes in, *After Chartism*, 237–240.
93. John Evans, "Mechanical Engineering," in *Reports of Artisans* (1867), 422.
94. *Ibid.*
95. *Ibid.*, 425.
96. Bramhall, "Saws and Tools," 51.
97. Hughes and Prior, "Carpenters and Joiners' Work," 214–215.
98. Connolly, "Masonry, &c.," 265.
99. Sinclair, "Tailor's Work," 369.
100. William Elliott, "Die-Sinking," in *Reports of Artisans* (1867), Part II, 341.
101. Hughes and Prior, "Carpenters and Joiners' Work," 213–214.
102. Edward Smith, Joseph Bird, and George Dexter, "Lace," in *Reports of Artisans* (1867), 147.
103. Hooper, "Cabinet Making," 2.
104. *Ibid.*, 23, 19.
105. *Ibid.*, 25.
106. *Ibid.*, 15.
107. *Ibid.*, 23.
108. *Ibid.*, 15.
109. Hooper may have been influenced by the Positivist Frederick Harrison, who was an active champion of working-class causes. In 1852, Harrison claimed that "It is true that Liberty is a mockery in France, but those other two, Equality and Fraternity are not a mockery, but living realities, those two without which liberty loses half its sweetness, & with which servitude loses half its pain ... That is I do think that a man is better and happier in Paris though a dragoon stops him at every street, than he is in London under the tyranny of our present state of society which wounds him worse than steel." Quoted in Finn, *After Chartism*, 200.
110. Hooper, "Cabinet Making," 11–12.
111. *Ibid.*, 6.
112. *Ibid.*, 12.
113. *Ibid.*, 21.
114. *Ibid.*, 20; Peter Gurney, "The Middle-Class Embrace."
115. Hooper, "Cabinet Making," 20, 22.
116. *Ibid.*, 16.
117. *Ibid.*, 4.

118. *Ibid.*, 6.
119. *Ibid.*, 7.
120. *Ibid.*, 19.
121. *Ibid.*, 3.
122. *Ibid.*, 2. Thomas Cook found much to fault in the incursion of middle-class lodgers at the barracks. The officers of the WMCIU, namely its Vice President, Hodgson Pratt, Cook argued, had permitted their "friends" to take advantage of the cut-rate prices they offered for transport and lodging in Paris. This enraged Cook who claimed that the scheme had compromised the integrity of his firm, which had negotiated the special rates with the railways for a specifically philanthropic cause. See *The Excursionist*, February 1, 1868.
123. Hooper, "Cabinet Making," 15.
124. *Ibid.*, 5.
125. *Ibid.*, 15.
126. *Ibid.*, 13.
127. *Ibid.*, 14.
128. *Ibid.*, 25.
129. *Ibid.*, 17.
130. *Ibid.*, 24.
131. *Ibid.*, 24.
132. *Ibid.*, 24.

4   "High Attainments": The Artisan Exhibition Tours and the Campaign for Technical Education, 1867–1889

1. "Fourth Ordinary Meeting," *The Journal of the Society of Arts* 15 (December 13, 1867): 57–67.
2. See Thomas Twining to Peter Le Neve Foster, April 18, 1868. RSA/18/R/36. Twining remarks: "if I rightly understand the proposal it will not have for its object to ferret out the secrets of foreign industry, but to study its organization, especially as concerns the mutual relations of the employers and employed; also the education of the latter, and their physical as well as social condition."
3. "Seventh Ordinary Meeting," *Journal of the Society of Arts* 16 (January 24, 1868): 177.
4. Throughout his professional life, Hooper encouraged employers, workers, and the state to develop educational travel. See the Samuelson London School of Economics, Pamphlet Collection. George N. Hooper, *An Address on General and Special Education delivered to the Students and Teachers of the Carriage Building Technical Class of the Young Men's Christian Association at the Royal Polytechnic, Regent Street, London*. (London: Waterloo & Sons Limited, 1894), Pamphlet Collection, London School of Economics. Hooper served as an International Juror at the 1855 Exhibition and in similar capacities at later exhibitions. See Edwards, *The Role of International Exhibition in Britain, 1850–1910*, 108, 130, fn.151.
5. George Hooper, "Workmen's Holidays," *The Journal of the Society of Arts* 16 (September 4, 1868): 729–730.
6. *Ibid.*
7. *Ibid.*
8. The announcements were enclosed in a letter from T.G. Atkins to Peter Le Neve Foster, secretary of the SA: "I have taken the liberty of forwarding the two papers enclosed, thinking it would please you to know that the Weavers of Spitalfields have some opportunity of learning of your proceedings by the perusal of some

of our local papers." February 8, 1873, A/RSA/23/A-H 1873 Box 1 RSA Archive 13: 23/A/59. The SA's history is recorded in its journal, which has been sustained throughout most of its history. In addition, see Sir Henry Trueman Wood, *A History of the Royal Society of Arts* (London: John Murray, 1913); and, Derek Hudson and Kenneth W. Luckhurst, *The Royal Society of Arts, 1754–1954* (London: John Murray, 1954).

9. Particular to London, Gareth Stedman-Jones describes the decade leading up to the depression as one of increasing immiseration for Spitalfield weavers who, reduced in numbers through a free-trade treaty with France, and cut off from dock work with the demise of the East London ship-building industry, took up casual employment when and where they could find it. Only a handful, if that, could have possibly made the time or produced the tuition funds to pursue a SA certificate. See Stedman-Jones, *Outcast London: A Study in the Relationship between Classes in Victorian Society* (Oxford: Oxford University Press, 1971; reprint, Harmondsworth: Penguin Books Inc., 1976), 101–105.

10. For a description of their duties from the perspective of an artisan reporter, see Joseph Leicester, "Report on Table and Fancy Glass," in *Artisan Reports on the Paris Universal Exhibition of 1878* (London: Sampson Low, Marston, Searle, & Rivington, 1879), 109.

11. *Reports of Artisans selected by a Committee Appointed by the Council of the Society of Arts to Visit the Paris Universal Exhibition*, 1867 (London: Bell and Daldy, 1867), iv.

12. "Seventh Ordinary Meeting," *Journal of the Society of Arts* 16 (January 24, 1868):161.

13. Anthony David Edwards also takes exhibitions as the launching point for an analysis of the technical education movement, emphasizing various governmental commissions as well as the SA in the organization of exhibitions and the rhetoric surrounding British economic decline in *The Role of International Exhibitions in Britain, 1850–1910*. See also, E.J.R. Eaglesham, *The Foundations of 20th-Century Education in England* (London: Routledge & Kegan Paul, 1972).

14. Jeffrey A. Auerbach identifies this dual purpose of the exhibition in *The Great Exhibition of 1851: A Nation on Display*, 10, 31.

15. The question of Britain's industrial (and thus economic) "decline" has been the subject of significant historical debate, but is not a concern of this book which accepts the premise that the perception of decline helped give rise to a technical educational reform movement. For a relatively recent analysis that argues against declension and offers a historiography of the debate, see Graeme Gooday, "Lies, Damned Lies and Declinism: Lyon Playfair, the Paris 1867 Exhibition and the Contested Rhetorics of Scientific Education and Industrial Performance," in Ian Inkster *et al.*, eds., *The Golden Age: Essays in British Social and Economic History, 1850–1870*, 105–120. Bernard Cronin muddies the waters further by arguing that upper-class agitation for technical education reform was too sporadic and driven by "market forces" to be properly called a "movement." See Cronin, *Technology, Industrial Conflict and the Development of Technical Education in 19th-Century England* (Aldershot: Ashgate, 2001), 3, 178. The analysis, here, however, links individuals, institutions, and networks across time invested in educational change. This suggests more continuity than Cronin allows, reflecting the importance of exhibitions to any analysis of nineteenth century educational change, a point in keeping with Anthony David Edwards in *The Role of International Exhibitions in Britain, 1850–1910*, xi–xiii.

16. Lara Kriegel examines "aesthetic reform," in the craft industries that produced the early schools of design and, after the 1851 Exhibition, the South Kensington

Museum, in *Grand Designs: Labor, Empire, and the Museum in Victorian Culture*. The history of the SA, which is not a significant feature of Kriegel's book, shows the intersection of design reform with the technical education movement.

17. Playfair titled his lecture "Industrial Education on the Continent." See A.S. Bishop, *The Rise of a Central Authority for English Education* (Cambridge; Cambridge University Press, 1971), 160. The lecture derived from his book of the same title. See L. Playfair, *Industrial Education on the Continent* (London: Royal School of Mines, 1852). The quotes from the lecture (reprinted here) derive from Samuel Smiles lecture delivered over ten years later in Smiles, "Industrial Education of Foreign and English Workmen," *Journal of the Society of Arts* 15 (December 13, 1867): 69.

18. As quoted in Smiles, "Industrial Education of Foreign and English Workmen," 69.

19. Sanderson, "French Influences on Technical and Managerial Education in England, 1870–1940," 112–113.

20. Michael Sanderson, *Education and Economic Decline in Britain, 1870s to the 1990s.* (Cambridge: Cambridge University Press), 1999, 14–15. For a listing of government reports by select Committees, Royal Commissions, Official committees and other governmental agencies on education see A.S. Bishop, "Select Bibliography" in *The Rise of a Central Authority for English Education*, 284–287; see also Edwards, *The Role of International Exhibitions in Britain*, which systematically analyses education commissions as well as exhibition commissions and their outcomes, and includes the names of committee members.

21. Smiles, "Industrial Education of Foreign and English Workmen," 69. This speech illustrates Asa Briggs' argument that Smiles was not a dogmatic *laissez faire* advocate. Briggs writes that Smiles was "attracted by the possibility of employing the machinery of the state to regulate some of the obvious social disharmonies of the middle years of the century." See Briggs, *Victorian People: A Reassessment of Persons and Themes 1851–1867* (Chicago: The University of Chicago Press, 1955; reprint, Chicago: The University of Chicago Press, 1972), 125 (page references are to reprint edition).

22. Thomas Twining, "Industrial and Scientific Education," *Journal of the Society of Arts*, 15 (December 20, 1867): 89.

23. Silvanus Phillips Thompson, "Apprenticeship: Scientific and Unscientific," *Journal of the Society of Arts*, 28 (December 5, 1879): 42.

24. Harry Butterworth, "The Society and the Department of Science and Art," *Journal of the Royal Society of Arts* 133 (March 1985): 300. See also Edward Alexander, "Henry Cole and the South Kensington (Victoria and Albert) Museum: The Museum of Decorative Art," in *Museum Masters: Their Museums and Their Influence* (Nashville, TN: The American Association for State and Local History, 1983), 143–175.

25. The DSA was effectively an extension of the Art Department (Department of Practical Art), which was founded in 1831 to teach industrial design at a time when silk imports from France had devastated Britain's weaving industry. See Bishop, *The Rise of a Central Authority*, 150–151.

26. Peter H. Hoffenberg, "Equipoise and its Discontents: Voices of Dissent During the International Exhibitions," in ed., Martin Hewitt, *An Age of Equipoise? Reassessing Mid-Victorian Britain* (Aldershot: Ashgate, 2000), 50–51.

27. See Bishop, *The Rise of a Central Authority*, 150–151, and *idem*.

28. Hudson and Luckhurst, *The Royal Society of Arts*, 237–238.

29. *Ibid.*, 236–238. See Sir Henry Trueman Wood, "The Society's Examinations," in *A History of the Royal Society of Arts*, 425–441; and *ibid.*, 356, 465–466. Harry

Butterworth, "The Society and the Department of Science and Art," 299–301, 365–7, 424–5. F.E. Foden, "Colleges, Schools and the Society's Examinations," *The Journal of the Royal Society of Arts* 140 (February 1992): 207–209. The Society began the examination system specifically for the "artisan class," which they defined as "commonly mechanics, artisans, labourers, clerks, tradesmen and farmers not in a large way of business, apprentices, sons and daughters of tradesmen and farmers, assistants in shops, and others, of various occupations, who are not Graduates, Undergraduates, or Students of a University nor following nor intending to follow a learned profession nor enjoying nor having enjoyed a liberal education." As Hudson and Luckhurst note, however, in 1861 the Society began to admit students of higher class and income levels, and charged them, unlike the others, with an entrance fee. See Hudson and Luckhurst, *The Royal Society of Arts*, 252.

30. Butterworth, "The Society and the Department of Science and Art," 300.
31. It should be noted that not all free traders and liberal anti-trade unionists disparaged the call for educational reform. Many shared the sentiments of the Society's Chairman, William Hawes, who deplored trade unions, but wanted a government system of national technical schools and subsidized education for the working classes. See "Fourth Ordinary Meeting," *Journal of the Society of Arts* (December 13, 1867): 66; and, "Seventh Ordinary Meeting: On the Reports of the Artisans selected to Visit the Paris Universal Exhibition of 1867," *Journal of the Society of Arts* 16 (January 24, 1868):176. Over a decade later, the *Reports of the Samuelson Commission* (1882–1884), recommended establishing new, voluntary, technical schools, but also government intervention if voluntarism fell short of the mark. See Edwards, *The Role of International Exhibitions in Britain 1850–1910*, 115–116.
32. Stephen F. Cotgrove, *Technical Education and Social Change* (London: George Allen & Unwin Ltd., 1958), 25.
33. Educationists also wanted to open day schools for technical instruction, as few youth seemed able to work a full day and study at night. See, for example, Henry Solly's comments to the Royal Commission on Technical Instruction (March 27, 1882) 208: "Evening classes meet the wants only of a few comparatively – quick, strong, hearty lads, ambitious and aspiring, who do not mind fatigue." First and Second Report (Vol. 1), The Royal Commission on Technical Instruction with Appendices, 1882–84 (Vol. 5), Education Scientific and Technical, *British Parliamentary Papers*, 208.
34. See George Howell's comments in "Discussion," *Journal of the Royal Society of Arts*," 23 (1875): 740.
35. This demand was later rectified with the 1889 Technical Instruction Act. However, a decade earlier the City and Guilds of London Institute, founded in 1878, offered 49 examination subjects between the years 1879 and 1889. See Foden, "Colleges, Schools and the Society's Examinations," 209; and, City and Guilds of London Institute, *City and Guilds of London Institute: A Short History, 1878–1992* (London: City and Guilds of London Institute, 1993).
36. Cotgrove, *Technical Education and Social Change*, 51. C.T. Millis enjoyed an exceptional career in education. An artisan reporter in 1878, Millis later became an instructor at the Regent Street Polytechnic, a director of the Artisan Institute, and the principal of the London, Borough Polytechnic. He also wrote extensively on technical education.
37. Cronin, *Technology, Industrial Conflict, and the Development of Technical Education in 19th-Century England*. Patrick Duffy similarly argues that skilled compositors resisted new measures for technical education that would violate the "sanctity

and mystery" of their "chapel" where knowledge was transferred from master to apprentice. See *The Skilled Compositor, 1850–1914: An Aristocrat Among Working Men* (Aldershot: Ashgate, 2000), 195.

38. Foucault, *Discipline and Punish*, 185, 189.
39. F.E. Foden, "The Founding of a Tradition: James Booth and the Society's Examinations," *Journal of the Royal Society of Arts* (June 1987): 528. See especially Hudson, *The Royal Society of Arts*, 246. Cotgrove writes that such employer support, however, was exceptional. See Cotgrove, *Technical Education and Social Change*, 50–51.
40. In the long term, these accommodations to industrial interests would tie the quality and character of technical education to the private demands of capital, rather than the public expectations of the academy. J. F. Donnelly, "Science, Technology and Industrial Work in Britain, 1860–1930: Towards a New Synthesis," *Social History* 16, no. 2 (May 1991): 200–201. Hudson and Luckhurst, *The Royal Society of Arts*, 246.
41. Incomplete figures for the Society of Arts' examinations are recorded in "Seventh Ordinary Meeting," *Journal of the Society of Arts* 16 (January 24, 1868): 161. Incomplete figures of the Department of Science and Art's external exams can be found in Foden, "Colleges, Schools and the Society's Examinations," 208.
42. Foden, "Colleges, Schools and the Society's Examinations," 209.
43. Prothero, *Radical Artisans in England and France, 1830–1870*, 86, 237; Biagini, *Liberty, Retrenchment and Reform: Popular Liberalism in the Age of Gladstone, 1860–1880*, 193.
44. *Ibid.*
45. Prothero, *Radical Artisans*, 235.
46. August, *The British Working Class: 1832–1940*, 70–71.
47. First introduced by Eric Hobsbawm in 1957, the term "Labour Aristocracy" has spurred a long debate over its utility in identifying a discrete sociological group within the Victorian working class. I find the term useful in the general sense of identifying workers who wished to convey or maintain their status as skilled, "respectable" workmen. For Hobsbawm's original essay on the labor aristocracy see Hobsbawm, *Labouring Men: Studies in the History of Labour* (New York: Basic Books, 1976). For an analysis of the controversy see Alastair Reid "Intelligent Artisans and Aristocrats of Labour: the Essays of Thomas Wright," in *The Working Class in Modern British History: Essays in Honour of Henry Pelling*, ed. Jay Winter (Cambridge: Cambridge University Press, 1983), 171–186; and, Henry Weisser, "The Labour Aristocracy, 1851–1914," *American Historical Review*, 101 (April 1996):490; With regard to technical exams, status, and identity see Christine M. Heward, "Education, Examinations and the Artisans: The Department of Science and Art in Birmingham, 1853–1902," in ed., Roy MacLeod, *Days of Judgement: Science, Examinations and the Organization of Knowledge in Late Victorian England* (Chester: Studies in Education, 1982), 45–64.
48. See, Clive Griggs, *The Trades Union Congress and the Struggle for Education: 1868–1925* (London: Falmer Press, 1983). See also the analysis of workers' testimony in government reports in Edwards, *The Role of International Exhibitions in Britain, 1850–1910*.
49. Recall, for example, T.J. Wilkinson's report which included the Flint Glass Makers' proposal to establish technical schools in districts associated with the glass trade. See Wilkinson, "Table and Fancy Glass," 156–157.
50. Robert Applegarth to Peter Le Neve Foster, March 4, 1868. A/RSA/18/A-J/1868 Box 1 (A-L) RSA archive 58. 18/A/97. The Workingmen's Club and Institute Union acknowledged the establishment of the ASCJ schools in "Report of the

Proceedings of the Workmen's Technical Education Committee" in *Workingmen's Club and Institute Union Reports* (1869), 8, The Workingmen's Club and Institute Union Archive, London.

51. The artisan reporter and labor leader, George Howell, expressed this conviction at a conference on apprenticeship held in 1879. He emphatically stated that trade unionists strongly supported technical education and that it was an imperative for industrial advance. See the discussion following a reading of Silvanus Phillips Thompson's paper on the apprenticeship system in Britain, in Thompson, "Apprenticeship: Scientific and Unscientific," *Journal of the Society of Arts* 28 (5 December, 1879): 43–44, 47.

52. Briggs, *Victorian People*, 179–80.

53. *Journal of the Society of Arts* 23 (July 2, 1875): 740.

54. Richard Bastow to Peter Le Neve Foster, March 3, 1873. A/RSA/23/A-H 1873/ Box 1 RSA Archive 13. 23/D/87. For a discussion of the antagonisms and occasional radical collaborations between trade and "non-society" men see Prothero, *Radical Artisans in England and France, 1830–1870*, 69.

55. William Larkins, "Introduction," in *Artisan Reports Upon the Vienna Exhibition* (Manchester: Society for the Promotion of Scientific Industry, 1873), ix.

56. "Eighth Ordinary Meeting," *Journal of the Society of Arts* 15 (February 1, 1867): 163.

57. For more on the SA's awards see Luckhurst, *The Royal Society of Arts,* passim. Of course, some ambitious artisans sought the recognition such prizes conferred. Robert Creaser Kingston, a gardener at Kew and the winner of the Prince Consort's Prize in 1868 wrote a letter to the Society in "gratitude" for the honor. See R. C. Kingston to P. Le Neve Foster, November 26, 1868. A/RSA/18/A-J/ 1868/ Box 1 (A-L) /RSA Archive 58. 18/I/5. For the Society's involvement with the Whitworth Awards see "Technical Education," *Journal of the Society of Arts* (June 26, 1868): 581. See also Henry Cole's letter to the Society (enclosed in a Whitehall Minute on the Whitworth Scholarships) in Henry Cole to P. Le Neve Foster, May 8, 1868, A/RSA/18/A-J 1868/Box 1 (A-L) RSA Box 58, 18/C/117; and, Cole to Foster, June 25, 1868, A/RSA/18/A-J. 1868/Box 1/ (A-L)/RSA Archive 58. 18/C/208. While the Whitworth Scholarships were open to all classes, a few were designated for the artisan classes "only." For a young machinist's negative impression of this system and his application to the Society for a Whitworth Prize, see Frederick Burton to P. Le Neve Foster, February 9, 1868, A/RSA/18/A-J 1868/Box 1 (A-L)/ RSA archive 58. For more on the Whitworth Prizes see, The Whitworth Society, *The Whitworth Book* (London: Longmans, Green and Co., 1926). The Science and Art Department also offered promising students of the artisan classes scholarships and prizes. For a summary of its prize and scholarship provisions see, "Technical Instruction," *Journal of the Society of Arts* (January 31, 1868), 321–22. Like the SA, the Science and Art Department eventually included trips to continental exhibitions in its prize system. For example, a Cornwall miner who had received a gold medal in Mineralogy, also received £10 to attend the 1867 Paris Exhibition. See Gordon Roderick and Michael Stephens, *Scientific and Technical Education in Nineteenth-Century England* (Newton Abbot: David & Charles, 1972) 28, n 45.d.

58. *Journal of the Society of Arts* 15 (February 1, 1867): 63. Butterworth notes that "The Society's science subject figures, even after a prize scheme was introduced, remained small. Entries for the subject of Chemistry, the most popular of the Society's science subjects, never exceeded 40, until 1862." See Butterworth, "The Society and the Department of Science and Art," 365.

59. "Fourteenth Ordinary Meeting," *Journal of the Society of Arts* 14 (March 9, 1866), 281–289. At this meeting, Coningsby read a paper titled "On the Late Anglo-French

Exhibition with a proposal for the Formation of an Anglo-French Association," in which he advocates international working men's exhibitions as one strategy to galvanize the Society's educational reform movement.

60. See Richard Whiteing's recollections of Coningsby in, Whiteing, *My Harvest* (New York: Dodd, Mead & Company, 1915), 45–57. Letters to the SA from Coningsby during the years 1866 and 1868, support Whiteing's descriptions of Coningsby's character and talents.

61. Meeting of the Central Council, May 30, 1865. *The Minute Book of the General Council of the First International, 30 May 1865* http://www.marxists.org/archive/marx/iwma/documents/1865/may.htm (accessed August 17, 2013). Coningsby, in the role of Secretary of the English Committee, defended the integrity of the Anglo-French Workingmen's Exhibition in *The Builder*, August 5, 1865. He remarked that "a report has gone abroad which has been very injurious to us," and denied its veracity, insisting that capital held no influence over the "self-reliant" working class organizers and their arrangements. See, Robert Coningsby, "Peace Jubilee! Anglo-French Exhibition," Newspaper Cuttings, V&A Museum. Miscellaneous. May 1862–January 1868 Vol. II, 1865. Pg 237.

62. Richard Whiteing, *My Harvest*, 53; and *Journal of the Society of Arts* 16 (July 3, 1868), 592.

63. "Fourteenth Ordinary Meeting," *Journal of the Society of Arts* 14 (March 9, 1866), 281–289. At this meeting, Coningsby read a paper titled "On the Late Anglo-French Exhibition with a proposal for the Formation of an Anglo-French Association," in which he advocates international working men's exhibitions as one strategy to galvanize the Society's educational reform movement. See, also, Richard Whiteing's description of the exhibition in *My Harvest*, 46–52.

64. *Ibid.*

65. *Ibid.*, 285. "Incapables" Coningsby knowingly added, "are cruelly treated, and held in great contempt; and if one such carries off a prize by accident, the result [to the prize system] is mischievous."

66. *Ibid.*

67. "Fourteenth Ordinary Meeting," *Journal of the Society of Arts* 14 (March 9, 1866): 282. They also discovered, however, that the organizational apparatus necessary to put such an exhibition together was more than working men, even collectively (their committee numbered 50 individuals), could do without the time, money, and influence that upper-class-exhibition organizers had at their disposal. The "experiment" thus failed to produce a surplus, putting the guarantors at a loss of some £500 to £600. See *ibid.*

68. *Ibid.*, 285.

69. *Ibid.*

70. *Ibid.*, 289. A separate working men's pavilion may not have conformed to organizers' conception of, in Tony Bennett's terms, a "rational public culture." It would have given symbolic power to a cosmopolitan working class, rather than to the organic social order, represented by individual worker-subjects and their firms within the nation. See Bennett, "The Exhibitionary Complex," 339.

71. Freda Fisher, "Unpublished Memoir of Sir Henry Trueman Wood Written by his Daughter, Freda Fisher (nee Wood)" (c. 1925–1940). Chapter VI, 1–2. RSA Archive.

72. *Ibid.*, 4. 1889 marked the centenary of the French Revolution, an event Republicans planned to celebrate at the Exhibition. Consequently, the British government refused to sanction an "official" British section as was customary. See *ibid.*, 29–31.

73. See Society of Arts, *Reports of Artisans to Visit the Paris Universal Exhibition, 1867* (London: Bell and Daldy, 1867).

74. The 1867 tours included artisans from London, Bradford, Nottingham, Sheffield, Coventry, Newcastle-under-Lyme, and Birmingham. The 1878 tours branched out further by including towns which supported their own artisan reporters, but that used the services of the SA and submitted reports for publication in the official volume of *Artisan Reports*. Dublin artisans, for instance, were also included.

75. W.C. Aitken, "Introductory Report," in *Artisan Reports Upon the Vienna Exhibition* (Manchester: Society for the Promotion of Scientific Industry, 1873), i–iv. The publishers divided this volume into two sections. The first is devoted to the *Artisan Reports* supported by the MSPSI with an introduction by William Larkins. The second section is devoted to the Birmingham Artisans and introduced by W.C. Aitken, as described above.

76. The Prince of Wales' contributions to the Tours are described in Sir Dighton Probyn Macnaghten to P. Le Neve Foster, May 15, 1878, A/RSA/28/L-V/1878/ Box 2. RSA archive 15. A/RSA/28/0/184. Many of these organizational methods had been perfected by the SA in drumming up support for the 1851 Exhibition. See Auerbach *The Great Exhibition of 1851: A Nation on Display*, 54–86.

77. "Artizans' Visits to Paris," *Journal of the Society of Arts* 15 (June 7, 1867): 475.

78. See the Circular of the "Committee for Organizing a Deputation of Irish Artisans to Visit and Report on the Forthcoming Paris International Exhibition of 1878." A/RSA/29/Y-MM 1879/Box 3/RSA Archive 18. A/RSA/29/EE/9.

79. Robert Pullar to Peter Le Neve Foster, July 30, 1878. A/RSA/28/L-V/1878/Box 2/ RSA Archive 15. A/RSA/28/0/20. The London, Brighton, and South Coast Railway was another firm that sent workers to the exhibition, in this case mechanics for their locomotive and engineer workshops. J. Knight, General Manager offered their reports to Sampson and Low, publishers of the *Artisan Reports* (1879). See J. Knight to Messrs. Sampson Low & Co., October 8, 1879. A/RSA/29/M-X/1879/ Box 2/RSA Archive 17. A/RSA/29/W/64.

80. James Samuelson to the SA, September 19, 1878. A/RSA/28/L-V/1878/Box 2 RSA Archive 15. A/RSA/28/Q8.

81. J. Knight to the SA, July 29, 1878. A/RSA/28/L-V/1878/ Box 2 RSA Archive 15. A/ RSA/28/L/1; J. Knight to the SA, August 9, 1878. A/RSA/28/L-V/1878 Box 2 RSA Archive 15. A/RSA/28/L/6.

82. F. Aumonier of the William Woollam's and Company Paper Stainers, for example, asked the SA for 14 proofs to distribute. F. Aumonier to Peter Le Neve Foster, July 5, 1878. A/RSA/28/A-K/1878/Box 1/ RSA Archive 61. 28/A/78.

83. See, for example, "The Sheffield Trades and the Paris Exhibition," *The Bee-Hive*, September 7, 1867. "To report upon the cutlery trade, the society has secured the assistance of the well-known Mr. John Wilson, penknife-grinder, in the employ of Messrs. Joseph Rogers and Sons; and the tool department is confided to Mr. W. Bramhall, an experienced sawmaker in the employ of Messrs. Spear and Jacksons."

84. W. Loveday to P. Le Neve Foster, March 2, 1879, A/RSA/29/M-X/1879/Box 2 RSA Archive 17.

85. "The Society of Arts and the Paris Exhibition," *The Bee-Hive*, October 19, 1867, 1.

86. Findlay to P. Le Neve Foster, November 11, 1878. A/RSA/28/A-K/1878/Box 1/ RSA Archive 61. A/RSA/28/H/25.

87. John Randall to P. Le Neve Foster, January 17, 1868. A/RSA/18/K-Z 1868/Box 2/(M-Z) RSA 50. 18/P/66. John Randall, "A Working Man's View of the Paris Exhibition," *The Times*, September 13, 1867, 8.

88. See Charles Saunderson to Henry Trueman Wood, May 23, 1879, A/RSA/29/ Y-MM/1879/Box 3/ RSA Archive 18. A/RSA/29/KK/5. The correspondence with the SA regarding publication and dissemination of the *Artisan Reports* is too numerous to cite in detail here. Scholars interested in the publication histories of Bell and Daldy (*Artisan Reports, 1867*), Eyre & Spottiswoode, and Sampson & Low (*Artisan Reports, 1878*), can consult the RSA archive in the years of the *Artisan Reports'* publication and the correspondence with the SA's editors (for the 1878 tours), Robert James Mann, Philip Cunliffe Owen, and Joseph Cundall. For the bookstall sales of the *Artisan Reports, 1878* see W.H. Smith & Son to Philip Cunliffe Owen, April 17, 1879, A/RSA/29/ NN-YY/ 1879/ Box 4 RSA Archive 59/A/RSA/29/XX/4c. For trade periodicals see, for example, A.H. Hill for *The Labour News and Employment Advertiser, & Co.* to Peter Le Neve Foster, June 24, 1878, A/RSA/28/A-K/ 1878/ Box 1 RSA Archive 61/A/RSA/28/J/28; and, W.E. Freil for the *Ironmonger and Metal trades' Advertiser* to Peter Le Neve Foster, June 18, 1878, A/RSA/28/A-K/ 1878/ Box 1 RSA Archive 61/A/RSA/28/H/51. The secretary of the Dublin committee for the 1878 artisan exhibition tours, Henry Parkinson, expressed similar concerns to that of Saunderson, but also criticized the Government Commission when it failed to live up to these expectations, an occasion for negative publicity. Writing to the Committee of Her Majesty's Commissioners, Parkinson complained that only three out of the twenty Irish reports submitted for publication were printed in the government's official volume, and moreover, that he was "distinctly given to understand ... that the reports of the Irish Artisans would be printed and published and if possible kept together in one portion of the book so as to preserve their Nationality." This neglect obviously infuriated Parkinson and had produced "great outcry amongst the Artizans." But, just as importantly, "it would be a pity" and a "disappointment," Parkinson added, if the Committee "were unable to distribute [the reports] in a cheap form amongst the working classes as it was intended." See Henry Parkinson to Earl Spencer, July 18, 1879, Dublin; and Ibid. (September 12, 1879). A/RSA/29/Y-MM/1879/Box 3/RSA Archive 18. A/ RSA/29/EE/9; A/RSA/29/Y-MM/1879/Box 3/RSA Archive 18. A/RSA/29/GG/6.
89. "Preface" in *Artisan's Reports*, 1867, v.
90. *Ibid.*
91. William Larkins, "Introduction," *Artisan Reports*, 1873, v–vi.
92. *Ibid.*, v.
93. William Larkins, "Introduction," in *Artisan Reports Upon the Vienna Exhibition*, 1873 (Manchester: Society for the Promotion of Scientific Industry, 1873), v.
94. W.C. Aitken, "Introductory Report," Part II (Birmingham Artisans' Reports) in *ibid.*, iv.
95. *Ibid.*
96. See Thomas Patterson to Peter Le Neve Foster, June 10, 1878, A/RSA/28/ L-V/1878/Box 2/ RSA Archive 15. A/RSA/29/O/120. Joseph Leicester to SA, July 25, 1878, A/RSA/28/L-V/ 1878/Box 2 RSA Archive 15. A/RSA/28/M/78. George Potter to P. Le Neve Foster July 10, 1878, A/RSA/28/L-V/1878/ Box 2/ RSA Archive 15. A/RSA/28/O/4; George Potter to Henry Trueman Wood, August 12, 1878, A/RSA/28/L-V/1878/Box 2/RSA Archive 15. A/RSA/28/O/106. The select group handed their list to Earl Spencer, see Earl Spencer to SA, May 27, 1878, A/ RSA/28/L-V/1878/Box 2/RSA Archive 15. A/RSA/28/Q/69.
97. If the SA lacked absolute faith in the ability of the special working men's committee to make suitable recommendations, it occasionally approved applications

simply on the recommendation of others within the reformist network. Hodgson Pratt wrote to the SA, for example, lauding the qualifications of a man he had met only once: "I mentioned to you [a member of the SA Committee] the other day the name of an artizan who is likely to make a valuable report if sent to the Paris Exhibition. His name is Henderson. He is a *Scotchman* (generally a guarantee for brains + for making good use of them!)." Pratt then described Henderson's colorful employment history as an engineer during the Crimean War, then abroad in Turkey and America, and finally for many years at the London, Woolwich Arsenal. "He is a man of great intelligence & quick energy & has done good ... work of his men and his class," Pratt noted, concluding – perhaps most importantly – that Henderson possessed a "Trade certificate of the first class as a Marine Engineer." Interestingly enough, Henderson's application became a case of mistaken identity. A little less than two weeks after receiving Pratt's recommendation, the SA received a letter from an artisan by the name of David Walker stating that he had been appointed an artisan reporter, but had not applied for the post. "There is some mistake," he wrote to the Committee. "I brought you the testimonials of my friend Mr. D. Henderson and his letter of application and afterwards introduced him to Mr. Hodgson Pratt as a most suitable man. Mr. Pratt mislaid his notes of the conversation, and asked me to give him some particulars of Mr. Henderson's career, which I did from my own knowledge but had no thought of applying for myself." The situation was readily resolved. Both men were appointed artisan reporters, but only Walker's report was accepted for publication, despite Pratt's emphatic endorsement of Henderson's abilities. See Hodgson Pratt to Mr. Morley, July 19, 1878, A/RSA/28/L-V/1878/Box 2/RSA Archive 15. A/RSA/28/0/97. David Walker to Peter Le Neve Foster, August 3, 1878, A/RSA/28/L-V/1878/Box 2/RSA Archive 15. A/RSA/28/U/105.

98. Peter Le Neve Foster to Henry Trueman Wood, July 11, 1878, A/RSA/28/A-K/1878/Box 1/RSA Archive 61. A/RSA/28/H/68.

99. "Introduction," in *Reports of Artisans*, 1889, ix–xii.

100. *Ibid.*, x.

101. John Askew to SA, July 29, 1878. A/RSA/ 28/A-K/ 1878/ box 1/RSA Archive 61. A/RSA/28/J/27.

102. Thomas Duckworth to P. Le Neve Foster, October 3, 1878. A/RSA/28/A-K/ 1878/ Box 1RSA Archive 61. A/RSA/28/F/94.

103. William Cross to SA, August 9, 1878. A/RSA/A-K/1878/Box 1/RSA Archive 61. A/RSA/28/E/106.

104. Joseph Leicester to Peter Le Neve Foster, March 16, 1878, A/RSA/28/L-V/1878/ Box 2/RSA Archive 15. A/RSA/28/M/99.

105. Joseph Leicester to SA, July 23, 1878. A/RSA/28/L-V/1878/Box 2/RSA Archive 15. 18/RSA/28/M/1878. See "Joseph Lynn Leicester," in Joyce M. Bellamy, ed. *Dictionary of Labour Biography* Vol. 3 (Basingstoke: Macmillan Press, 1972) 133–134.

106. John Askew to SA, August 13, 1878. A/RSA/28/A-K/1878/Box 1/RSA Archive 61. 28/A/53.

107. Edwin Robbins to P. Le Neve Foster, August 15, 1878, A/RSA/ 28/L-V/1878/ Box RSA Archive 15 A/RSA/ 28/P/84 and see the fragment n.d. A/RSA/28/P/100.

108. Samuel R. Dermott to the Society of Arts, August 23, 1878. A/RSA/28/A-K/Box 1/ RSA Archive 61. A/RSA/28/F44.

109. W. J. Fleming to P. Le Neve Foster, August 9, 1878. A/RSA/28/ A-K/1878/ Box 1/ RSA Archive 61. A/RSA/28/ H/5.

110. J. Murray to SA, September 26, 1868. A/RSA/18/K-Z/1868/ Box 2 (M-Z). RSA Archive 50. 18/K/113.
111. Thomas Warsop to Peter Le Neve Foster, August 27, 1878. A/RSA/28/L-V/1878/ Box 2 RSA Archive 15. A/RSA/28/0/77.
112. Throughout most of the second half of the nineteenth century, "Science" teachers, which the SA paid by students' examination "results," derived from the ranks of "intelligent artisans" and elementary school teachers. See Butterworth, "The Science and Art Department Examinations," 37.
113. Because the tours were funded in part by government grant, the SA would likely have had to abide by the rules of the Department of Science and Art. See RSA file titled "1867 Scholarships Artizans South Ken" for a circular titled "Council on Education, South Kensington: Scientific Instruction. Local and Central Scholarships. At Whitehall the 21st Day of December 1867". A/RSA/ 18/K-Z 1868/Box 2/(M-Z) RSA 50 – folded in a letter from MacLeod 29/10/68 18/K/197a.
114. John Rogers to P. Le Neve Foster, August 26, 1878. A/RSA/28/L-V/ 1878/ Box 2. RSA Archive 15. A/RSA/28/P/67.
115. "Benjamin Lucraft," in *Dictionary of Labour Biography* Vol. 3, 152.
116. See, for instance, the struggle for "self-education" in Joseph Gutteridge, *Lights and Shadows in the Life of an Artisan* (Coventry: Curtis and Beamish, 1893); and Leventhal, *Respectable Radical*.
117. Gutteridge had likely participated in strike action protesting changes in the silk industry following the free trade agreement with France in 1860. Free trade destroyed his livelihood. And yet, he supported free trade as the "poor man's best hope," which, Biagini explains, was, at core, a reaction to the abuses of protectionist aristocratic privilege, such as the Corn Laws. See, Eugenio Biagini, *Liberty, Retrenchment, and Reform: Popular Liberalism in the Age of Gladstone, 1869–1880*, 100. See also Gutteridge, *Lights and Shadows*, and the "Introduction" by Valerie E. Chancellor, ed., in *Master and Artisan in Victorian England: The Diary of William Andrews and the Autobiography of Joseph Gutteridge* (New York: Augustus M. Kelley, Publishers, 1969), 1–9.
118. Gutteridge, *Lights and Shadows*.
119. See John Randall, "On Technical Education" *Journal of the Society of Arts* 16 (March 6, 1868), 294–297). Several more of his publications on education, geology, and a regional history of Shropshire can be found at the British Library. For a short biography of John Randall see *The Proceedings of the Geological Society* (May 1911), liii.
120. "Freedom of Wenlock Conferred on Mr. John Randall," *The Shrewsbury Chronicle* (June 11, 1909).
121. See the biographical summary of Hems's life, work, and travels in *The Decorator* (October 22, 1905): 94, Devon Record Office, UK, 4270/Z, Z 8. Although he used the SA's services for artisan reporters in 1878, the SA did not publish Hems's report, which was funded, and presumably published by the Exeter Chamber of Commerce. See Hems to Peter Le Neve Foster, August 7, 1878, A/ RSA/28/A-K/1878/Box 1 RSA Archive 61, A/RSA/28/J/61.
122. For Mondy, see Robert Coningsby to P. Le Neve Foster, November 17, 1868. RSA/ 18/C/155.
123. Edmond Mondy to P. Le Neve Foster, January 6, 1868. A/RSA/18/ K-Z 1868/Box 2/M-Z/ RSA Archive 50. 18/K/81; *ibid.*, 18/K/100.
124. John Heywood to P. Le Neve Foster, February 20, 1878. A/RSA/28/A-K/1878/Box 1/RSA Archive 61. A/RSA/28/K/71. *Ibid.*, March 3, 1878, A/RSA/28/J/72. *Ibid.*, March 29, 1878, A/RSA/28/J/35. John Heywood to RSA, September 18, 1879, A/

RSA/29/M-X/1879/Box 2. RSA Archive 17. A/RSA/29/R/ 72. *Ibid.*, April 20, 1880, A/ RSA/29/Q/37.

125. Archive of George Bell and Sons, "Brief Description: Administrative/Biographical History," Reading University Special Collection http://archiveshub.ac.uk/data/ gb006-rulmss1640etc (accessed August 8, 2013).

126. *Artisan Reports' Upon the Vienna Exhibition* (Manchester: Society for the Promotion of Scientific Industry, 1873), ix.

127. R. Francis, "Carving and Gilding," in *Reports of Artisans Selected by the Mansion House Committee to Visit the Paris Universal Exhibition, 1889*, 188, 191.

128. T. Vest, "Carpentry and Joinery," in *Reports of Artisans (1889)*, 167.

129. W. H. Edmunds, "Bookbinding," in *Reports of Artisans* (1889), 20–21, 19.

130. F.S. Knowles, "Hatters' Work" in *Reports of Artisans* (1889), 441.

131. See Roger Price, *A Concise History of France* (Cambridge: Cambridge University Press, 1993), 196–197, 204–205. For a more detailed history of workers and the revival of French socialism in the 1880s see Roger Magraw, *A History of the French Working Class*, Volume II: *Workers and the Bourgeois Republic* (Oxford: Blackwell Publishers, 1992).

132. Joseph Leicester, "Report upon Table and Fancy Glass," in *Artisan Reports on the Paris Universal Exhibition of 1878*, 156.

133. T.D. Wright, "Clockmaking," in *Reports of Artisans Selected by the Mansion House Committee to Visit the Paris Universal Exhibition, 1889*, 230.

134. W.H. Edmunds, "Bookbinding" in *Reports of Artisans Selected by the Mansion House Committee to Visit the Paris Universal Exhibition, 1889*, 19–20.

135. T.D. Wright, "Clockmaking," 230.

136. Summers makes this observation with respect to the *Bourses du Travail*, which, he writes, invited public discussions on labor and political questions. See G. Summers, "Bread and Biscuit Making," in *Reports of Artisans Selected by the Mansion House Committee to Visit the Paris Universal Exhibition, 1889*, 107–108. Summers makes an interesting observation given that the 1884 Act stipulated that unions could only discuss "economic" issues. See Magraw, *A History of the French Working Class*, Volume II: *Workers and the Bourgeois Republic*, 22.

137. G. Summers, "Bread and Biscuit Making," 78.

138. Roger Magraw writes that "there were strings attached" to these institutions. If workers used the BT to organize strike actions or harbored labor militants, the municipal council withheld the funding that kept the BTs alive. The BTs, in other words, were part of the ruling establishment's overall strategy to defuse the revolutionary implications of the socialist resurgence by appropriating socialists' aims into their own party platforms. "Was not British trade-unionism moderate precisely because it was tolerated by state and employers?" strategists conjectured. Rather than let socialist "hot heads" take control of labor aspirations, they presumed that "legalized unionism [through new laws and institutions such as the BT] would draw in the mass of ordinary, realistic workers, the 'timid' who would neutralize the danger for the 'bold.'" See Magraw, *Workers and the Bourgeois Republic*, vol. II (1992), 22–23.

139. Summers, "Bread and Biscuit Making," 107–108.

140. D. Toomey, "Boiler Making and Iron Shipbuilding," in *Reports of Artisans Selected by the Mansion House Committee to Visit the Paris Universal Exhibition, 1889*, 8.

141. C. Kinggate, "Coachbuilding," in *Reports of Artisans Selected by the Mansion House Committee to Visit the Paris Universal Exhibition, 1889*, 252.

142. T. Vest, "Carpentry and Joinery," in *Reports of Artisans Selected by the Mansion House Committee to Visit the Paris Universal Exhibition, 1889*, 187.

143. Malcolm Macleod, "Social and Working Habits and Customs of German Workmen," *Artisan Reports Upon the Vienna Exhibition* (Manchester: Society for the Promotion of Scientific Industry, 1873), 51. MacLeod's report stands out from the rest in this volume by focusing exclusively on the work culture and social aspects of German workers. His own particular trade goes unmentioned, both in his own report and in the introduction to the volume. Macleod may have been a professional reporter with working-class credentials, much like Coningsby and Whiteing, who also contributed "special reports" to the 1867 volume.
144. *Ibid.,* 55.
145. For more on the liberal trajectory of French education for the working classes see Sandra Horvath-Peterson, *Victor Duruy and French Education: Liberal Reform in the Second Empire* (Baton Rouge: Louisiana State University Press, 1984).
146. James Hopps, "Report on Mechanical Engineering," in *Artisan Reports on the Paris Universal Exhibition of 1878*, 256, 516.
147. William H. Howard, "Report on Wood Carving," *Artisan Reports on the Paris Universal Exhibition of 1878*, 221.
148. J. Brooke, "Tile and Mosaic Working," in *Reports of Artisans Selected by the Mansion House Committee to Visit the Paris Universal Exhibition, 1889*, 640–641.
149. K. M'Crae, "Boot and Shoe Making: Men's" in *Reports of Artisans Selected by the Mansion House Committee to Visit the Paris Universal Exhibition, 1889*, 73.
150. W. H. Edmunds, *Reports of Artisans Selected by the Mansion House Committee to Visit the Paris Universal Exhibition, 1889*, 38–39. Indeed, the results of a ten-year investigation by the London School Board (headed by George Potter and Benjamin Lucraft) into the disbursement of the City Parochial Charities funds had recently been disclosed, showing that much of its educational endowments for the poor had gone into funding middle-class schools and lavish entertainments by and for the City's livery companies. See Brian Simon, *Education and the Labour Movement, 1870–1920* (London: Lawrence & Wishart, 1974), 129.
151. W. H. Edmunds, *Reports of Artisans* (1889), 40.
152. *Ibid.,* 39–40.
153. Vest, "Carpentry and Joinery," 186.
154. For the "workingman's Grand Tour" see Judith Adler, "Youth on the Road: Reflections on the History of Tramping," in *Annals of Tourism Research*, 12 (1985): 335–354. G. Summers links the French travel scholarships for apprentices to the older practice of the journeyman's tramp, in "Bread and Biscuit Making," 110.
155. *Reports of Artisans Selected by the Mansion House Committee*, xi–xii.
156. *Ibid.*
157. Although artisan exhibition tours had passed their heyday, this did not preclude other kinds of "artisan reports." See, for example, *Life Under Tariffs: What We Saw In Germany. The Sheffield Daily Telegraph Tour, September, 1910, Reports of Delegates*. Pamphlet Collection, London School of Economics, HC (43) E10. The legacy of the artisan tours and the journeyman's tramp can also be found in such busman's holiday memoirs as a mechanic's study of France, in Henry Steele, *The Working Classes in France* (London: Twentieth Century Press, 1904); In addition, see Henry Mulliner *A Carriage Builder's Tour in America* (Leamington: B. Sarney, 1883). Mulliner's pamphlet reproduced a speech he gave at the Institute of British Carriage Builders which was made at George Hooper's request. See T. Lowe, *A Mechanic's Tour Round the World* (London: Wyman & Sons, 1886), British Library; A Birmingham Working Man (H. Smith), *A Tour through the Land of the West, and a Visit to the Columbian Exposition* (London: Simpkin, Marshall,

1894.); William Will, "A Working Man's Trip to Canada," in *The People's Journal* (Dundee) August 21, 1897.

158. The 1889 Technical Instruction Act gave tax monies derived from a "penny rate" to technical education committees, and the Local Taxation Act of 1890 augmented these funds from a duty on beer and spirits, familiarly called "whisky money." See Roger Fieldhouse, "The Nineteenth Century," in *A History of Modern British Adult Education*, Roger Fieldhouse, ed. (Leicester: National Institute of Adult Continuing Education, 1996), 43. M. Sanderson, *The Missing Stratum, Technical School Education in England, 1900–1990s* (London: Athlone Press, 1994).

159. Michael Sanderson, *Education and Economic Decline*, 41–42. In 1879, Professor Ayrton defined four classes in Britain that required technical instruction: "apprentices," "artisans already following or learning a trade," "sons of rich manufacturers who will become mangers of works," "and ... specialists to give all these three classes technical education." Ayrton had supposed that the new City and Guilds of London Institute would train all four classes. But, as discussed above, the latter two would be accommodated by elite universities, leaving the artisan classes to the London Institute. See the discussion following a paper read by Silvanus Phillips Thompson at the Society of Arts in "Apprenticeship: Scientific and Unscientific," *Journal of the Society of Arts* 28 (December 5, 1879): 46.

160. In 1870 the SA abandoned their courses held in common with the department, and, at Donnelly's suggestion, took a further step in the development of industrial education when in 1873 they began to oversee "technological" examinations in the "scientific background [theory] and actual practice of specific trades." See Hudson, *The Royal Society of Arts*, 254. The SA's recent educational expansion, however, was short-lived. By the late 1870s, other voluntary institutions had taken it upon themselves to provide workers with technical instruction. The SA, which preferred the role of "initiator" to that of permanent superintendent of public projects, willingly divested its technical exam system to the largest of these new institutions: The City and Guilds of London Institute for the Advancement of Technical Education. At the helm of the transfer stood Henry Trueman Wood, who had been deeply involved in the City and Guilds efforts to develop a national system of technical education. Devoted to providing education "adapted to the requirements of all classes of persons engaged, or preparing to engage, in manufacturing or other industries," the City and Guilds Institute maintained not only the centralizing function of the SA's examination system and its links to the Science and Art Department, but the SA's base of funding – charitable support. Therefore, the creation of the City and Guilds' Institute helped forestall the implementation of a truly national, state-funded system of technical education as advocated decades earlier by Playfair and others. See John A. Barnes, *City and Guilds of London Institute: A Short History, 1878–1992* (London: City and Guilds of London Institute, 1993), 17–18.

161. Andy Green, *Education and State Formation: The Rise of Education Systems in England, France and the USA* (New York: St Martin's Press, 1990), 299.

162. Thomas Cook, "The Excursion Season of 1870," *The Excursionist*, May 7, 1870, 8–9.

163. Albert Harris, "Workers on Holiday," *The Strand Magazine* 34, no. 199 (August 1907): 43–48. http://books.google.com/books?id=4JMkAQAAIAAJ&pg=PA44& lpg=PA44&dq=lever+brothers+paris+excursion&source=bl&ots=TBMcaaiM_-& sig=mcOYODsIqfS4HCDPijgYtRiJRUE&hl=en&sa=X&ei=2d8_UbrpBdH8yAGk jYCYDg&ved=0CFYQ6AEwAg#v=onepage&q=lever%20brothers%20paris%20 excursion&f=false (accessed May 23, 2013).

164. For the French police reports see, "Reports de Surveillance," File DA772 (May 25, 1900), in *Rapport Sur les Municipale à l'Exposition de 1900*, the Préfecture de Police Museum, Paris, France. See the Unilver Archives, Port Sunlight Heritage Centre, for menus, handbooks, excursion tickets, and passages from the writing contests in the company's *Progress Magazine*, July 1900 "Port Sunlight to Paris and Back, in Two Days"; 1905 "To Brussels and Liege"; and October 1910, "Our Brussels Excursion." For more on Unilever, see Brian Lewis, *So Clean: Lord Leverhulme, Soap and Civilization* (Manchester: Manchester University Press, 2008).

165. For descriptions of Working Men's College tours, see *The Working Men's College Magazine*, Working Men's College Archive, London. The Toynbee Travellers' Club was founded in 1888 and The Workmen's Travelling Club in 1902. Records of their tours can be located in *The Toynbee Record*, British Library. Additionally, see Toynbee Travellers' Club logbooks of their expeditions in Toynbee Hall Papers, London Metropolitan Archive.

5   Class Trips and the Meaning of British Citizenship: The Regent Street Polytechnic at Home and Abroad, 1871–1903

1. John Mason Cook, to Sir John Gorst, May 5, 1896, University of Westminster Archive, Polytechnic Touring Association (hereafter UWA, PTA), 1/2/2.

2. [R. J. Mitchell], to A.J. Mundella, unsigned letter, June 2, 1896, UWA, PTA 1/2/4. Polytechnics Sub Committee Minutes, May 13, 1896, LMA (London Metropolitan Archives), Technical Education Board (TEB) 36, September26, 1894 to November 10, 1897, London Metropolitan Archives (LMA); Quintin Hogg, to [the Secretary, Department of Science & Art], [1897], UWA, PTA 1/2/6. The Charity Commission distributed funds for leisure activities, but there is no record of Polytechnic tours in the minute books of the Foundation's Central Governing Body, City Parochial Foundation, London. In addition, see the provisions of the Parochial Charities Act outlined by the principal of the Chelsea Polytechnic, F. J. Harlow, "Notes on the Legal Aspect of Polytechnic Schemes," March 10, 1936, Woolwich Polytechnic: Trust Deed & Charity Commission Orders, Riverside House Library Archive. See also Education Department, "The London Polytechnics," in *Special Reports on Educational Subjects*, vol. 2, 1898, Riverside House Library Archive. For John Cook, see Brendon, *Thomas Cook*. For Hogg's "ruthless" business demeanor, see Ethel M. Hogg, *Quintin Hogg: A Biography*, 2nd edition. (London, 1904), 324–25.

3. Brian Simon, "The Background to Legislation, 1897–1900," chap. 6 in *Education and the Labour Movement* (London, 1965); E.J.R. Eaglesham, "Administrative Muddle," chapter 2 in *The Foundations of 20th-Century Education in England* (London, 1967).

4. Other non-aristocratic links to educational travel are illuminated in Margaret Hunt, "Racism, Imperialism, and the Traveler's Gaze," *Journal of British Studies* 32, no. 4 (October 1993): 333–57; and Judith Adler, "Youth on the Road: Reflections on the History of Tramping," *Annals of Tourism Research* 12, no. 3 (1985): 335–54.

5. In this context, I draw on Alison Games's use of "cosmopolitanism" to refer to a pragmatic form of "accommodation" that Grand Tour students and merchants used to gain new knowledge or experience in the world. It does not refer to an ideological or philosophical affinity with enlightenment universalism or liberal internationalism. See Alison Games, "Introduction," and "The Mediterranean Origins of the British Empire," chapter 1 in *The Web of Empire: English Cosmopolitans in an Age of Expansion, 1560–1660* (New York: Oxford University Press, 2008).

6. For John Cook's pursuit of royal clients, see Brendon, *Thomas Cook*, 183–85. The Toynbee Settlement House developed tours for its primarily lower-middle-class members but on a far smaller scale than the Polytechnic. See Joan D. Browne, "The Toynbee Travellers' Club," *History of Education* 15, no. 1 (1986): 11–17.

7. David Sutton, "Liberalism, State Collectivism and the Social Relations of Citizenship," in *Crisis in the British State, 1880–1930*, 63–79, esp. 64. See also Andrew Vincent, "The New Liberalism and Citizenship," in *The New Liberalism: Reconciling Liberty and Community*, ed. Avital Sihmony and David Weinstein (Cambridge University Press, 2001), 205–27; and Stuart Hall and Bill Schwarz, "State and Society, 1880–1930," in *Crisis in the British State, 1880–1930*, 7–32. For the new liberalism in education, see Stephen Heathorn, *For Home, Country, and Race: Constructing Gender, Class, and Englishness in the Elementary School, 1880–1914* (University of Toronto Press, 2000); and Harry Hendrick, *Images of Youth: Age, Class, and the Male Youth Problem, 1880–1920* (Oxford University Press, 1990).

8. Hall and Schwartz, "State and Society," 11, 21. See also Keith McClelland and Sonya Rose, "Citizenship and Empire, 1867–1928," in *At Home with the Empire: Metropolitan Culture and the Imperial World*, ed. Catherine Hall and Sonya O. Rose (Cambridge University Press, 2006), 275–97.

9. Aihwa Ong, "Cultural Citizenship as Subject-Making: Immigrants Negotiate Racial and Cultural Boundaries in the United States," *Anthropology* 37, no. 5 (December 1996): 737–62, esp. 738. Ong draws on Foucault's concept of "governmentality" as a corrective to the state-centered analysis of Philip Corrigan and Derek Sayer in *The Great Arch*.

10. For some students, the Polytechnic's dynamism would have encouraged a consciousness of the present as a "period of both transformation and transition." It followed then that class realities were also subject to change. For the modern consciousness of the present as always in transition, see Martin Daunton and Bernhard Rieger, "Introduction," in *Meanings of Modernity: Britain from the Late-Victorian Era to World War II*, eds. Martin Daunton and Bernhard Rieger (Oxford University Press, 2001), 1–21, esp. 5.

11. Some students were successful in changing their economic status and even crossing class boundaries. See Julie Stevenson, "'Among the qualifications of a good wife, a knowledge of cookery certainly is not the least desirable' (Quintin Hogg): Women and the Curriculum at the Polytechnic at Regent Street, 1888–1913," *History of Education* 26, no. 3 (1997): 267–86, esp. 285. For an analysis of modernity with reference to upwardly mobile youth who "straddled" working- and lower-middle-class identities, see A. James Hammerton, "Pooterism or Partnership? Marriage and Masculine Identity in the Lower Middle Class, 1870–1920, *Journal of British Studies* 38, 3 (July 1999): 291–321, esp. 313–14; and Peter Bailey, "White Collars, Gray Lives? The Lower Middle Class Revisited," *Journal of British Studies* 38, 3 (July 1999): 273–90, esp. 288.

12. This approach draws on the insights of scholars who have complicated T. H. Marshall's classic teleology of civil, political, and social rights and the "fixed" quality of judicial and legal status. See Kathleen Canning and Sonya Rose, "Introduction: Gender, Citizenship and Subjectivity: Some Historical and Theoretical Considerations," *Gender and History* 13, no. 3 (November 2001): 427–43, esp. 428.

13. Charles J. Finger, *Seven Horizons* (Garden City, NY: Country Life Press, 1930), 82–91. Finger omits most dates from his autobiography. The earliest (but, by no means definitive) reference I have found for Finger at the Polytechnic is 1887, when he gave a paper to the Mutual Improvement Society in defense of women's

suffrage. See *Home Tidings* 10 (April 2, 1887), 117 (UWA). All issues of *Home Tidings* and the *Polytechnic Magazine* are located at AWA.
14. Finger, *Seven Horizons*, 83.
15. Finger became a successful author of young adult adventure stories, winning a Newbery Medal in 1924. See Finding Aid, "Information about Charles J. Finger: Correspondence, Diaries, and Manuscripts, 1893–1987," processed in 1989, University of Arkansas Library, Special Collections, Manuscript Collection 639. http://libinfo.uark.edu/specialcollections/findingaids/finger.html#INFORMATION_ ABOUT_ CHARLES J. (accessed August 17, 2013).
16. Finger, *Seven Horizons*, 83, 90–91, 129, 136. Hogg announced the party's departure for Chile in *Polytechnic Magazine* 16 (February 20, 1890): 111. Hogg later recalls this event in *Polytechnic Magazine* 30 (January 6, 1897): 2. Finger, however, does not mention the party in his autobiography.
17. Alys L. Douglas Hamilton, *Kynaston Studd* (London, 1953), 38–40, 49–57; R. G. Studd, *The Holiday Story* (London: London Polytechnic, 1950), 18, 87–89.
18. Viscount Hailsham, "Introduction," in *Robert Mitchell: A Life of Service*, by Ethel M. Wood (London, 1934), ix; and Wood, *Robert Mitchell*, 1.
19. Finger, *Seven Horizons*, 129; see also the annual testimonials in the *Polytechnic Magazine* given at Founder's Day celebrations following Hogg's death in 1903.
20. Very few of Hogg's papers remain. Ethel M. (Hogg) Wood's two biographies of her father are the richest source of information on his private life. See Hogg, *Quintin Hogg*; and Ethel M. (Hogg) Wood, *The Polytechnic and Its Founder Quintin Hogg* (London, 1932). Other rich sources for Hogg's views are the *Polytechnic Magazine* and its predecessor *Home Tidings*. See also Henry S. Lunn's remarks in *Chapters from My Life: With Special Reference to Reunion* (London: Cassell, 1918), 137–41.
21. Ethel Hogg writes extensively about Hogg's religious beliefs in *Quintin Hogg*. See also Lunn, *Chapters from My Life*, 140–41.
22. Quintin Hogg's Eton friends, Thomas Pelham and Arthur Kinnaird, became important philanthropists in their own rights. Hogg worked in this capacity with Lord Shaftsbury and his "shoeblack brigade." See Hogg, *Quintin Hogg*, 47–63.
23. *Ibid.*, 79, 91–94, 225.
24. Hogg, *Quintin Hogg*, 206, 224–25.
25. This classical motto for personal development was expressed by many educational and social reformers, including Reverend Henry Solly, who viewed the Polytechnic as a successor to the WMCI. See, Richard Price, "The Working Men's Club Movement and Victorian Social Reform Ideology," *Victorian Studies* 15 (1971): 121; and Solly, "The London Polytechnic Redivivus," *Leisure Hour* (1884) no visible page numbers, University of Westminster Archive.
26. Hogg, *Quintin Hogg*, 71–100; Brenda Weeden, *History of the Royal Polytechnic Institution 1838–1881: The Education of the Eye* (Cambridge: Granta Editions 2008).
27. For a discussion of students, members, fees, and population numbers at the Polytechnic, see Hogg, *Quintin Hogg*, 228. With regard to public funds, Hogg still wielded considerable influence as a charity commissioner and chairman of the Technical Education Board of the LCC. See Hogg, *Quintin*, 224, 255. For the governance of the Polytechnic and distribution of grants, see Wood, *A History of the Polytechnic*, 138–42. See also Victor Belcher, *The City Parochial Foundation, 1891–1991: A Trust for the Poor of London* (London: Scolar Press, 1991). The LCC took an interest in (without, it seems, funding) the travel initiatives of the Polytechnics. See Polytechnics Sub Committee, Minutes, Battersea Polytechnic, May 13, 1896, LMA, TEB 36, September 26, 1894 to November 10, 1897. For the 1894 statistics, see Reverend Isidore Harris, M.A., "An Interview with Mr. Quintin

Hogg, Founder and President of the Polytechnic," *Great Thoughts* 12 (July 1894): 216–18.

28. For the YWCI, see Hogg, *Quintin Hogg*, 237–39; Wendy Jackson, "The Development of Commercial Education in London between 1870 and 1920, with Particular Reference to Women and Girls" (Master's dissertation, Institute of Education, University of London, 1997); Julie Stevenson, "A Neglected Issue in the History of Education and Training: Women Students of University College London and the Polytechnic at Regent Street, ca. 1870–1930" (PhD dissertation, Thames Valley University, London, 1996), and "Among the qualifications of a good wife," 267–86. For Hogg's views on "mixing the sexes," see Harris, "An Interview with Mr. Quintin Hogg," 217. For "rescue" work and the problem of "girls," see Hendrick, *Images of Youth*, 174.

29. Brad Beaven, *Leisure, Citizenship and Working-Class Men in Britain, 1850–1945* (Manchester University Press, 2005), 7; Henry Lunn, "Letters to the Editor," *Polytechnic Magazine* 17 (October 30, 1890): 288; Archdeacon Farrar marshals police statistics to support these views in "The Regent Street Polytechnic," *Magazine of Christian Literature* 7 (November 1892): 97–109.

30. For reformers' emphasis on civic over class identities and social citizenship over political citizenship, see Hendrick, *Images of Youth*, 237–38; and Heathorn, *For Home, Country, and Race*, 24–26. This was the identical aim of progressives on municipal boards that controlled the distribution of grants to the Polytechnic, such as the LCC. See Chris Waters, "Progressives, Puritans, and the Cultural Politics of the Council, 1889–1914," in *Politics of the People of London: The London County Council, 1889–1965*, ed. Andrew Saint (London, 1989), 49–70, esp. 57.

31. Hendrick, *Images of Youth* (Oxford, 1990), 164–65. Lunn drew links between nationalism, citizenship, and muscular Christianity, e.g., in "The Survival of the Fittest," *Polytechnic Magazine* 17 (October 23, 1890), 261.

32. Lauren M. E. Goodlad, *Victorian Literature and the Victorian State: Character and Governance in a Liberal Society* (Baltimore: Johns Hopkins University Press, 2003), 37–39. For the Polytechnic's "pastoral" work, see Quintin Hogg, "Polytechnics," *Journal of the Society of Arts* 45 (July 1896–97): 857–63, esp. 62; Reverend A. R. Buckland, "Apostles to Young Men," *Quiver* 12 (1894): 883–86, esp. 886; Archdeacon Farrar, "The Regent Street Polytechnic," *Magazine of Christian Literature* 7 (November 1892): 97–109; and Harris, "An Interview with Mr. Quintin Hogg," 216–18. For Hogg and identity, see Hogg, *Quintin Hogg*, 206, 285–91.

33. Hogg, *Quintin Hogg*, 369; Harris, "An Interview with Mr. Quintin Hogg," 216; Sarah A. Tooley, "The Polytechnic Movement: An Interview with Mr. Quintin Hogg," *Young Man*, no. 1 (May 1895): 145–50, esp. 147.

34. Lunn, *Chapters From My Life*, 138; Seth Koven, *Slumming: Sexual and Social Politics in Victorian London* (Princeton, NJ, 2004), 4–6.

35. Hogg, *Quintin Hogg*, 291.

36. *Ibid.*, 405–6.

37. George Ives Diaries, June 7, 1903, Harry Ransom Center, no. 43, 15–16. I am grateful to Brian D. A. Lewis for providing this information from his current research on Ives and "interpreting" Ives's compelling (but, as yet, inconclusive) evidence.

38. For the criminalization of homosexuality, see H. G. Cocks, *Nameless Offences: Homosexual Desire in the Nineteenth Century* (London: I.B. Tauris, 2003). For the conjoining of religion and sex that youth-oriented, homosocial environments facilitated, see John Donald Gustav-Wrathall, "Intense Friendship," in *Take the Young Stranger by the Hand: Same-Sex Relations and the YMCA* (Chicago University

Press, 1998); and H. G. Cocks, "A Strange and Indescribable Feeling: Unspeakable Desires in Late Victorian England," chapter 5 in Cocks, *Nameless Offences*.

39. For Ives's comment on homosexual encounters at the Polytechnic, see Matt Cook, *London and the Culture of Homosexuality, 1885–1914* (Cambridge University Press, 2003), 147.
40. Remarking on this partnership, Hogg commended the "Poly Council" for their "self sacrificing lives ... who have thought the Institute worth living for and working for." See "The Quintinian," supplement, *Polytechnic Magazine* 21 (November 1892): ii.
41. Tooley, "The Polytechnic Movement, 145–50, esp. 146–47; Hogg, *Quintin Hogg*, 237.
42. The magazine had its start as *Home Tidings* at the YMCI's earlier location at Long Acre. Hogg originally edited it himself but later hired Samson Clark, a professional editor and possibly a Polytechnic member.
43. "A Chat with Dr. H. S. Lunn," *Polytechnic Magazine* 26 (March 13, 1895):159. On the Polytechnic's global community, see, in addition to the above, Lunn, *Chapters from My Life*, 140. For the Polytechnic's broader social mission, see Lunn, in "Letters to the Editor," *Polytechnic Magazine* 17 (October 30, 1890): 288.
44. A Good Englishman, "Going to Europe," *Polytechnic Magazine* 25 (August 29, 1894): 115.
45. See, e.g., *Home Tidings* 10 (January 22, 1887): 29; 10 (March 26, 1887): 109; and 13 (September 6, 1888): 155. See also *Polytechnic Magazine* 14 (February 28, 1889): 122; 14 (May 23, 1889): 297; 16 (August 21, 1890): 122; 16 (January 16, 1890): 34–35; 16 (May 15, 1890): 315; 20 (February 26, 1892): 141; 22 (April 26, 1893): 326; and 40 (January 22, 1902): 33.
46. Good Englishman, "Going to Europe," 115. George Holyoake, *The Good of Going to Paris to See the Exhibition: A Letter to Willis Chater, Weaver, of Mytholmroyd*. London: London Book Store, 1867.
47. "What Our Neighbors Are Doing," *Polytechnic Magazine* 41 (July 9, 1902): 20. See the extended discussion of German industry in "Made in Germany," *Polytechnic Magazine* 29 (September 23, 1896): 124. *Polytechnic Magazine* complains about the Education Department's laissez-faire approach to educational travel in comparison with other "governments" in its issue 35 (November 29, 1899): 280.
48. *Home Tidings* 232 (December 17, 1887): 208.
49. See periodic lists of library acquisitions in the *Polytechnic Magazine*; newspaper clipping, January 22, 1896, UWA, Reading Circle Press Cuttings, v. 1893–1899, 67.
50. "Mr. C. E. Musgrave: Lecture," *Polytechnic Magazine* 12 (March 1, 1888): 92.
51. Lydia Murdoch describes a similar educational environment in poor law schools in *Imagined Orphans: Poor Families, Child Welfare, and Contested Citizenship in London* (New Brunswick, NJ: Rutgers University Press, 2006), 130–36.
52. *Polytechnic Magazine* 32 (January 10, 1898): 19; and 30 (January 27, 1897): 34.
53. *Polytechnic Magazine* 40 (January 22, 1902): 33, 38. See also *Polytechnic Magazine* 40 (January 29, 1902): 47. In addition, see Cecilia Morgan, "'A Wigwam to Westminster': Performing Mohawk Identity in Imperial Britain, 1890–1990s," *Gender and History* 15, no. 2 (August 2003): 319–41, esp. 320; and Brant-Sero's interview with the *Daily News*, republished in the *Journal of American Folk-Lore* 18 (April–June 1905): 160–62. For Britain's racial diversity, see Laura Tabili, "A Homogeneous Society? Britain's Internal 'Others,' 1800–Present," in Hall and Rose, *At Home with the Empire*, 53–76.
54. For government oversight of language courses at the Polytechnic, see London Polytechnic Council, "'A' Entries for the Current Session Minutes for the Years

1897–1900," November 19, 1897, 6, LMA, TEB 33. Earlier in the decade, the LCC refused to fund the Polytechnic's modern language classes as they were not deemed "technical." See Polytechnics Sub Committee, Minutes, Regent Street Polytechnic, July 7, 1897, LMA, TEB 36, September 26, 1894 to November10, 1897.

55. For George Hooper and the SA, see Chapter 4.

56. George N. Hooper, *An Address on General and Special Education Delivered to the Students and Teachers of the Carriage Building Technical Class of the Young Men's Christian Association* (London: private publication), 1894, London School of Economics (LSE) Pamphlet Collection, L/289. The Polytechnic's Labour Bureau offered similar advice in C. J. Peer and P. H. Clephane, *Business Guide and Civil Service Guide (1906)*, BL.

57. *Polytechnic Magazine* 2 (May 25, 1898): 245. Similar stories of students using their language skills for professional advancement can be found in *Home Tidings* 7 (November 21, 1885): 363–64; and *Polytechnic Magazine* 34 (June 21, 1899): 312.

58. *Home Tidings* 10 (March 13, 1886): 243.

59. Administrators and students tried to formalize the idea of "Poly consuls" and periodically printed the names and addresses of students abroad. See, e.g., *Polytechnic Magazine* 38 (January 30, 1901): 50; and "Our Foreign Legion," *Polytechnic Magazine* 52 (January 1913): 221. See also "Our Foreign Legion" in *Polytechnic Magazine* 46 (June 1906): 58, and 52 (January 1913): 221. For instances of networking, see, e.g., Ralph May's offer to help "especially Poly boys" in *Polytechnic Magazine* 41 (July 9, 1902): 15. Similar networks for an earlier period are analyzed in Alan Lester, *Imperial Networks: Creating Identities in Nineteenth- Century South Africa and Britain* (London: Routledge, 2001).

60. For the "Poly colony" in Fort Collins, Colorado, see Hogg, *Quintin Hogg*, 405; and *Home Tidings* 7 (November 21, 1885): 363. Hogg also founded a "Poly colony" in Fort Qu'Appelle, Assiniboia, Canada, ca. 1884; see *Polytechnic Magazine* 41 (July 9, 1902): 15.

61. Newspaper clipping (n.d.) UWA, Reading Circle Press Cuttings, v. 1893–1899, P157a, 58.

62. "The Quintinian," supplement, *Polytechnic Magazine* 28 (February 5, 1896): 74.

63. Quintin Hogg to the Secretary, Department of Science & Art, South Kensington [1897], UWA, pt 1/2/6.

64. See, e.g., *Home Tidings* 7 (August 15, 1885): 97.

65. *Home Tidings* 11 (August 6, 1887): 42; "Holiday Resorts," *Polytechnic Magazine* 12 (May 31, 1888): 302.

66. "Strangers in a Foreign Land," *Home Tidings* 9 (July 24, 1886): 53–55.

67. J.W. Andrew quoted in L.C.B. Seaman, *The Quintin School, 1886–1956: A Brief History*, pt. 3, *Pioneers, 1886–1919* (Chertsey: Burrell & Son, 1957), 1. This was reformatted for online access in 2005 by A. E. Beck (1939–46) and H. V. Beck (1935–42) at http://www.polyboys.org.uk/X08_RSP/X08B_QSH/X08B_QSH_000.htm.

68. Studd, *The Holiday Story*, 5, 13.

69. For the Paris Exhibition tour statistics, see Henry Lunn, "The Polytechnic Invasion of Norway," in *Review of Reviews* (London) 4 (August 1891): 181–84, esp. 181.

70. *Polytechnic Magazine* 14 (January 3, 1889): 59. Also see "The Plumbers' Week in Paris: By One of Them," *Polytechnic Magazine* 15 (July 18, 1889): 33–34.

71. See, e.g., *Polytechnic Magazine* 32 (March 23, 1898): 150; 47 (November 1907): 148; "German Class Students' Tour to the Rhine" 34 (February 15, 1899): 79; and "French," 53 (June 1913): 101. For the tour of Vienna, see "Students' Tour," *Polytechnic Magazine* 53 (March 1913): 24. For more on the involvement of the

Polytechnic's faculty in conducting study-abroad tours, see Seaman, *Pioneers, 1886–1919*, 4; For other student and faculty tours, see *Polytechnic Magazine* 47 (November 1907): 148; and 14 (January 3, 1889): 59.

72. Printed pamphlet (1892) in section titled "The Power Institute for Technical Education, Its Genesis and Status," UWA, Reading Circle Press Cuttings, v. 1893–99, P157a, 47.

73. William Stead, "Co-Operative Travelling: The Work of the Toynbee Travellers' Club and the Polytechnic Cheap Trips," *Review of Reviews* (London) 5 (June 1892): 619–28. The new liberal theme of "mutual respect" and "reliance" is echoed in student travel reports. See, e.g., E.W.W., "The Rhine Tour," *Polytechnic Magazine* 35 (September 27, 1899): 151. For middle-class travel collectivities in a broader European context, see Rudy Kosher, *German Travel Cultures* (Oxford: Berg Publishers, 2000), 22–23. Lest some students neglect to make the most of their holidays, J.S. Dexter argues that healthful recreation produces better workers in "Educational Advantages of the Summer Holidays," *Polytechnic Magazine* 35 (November 1, 1899): 227.

74. Hogg, *Quintin Hogg*, 235.

75. "Co-Operative & Educational Holiday Tours, 1895." See also the collection of Polytechnic Co-Operative and Educational Brochures for 1897 at the Thomas Cook Archive, TCG/BK 12/1. In 1896 the P.T.A. arranged the tours for about 12,000 tourists. See Wood, *The Polytechnic and Its Founder Quintin Hogg*, 155.

76. Studd, *The Holiday Story*, 36. For the "anti-tourist," see James Buzard, *The Beaten Track*.

77. The brochure makes special reference to the "educational experts" Lyon Playfair and Anthony Mundella. See the *Polytechnic Co-Operative and Educational Brochures* for 1897, Thomas Cook Archive, Peterborough, TCG/BK12/1. For the Polytechnic's hostility toward Thomas Cook & Son, see Studd's reference to Cook's travel "monopoly" and luxurious "European Tours" for the upper classes in Studd, *Holiday Story*, 16–17. See also "Co-Operative & Educational Holiday Tours, from February till September 1895," 15. See similar testimonials in *Polytechnic Magazine* 23 (August 30, 1893), 576: 27 (July 10, 1895), 20; and 30 (March 24, 1897): 147. For the significance of mass tours in ordinary tourists' lives, see Orvar Löfgren, *On Holiday: A History of Vacationing* (Berkeley: University of California Press, 1999).

78. Studd, *The Holiday Story*, 33, 35, 113. For a contemporary description of a "reunion," see "Grand Conversazione and Reunion of the Norway and Swiss Parties," *Polytechnic Magazine* 25 (November 28, 1894): 304–7.

79. George Wiles, "The Quintinian," *Polytechnic Magazine* 29, suppl. (August 5, 1896): 63.

80. Arthur Beckham, "Bad Luck," in "The Quintinian," supplement, *Polytechnic Magazine* 35 (October 4, 1899): 167. For a nuanced textual analysis of colonial "failures," see Nicholas Thomas and Richard Eves, *Bad Colonists: The South Seas Letters of Vernon Lee Walker and Louis Becke* (Durham, NC: Duke University Press, 1999).

81. Here, Hogg referred to the letters of East End working men, printed in the *Polytechnic Magazine*, who had tried their fortunes in the colonies. See *Home Tidings* 8 (March 13, 1886): 242–44.

82. For British youth and imperial identities, see John Tosh, "Manliness, Masculinities and the New Imperialism, 1880–1900," chapter 9 in *Manliness and Masculinities in Nineteenth-Century Britain* (Harlow: Pearson, 2005).

83. For the characteristics of boys' literature or "romances" in the context of collaborative authorship, see Wayne Koestenbaum, *Double Talk: The Erotics of Male Literary Collaboration* (New York: Routledge, 1989).

84. Don Homfray, "The Quintinian," *Polytechnic Magazine* 35, suppl. (August 1899). 66. Homfray's reference to the "rough" passengers asserts his own respectability by comparison. For working-class respectability, see Peter Bailey, "A Role Analysis of Working-Class Respectability: Will the Real Bill Banks Please Stand Up," chapter 2 in *Popular Culture and Performance in the Victorian City*.

85. Don Homfray, "The Quintinian," *Polytechnic Magazine* 35, suppl. (November 1, 1899): 220.

86. Frederick Slade, "The Quintinian," *Polytechnic Magazine*, 24, suppl. (January 3, 1894), 18; "The Quintinian," *Polytechnic Magazine*, 26, suppl. (March 6, 1895), 143, 158–159. Slade's students took music and history lessons, participated in social and sporting activities, controlled their spending through a saving's club, and attended bible classes. See, "The Quintinian," *Polytechnic Magazine*, 29, suppl. (July 1, 1896), 7.

87. For an example, see Sid Lello's travels and death in *Polytechnic Magazine* 31 (September 15, 1897): 97–98; also see "The Quintinian," *Polytechnic Magazine* 31, suppl. (November 1897): 182.

88. James Hubbard, *Polytechnic Magazine* 45 (May 1905): 41; and 52 (January 1913): 221.

89. For the Polytechnic's imperial tone in continental travel reports, see printed pamphlet (1892) in section titled "The Power Institute for Technical Education, Its Genesis and Status," UWA, Reading Circle Press Cuttings, v. 1893–99, P157a, 47; see also *Home Tidings* (August 8, 1885): 84; 7 (10 October 1885): 235–37; 9 (July 24, 1886): 53–55; and 10 (April 16, 1887): 130–31, continued in (May 28, 1887): 178–79.

90. See, "Patriotism or ?" *Polytechnic Magazine* 35 (November 1, 1899): 225. Archdeacon Sinclair preached humility, as English travelers tend to "march about as if everything belonged to themselves," in "Notes of Last Sunday's Address" in *Polytechnic Magazine* 28 (January 29, 1896): 57.

91. Authorial anonymity, collaborative or otherwise, conferred the symbolic power of a collective identity to the Polytechnic's travel narratives. For more on collaborative authorship see Koestenbaum, *Double Talk*. More generally, British travel guides that encompassed the colonies and beyond constructed a collective identity, one that John Mackenzie identifies as the myth of a "supra-nationality which embraced the world through travel and the traveller's gazetteer," in "Empires of Travel: British Guide Books and Cultural Imperialism in the 19th and 20th Centuries," in *Histories of Tourism: Representation, Identity, and Conflict*, ed. John K. Walton, 21. For more on the development of travel journalism that takes in account, in small measure, the Polytechnic, Lunn, and women travel writers, see Jill Steward, " 'How and Where to Go': The Role of Travel Journalism in Britain and the Evolution of Foreign Tourism, 1840–1914," in *Histories of Tourism: Representation, Identity, and Conflict*, 49.

92. The reading circle described its group tour and collaborative report as a community-building process in "The Rhine Tour," *Polytechnic Magazine* 35 (September 27, 1899): 151.

93. *Home Tidings* 9 (September 4, 1886): 156–57.

94. David Chirico, "The Travel Narrative as a (Literary) Genre," in *Under Eastern Eyes: A Comparative Introduction to East European Travel Writing on Europe*, eds. Wendy Bracewell and Alex Drace-Francis (Budapest: Central European University Press, 2008), 27–59, esp. 50.

95. Brochure of the *Polytechnic Co-Operative & Holiday Tours, 1895*, BL. For the language of travel communities, see, as well, "Swiss Trips" and "Madeira Trips," *Polytechnic*

Magazine 17 (June 26, 1890): 408–15; Lunn, "The Polytechnic Invasion of Norway," 181–84; and Hogg, "Social Salvation," in Letters to the Editor, *Polytechnic Magazine* 17 (November 13, 1890): 317.

96. Hogg, *Polytechnic Magazine* 32 (March 23, 1898): 150.
97. *Home Tidings* 2 (January 1881): 18–20. The meeting concluded with a resolution in the mechanic's favor, although it was amended the following meeting giving each class and occupational group 20 percent membership. Student-members enjoyed access to various educational courses, as well as clubs, athletic facilities, and other institutional amenities.
98. Manual workers comprised 85 percent of the student body in the early 1880s. See *Home Tidings* 2 (January 1881): 18. See also Steven Cotgrove, *Technical Education and Social Change*, 61. However, by 1900, the occupational ratio shifted in favor of clerks and professions. See Jackson, "The Development of Commercial Education," 59. For further statistics related to students' social class and income, see Stevenson, "A Neglected Issue," 126–27.
99. "Regent Street," in *The London Encyclopedia*, revised edition, Ben Weinreb and Christopher Hibbert (London, 1995), 660–62; Hermoine Hobhouse, "An Avenue of Superfluities," in *A History of Regent Street* (London, 1975), 82–107.
100. For an analysis of the "popular tropes" that likened university settlements to colonies and slums to jungles, see Koven, *Slumming*, 236–37; and Judith R. Walkowitz, "Urban Spectatorship," chapter 1 in *City of Dreadful Delights*. For the class composition of the Polytechnic Day School, see Seaman, *The Quintin School, 1886–1956: A Brief History*, 2.
101. Seaman, *Pioneers, 1886–1919*, 12–15; Hogg, *Quintin Hogg*, 151–53.
102. Seaman, Pioneers, 1886–1919, 5.
103. Inquisitor, "Things I Would Like to Know," *Polytechnic Magazine* 40 (June 25, 1902): 266.
104. *Ibid.*, *Polytechnic Magazine* 40 (June 18, 1902): 207.
105. *Polytechnic Magazine* 32 (March 23, 1898): 150.
106. Inquisitor, "Things I Would Like to Know," *Polytechnic Magazine* 40 (June 18, 1902): 257.
107. "Holidays – A Suggestion," *Polytechnic Magazine* 16 (June 5, 1890): 364.
108. F.G.H., "Letter to the Editor," *Polytechnic Magazine* 26 (June 12, 1895): 301; Robert Dredge, "Re Holiday Homes," in Letters to the Editor, *Polytechnic Magazine* 26 (June 19, 1895): 320.
109. H. Morley, "Is the Social Element in the Poly Neglected?" in Letters to the Editor, *Polytechnic Magazine* 21 (December 21, 1892): 425. See also, Morley, "Social Life in the Institute," in Letters to the Editor, *Polytechnic Magazine* 22 (February 15, 1893): 144; and Herbert J. Flower, "The Social Question," in Letters to the Editor," *Polytechnic Magazine* 29 (September 23, 1896): 124.
110. Hogg, *Polytechnic Magazine* 29 (October 7, 1896): 146. In 1899, the Poly home at Westcliff-on-Sea offered a "free holiday" to Polytechnic students unable to afford its nominal rates. See *Polytechnic Magazine* 35 (July 26, 1899): 57.
111. Hogg, *Polytechnic Magazine* 29 (October 7, 1896): 146.
112. See the reference to "one of our lady students" who had passed the Royal College of Surgeons exam, in *Polytechnic Magazine* 21 (September 29, 1892): 146; Albert Shaw, "A Model Working-Girls' Club," *Scribner's Magazine* 11 (February 1892): 169–77, esp. 173.
113. For YWCI student suffrage demands, see a series of Letters to the Editor titled "Why Not?" in *Polytechnic Magazine*, including 21 (September 8, 1892): 116; 21 (September 29, 1892): 152; 21 (November 30, 1892): 347; and 21 (November 9,

1892): 279. For the Polytechnic's parliamentary debates on the "Women Question," see "In Parliament," Society & Club Reports, *Polytechnic Magazine* 14 (January 31, 1889): 65; The Clerk of the House, "Sisters and Sociability," Letters to the Editor, *Polytechnic Magazine* 36 (February 14, 1900): 84; "Polytechnic Parliament," *Polytechnic Magazine* 21 (October 27, 1892): 230.

114. Sister, "Why Not," Letters to the Editor, *Polytechnic Magazine* 21 (September 8, 1892): 116. After Hogg's death in 1903, fewer debates appeared in the magazine. The magazine's publishing schedule changed from a weekly to a monthly publication, and the page reserved for the sister institute was reduced to a column and sometimes expunged altogether. Occasionally, however, references to the women's suffrage movement managed to surface, such as a report on the sisters' meeting of the Mutual Improvement Society, in which a Miss Buckner gave a paper in support of the suffragists "militant tactics." See *Polytechnic Magazine* 48 (February 27, 1909): 222.

115. Stead, "Co-Operative Travelling." In contrast, women played a central role in the development of the Toynbee Settlement's travel programs. See Dina Copelman, *London's Women Teachers: Gender, Class and Feminism, 1870–1930* (London: Routledge, 1996), 174.

116. YWCI students complained that there was little news in the *Polytechnic Magazine* that concerned them, which they interpreted as another exclusion. See *Polytechnic Magazine* 17 (November 20, 1890): 327. For a group tour, see "How a Lady Views It," *Polytechnic Magazine* 17 (September18, 1890): 179. For discursive considerations, see Shirley Foster and Sara Mills, "Introduction," in *An Anthology of Women's Travel Writings* (Manchester University Press, 2002). For "Miss Milligan," see *Polytechnic Magazine* 32 (April 27, 1898): 202.

117. Sidney Webb commended those who rose out of the "ranks" in "Distribution of Prizes to the Architectural and Engineering Students," *Polytechnic Magazine* 32 (January 12, 1898): 32. Even the Polytechnic's career guide recommended migration as the only certain relief from the "rule" of "caste." See C. J. Peer and P. H. Clephane, *Business Guide and Civil Service Guide* (1906), 11, BL. Note, too, that social stratification riddled the tours. Hogg stated that "poorer lads" had access to Brighton holidays with "people of their own station," while the "better off" enjoyed "foreign trips." See Harris, "An Interview," 218.

118. Albert J. Spalding, "The Employment of Women," *Polytechnic Magazine* 16 (June 5, 1890): 364. Seth Koven shows how "sex wars" reconfigured masculine identities in *Slumming*, 229. For lower- middle-class masculine identities that adjusted to modernity by dignifying married life in the suburbs, see Hammerton, "Pooterism or Partnership?" This perspective rarely surfaces in the *Polytechnic Magazine*, except in marriage announcements accompanied by "ball and chain" quips that poked fun at the groom. These marriage announcements competed with frequent references to the Polytechnic's "Bachelor Club."

119. Quintin Hogg, "Polytechnics," 862.

120. "Radical Notes," *Polytechnic Magazine* 23 (November 1, 1893): 709.

121. C. J. Peer, "Social Salvation," *Polytechnic Magazine* 17 (October 23, 1890): 262–63.

122. See Wim Neetens for Besant's "optimistic" (if more ambivalent) perspective on social change in "Problems of a 'Democratic Text': Walter Besant's Impossible Story," *Novel* 23 (Spring 1990): 247–64. For Besant and the People's Palace, see Simon Joyce, "Castles in the Air: The People's Palace, Cultural Reformism, and the East End Working Class," *Victorian Studies* 39, no. 4 (Summer 1996): 513–38; Beaven, *Leisure, Citizenship and Working-Class Men*, 30–33.

123. Walter Besant, "The Upward Pressure (A Chapter from the *History of the Twentieth Century*)," *Scribner's Magazine* 13, no. 5 (May 1893): 585–96, esp. 596.

124. *Ibid.*, 592.

125. LCC, TEB, "Regent Street Polytechnic," Minutes of the Polytechnics Sub Committee, Minutes, May 13, 1896, LMA, TEB 36, September 26, 1894 to November 10, 1897.

126. Hugh Oakeley Arnold-Forster, *The Citizen Reader* (London: Cassell, 1904), 164. Heathhorn discusses the influence of Arnold-Forster and *The Citizen Reader* in elementary education, in *For Home, Country, and Race*, 49–50.

127. State and private organizations financed scholarships for study abroad. See, for example, the Education Department's development of study abroad teaching assistantships in France and Germany in 1905, ED 121/227 74844, Public Record Office; Education Department, *Special Reports on Educational Subjects*, vol. I of *Education in the United Kingdom and the European Continent* (London: Wyman and Sons, Ltd., 1897; Reprint: Kyoto: Rinsen Book Company, 1974); "Third Year Students Abroad," *The Schoolmistress*, August 16, 1900, 309; "Gilchrist Scholarships and Studentships for Women," *Technical Education Gazette*, June 1902, 99; Elizabeth Healey, *The Educational Systems of Sweden, Norway, and Denmark, with Special Reference to the Education of Girls and Adults Being The Report presented to the Trustees of the Gilchrist Educational Trust on a visit to Scandinavia in 1892, as Gilchrist Travelling Scholar* (London: Taylor and Francis, 1892), Pamphlet Collection, London School of Economics. Additionally, see notices on available foreign commercial scholarships in "Foreign Commercial Institutes," *Technical Education Gazette*, February 1900, 45. For a contemporary discussion of the development of international student-exchange programs see "The Practical Side of Educational travel, *The Sphinx* 18 (October 28, 1910): 11–12, University of Liverpool Archive. Precedents for these scholarships can also be found in early exhibition literature. See for example, "Paris Exhibition. Visits of Teachers," *Journal of the Society of Arts* 15 (May 3, 1867): 391, which stated that "A minute passed by the Committee of Council on Education in accordance with the practice of the Science and Art Department at the International Exhibition at Paris in 1855 and in London 1862, offer encouragement to the masters (and mistresses) certified teachers to go to study objects in science and art which may be likely to benefit the instruction given in such schools. £5 expenses, £2 for reports." See also "Report of M. Haussoullier," in Henry Cole *Reports on the Paris Exhibition* (1867), RSA Archive. For the new technological class, see Tom Jeffrey, "A Place in the Nation: The Lower Middle Class in England," in *Splintered Classes: Politics and the Lower Middle Class in Interwar Europe*, ed. Rudy Koshar (New York: Holmes & Meier, 1990), 70–95.

128. *Polytechnic Magazine* records travel scholarships awarded to its students by outside governmental or civic bodies, such as a "travelling studentship" to learn foreign languages awarded by the Salters' Company. See *Polytechnic Magazine* 40 (April 30, 1902): 188. For the conceptualization of the Hodgson Pratt Memorial," see, *The Working Men's College Journal: Conducted by Members of the Working Men's College* 10: 167–188 (London, 1907), 373. http://books. google.com/books?id=FC4BAAAAYAAJ&pg=PA373&lpg=PA373&dq=Hodgson+p ratt+memorial+travelling+scholarship&source=bl&ots=8bPCI2nJLI&sig=_Czg79 aHn8Uz3D6wLElaqc3UIao&hl=en&sa=X&ei=s_RrUKTQHfGgyAH6moC4AQ&v ed=0CCIQ6AEwAQ#v=onepage&q=Hodgson%20pratt%20memorial%20travel-ling%20scholarship&f=false (accessed August 17, 2013). See, also, the report of one scholarship recipient, Fred Longden (Hodgson Pratt Student at Ruskin College, Oxford) *Apprenticeship in Ironmoulding: A Comparison of Apprenticeship*

Conditions in English and Belgian Foundries (London: Hodgson Pratt Memorial Ltd., 1914), Pamphlet Collection, London School of Economics. For additional information on the Hodgson Pratt Memorial Travelling Scholarships, see the *Annual Reports* at the British Library. For similar scholarships conferred to students by philanthropic and co-operative institutions see, for example, notice of "Travelling Scholarships" provided by Herbert Henry Asquith in "Toynbee Travellers Club: List of Members," London Metropolitan Archive; See also, Thomas Dawe (Blandford Scholar) *A Co-operative Tour in Belgium and France*, (Manchester: The Co-Operative Union Limited), 1901, Pamphlet Collection, London School of Economics.

129. Besant condemned the "scholarship system" as undemocratic in *Upward Pressure*, 594.
130. I have drawn this summation from Canning and Rose, "Identity," 429.
131. Studd's father became chairman of both the institute and the PTA, maintaining the PTA's ties to the Polytechnic. See Studd, *The Holiday Story*, 60, 104–5.
132. John Urry, *The Tourist Gaze*, 27; also see John Urry, *Consuming Places* (London: Routledge, 1995), 165; Hartmut Berghoff develops Urry's observations further in examining the multiple meanings given to tourism and consumption in "From Privilege to Commodity? Modern Tourism and the Rise of the Consumer Society," in *The Making of Modern Tourism: The Cultural History of the British Experience, 1600–2000*, eds., Barbara Korte Berghoff, Ralf Schneider and Christopher Harvie (Basingstoke: Palgrave, 2002), 159–178; see also, Beaven, *Leisure, Citizenship and Working-Class Men*, 44; Sandra Dawson shows that trade unionists viewed paid holidays as a "symbol of social as well as political citizenship" in "Working-Class Consumers and the Campaign for Holidays with Pay," *Twentieth Century British History*, 18, no. 3 (January 2007): 1–29, esp. 5–6. The Workers' Travel Association (WTA) also shares a place in this history. The WTA was a voluntary association founded in 1921 by a former member of the Toynbee Settlement and backed by the cooperative movement, trade unions, and Labour politicians. One strong supporter was foreign secretary, Ernst Bevin, who accompanied the tourists on numerable holidays abroad, sometimes in the capacity of WTA President. The WTA aimed to encourage international understanding by providing ordinary people with cheap, pleasurable, and educational experiences abroad. Indeed, the W.T.A. produced the First International Conference on Workers' Travel in London in 1927, to facilitate exchanges between British and continental workers' organizations. Most travelers, however, rejected the WTA's initial attempts to "educate" them with didactic tours that highlighted socialist and labor history, institutions, and values. See, Francis Williams, *Journey into Adventure: the Story of the Workers' Travel Association:* (London: Odhams Press Limited, 1960), 59, 71–77.
133. The difficulty, of course, is that scholars have justly derided reformers attempts at social control through social citizenship, which tended to subordinate political rights to civic duty. The conundrum, as Vincent shows, is that by delinking social rights from civic duty in the twentieth century, passive entitlements have won out over active responsibility to one's community and "social solidarity." Simhony and Weinstein distill Vincent's argument in "Introduction," in *The New Liberalism*, 24. One implication of this is that study abroad students who construct identities as "global citizens" today do so as an elite privilege.
134. "Royal Commission on University Education in London," First Report, British Parliamentary Papers, 1910, xxiii, 199–202, quoted in Cotgrove, *Technical Education and Social Change*, 64.

135. Crees, "Introduction," in *First Annual Report of the Association for the International Interchange of Students, 1909–10*, ed. Henry W. Crees (London: Association for the International Interchange of Students, 1910),ix. Googlebooks, http://babel. hathitrust.org/cgi/pt?id=wu.89093690436;view=1up;seq=4 (accessed May 11, 2013). When the AIIS launched in 1909, it set its sights on the wider world, but focused for the time being on England, Canada, and the United States.

136. *Ibid.*, vii–xii.

137. Scholars and students routinely traveled to seats of learning during the Middle Ages, such as Desiderius Erasmus, the namesake of the European Union's student exchange program. More germane to the modern era was the pattern of student mobility during the nineteenth century that would encourage institutional and government interest in study abroad. This was the flow of male as well as female students, mostly from the USA, to German and other European universities, where they sought new learning experiences and credentials that could not be attained at home. These students, such as women who sought medical degrees or studio instruction in painting and sculpture, thus acted independently, without institutional support, to acquire degrees at foreign institutions. See, Konrad H. Jarausch, ed., *The Transformation of Higher Learning, 1860–1930* (Chicago: University of Chicago Press, 1983); Sandra L. Singer, *Adventures Abroad: North American Women at German Speaking Universities, 1868–1915* (Westport: Praeger, 2003); Thomas Neville Bonner, *To the Ends of the Earth: Women's Search for Education in Medicine* (Cambridge: Harvard University Press, 1992); Jane R. Becker and Gabriel P. Weisberg, eds., *Overcoming All Obstacles: The Women of the Académie Julian* (New Brunswick, NJ: Rutgers University Press, 1999).

138. See, for example, Walter Runciman, "Agreement Relating to the Exchange of German and English Women Teachers, with the Object of Improving the Modern Language Teaching in Secondary Schools for Girls in Both Countries," Board of Education for England and Wales (May 29, 1908) PRO, ED 121/227 74844; Hoffa, *A History of US Study Abroad: Beginnings to 1965*, 47–48.

139. Cecil John Rhodes, *The Last Will and Testament of Cecil John Rhodes with Elucidatory Notes*, ed. W.T. Stead (London: Review of Reviews Offices, 1902), 35–38.

140. Education Department, "NOTE by Miss Williams (the Official Representative of the French Ministry of Public Instruction in this matter) on English Répétitrices in French Training Colleges," in *Special Reports on Educational Subjects*, vol. I, 76–79.

141. Hoffa, *A History of US Study Abroad*, 67.

142. De Witt, *Internationalization of Higher Education in the United States of America and Europe*, 10–16, 88. Although the language of international "peace and understanding" underpinned these programs and had existed as a discourse since the nineteenth century, De Witt rightly cautions that the foreign policy initiatives of hegemonic states and geo political blocs determine what is a viable "peace" and what is meant by "understanding" in the world.

143. Hoffa, *A History of US Study Abroad*, 113–114. For an extensive list British educational travel opportunities see, Central Bureau for Educational Visits and Exchanges established by UNESCO National Co-Operating Body for Education, *Survey of British Organizations Concerned in Furthering Educational Travel*, (London: Hamilton House, July 1949).

144. Hans de Wit, *Internationalization of Higher Education in the United States of America and Europe: A Historical, Comparative, and Conceptual Analysis* (Boston: Greenwood Press, 2002), 6.

145. *Ibid.*, 48–49, 67, 73, n.8, 223.

Conclusion: Goody, Gordon, and Shilpa Shetty "Poppadom": The Politics of Study Abroad from the New Liberalism to New Labour

1. Jade recalls her days in CBB and her time in India in Jade Goody, *Jade: Fighting to the End. My Autobiography* (London: John Blake Publishing, Ltd., 2009).
2. *Ibid.*, 103.
3. Arjun Appadurai, *Modernity at Large: Cultural Dimension of Globalization* (Minneapolis: University of Minnesota Press, 1996).
4. See, for example, "Big Brother's Jade: Harsh or Fair?" BBC News (World Edition), July 19, 2002, http://news.bbc.co.uk/2/hi/entertainment/2097691.stm (accessed August 17, 2013).
5. Owen Jones writes that in 2005, the English Dictionary defined "Chav" as "a young working-class person who dresses in casual sports clothing," but that its broader meaning and use is as a metonym for "any negative traits associated with working-class people". See, Jones, *Chavs: The Demonization of the Working Class* (London: Verso Books, 2011), 8.
6. Jones, *Chavs*, 1-12. See also Johann Hari's sensitive assessment of Jade Goody in, "Jaded Contempt for the Working Class: By any tangible measure, the white working class is the least racist part of British society," *The Independent*, January 22, 2007, http://www.independent.co.uk/opinion/commentators/johann-hari/ johann-hari-jaded-contempt-for-the-working-class-433182.html (accessed August 17, 2013). Lucy Mangan provides an insightful class analysis in, "Jade Goody: At peace – and finally out of the limelight," *The Guardian*, March 23, 2009, http:// www.guardian.co.uk/media/2009/mar/22/lucy-mangan-on-jade-goody (accessed August 17, 2013).
7. Jones, *Chavs*, 71–72.
8. "Big Brother's Jade: Harsh or Fair?"
9. Mangan, "Jade Goody: At peace – and finally out of the limelight"; Goody, *Jade: Fighting to the End*, 101–104.
10. Owen Gibson, Vikram Dodd and Randeep Ramesh in Delhi, "Racism, ratings and reality TV: now Big Brother creates a diplomatic incident," *The Guardian*, January 18, 2007, http://www.guardian.co.uk/media/2007/jan/18/bigbrother. politics (accessed August 17, 2013).
11. Lucy Mangan, "Jade Goody: At peace – and finally out of the limelight."
12. Goody, *Jade: Fighting to the End*, 143–148.
13. Goody was more travelled than her detractors assumed. She and her mother took a number of foreign holidays that were funded through a legal settlement awarded for a motorcycle accident that killed her uncle and disabled her mother. In her first autobiography, Goody notes that her mother was a "free spirit" and wanted to travel the world as an adventure, not on a time table set by a Cook's package tour. Thus, Goody spent time in Spain, Nigeria, and even attended school in Egypt, where she learned to read "backwards" while her mother smoked hookah pipes at the cafes. See, Jade Goody, *Jade: How it all Began, My First Book* (London: John Blake Publishing, Ltd., 2006), 34-37. Goody admitted that she regarded Shetty as a "posh, up-herself princess." See, Johann Hari, "Jade Goody Showed the Brutal Reality of Britain," *The Independent*, March 23, 2009, http://www.independent.co.uk/opinion/commentators/johann-hari/ johann-hari-jade-goody-showed-the-brutal-reality-of-britain-1651722.html (accessed August 17, 2013).

14. The EMA's helped low-income students stay in school or go to college. See, for example, Sarah Hartley, "Leeds students hard hit by scrapping of Education Maintenance Allowance," Guardian (Leeds), December 30, 2010, http://www.guardian.co.uk/leeds/2010/dec/17/leeds-students-education-maintenance-allowance (accessed August 17, 2013).

15. Sanjoy Majumder, "Sea Change in UK–India Relations," *BBC News*, January 16, 2007, http://news.bbc.co.uk/2/hi/south_asia/6267387.stm (accessed August 17, 2013). This discourse of the economic threat to Britain (one that echoes nineteenth century calls to improve education and develop study abroad opportunities) is also expressed in the following report, A.M. Findlay and R. King *et al.*, "Motivations and Experiences of UK Students Studying Abroad," *BIS Research Paper No. 8* (University of Dundee: Department for Business Innovation & Skills, 2010), http://www.bis.gov.uk/assets/BISCore/corporate/MigratedD/publications/B/BIS-RP-008.pdf, esp. 5–6, 43 (accessed August 17, 2013).

16. Sunder Katwala, "The Education of Jade Goody," *The Guardian* January 19, 2007, http://www.guardian.co.uk/commentisfree/2007/jan/19/post955 (accessed August 17, 2013); see also Majumder, "Sea Change in UK–India Relations."

17. "Neet England: how many young people are Not in Employment Education or Training?" *The Guardian*, February 24, 2011, http://www.guardian.co.uk/news/datablog/2011/feb/24/neets-statistics (accessed August 17, 2013).

18. Immanuel Wallerstein, "Social Science and the Communist Interlude, or Interpretations of Contemporary History." (Paper given at ISA Regional Colloquium, "Building Open Society and Perspectives of Sociology in East-Central Europe," Krakow, Poland, Sept. 15–17, 1996.) 1997. http://www2.binghamton.edu/fbc/archive/iwpoland.htm (accessed August 17, 2013).

19. Lisa W. Foderaro, "Former Prime Minister of Britain Embarks on a Global Opportunity at N.Y.U." *New York Times, N.Y. Region Section.* December 14, 2010 http://www.nytimes.com/2010/12/15/nyregion/15brown.html (accessed August 17, 2013).

20. Donnelly, "Science, Technology, and Industrial Work in Britain, 1860–1930: Towards a New Synthesis," 191–201.

21. Findlay *et al.*, "Motivations and Experiences of UK Students Studying Abroad," 19–21.

22. *Ibid.*, 43.

23. Johanna Waters and Rachel Brooks, "Accidental Achievers? International Higher Education, Class Reproduction and Privilege in the Experiences of UK Students Overseas," *British Journal of Sociology of Education* 31 issue 2 (2010): 217–228.

24. Lynette Shultz, "Educating for Global Citizenship: Conflicting Agendas and Understandings," *The Alberta Journal of Educational Research* 53, No. 3 (Fall 2007): 248–250.

25. Structural, economic, and cultural impediments to the democratization of study abroad (and, by implication the ideal of "global citizenship") are addressed in Russell Deacon, *Why The Post-1992 Welsh Universities Students aren't Engaging with ERASMUS (Study Abroad): A Case Study on UWIC's Department of Humanities 3.* No. 1 (February 2011): 2–19. http://www.educationstudies.org.uk/journal/vol_23/ (accessed August 17, 2013); and, for the American (but related) context see, Mark Salisbury *et al.*, "Going Global: Understanding the Choice Process of the Intent to Study Abroad, *Research in Higher Education* 50, no. 2 (2009): 119–143.

26. Note too that this perception is not lost on economically and ethnically marginalized groups in other capitalist societies. See, Kevin R. McClure, Katalin Szelényi *et al.* "We Just Don't Have the Possibility Yet": U.S. Latina/o Narratives on Study Abroad," *Journal of Student Affairs Research and Practice* 47, No. 3 (2010): 367–386.

27. Goody, *Jade: Fighting to the End*, xxi.

28. Jade Goody, *Jade Forever in my Heart: The Story of my Battle against Cancer* (London: Harper Collins, 2009), 277–278.

References

Unpublished and Archival Sources

Bishopsgate Institution and Library, London
  George Howell Letter Books
  Minutes of the International Workingmen's Association
Bodleian Library, Oxford
  Hine, Frederick *A Week in Paris* (1867)
British Library Manuscript Collection, London
  Layard Papers
City Parochial Foundation, London
  Minute Books
Devon Record Office
  The Decorator
Archive of George Bell and Sons, Reading University Special Collection
  http://archiveshub.ac.uk/data/gb006-rulmss1640etc
London School of Economics Pamphlet Collection. London
  Dawe, Thomas. *A Co-operative Tour in Belgium and France*. Manchester: The Co-Operative Union Limited, 1901.
  Healey, Elizabeth. *The Educational Systems of Sweden, Norway, and Denmark, with Special Reference to the Education of Girls and Adults Being The Report presented to the Trustees of the Gilchrist Educational Trust on a visit to Scandinavia in 1892, as Gilchrist Travelling Scholar*. London: Taylor and Francis, 1892.
  Hooper, George N. *An Address on General and Special Education Delivered to the Students and Teachers of the Carriage Building Technical Class of the Young Men's Christian Association at the Royal Polytechnic, Regent Street, London*. London: Waterloo & Sons Limited, 1894
  Life Under Tariffs: What We Saw In Germany. The Sheffield Daily Telegraph Tour, September, 1910, Reports of Delegates.
  Longden, Fred. *Apprenticeship in Ironmoulding: A Comparison of Apprenticeship Conditions in English and Belgian Foundries*. London: Hodgson Pratt Memorial Ltd., 1914.
London Metropolitan Archives, London
  London County Council Technical Education Board, Minutes of the Polytechnics Sub Committee
  Toynbee Hall Papers
Préfecture de Police Museum, Paris
  Rapport Sur les Services de la Police Municipale à l' Exposition de 1900
Public Record Office (PRO), London
  Cowley Papers
  Universal Tourist Company Records
  Education Department Records
  Board of Education Papers for England and Wales
Royal Society of Arts Archive (RSA), London
  Note: At the time of research at the RSA, the Archive was in the process of reorganization. Individual manuscript and box numbers may have changed.

Freda Fisher. Unpublished Memoir of Sir Henry Trueman Wood, Written by his Daughter, Freda Fisher (née Wood) (c. 1925–1940).
Solly, Henry Rev. "The London Polytechnic Redivivus." *The Leisure Hour: An Illustrated Magazine for Home Reading* (1884). London: W. Stevens.

Correspondence

Ephemera

Journal of the Society of Arts.
Reports on the Paris Universal Exhibition, 1867. Volume I Containing the Report by the Executive Commissioner, and Appendices Presented to Both Houses of Parliament by Command of Her Majesty.
Reports of Artisans Selected by a Committee Appointed by the Council of the Society of Arts to Visit the Paris Universal Exhibition 1867. London: Bell and Daldy, 1867.
Reports of Artisans Selected by the Mansion House Committee to Visit the Paris Universal Exhibition, 1889. London: C.F. Roworth, 1889.
Artisan Reports Upon the Vienna Exhibition. Manchester: Society for the Promotion of Scientific Industry, 1873.
Artisan Reports on the Paris Universal Exhibition of 1878. London: Sampson Low, Marston, Searle, & Rivington, 1879.
Surrey History Centre
Broadwood and Sons, "Paris Exhibition, Return Thanks of the Men," (1867).
Thomas Cook Archive, Peterborough
The Excursionist.
Pamphlet Literature.
Ephemera
Unilever Archives, Merseyside
Ephemera and *Progress Magazine*
University of Arkansas Library, Special Collections, Manuscript Collection
Charles J. Finger: Correspondence, Diaries, and Manuscripts
University of Greenwich Archives
Woolwich Polytechnic Ephemera
Education Department: *Special Reports on Educational Subjects*, vol. I of *Education in the United Kingdom and the European Continent.* London: Wyman and Sons, Ltd., 1897; Reprint: Kyoto: Rinsen Book Company, 1974
University of Liverpool Archive
The Sphinx
University of Westminster Archive, London
Correspondence
Pamphlet Literature
Ephemera
Home Tidings (London)
The Polytechnic Magazine (London)
Reading Circle Press Cuttings
Victoria & Albert Museum Archive, Blythe House
Exhibition Foreign and Colonial Paris 1866–1870
Newspaper Cuttings: Paris Exhibition 1867
Report of the Paris Excursion Committee (1868), Exhibition Foreign and Colonial Paris, 1866–1870

The Working Men's Club and Institute Union Archive, London
Working Men's Club and Institute Reports
The Working Men's College Archive, London
The Working Men's College Magazine (London)

Newspapers & Selected Periodicals

The Bee-Hive (London)
The British Lion (London)
The Daily Telegraph (London)
The Illustrated London News
Journal of the Royal Society of Arts (London)
Journal of the Society of the Arts (London)
The People's Journal (Dundee)
The Proceedings of the Geological Society (London)
Reynolds's Newspaper
Review of Reviews
Scribner's Magazine
The Schoolmistress (London)
The Shrewsbury Chronicle
The Technical Education Gazette (London)
The Times
The Toynbee Record (London)

Published Primary Source Documents

Arnold-Forster, Hugh Oakeley. *The Citizen Reader.* London: Cassell & Co., 1904.
Besant, Walter. "The Upward Pressure (A Chapter from the *History of the Twentieth Century*)." *Scribner's Magazine* 13, no. 5 (May 1893): 585–96.
A Birmingham Working Man (Pseudonym). *A Tour through the Land of the West, and a Visit to the Columbian Exposition.* London: Simpkin, Marshall, 1894.
Brant-Sero, John Ojijatekha. Interview (reprint from *Daily Mail*). *Journal of American Folk-Lore* 18 (April–June 1905): 160–62.
British Parliamentary Papers, Vol. 1 & 5. London.
Buckland, Reverend A. R. "Apostles to Young Men." *Quiver* 12 (1894): 883–86.
Central Bureau for Educational Visits and Exchanges. Established by UNESCO National Co-Operating Body for Education. "Survey of British Organizations Concerned in Furthering Educational Travel." London: Hamilton House, July 1949.
Crees, Henry W. "Introduction." In *First Annual Report of the Association for the International Interchange of Students, 1909–10*, edited by Henry W. Crees, vii–xii. London: Association for the International Interchange of Students, 1910.
Dent, Joseph Malaby and Hugh Railton Dent. *The Memoirs of J.M. Dent, 1849–1926.* London: J.M. Dent and Sons, 1928.
Dent, J.J. *Hodgson Pratt and His Memorial.* London: Hodgson Pratt Memorial Ltd., 1918.
Dyer, George. "Benjamin Lucraft." In *Six Men of the People: Biographical Sketches with Portraits*, by William Catchpool and George Dyer. London: Dyer Brothers, 1882.
Farrar, Archdeacon. "The Regent Street Polytechnic." *Magazine of Christian Literature* 7 (November 1892): 97–109.
Finger, Charles J. *Seven Horizons.* Garden City, NY: Country Life Press, 1930.

Goody, Jade. *Jade: How it all Began, My First Book.* London: John Blake Publishing, Ltd, 2006.

Goody, Jade. *Jade: Fighting to the End. My Autobiography.* London: John Blake Publishing, Ltd, 2009.

Goody, Jade. *Jade Forever in my Heart: The Story of my Battle against Cancer.* London: Harper Collins, 2009.

Gutteridge, Joseph. *Lights and Shadows in the Life of an Artisan.* Coventry: Curtis and Beamish, 1893.

Hall, B.T. *Our Fifty Years: The Story of the Working Men's Club and Institute Union: Together with Brief impressions of the Men of the Movement.* London: Working Men's Club and Institute Union, 1912, 45.

Hamilton, Alys L. Douglas, *Kynaston Studd.* London: London Polytechnic, 1953.

Hansard's Parliamentary Debates, Ser. 3, V. 182, 1400–1403.

Harris, Reverend Isidore Harris, M.A. "An Interview with Mr. Quintin Hogg, Founder and President of the Polytechnic." *Great Thoughts* 12 (July 1894): 216–18.

Hogg, Ethel M. *Quintin Hogg: A Biography.* 2nd edition. London: Archibald Constable & Co. Ltd., 1904.

Hogg, Quintin. "Polytechnics." *Journal of the Society of Arts* 45 (July 1896–97): 857–63.

Holyoake, George. *The Good of Going to Paris to See the Exhibition: A Letter to Willis Chater, Weaver, of Mytholmroyd.* London: London Book Store, 1867.

Layard, Sir A. Henry. *Sir Henry Layard: Autobiography and Letters.* Vol. 2. London: John Murray, 1903.

Lowe, T. *A Mechanic's Tour Round the World.* London: Wyman & Sons, 1886.

Lunn, Henry S. "The Polytechnic Invasion of Norway." *Review of Reviews* (London) 4 (August 1891): 181–84.

Lunn, Henry S. *Chapters from My Life: With Special Reference to Reunion.* London: Cassell & Co., 1918.

Marx, Karl. *The First International and After: Political Writings: Volume 3.* Edited with an Introduction by David Fernbach. New York: Penguin Classics, 1992.

Melville, Herman. *Moby Dick and the Whale.* New York: Penguin Books, 1992.

Millis, C. T. *Technical Education: Its Development and Aims.* London: Edward Arnold & Co., 1925.

Mulliner, Henry. *A Carriage Builder's Tour in America.* Leamington: B. Sarney, 1883.

Peer, C.J. and P. H. Clephane. *Business Guide and Civil Service Guide.* London: Pollock & Co., 1906.

Peppin, T.S. *Club-land of the Toiler: Exemplified by the Workmen's Club and Institute Union.* London: J.M. Dent & Co. 1895. Googlebooks http://books.google.com/books?id=7IwZAAAAYAAJ&dq=club+land+of++the+toiler&source=gbs_navlinks_s (accessed August 17, 2013).

Playfair, Lyon. *Industrial Education on the Continent.* London: Royal School of Mines, 1852.

Pratt, Hodgson. *University Education in England for Natives of India, Considered with a View to Qualify them for the Learned Professions or the Public Service and to create a Class who shall mediate between the Indian People and their English Rulers.* London: James Ridgeway, 1860.

Pratt, Hodgson. "The Working Men's Club and Institute Union." *Lend a Hand: Record of Progress* XVIII, no. 1 (January 1897): 30–40. http://books.google.com/books?id=K7FCAQAAIAAJ&pg=PA30&dq=Hodgson+Pratt&hl=en&sa=X&ei=e4yUT_HkMsiigwefqLjZBA&ved=0CGUQ6AEwCDgK#v=onepage&q=Hodgson%20Pratt&f=false (accessed August 17, 2013).

Rhodes, Cecil John. *The Last Will and Testament with Elucidatory Notes*. Edited by W.T. Stead. London: Review of Reviews Office, 1902.

Shaw, Albert. "A Model Working-Girls' Club." *Scribner's Magazine*, 11 (February 1892): 169–77.

Stead, William. "Co-Operative Travelling: The Work of the Toynbee Travellers' Club and the Polytechnic Cheap Trips." *Review of Reviews* (London) 5 (June 1892): 619–28.

Steele, Henry. *The Working Classes in France*. London: Twentieth Century Press, 1904.

Studd R. G. *The Holiday Story*. London: P. Marshall, 1950.

Tooley, Sarah. "The Polytechnic Movement: An Interview with Mr. Quintin Hogg." *Young Man*, no. 1 (May 1895): 145–50.

Whiteing, Richard. *My Harvest*. New York: Dodd, Mead & Company, 1915.

The Whitworth Society. *The Whitworth Book*. London: Longmans, Green and Co., 1926.

Wood, Sir Henry Trueman. *A History of the Royal Society of Arts*. London: John Murray, 1913.

Wood, Ethel M. *Robert Mitchell: A Life of Service*. London: Frederick Muller, Ltd., 1934.

Wood, Ethel M. *The Polytechnic and Its Founder Quintin Hogg*. London: Nisbet & Co., 1932.

Working Men's Club and Institute Union, Paris Excursion Committee. *Modern Industries: A Series of Reports on Industry and Manufactures as Represented in the Paris Exposition in 1867, by Twelve British Workmen, Visiting Paris under the Auspices of the Paris Excursion Committee*. London: MacMillan and Co, 1868. (GoogleBooks, http://books.google.com/books?id=OxZAAAAAYAAJ&dq=inauthor:%22Working+Men's+Club+and+Institute+Union%22&source=gbs_navlinks_s (accessed August 17, 2013).

"The Commune of Paris," *The Edinburgh Review or Critical Journal* (American Edition). New York: Leonard Scott Publishing Company, 1871) CXXXIV(July–October, 1871): 263–290, 263, 271. Open Library. http://ia600305.us.archive.org/22/items/edinburghreview45coxgoog/edinburghreview45coxgoog.pdf (accessed September 22, 2013).

"History of the Prohibition of the Co-operative Congress of Paris," *The Social Economist, Industrial Partnerships Record & Co-operative Review* (1867): 129–30. http://books.google.com/books?id=X3UOAAAAQAAJ&pg=PA26-IA7&lpg=PA26-IA7&dq=cooperative+meeting+1867+exhibition&source=bl&ots=yWTK2GAXEm&sig=zGX2A5eSVLmhDSRjcREm14r9DDc&hl=en&sa=X&ei=rbVQUP7WDYm0yQHThIF4&ved=0CC8Q6AEwAA#v=onepage&q=cooperative%20meeting%201867%20exhibition&f=false (accessed August 17, 2013).

Secondary Sources

Anon. "Big Brother's Jade: Harsh or Fair?" *BBC News* (World Edition). 19 July 2002. http://news.bbc.co.uk/2/hi/entertainment/2097691.stm (accessed August 17, 2013).

Anon. "Neet England: how many young people are Not in Employment Education or Training?" *Guardian*. 23 February 2012. http://www.theguardian.com/news/datablog/2011/feb/24/neets-statistics (accessed August 17, 2013).

Adler, Judith. "Travel as Performed Art." *American Journal of Sociology* 94, No. 6 (May 1989): 1366–91.

Adler, Judith. "Youth on the Road: Reflections on the History of Tramping." *Annals of Tourism Research* 12 (1985): 335–354.

Allan, D. G. C. "The 'Red Doctor' Amongst the Virtuosi: Karl Marx and the Society." *Journal of the Royal Society of Arts* 129, No. 5297, Part 1 (March, 1981): 259–261; Part 2 (April, 1981): 309–311.

Alexander, Edward. "Henry Cole and the South Kensington (Victoria and Albert) Museum: The Museum of Decorative Art." In *Museum Masters: Their Museums and Their Influence*. Nashville, TN: The American Association for State and Local History, 1983.

Anderson, Benedict. *Imagined Communities: Reflections on the Origin and Spread of Nationalism*. London: Verso, 1983.

Arjun Appadurai. *Modernity at Large: Cultural Dimensions of Globalization*. Minneapolis: University of Minnesota Press, 1996.

Auerbach, Jeffrey A. *The Great Exhibition of 1851: A Nation on Display*. New Haven: Yale University Press, 1999.

August, Andrew. *The British Working Class, 1832–1940*. Harlow: Pearson Longman, 2007.

Auslander, Leorna. "Perceptions of Beauty and the Problem of Consciousness: Parisian Furniture Makers." In *Rethinking Labor History: Essays on Discourse and Class Analysis*, edited by Lenard R. Berlanstein, 149–181. Urbana: University of Illinois Press, 1993.

Auslander, Leorna. *Taste and Power: Furnishing Modern France*. Berkeley: University of California Press, 1996.

Bailey, Peter. *Leisure and Class in Victorian England: Rational Recreation and the Contest for Control, 1830–1885*. London: Routledge & Kegan Paul, 1978.

Bailey, Peter. *Popular Culture and Performance in the Victorian City*. Cambridge: Cambridge University Press, 1998.

Bailey, Peter. "White Collars, Gray Lives? The Lower Middle Class Revisited." *Journal of British Studies* 38, 3 (July 1999): 273–90.

Barton, Susan. "'Why Should Working Men Visit the Exhibition?': Workers and the Great Exhibition and the Ethos of Industrialism." In *The Golden Age: Essays in British Social and Economic History, 1850–1870*, edited by Ian Inkster *et al.*, 146–163. Aldershot: Ashgate, 2000.

Barton, Susan. *Working-Class Organisations and Popular Tourism, 1840–1970*. Manchester: Manchester University, 2005.

Barnes, John A. *City and Guilds of London Institute: A Short History, 1878–1992*. London: City and Guilds of London Institute, 1993.

Beaven, Brad. *Leisure, Citizenship and Working-Class Men in Britain, 1850–1945*. Manchester: Manchester University Press, 2005.

Becker, Jane R. and Gabriel P. Weisberg, eds. *Overcoming all Obstacles: The Women of the Académie Julian*. New Brunswick: Rutgers University Press, 1999.

Belchem, John. *Popular Radicalism in Nineteenth-Century Britain*. New York: St Martin's Press, 1996.

Belcher, Victor. *The City Parochial Foundation, 1891–1991: A Trust for the Poor of London*. London: Scolar Press, 1991.

Bennett, Tony. *The Birth of the Museum: History, Theory, Politics*. London: Routledge, 1995.

Bennett, Tony. *Culture, A Reformer's Science*. London: Sage Publications, 1998.

Bennett, Tony. "The Exhibitionary Complex." In *Representing the Nation: Reader, Histories, Heritage and Museums*, edited by David Boswell and Jessica Evans. London: Routledge, 1999.

Bennett, Tony. *Pasts Beyond Memory: Evolution, Museums, Colonialism*. London: Routledge, 2004.

Benson, John. *The Rise of Consumer Society in Britain, 1880–1980*. London: Longman, 1994.

Berghoff, Hartmut. "From Privilege to Commodity? Modern Tourism and the Rise of the Consumer Society." In *The Making of Modern Tourism: The Cultural History of the British Experience, 1600–2000*, edited by Barbara Korte Berghoff, Ralf Schneider and Christopher Harvie, 159–178. Basingstoke: Palgrave, 2002.

Biagini, Eugenio. *Liberty, Retrenchment, and Reform: Popular Liberalism in the Age of Gladstone, 1869–1880*. Cambridge: Cambridge University Press, 1992.

Bishop, A.S. *The Rise of a Central Authority for English Education*. Cambridge: Cambridge University Press, 1971.

Black, Jeremy. *The British and the Grand Tour*. London: Croom Helm, 1985.

Bonnell, Victoria and Lynn Hunt, eds. *Beyond the Cultural Turn: New Directions in the Study of Society and Culture*. Berkeley: University of California Press, 1999.

Bonner, Thomas Neville. *To the Ends of the Earth: Women's Search for Education in Medicine*. Cambridge, MA: Harvard University Press, 1992.

Böröcz, József. "Travel-Capitalism: The Structure of Europe and the Advent of the Tourist." *Comparative Studies in Society and History*. 34 (1992): 708–741.

Brauer, George C. *The Education of a Gentleman: Theories of Gentlemanly Education in England, 1660–1775*. New York: Bookman, 1959.

Brendon, Piers. *Thomas Cook: 150 Years of Popular Tourism*. London: Secker & Warburg, 1991.

Briggs, Asa. *Victorian People: A Reassessment of Persons and Themes 1851–1867*. 1955. Reprint, Chicago: University of Chicago Press, 1972.

Brooke, Michael Z. *Le Play: Engineer and Social Scientist. The Life and Work of Frédéric Le Play*. New Brunswick, NJ: Transaction, 1970.

Brown, Heloise. *"The Truest Form of Patriotism": Pacifist Feminism in Britain, 1870–1902*. Manchester: Manchester University Press, 2003.

Browne, Joan D. "The Toynbee Travellers' Club." *History of Education* 15, no. 1 (1986): 11–17.

Burchell, S.C. *Imperial Masquerade: the Paris of Napoleon III*. New York: Atheneum, 1971.

Burton, Antoinette. *At the Heart of the Empire: Indians and the Colonial Encounter in Late-Victorian England*. Berkeley: University of California Press, 1998.

Butterworth, Harry. "The Science and Art Department Examinations: Origins and Achievements." In *Days of Judgment*, edited by Roy MacLeod. Chester: Studies in Education, 1982.

Buzard, James. *The Beaten Track: European Tourism, Literature, and the Ways to 'Culture': 1800–1918*. Oxford: Oxford University Press, 1993.

Canning, Kathleen and Sonya Rose. "Introduction: Gender, Citizenship and Subjectivity: Some Historical and Theoretical Considerations." *Gender and History* 13, no. 3 (November 2001): 427–43.

Ceadel, Martin. *Semi-Detached Idealists: The British Peace Movement and International Relations, 1854–1945*. Oxford: Oxford University Press, 2000.

Chancellor, Valerie, E., ed. *Master and Artisan in Victorian England: The Diary of William Andrews and the Autobiography of Joseph Gutteridge*. New York: Augustus M. Kelley, Publishers, 1969.

Charlton, Kenneth. *Education in Renaissance England*. London: Routledge & Kegan Paul, 1965.

David Chirico. "The Travel Narrative as a (Literary) Genre." In *Under Eastern Eyes: A Comparative Introduction to East European Travel Writing on Europe*, edited by Wendy Bracewell and Alex Drace-Francis, 27–59. Budapest: Central European University Press, 2008.

Clark, Anna. *The Struggle for the Breeches; Gender and the Making of the British Working Class*. Berkeley: University of California Press, 1995.

Cleve, Ingeborg. "Dem Fortschritt entgegen. Ausstellungen und Museen im Modernisierungsprozess des Königreichs Württemberg, 1806–1918." In *Historische Anthropometrie* (Jahrbuch für Wirtschaftsgeschichte 9/1, 2000/1):149–169.

Clifford, James. *Routes: Travel and Translation in the Late Twentieth Century.* Cambridge, MA: Harvard University Press, 1997.

Cocks, H. G. *Nameless Offences: Homosexual Desire in the Nineteenth Century.* London: I.B. Tauris, 2003.

Colley, Linda. *Britons: Forging the Nation 1707–1837.* New Haven, CT: Yale University Press, 1992.

Collini, Stefan. *English Pasts: Essays in History and Culture.* Oxford: Oxford University Press, 1999.

Collins, Henry. "Karl Marx, the International and the British Trade Union Movement." *Science & Society* 26, No. 4 (Fall 1962): 400–421.

Cook, Matt. *London and the Culture of Homosexuality, 1885–1914.* Cambridge: Cambridge University Press, 2003.

Copelman, Dina. *London's Women Teachers: Gender, Class and Feminism, 1870–1930.* London: Routledge, 1996.

Corrigan, Philip and Derek Sayer. *The Great Arch: English State Formation as Cultural Revolution.* Oxford: Basil Blackwell, 1985.

Cotgrove, Stephen F. *Technical Education and Social Change.* London: George Allen & Unwin Ltd., 1958.

Cunningham, Hugh. *Leisure in the Industrial Revolution, c. 1780–c.1880.* London: Croom Helm, 1980.

Davidoff, Leonore and Catherine Hall. *Family Fortunes: Men and Women of the English Middle Class, 1780–1850.* Chicago: University of Chicago Press, 1987.

Davis, John R. "The Great Exhibition and the German States." In *Britain, the Empire, and the World at the Great Exhibition of 1851*, edited by Jeffrey A. Auerbach and Peter A. Hoffenberg, 147–172. Aldershot: Ashgate, 2008.

Dawson, Susan. *Holiday Camps in Twentieth-Century Britain.* Manchester: Manchester University Press, 2011.

Dawson, Susan. "Working-Class Consumers and the Campaign for Holidays with Pay." *Twentieth Century British History*, 18, no. 3 (January 2007): 1–29.

Dent, K.S. "Travel as Education: The English Landed Classes in the Eighteenth Century." *Educational Studies* 1 (1975): 171–180.

de Wit, Hans. *Internationalization of Higher Education in the United States of America of Europe: A Historical, Comparative, and Conceptual Analysis.* Boston: Greenwood, 2002.

Deacon, Russell. *Why The Post-1992 Welsh Universities Students aren't Engaging with ERASMUS (Study Abroad): A Case Study on UWIC's Department of Humanities* 3. No. 1 (February 2011): 2–19. http://www.educationstudies.org.uk/journal/vol_23/ (accessed August 17, 2013).

Donnelly, J. F. "Science, Technology and Industrial Work in Britain, 1860–1930: Towards a New Synthesis." *Social History* 16, no. 2 (May 1991): 191–201.

Daunton, Martin and Bernhard Rieger. "Introduction." In *Meanings of Modernity: Britain from the Late-Victorian Era to World War II.* Edited by Martin Daunton and Bernhard Rieger, 1–21. Oxford: Berg, 2001.

Duffy, Patrick. *The Skilled Compositor, 1850–1914: An Aristocrat Among Working Men.* Aldershot: Ashgate, 2000.

Eagles, Robin. *Francophilia in English Society, 1748–1815.* Basingstoke: Palgrave, 2000.

Eaglesham, E.J.R. "Administrative Muddle," chapter 2 in *The Foundations of 20th Century Education in England*. Routledge & Kegan Paul: London, 1967.

Edwards, Anthony David. *The Role of International Exhibitions in Britain, 1850–1910: Perceptions of Economic Decline and the Technical Education Issue*. Cambria: Cambria Press, 2008.

Eyffinger, Arthur. *The 1899 Hague Peace Conference: "The Parliament of Man, the Federation of the World."* The Hague: Kleuwer Law International, Martinus Nijhoff Publishers, 1999.

Eley, Geoff. "Rethinking the Political: Social History and Political Culture in Eighteenth and Nineteenth Century Britain." *Archiv für Sozialgeschichte* 21 (1981): 427–457.

Engerman, David. "Research Agenda for the History of Tourism: Towards an International Social History." *American Studies International*, 32 (1994): 3–31.

Fernbach, David. "Introduction." In Karl Marx, *The First International and After: Political Writings: Volume 3*. Edited by David Fernbach. New York: Penguin Classics, 1992: 9–72.

Fieldhouse, Roger. *A History of Modern British Adult Education*. Leicester: National Institute of Adult Continuing Education, 1996.

Findlay, A.M. and R. King, A. Geddes, F. Smith, A. Stam, M. Dunne, R. Skeldon, J. Ahrens. "Motivations and Experiences of UK Students Studying Abroad." *BIS Research Paper No. 8*. University of Dundee: Department for Business Innovation & Skills, 2010. http://www.bis.gov.uk/assets/biscore/corporate/migratedd/publications/b/bis-rp-008.pdf (accessed August 17, 2013).

Finer, Samuel. *The Life and Times of Sir Edwin Chadwick*. London: Methuen, 1952.

Finn, Margot C. *After Chartism: Class and Nation in English Radical Politics, 1848–1874*. Cambridge: Cambridge University Press, 1993.

Flett, Keith. *Chartism after 1848: the Working Class and the Politics of Radical Education*. Monmouth: Merlin Press, 2006.

Foderaro, Lisa W. "Former Prime Minister of Britain Embarks on a Global Opportunity at N.Y.U." *New York Times, N.Y. Region Section*. 14 December 2010 http://www.nytimes.com/2010/12/15/nyregion/15brown.html (accessed August 17, 2013).

Foster, Shirley and Sara Mills. *An Anthology of Women's Travel Writings*. Manchester: Manchester University Press, 2002.

Foucault, Michel. *Discipline and Punish: The Birth of the Prison*. Translated by Alan Sheridan. New York: Vintage Books, 1979.

Foucault, Michel. "Governmentality." In *The Foucault Effect: Studies in Governmentality*, edited by Graham Burchell, Colin Gordon and Peter Miller. Chicago: University of Chicago Press, 1991.

Foucault, Michel. *Technologies of the Self: A Seminar with Michel Foucault*. Edited by L.H. Martin and P.H. Hutton. Amherst: University of Massachusetts Press, 1988.

Foucault, Michel. *Politics, Philosophy, Culture; Interviews and other writings, 1977–1984*. Translated by Alan Sheridan. New York: Routledge, 1988.

Gagnier, Regenia. *Subjectivities: A History of Self-Representation in Britain, 1832–1920*. New York: Oxford University Press, 1991.

Games, Alison. *The Web of Empire: English Cosmopolitans in an Age of Expansion, 1560–1660*. New York: Oxford University Press, 2008.

Gibson, Owen, Vikram Dodd and Randeep Ramesh in Delhi. "Racism, ratings and reality TV: now Big Brother creates a diplomatic incident." *The Guardian*. 18 January 2007. http://www.guardian.co.uk/media/2007/jan/18/bigbrother.politics (accessed August 17, 2013).

Gore, Joan. *Dominant Beliefs and Alternative Voices: Discourse, Belief, and Gender in American Study Abroad.* New York: Routledge, 2005.

Gooday, Graeme. "Lies, Damned Lies and Declinism: Lyon Playfair, the Paris 1867 Exhibition and the Contested Rhetorics of Scientific Education and Industrial Performance." In *The Golden Age: Essays in British Social and Economic History, 1850–1870,* edited by Ian Inkster, *et al.* Aldershot: Ashgate, 2000.

Goodlad, Lauren M.E. *Victorian Literature and the Victorian State: Character & Governance in a Liberal Society.* Baltimore: Johns Hopkins University Press, 2003.

Green, Andy. *Education and State Formation: The Rise of Education Systems in England, France and the USA.* New York: St Martin's Press, 1990.

Greenhalgh, Paul. *Ephemeral Vistas: The Expositions Universelles, Great Exhibitions, and World's Fairs, 1851–1939.* Manchester: Manchester University Press, 1988.

Gurney, Peter. "The Middle-Class Embrace: Language, Representation, and the Contest Over Co-operative Forms in Britain, c. 1860-1914." *Victorian Studies* 37, No. 2 (Winter, 1994): 253-286.

Gurney, Peter. *Co-operative Culture and the Politics of Consumption in England, 1870–1930.* Manchester: Manchester University Press, 1996.

Gustav-Wrathall, John Donald. *Take the Young Stranger by the Hand: Same-Sex Relations and the YMCA.* Chicago: University of Chicago Press, 1998.

Haine, W. Scott. *The World of the Paris Café: Sociability among the French Working Class, 1789–1914.* Baltimore: Johns Hopkins University Press, 1996.

Hall, Stuart, and Bill Schwarz. "State and Society, 1880–1930." In *Crisis in the British State, 1880–1930,* edited by Mary Langan and Bill Schwarz 7–32: London, Hutchinson and Co., 1985.

Hammerton, James A. "Pooterism or Partnership? Marriage and Masculine Identity in the Lower Middle Class, 1870–1920." *Journal of British Studies* 38, 3 (July 1999): 291–321.

Hari, Johann. "Jade Goody Showed the Brutal Reality of Britain." *The Independent.* 23 March 2009. http://www.independent.co.uk/opinion/commentators/johann-hari/johann-hari-jade-goody-showed-the-brutal-reality-of-britain-1651722.html (accessed August 17, 2013).

Hari, Johann. "Jaded Contempt for the Working Class: By any tangible measure, the white working class is the least racist part of British society." *The Independent,* 22 January 2007. http://www.independent.co.uk/opinion/commentators/johann-hari/johann-hari-jaded-contempt-for-the-working-class-433182.html (accessed August 17, 2013).

Harris, Albert. "Workers on Holiday." *The Strand Magazine* 34, No. 199 (August 1907): 43–48. http://books.google.com/books?id=4JMkAQAAIAAJ&pg=PA44&lpg=PA44&dq=lever+brothers+paris+excursion&source=bl&ots=TBMcaaiM_-&sig=mcO YODsIqfS4HCDPijgYtRiJRUE&hl=en&sa=X&ei=2d8_UbrpBdH8yAGkjYCYDg&ved =0CFYQ6AEwAg#v=onepage&q=lever%20brothers%20paris%20excursion&f=false (accessed August 17, 2013).

Harrison, Royden. *Before the Socialists: Studies in Labour and Politics, 1861–1881.* London: Routledge & Kegan Paul, 1965.

Harrison, Royden. "E. S. Beesly and Karl Marx." *International Review of Social History* 4 (1959): 208–238.

Hartley, Sarah. "Leeds students hard hit by scrapping of Education Maintenance Allowance." *The Guardian,* December 30, 2010. http://www.guardian.co.uk/leeds/2010/dec/17/leeds-students-education-maintenance-allowance (accessed August 17, 2013).

Hendrick, Harry. *Images of Youth: Age, Class, and the Male Youth Problem, 1880–1920.* Oxford; Clarendon Press, 1990.

Heathorn, Stephen. *For Home, Country, and Race: Constructing Gender, Class, and Englishness in the Elementary School, 1880–1914*. Toronto: University of Toronto Press, 2000.

Heward, Christine M. "Education, Examinations and the Artisans: The Department of Science and Art in Birmingham, 1853–1902." In *Days of Judgment: Science, Examinations and the Organization of Knowledge in Late Victorian England*, edited by Roy MacLeod. Chester: Studies in Education, 1982.

Hobhouse, Hermoine. *A History of Regent Street*. London: MacDonald and Jane's, 1975.

Hobsbawm, Eric. *Labouring Men: Studies in the History of Labour*. New York: Basic Books, 1976.

Hoffa, William W. "A History of US Study Abroad: Beginnings to 1965." Special Issue of *Frontiers: The Interdisciplinary Journal of Study Abroad*. Carlisle: Dickenson College, 2007.

Hoffenberg, Peter. *An Empire on Display: English, Indian, and Australian Exhibitions from the Crystal Palace to the Great War*. Berkeley: University of California Press, 2001.

Hoffenberg, Peter H. "Equipoise and its Discontents: Voices of Dissent during the International Exhibitions." In *An Age of Equipoise?: Reassessing Mid-Victorian Britain*, edited by Martin Hewitt. Aldershot: Ashgate, 2000.

Hoffenberg, Peter H. *An Empire on Display: Indian, and Australian Exhibitions from the Crystal Palace to the Great War*. Berkley: California University Press, 2001.

Horvath-Peterson, Sandra. *Victor Duruy & French Education: Liberal Reform in the Second Empire*. Baton Rouge: Louisiana State University Press, 1984.

Hudson, Derek and Kenneth W. Luckhurst. *The Royal Society of Arts, 1754–1954*. London: John Murray, 1954.

Hunt, Margaret. "Racism, Imperialism, and the Traveler's Gaze." *Journal of British Studies* 32 (October 1993): 333–357.

Hunter, Ian. *Rethinking the School: Subjectivity, Bureaucracy, Criticism*. New York: St. Martin's Press, 1994.

Jarausch, Konrad H., ed. *The Transformation of Higher Learning, 1860–1930*. Chicago: University of Chicago Press, 1983.

Jeffrey, Tom. "A Place in the Nation: The Lower Middle Class in England." In *Splintered Classes: Politics and the Lower Middle Classes in Interwar Europe*, edited by Rudy Koshar, 70–96. New York: Holmes & Meier, 1990.

Jones, Owen. *Chavs: The Demonization of the Working Class*. London: Verso Books, 2011.

Joyce, Patrick. *Democratic Subjects: The Self and the Social in Nineteenth-Century England*. Cambridge: Cambridge University Press, 1994.

Joyce, Patrick. *The Rule of Freedom: Liberalism and the Modern City*. London: Verso, 2003.

Joyce, Patrick. *Work, Society and Politics. The Culture of the Factory in Later Victorian England*. New Brunswick: Rutgers University Press, 1980.

Joyce, Simon. "Castles in the Air: The People's Palace, Cultural Reformism, and the East End Working Class." *Victorian Studies* 39, no. 4 (Summer 1996): 513–38.

Kalinowski, Katherine, and Betty Weiler. "Educational Travel." In *Special Interest Tourism*, edited by Betty Weiler and Colin Michael Hall. London: Belhaven Press, 1992.

Katwala, Sunder. "The Education of Jade Goody." *The Guardian*, January 19, 2007. http://www.guardian.co.uk/commentisfree/2007/jan/19/post955 (accessed August 17, 2013).

Keane, Patrick. "The Work/Leisure Ethic in Adult Education." *Dalhousie Review* 75 (1977): 28–46.

Kelly, Thomas. *The History of Public Libraries in Great Britain, 1845–1965*. London: Library Association, 1973.

Kosher, Rudy. *German Travel Cultures*. Oxford: Berg Publishers, 2000.

Koestenbaum, Wayne. *Double Talk: The Erotics of Male Literary Collaboration*. New York: Routledge, 1989.

Koven, Seth. "The Whitechapel Picture Exhibitions and the Politics of Seeing." In *Museum Culture: Histories, Discourses, Spectacles*, edited by Daniel J. Sherman and Irit Rogoff. Minneapolis: University of Minnesota Press, 1994.

Koven, Seth. *Slumming: Sexual and Social Politics in Victorian London*. Princeton, NJ: Princeton University Press, 2004.

Kramer, Lloyd. "Victor Jacquemont and Flora Tristan: Travel, Identity and the French Generation of 1820." *History of European Ideas* 14 (1992): 789–816.

Kramer, Lloyd. *Lafayette in Two Worlds: Public Cultures and Personal Identities in an Age of Revolutions* (Chapel Hill: The University of North Carolina Press, 1996).

Kriegel, Lara. *Grand Designs: Labor, Empire, and the Museum in Victorian Culture*. Durham, NC: Duke University Press, 2007.

Kulstein, David I. *Napoleon III and the Working Class: A Study of Government Propaganda under the Second Empire*. Los Angeles: California State Colleges, 1969.

Layard, A.H. *Austen Henry Layard. Autobiography and Letters from his Childhood until his Appointment as H.M. Ambassador at Madrid*. Vol. 2. London: John Murray, 1903.

Lemon, Rebecca, Emma Mason, Jonathan Roberts, Christopher Roland. *The Blackwell Companion to the Bible in English Literature*. Oxford: Wiley-Blackwell, 2009.

Lester, Alan. *Imperial Networks: Creating Identities in Nineteenth-Century South Africa and Britain*. Routledge: London, 2001.

Leventhal, F.M. *Respectable Radical: George Howell and Victorian Working Class Politics*. London: Weidenfeld & Nicolson, 1971.

Lewis, Brian. *So Clean: Lord Leverhulme, Soap and Civilization*. Manchester: Manchester University Press, 2008.

Löfgren, Orvar. *On Holiday: A History of Vacationing*. Berkley: University of California Press, 1999.

MacCannell, Dean. *The Tourist: A New Theory of the Leisure Class*. New York: Schocken Books, 1976.

Mackenzie, John M. "Empires of Travel: British Guide Books and Cultural Imperialism in the 19th and 20th Centuries." In *Histories of Tourism: Representation, Identity, and Conflict*, edited by John K. Walton, 19–38. Clevedon: Channel View Publications, 2005.

Magraw, Roger. *A History of the French Working Class, Volume II: Workers and the Bourgeois Republic*. Oxford: Blackwell Publishers, 1992.

Majumder, Sanjoy. "Sea Change in UK–India Relations," *BBC News*, 16 January 2007. http://news.bbc.co.uk/2/hi/south_asia/6267387.stm (accessed August 17, 2013).

Mangan, Lucy. "Jade Goody: At peace – and finally out of the limelight." *The Guardian*. 23 March 2009. http://www.guardian.co.uk/media/2009/mar/22/lucy-mangan-on-jade-goody (accessed August 17, 2013).

McClelland, Keith and Sonya Rose. "Citizenship and Empire, 1867–1928." In *At Home with the Empire: Metropolitan Culture and the Imperial World*. Edited by Catherine Hall and Sonya O. Rose, 275–97. Cambridge: Cambridge University Press, 2006.

McClure, Kevin R. and Katalin Szelényi, Elizabeth Niehaus, Aeriel A. Anderson, and Jeffrey Reed. "We Just Don't Have the Possibility Yet": U.S. Latina/o Narratives on Study Abroad." *Journal of Student Affairs Research and Practice* 47, No. 3 (2010): 367–386.

Mills, Sara. *Discourses of Difference: An Analysis of Women's Travel Writing and Colonialism*. London: Routledge, 1991.

Mitchell, Timothy. *Colonizing Egypt*. Berkeley: University of California Press, 1988.

Morgan, Cecilia. "'A Wigwam to Westminster': Performing Mohawk Identity in Imperial Britain, 1890–1990s." *Gender and History* 15, no. 2 (August 2003): 319–41.

Morgan, Marjorie. *National Identities and Travel in Victorian Britain*. Basingstoke: Palgrave, 2001.

Murdoch, Lydia. *Imagined Orphans: Poor Families, Child Welfare, and Contested Citizenship in London*. New Brunswick, NJ: Rutgers University Press, 2006.

Neetens, Wim. "Problems of a 'Democratic Text': Walter Besant's Impossible Story." *Novel* 23 (Spring 1990): 247–64.

Ong, Aihwa. "Cultural Citizenship as Subject – Making: Immigrants Negotiate Racial and Cultural Boundaries in the United States." *Anthropology* 37, no. 5 (December 1996): 737–62.

O'Connor, Maura. *The Romance of Italy and the English Political Imagination*. New York: St Martin's Press, 1998.

Parker, Julia. *Citizenship, Work and Welfare; Searching for the Good Society*. New York: St Martin's press, INC., 1998.

Parratt, Catriona M. *"More than Mere Amusement": Working-Class Women's Leisure in England, 1750–1914*. Boston: Northeastern University Press, 2001.

Pollard, Sidney. *Britain's Prime and Britain's Decline: The British Economy 1870–1914*. London: Edward Arnold, 1989.

Porter, Bernard. *The Absent-Minded Imperialists: What the British Really Thought About Empire*. Oxford: Oxford University Press, 2004.

Price, Richard. "The Working Men's Club Movement and Victorian Social Reform Ideology." *Victorian Studies* 15 (1971): 117–147.

Richard Price. *Labour in British Society: An Interpretive History*. London: Routledge, 1986.

Price, Roger. *A Concise History of France*. Cambridge: Cambridge University Press, 1993.

Prokhorov, A.M. and M. Waxman, eds. *Great Soviet Encyclopedia*, 3rd Edition. New York: Macmillan, 1973.

Prothero, Iorwerth. *Radical Artisans in England and France, 1830–1870*. Cambridge: Cambridge University Press, 1997.

Pudney, John. *The Thomas Cook Story*. London: Michael Joseph, 1953.

Rancière, Jacques and Patrick Vauday. "Going to the Expo: The Worker, his Wife and Machines." In *Voices of the People: The Social Life of "La Sociale" at the End of the Second Empire*, edited by Adrian Rifkin and Roger Thomas. London: Routledge & Paul Kegan, 1988.

Reid, Alastair. "Intelligent Artisans and Aristocrats of Labour: the Essays of Thomas Wright." In *The Working Class in Modern British History: Essays in Honour of Henry Pelling*, edited by Jay Winter. Cambridge: Cambridge University Press, 1983.

Reid, Donald. *Paris Sewers and Sewermen: Realities and Representations*. Cambridge, MA: Harvard University Press, 1991.

Roderick, Gorden and Michael Stephens. *Scientific and Technical Education in Nineteenth-Century England*. Newton Abbot: David & Charles, 1972.

Rodrick, Anne. *Self Help and Civic Culture: Citizenship in Victorian Birmingham*. Aldershot: Ashgate, 2004.

Rojek, Chris and John Urry, eds. *Touring Cultures: Transformations of Travel and Theory*. London: Routledge, 1997.

Rose, Jonathan. *The Intellectual Life of the British Working Classes*. New Haven, CT: Yale University Press, 2001.

Rose, Sonya. *Limited Livelihoods: Gender and Class in Nineteenth-Century England*. Berkeley: University of California Press, 1992.

Ross, Ellen. *Slum Travelers: Ladies and London poverty, 1860–1920*. Berkeley: University of California Press, 2007.

Royle, Edward. "George Jacob Holyoake." In *Religion, Radicalism, and Freethought in Victorian & Edwardian Britain: Selected Pamphlets by G.J. Holyoake, 1841–1904*, edited by Edward Royle. East Ardsley: EP Microform Ltd., n.d.

Saab, Ann Pottinger. *Reluctant Icon: Gladstone, Bulgaria, and the Working Classes*. Cambridge, MA: Harvard University Press, 1991.

Salisbury, Mark H., Paul D. Umbach, Michael B. Paulsen and Ernest T. Pascarella. "Going Global: Understanding the Choice Process of the Intent to Study Abroad."*Research in Higher Education* 50, No 2 (2009): 119–143.

Sanderson, Michael. *Education and Economic Decline in Britain, 1870s to the 1990s*. Cambridge: Cambridge University Press, 1999.

Sanderson, Michael. "French Influences on Technical and Managerial Education in England, 1870–1940." In *Management and Business in Britain and France: The Age of Corporate Economy*, edited by Youssef Cassis *et al*. Oxford: Clarendon Press, 1995.

Sanderson, Michael. *The Missing Stratum, Technical School Education in England, 1900–1990s*. London: Athlone Press, 1994.

Seaman, L.C.B. *The Quintin School, 1886–1956: A Brief History*. Chertsey: Burrell & Son, 1957. This was reformatted for online access in 2005 by A. E. Beck (1939–46) and H. V. Beck (1935–42) at http://www.polyboys.org.uk/X08_RSP/X08B_QSH/X08B_QSH_000.htm (accessed August 17, 2013).

Shennan, Margaret. *Teaching About Europe*. London: Cassell Educational, 1991.

Shultz, Lynette. "Educating for Global Citizenship: Conflicting Agendas and Understandings." *The Alberta Journal of Educational Research*. 53, No. 3 (Fall 2007): 248–258.

Simon, Brian. *Education and the Labour Movement, 1870–1920*. London: Lawrence & Wishart, 1974.

Singer, Sandra L. *Adventures Abroad: North American Women at German Speaking Universities, 1868–1915*. Westport, CT: Praeger, 2003.

Small, Robin. *Marx and Education*. Aldershot: Ashgate, 2005.

Stedman Jones, Gareth. *Languages of Class: Studies in English Working Class History*, Cambridge: Cambridge University Press, 1983.

Stedman Jones, Gareth. *Outcast London: A Study in the Relationship between Classes in Victorian Society*. 1971. Reprint, Middlesex: Penguin Books Inc., 1976.

Steedman, Carolyn. *The Radical Soldier's Tale*. London: Routledge, 1988.

Stevenson, Julie. "'Among the qualifications of a good wife, a knowledge of cookery certainly is not the least desirable' (Quintin Hogg): Women and the Curriculum at the Polytechnic at Regent Street, 1888–1913." *History of Education* 26, no. 3 (1997): 267–86.

Steward, Jill. "'How and Where to Go': The Role of Travel Journalism in Britain and the Evolution of Foreign Tourism, 1840–1914." In *Histories of Tourism: Representation, Identity, and Conflict*, edited by John K. Walton, 39–54. Clevedon: Channel View Publications, 2005.

Stokes, Eric. *The English Utilitarians and India* (1959; reprint, Oxford: Oxford University Press, 1989).

Stone, Wilbur Fiske, ed. "Biographical Sketches: Ernst le Neve Foster." *History of Colorado*, Vol. II. Chicago: S.J. Clarke, 1918.

Subotsky, Fiona. "Armadale (1866), Wilkie Collins – Psychiatrists in 19th-century Fiction." *The British Journal of Psychiatry* 194 (2009): 445.

Sutton, David. "Liberalism, State Collectivism and the Social Relations of Citizenship." In *Crisis in the British State, 1880–1930*, edited by Mary Langan and Bill Schwarz, 63–79. London: Hutchinson & Co., 1985.

Swinglehurst, Edmund. *The Romantic Journey: The Story of Thomas Cook and Victorian Travel*. New York: Harper & Row, 1974.

Tabili, Laura. "A Homogeneous Society? Britain's Internal 'Others,' 1800–Present." In *At Home with the Empire*, edited by Catherine Hall and Sonya Rose, 53–76. Cambridge: Cambridge University Press, 2006.

Nicholas Thomas and Richard Eves. *Bad Colonists: The South Seas Letters of Vernon Lee Walker and Louis Becke*. Durham, NC: Duke University Press, 1999.

Thompson, E.P. "The Making of a Ruling Class." *Dissent* (Summer 1993): 377–382.

Thompson, E.P. *The Making of the English Working Class*. New York: Vintage Books, 1966.

Thompson, F.M.L. *The Rise of Respectable Society: A Social History of Victorian Britain, 1830–1900*. Cambridge, MA: Harvard University Press, 1988.

Thorne, Susan. *Congregational Missions and the Making of an Imperial Culture in 19th-Century England*. Stanford, CA: Stanford University Press, 1999.

John Tosh. *Manliness and Masculinities in Nineteenth-Century Britain*. Harlow: Pearson Longman, 2005.

Towner, John. "The Grand Tour: A Key Phase in the History of Tourism." *Annals of Tourism Research* 12 (1985): 297–333.

Tremlett, George. *Clubmen: the History of the Working Men's Club and Institute Union* London: Secker & Warburg, 1987.

Truesdell, Matthew. *Spectacular Politics: Louis-Napoleon Bonaparte and the Fête Impériale, 1849–1870*. New York: Oxford University Press, 1997.

Urry, John. *The Tourist Gaze: Leisure and Travel in Contemporary Societies*. London: Sage Publications, 1990.

Urry, John. *Consuming Places*. London: Routledge, 1995.

Van Wesemael, Pieter. *Architecture of Instruction and Delight: A Socio-historical Analysis of World Exhibitions as a Didactic Phenomenon (1798–1851–1970)*. Rotterdam: 010 Publishers, 2001.

Varouxakis, Georgios. *Victorian Political Thought on France and the French*. Basingstoke: Palgrave, 2002.

Vincent, Andrew. "The New Liberalism and Citizenship." In *The New Liberalism: Reconciling Liberty and Community*, edited by Avital Simhony and David Weinstein, 205–27. Cambridge: Cambridge University Press, 2001.

Vincent, David. *Bread, Knowledge and Freedom: A Study of Nineteenth-Century Working Class Autobiography*. London: Europa Publications Ltd., 1981.

Viswanathan, Guari. *Masks of Conquest: Literary Study and British Rule in India*. New York: Columbia University Press, 1989.

Viswanathan. Guari. "Raymond Williams and British Colonialism." *The Yale Journal of Criticism*. Vol. 4, no. 2 (1991): 47–66.

Walkowitz, Judith. *City of Dreadful Delight: Narratives of Sexual Danger in Late Victorian London*. Chicago: Chicago University Press, 1992.

Wallerstein, Immanuel. "Social Science and the Communist Interlude, or Interpretations of Contemporary History." (Paper given at ISA Regional Colloquium, "Building Open Society and Perspectives of Sociology in East-Central Europe," Krakow, Poland, Sept. 15–17, 1996.) 1997. http://www2.binghamton.edu/fbc/archive/iwpoland.htm (accessed August 17, 2013).

Walton, John K., ed. *Histories of Tourism: Representation, Identity, and Conflict*. Clevedon: Channel View Publications, 2005.

Walton, John K. *The Blackpool Landlady: A Social History*. Manchester: Manchester University Press, 1983.

Walton, John K. "The Demand for Working-Class Seaside Holidays in Victorian Britain." *Economic History Review [Great Britain]* 34 (1981): 249–265.

Walton, John K. *The English Seaside Resort: A Social History 1750–1914.* Leicester: Leicester University Press, 1983.

Walton, Whitney. *Internationalism, National Identities, and Study Abroad: France and the United States 1890–1970.* Palo Alto: Stanford University Press, 2010.

Ward, C. and D. Hardy. *Goodnight Campers! The History of the British Holiday Camp.* London: Mansell, 1986.

Waterfield, Gorden. *Layard of Nineveh.* New York: Frederick A. Praeger, 1968.

Waters, Chris. "Progressives, Puritans, and the Cultural Politics of the Council, 1889–1914." In *Politics of the People of London: The London County Council, 1889–1965,* edited by Andrew Saint, 49–70. London: Hambledon Press, 1989.

Waters, Johanna and Rachel Brooks. "Accidental Achievers? International Higher Education, Class Reproduction and Privilege in the Experiences of UK Students Overseas." *British Journal of Sociology of Education.* 31 issue 2 (2010): 217–228.

Weeden, Brenda. *History of the Royal Polytechnic Institution 1838–1881: The Education of the Eye.* Cambridge: Granta Editions, 2008.

Weinreb, Ben and Christopher Hibbert. *The London Encyclopedia.* Revised Edition. London: Macmillan, 1995.

Weisser, Henry. "The Labour Aristocracy, 1851–1914." *American Historical Review,* 101 (April 1996): 490.

Williams, Raymond. *The Long Revolution: An Analysis of the Democratic, Industrial, and Cultural Changes Transforming our Society.* New York: Columbia University Press, 1961.

Williams, Francis. *Journey into Adventure: the Story of the Workers Travel Association.* London: Odhams Press Limited, 1960.

Windscheffel, Alex. *Popular Conservatism in Imperial London, 1868–1906.* Woodbridge: Boydell Press, 2007.

Unpublished Material: Theses and Dissertations

Jackson, Wendy. "The Development of Commercial Education in London between 1870 and 1920, with Particular Reference to Women and Girls." Master's dissertation. Institute of Education, University of London, 1997.

Major, Susan. " 'The Million go Forth': Early Railway Excursion Crowds, 1840–1860." Ph.D. dissertation, University of York, 2012.

Stevenson, Julie. "A Neglected Issue in the History of Education and Training: Women Students of University College London and the Polytechnic at Regent Street, ca. 1870–1930." Ph.D. dissertataion, Thames Valley University, London, 1996.

Index

Page numbers in *italics* refer to illustrations. Page numbers followed by n refer to notes.

Printed and bound by CPI Group (UK) Ltd, Croydon, CR0 4YY